"NOT IN HEAVEN"

Indiana Studies in Biblical Literature

Herbert Marks and Robert Polzin,
general editors

"NOT IN HEAVEN"

Coherence and Complexity in Biblical Narrative

EDITED BY

JASON P. ROSENBLATT

AND

JOSEPH C. SITTERSON, JR.

INDIANA UNIVERSITY PRESS
BLOOMINGTON & INDIANAPOLIS

This volume is part of a series
of publications resulting from the
Bicentennial celebration
of Georgetown University
(1789–1989).
The conference
on which it draws was
sponsored and supported by
Georgetown University's
Bicentennial Office.

The paper used in this publication meets the minimum requirements
of American National Standard for Information Sciences—Permanence of
Paper for Printed Library Materials, ANSI Z39.48-1984.
⊗™

Manufactured in the United States of America

Library of Congress Cataloging-in-Publication Data

Not in heaven : coherence and complexity in Biblical narrative /
edited by Jason P. Rosenblatt and Joseph C. Sitterson, Jr.
    p.   cm. — (Indiana studies in Biblical literature)
    ISBN 0-253-35036-0 (cloth : alk. paper)
    1. Narration in the Bible.   2. Bible—Criticism, Narrative.
3. Bible—Hermeneutics.   4. Bible and literature.   5. Bible as
literature.   6. Bible—Criticism, interpretation, etc.
I. Rosenblatt, Jason Philip, date.   II. Sitterson, Joseph C.,
date.   III. Series.
BS521.7.N67   1991
220.6′6—dc20   91-6317
ISBN 0-253-20678-2 (pbk. : alk. paper)
1 2 3 4 5   95 94 93 92 91

CONTENTS

ACKNOWLEDGMENTS

This volume grew out of a conference entitled "The Bible and Contemporary Literary Theory," held at Georgetown University, Washington, D.C., April 28–29, 1989. We are delighted to acknowledge large debts of gratitude to the *sine qua non* Kathy Kizer, whose talent for organization attained to a kind of wisdom; to our sponsors at the Bicentennial Office, especially its director, Rev. Charles L. Currie, S.J., and special assistant, Dr. Kathleen Lesko, who provided a perfect mix of support and independence; and to the Georgetown English Department: its chair, James Slevin, for strong encouragement from the outset, and Lynne Hirschfeld, administrative officer, and Joan Reuss, secretary, for manifold kindnesses. Other members of the Georgetown community who enhanced the quality of the conference are Rev. John B. Breslin, S.J., Michael Feinstein, Robin Smith, and Rev. James P. Walsh, S.J.

In the preparation of *"Not in Heaven,"* we have benefited much from the advice of Robert Polzin and Herbert Marks, coeditors of the Indiana Studies in Biblical Literature series at Indiana University Press. Rabbis William Altshul and Benjamin Mintz offered scholarly suggestions. Finally, because enduring love blurs distinctions between earth and heaven, we want to mention our wives: Zipporah Marton Rosenblatt and Donna Maulsby Sitterson.

J.P.R.
J.C.S., JR.

"NOT IN HEAVEN"

INTRODUCTION

Jason P. Rosenblatt and Joseph C. Sitterson, Jr.

"For this commandment . . . is not hidden from thee, neither is it far off. It is not in heaven. . . . Neither is it beyond the sea. . . . But the word is very nigh unto thee, in thy mouth, and in thy heart, that thou mayest do it." (Deut. 30:11–14)

Many centuries ago biblical exegesis generated the secular discipline of literary analysis, and today the child repays the parent, applying the insights and methods of that derived discipline to its original source, the Bible. The deuteronomic phrase that gives this volume its title can be read to sanction divergent approaches: the three bare words themselves authorizing the independent, earthbound arguments of literary critics; the quotation marks indicating their divine source and context, and authorizing the piety of more traditional biblical scholars. In order for the phrase "not in heaven" to legitimize secular literary interpretation, it must be wrenched from its immediate context, where it emphasizes the Torah's clarity and accessibility. Precedent for reinscribing this very phrase is set in a great talmudic scene of interpretation. The scene addresses topics of narrative coherence, poetics and hermeneutics, and ideology that help us to read the essays in this volume as a group, and it illustrates the irreducible interpretive tensions generated by these topics.

The Babylonian Talmud records what amounts to a difference of opinion between God and the sages on a legal matter, the purity or impurity of the oven of Akhnai, constructed of burnt clay cut into tiles, each layer separated by sand.[1] Rabbi Eliezer ben Hyrcanos, concentrating on the individual layers separated by sand, holds that the oven is an incomplete vessel and therefore not liable to uncleanness. The sages, concentrating on the unifying outer coating of mortar, see it as a complete vessel in full working order and thus liable to impurity. After citing this difference of opinion, the Talmud asks why this oven is given the name of Akhnai, literally, an annulated serpent:

[Because] on that day [the sages] encompassed [R. Eliezer like a coiled serpent] with [irrefutable] arguments and pronounced the oven unclean. . . . On that day R. Eliezer brought forward all the arguments in the world to prove his claim, but [the sages] would not accept them.

1

Finally, [his arguments exhausted,] he said [to the sages]: "If the law
agrees with me, let this carob [tree] prove it." The carob was torn
a hundred cubits from its place—some affirm, four hundred cubits.
They said to him, "One does not bring proof [in a matter of law]
from a carob." [R. Eliezer performs additional miracles in support
of his claim, making water flow backwards and the walls of the house
of study incline to fall; the sages remain unimpressed, R. Joshua in
fact rebuking the walls for daring to interfere in a scholarly dispute.]
The walls did not fall, in honor of R. Joshua, nor did they raise themselves up, in honor of R. Eliezer; and they still remain standing in-
clined. Again [R. Eliezer] said to them, "If the law agrees with me,
let it be proven from Heaven." Whereupon a heavenly voice cried
out [to the sages], "What are you next to R. Eliezer, seeing that in
all matters the law agrees with him?" R. Joshua stood up and said,
"It is not in heaven." What did he mean by this? Said R. Jeremiah,
"The Torah has already been given at Mount Sinai, and we therefore
pay no attention to a heavenly voice; since you already wrote in the
Torah at Mount Sinai, 'Incline after the majority' [Exod. 23:2]." [Many
years after this event,] R. Nathan met [the prophet] Elijah and asked
him: "What did the Holy One, Blessed be He, do at that hour [when
R. Joshua said what he said]?" "He laughed and said, 'My children
have defeated me, My children have defeated me.'" It was said that
on that day all objects that R. Eliezer had declared clean were brought
and burned in fire [as unclean]. Then they took a vote and excommunicated him [lit., "blessed him," a euphemism for excommunication].²

The argument over whether the oven is an imperfectly connected series of fragments or a single unified construct adumbrates contemporary
critical argument about textual coherence.³ Certainly the figurative
structure of the scene sets images of fragmentation (an irregular oven,
not made in one piece; a snake with its linked vertebrae, and an annulated one at that) against those of coherence (the oven's outer coating
of mortar or cement; the encompassing, inescapable arguments, coiled,
according to Rashi, like a snake "with its tail in its mouth," a traditional
emblem of eternity). As clay encompasses the fragmented tiles of the
oven, conferring on them the unity necessary if they are to be capable,
literally, of "receiving uncleanness," so the sages attempt to encompass
the solitary R. Eliezer, who will remain resistant to authority and therefore outside the community.⁴ But in this problematic scene, R. Eliezer's
association with images of fragmentation belies his assumption of textual
coherence; while R. Joshua, whose association with images of coherence
represents the all-encompassing legal opinion of the majority, makes
his point through an act of textual disruption. R. Eliezer strove always
to follow the traditions of his teachers, never adding to their words.
Unsurprisingly for so conservative a scholar, he assumes the determina-

bility and the identity of meaning and authorial intention. And the miraculous intervention of God himself supports that view. R. Joshua rips the phrase "not in heaven" from its immediate context and claims it for his own, denying the deuteronomic chain of verses the shaping power which that context provides. And God's laugh of endorsement at the scene's end indicates that this new meaning is also a part of his eternal Torah. Finally, R. Jeremiah can be said to occupy a less radical position than R. Joshua, since he midrashically reinscribes the deuteronomic phrase in the context of the written Torah, forcing it to comply with an assertion in Exodus of majority rule. For him, the miraculous revelation at Sinai supersedes the smaller-scale miracle supporting R. Eliezer's view.

From a different angle, the argument over the purity or impurity of an oven of burnt clay becomes a struggle for primacy between poetics and hermeneutics. R. Eliezer can be said to have accurately recovered heavenly poetics when Heaven itself, the divine author of scripture, intervenes on his behalf. But R. Joshua as interpreter in effect asserts the primacy of hermeneutics over poetics when he counters with a scriptural citation that removes the text beyond the reach of the author. The words "not in heaven" become R. Joshua's at the moment he pronounces them; hence the shocked midrashic question that follows immediately— "What did he mean by this?" Uttering the phrase thus constitutes a sort of violation, replacing the authority of the fixed, written Torah (Deut. 30:12) with that of the fluid, oral Torah, in which R. Joshua is saying that those commandments are in fact beyond God's reach. And yet, of course, this is a violation with a difference. By repeating scripture, R. Joshua pays pious tribute to the past and thus maintains continuity with it. When the rabbis ask why the opinion of his opponents made God laugh, their answer plays on the root *n'tz'ch*, which means "eternity" as well as "defeat": "My children have eternized me," rejecting even the directive of a heavenly voice through their faith in the Torah's everlastingness. Not even a prophet could change their minds, and therefore God rejoiced in their insistence.[5]

Centuries later Maimonides's reinterpretation of "not in heaven" reverses the bold spirit of R. Joshua's pronouncement while recognizing its repressive ideological application. For Maimonides—who may be thinking not only of R. Eliezer but also of another first-century wonderworking rabbi—this very pronouncement proves that "the precepts of the Torah are not subject to change," and anyone who opposes authoritative tradition on the basis of divine inspiration—"even though he authenticates his opinion by means of a sign"—"is a false prophet . . . since he has come to repudiate the Torah, which stated, 'It is not in heaven.'"[6]

In the act of reinscribing R. Joshua's interpretation, Maimonides syn-
ecdochically represents normative Judaism, which reconciles potentially
disruptive oppositions within the problematic talmudic passage. The law
(*halakha*) generated by this text provides the key to the interpretation
of the narrative (*aggadah*), and both favor R. Joshua and the sages. An
oven cut up breadthwise into rings and subsequently plastered over with
clay becomes susceptible to uncleanness; and "Not in heaven" teaches
us that no prophet—not even one who works signs and wonders—is
entitled to establish a new *halakha*.

If we read the deuteronomic text as plain sense (*peshat*) and the talmudic text as exegesis (*derash*), the two appear to coexist harmoniously:
one places the Torah within the human mouth and heart, while the
other removes it from God's reach. The rabbis interpret the benign
laugh of the heavenly father delighted with his children's ingenuity not
as mere permission but rather as a positive commandment to read scripture independently.[7] The talmudic text of interpretation becomes itself
poetic by means of R. Eliezer's miracles and R. Joshua's reconstitution
of the deuteronomic phrase; and hermeneutics and poetics converge
in the rabbinic assertion that complete interpretive freedom conforms
to the will of God. Not only R. Eliezer's written and R. Joshua's oral
Torah but all future interpretations were already revealed by God to
Moses at Sinai.[8]

Such large reconciliations should not surprise us when we recall that
midrash originated in circumstances of discontinuity. It is a system that
attempts to maintain continuity between the ancient biblical text and
readers living in the new world of Hellenistic Judaism. Our talmudic
passage provides two spatial symbols of midrashic inclusiveness: the
walls of the house of study, neither erect nor fallen but permanently
bent over in deference to the opponents who dwelled within them; and
the infinitely capacious mind of God, which contains the declarative
heavenly voice and the concessive laugh, and which asserts simultaneously defeat and victory.

But we need not look outside of normative Judaism to begin a critique
of midrashic coherence. The *halakha* in this passage demonstrates the
practical use of division. Once an oven has become impure, it cannot
be used unless its owner places sand or gravel as a barrier between
the encompassing outer layers of plaster and the sides of the oven.[9]
The owner of the oven of Akhnai has cut it into tiles, relying on its
fragmented status to keep it insusceptible to uncleanness. Moreover,
a rabbinic minority, impressed by the heavenly voice, holds that R. Eliezer's view is in fact legally correct, and the oven is clean; but the rabbis
declared it unclean as a preventive measure, lest someone else build

in ignorance a similar one that is indisputably unclean, because its tiles are not separated by sand.[10]

Our text becomes even more problematic when we consider its primary talmudic context: a discussion of the damage done by hurtful words, which occupies the pages that immediately precede and follow the story of the oven of Akhnai. In this larger context, R. Joshua and the sages recede in importance, while R. Akiba becomes the exemplary, R. Eliezer the powerful figure. The sages, afraid that if an unworthy person were to inform R. Eliezer of his ostracism in a hurtful way the entire world might be destroyed, appoint R. Akiba his student, who loves him, to carry the bad news. The talmud goes on to describe R. Akiba's delicacy of behavior, his mourning garb and tentative opening words, which suggest that he and not R. Eliezer had been excommunicated. Finally, the text concentrates on the sheer power, even over life and death, of R. Eliezer's pain, and concludes that all other gates to heaven can be locked except the gates of pain. Reading the story of the oven of Akhnai in this larger context makes identifying its main purpose more difficult.[11]

However unclear its main purpose, the talmudic text can be read in terms of the legal uses of division; as we turn to the essays in this volume, we might also keep in mind the aesthetic uses of division. When the impulse to preserve the autonomy of the text becomes too strong, it can undermine the desire to shape an aesthetics receptive to both the disruptions that threaten autonomy and the coherences that preserve it. Disruptions can become satisfying as a result of the coherences, much as prosodic irregularities can become identifiable and fraught with critical as well as phonetic implication only by being measured against an existing metrical norm.

The fundamental overt disagreement among the readers in this volume regards the question of coherence in narrative point of view. Alter, Sternberg, Nohrnberg, and Drury all assume or discover coherent and unitary narratives and narrators; Berlin, Levinson, and Sanders explicitly or implicitly critique this assumption; Trible, Schwartz, and McBride assume or discover its opposite. But there are differences worth noticing in all three groups. The nature of the evidence for and against coherence varies. Robert Alter finds narrative purpose, albeit "literary" and not "religious" purpose, in the minutest details of stylistic repetition in three short passages from Genesis 18, Judges 4, and Esther—repetition that in every case turns out to reflect the narrator's sophisticated understanding of human psyche and motive. Meir Sternberg finds a similar purpose in similar details and even in the silences or "gaps" in Genesis 23; what Abraham and the Hittites say, how they say it, even

what they do not say, and especially what the narrator does not say
—all are the meaningful products of a purposeful narrator. Sternberg's
narrator is both purposeful and "all- knowing," a "scriptwriter and stage
manager rolled into one."[12] Alter's narrator is not. Even though they
both seek, in Alter's words, "to uncover a distinctive poetics of biblical
narrative fashioned for the special ends of the Bible's new monotheistic
understanding of history and human nature," biblical narrators as Alter
characterizes them seem sometimes to be at odds with that understanding. In Esther, for example, what he shows to be "the inventive deployment of sexual comedy in the story"—Ahasuerus is in a double sense
"a man with a shaky scepter"—"is not readily reconciled with the sober
purposes of covenantal faith."

James Nohrnberg, like Sternberg, finds a virtually godlike narrator:
the dizzying typologies of the Joseph and David stories implicitly reflect
an omniscient and transhistorical narrator. For John Drury, Mark's numerological typology has been nearly buried by two thousand years of
cultural change, but it can be recovered and seen as purposeful when
we study it closely from an almost formalist perspective, which Drury
observes is likely also to have been the perspective of Mark and his
earliest readers, for whom the Bible was the central cultural text, their
world uncluttered and their attention undistracted by the many subsequent texts that fill our world. Drury's Mark, then, is firmly if hypotheti-
cally grounded in his own time.

Trible, Schwartz, and McBride all locate narrative fault-lines, but different ones. Phyllis Trible grants Genesis 22 its official coherence, and
then juxtaposes to it and to its narrator's intent the text's own silence
about, its failure to tell, the story of Sarah. For Regina Schwartz, history
"as we know it and as we live it" and history as it is told in Samuel
are discontinuous, in the biblical instance reflected in the text's radical
ambivalence toward David and even the monarchy itself; this ambivalence implicitly undermines the narrator's attempts to impose official
coherence on his story. For her, what coherence there is reflects not
narrative omniscience but narrative self-deception. William McBride
dispenses altogether with a single narrator in his midrash-like mingling
of biblical text and subsequent commentary, without assigning priority
to any single text involved.

"Narrative point of view" might remain theoretically useful to both
camps, if we could agree that biblical narrators are complex, and that
their complexity is made up to an important degree of their certainty
and their uncertainty, their coherence and their incoherence, and the
resulting intrasubjective tensions which are then reflected in their texts.
This agreement might also bring narrator and author closer together
conceptually, as long as we admit authors and redactors to be complex,

without a unitary, pure, uncomplicated purpose (even when such a purpose might accurately be called a "main purpose"). The advantage of this way of talking about narrators is that it makes everyday sense to us. Its disadvantage is that it ignores the specialized discourse about narrators among many literary critics today, which sees the narrator as a construction of and by the text, which text itself might be created by any number of authors and redactors. (The difficulty in talking about biblical narrators may be attributed in part to their reticence, about which Sternberg has written so well;[13] we find it hard to imagine "the narrator" when he is self-effacing, and so we identify him with "the author," or at least with "the implied author.") We cannot resolve this particular theoretical tension, but we can observe that both ways of talking about narrators, everyday and specialized, admit narrators who can be unified and disunified, centered and decentered, constructed and deconstructed. In addition, since the text in most biblical cases has been produced over time, by more than one human subject, any "narrator" constructed from that historically layered text will also be similarly layered. Put another way, if a text embodies diachronic as well as synchronic features, one of them being irreducible complexity, so may its narrator.

Adele Berlin and Bernard Levinson critique Alter and Sternberg, respectively, as the two exemplary literary readers of the Hebrew Bible today. To Berlin, the problem of narrative coherence cannot always be resolved by a decontextualized close reading, because such a reading may confuse hermeneutics, the reader's act of interpretation, with poetics, the author's act of creation. And even in Alter's work she finds an occasional confusion of the two. But can they be distinguished from one another so clearly? Here contemporary literary theory's use of midrash as metaphor for all literary texts comes into play. We do not have to admit the metaphor as absolute—as in Northrop Frye's all literature is written out of literature, or Harold Bloom's every poem rewrites a previous poem—to accept its relevance to biblical interpretation: namely, that the biblical texts we possess are midrashic insofar as they interpret earlier texts by means of narrative augmentation. This does not require us to ignore distinctions between earlier and later interpretations when we can make them, and as long as we know why we are making them. But it does mean that Berlin's important distinction between poetics and hermeneutics depends for its clarity on a conception of poetics limited to original authorial composition to the exclusion of any subsequent redaction of that composition.

Levinson's intended task might be the more theoretically daunting —namely, a reconciliation of literary with form-historical interpretation. He asserts that both together are needed to make up adequate interpretation, "the right chorale." We would agree, if chorale could be updated and heard to include not only, say, the counterpoint of literary and form-historical melodic lines, but also their possible atonality. But for most of us atonality does not make such a traditional harmony. Nor does it for Levinson, who finds Sternberg's conception of narrator incompatible with form-historical conceptions of author and redactor. The only way we see to make them at least theoretically compatible is through our barely adumbrated description above of the complex narrator. And this does not resolve particular narrative contradictions and confusions; it only provides us a conceptual frame for them.

James Sanders's argument for biblical pluralism takes a different tack, by turning the methods of form-historical criticism against itself. He argues that most form-historical critics have used the cultural and manuscript evidence of layer upon layer of author and redactor (tradent) to establish ur-texts reflecting their own biases in favor of one or another canon-within-the-canon; "such a procedure in effect decanonized the text because it bypassed the actual manuscripts inherited from ancient communities of faith, instead attempting to reach back of them to so-called original speeches and compositions." But the same evidence, he argues, shows that original authorial composition appears not to have been a major factor in the importance of biblical texts to believing communities. Instead, their importance is partly a function of the "multiple voices" that derive not only from the Bible's different books but from their multiple and layered composition. The pluralism of these voices, he suggests, has ensured the Bible's canonical survival: "no one community of faith or mode of theology can encompass the whole canon any more than one theology can encompass the concept of God."

Perhaps the most prevalent form of this pluralism in the Bible is its intratextual stylistic tension: parataxis and repetition, which Gabriel Josipovici has argued to be the defining mode of the Hebrew and Christian Bibles because it "allows even the most antagonistic views to be placed side by side within a larger whole."[14] Several essays in this volume explore in persuasive detail textual moments of such incremental repetition. Alter shows that the "near-verbatim repetition" in the annunciation of the birth of Isaac in Genesis 18 reveals, in addition to the "covenantal promise of progeny and future national greatness," the narrator's human and artistic interest in "imagining Sarah, Abraham, and the angel . . . as *characters*." Sternberg argues that in the *machpelah* episode of Genesis 23 the Bible's pervasive "poetics of repetition with variation" works in opposite ways: "when the Hittites echoed Abraham's plea, their variations masqueraded as the repetitions of compliance or even over-compliance, while underground sharpening into dissent. On the other hand, so far from contradicting the original request, Abraham's self-variants reinforce it by way of specification and pinpointing."

This recognition, that parataxis and repetition are not necessarily marks of earlier, oral culture, rather than later, literate culture, marks a fundamental difference between much contemporary literary biblical interpretation and form-historical interpretation.[15] Like parataxis and stylistic repetition, thematic repetition—typology—also is open to diametrically opposed readings. For Nohrnberg it evidences a masterful intelligence able to see pattern and repetition transcending any single historical moment. For Schwartz this very ability is deluded—the source of all coherent narratives, it imposes pattern where there is none. For Drury, typology, like parataxis for most of the interpreters in this volume, is repetition with a difference; thus, history does not reduce to typological sameness. Drury's remarks on typology bear on R. Joshua's bold pronouncement in the talmudic scene of interpretation: the words "not in heaven" become R. Joshua's at the moment he pronounces them, just as Christ's repetitions throughout the Gospels of phrases from the Hebrew Bible constitute a sort of hostile takeover. Typology, like gossip, succeeds only when it is accompanied by a sense of violation. The use of types in Mark becomes an archetype of the creation of any work of art, which requires a peculiar sort of transgression that pays its dues to tradition at the same time that it violates it. Drury's essay on Mark thus casts its New Testament light into a dark corner of this talmudic scene, allowing us to read it, with a sense of violation, as mimetic of the Gospel. "Thus," says Mark of Jesus, "he declared all things clean." And in the scene R. Eliezer, a single miracle worker, pronounces all foods prepared in the oven of Akhnai to be clean, in the face of pharisaic obstinacy.

Interpreting the talmudic scene as a remarkable assertion of the independence of human reasoning, contemporary readers concentrate on R. Joshua's pronouncement and the divine laughter that confirms it. But in ostracizing R. Eliezer for his unwillingness to accept the majority opinion, the sages demonstrate their power to stifle one who Heaven asserts surpasses them all. The power of the interpretive community to substitute authoritative opinion for absolute truth reminds us that ideology informs our readings. Sternberg emphasizes the heavy price exacted for a piece of land "in Kiryat-Arba, which is Hebron," and however strong his desire to keep the ancient text free from contamination by contemporary politics, those place-names are for some readers so highly charged that they become impossible to control.

In her radically iconoclastic feminist Protestant reading of Sarah's absence from Genesis 22, Trible advocates a sort of guerrilla warfare on the biblical text, suggesting that readers listen for the still small voice that exposes patriarchy and that gives them the means by which they may subvert it. In the discussion following her presentation at the con-

ference, Trible cited as her hermeneutic base a deuteronomic text that
inhabits the same textual neighborhood as R. Joshua's: "I have set before
you life and death, blessing and cursing: therefore choose life" (30:19).[16]
For Trible, the traditional patriarchal reading of the binding of Isaac
is death, while the readers' discernment of idolatrous attachment as one
of the costs of patriarchy, which permits them to reject attachment and
thus to undercut the main line of the narrative, is life.

Schwartz, following Foucault, seeks to "disrupt . . . the fiction of the
unity of the subject, and to break . . . the commitment of seeking origins
and ends" by means of his Nietzschean distinction between "effective"
and "traditional" history: "Traditional history is devoted to searching
out sources, establishing continuity, finding resemblances, and charting
development, with some goal ever in sight. 'Effective history,' in contrast,
is devoted to charting ruptures and discontinuities. . . . " What effective
history does to our subjectivity, Schwartz does to the text of Samuel,
revealing its thematic tensions, teasing duplications, and provocative
contradictions.

In his midrashic reading of the book of Esther, McBride stresses difference and dissymmetry not only as textual features but as moral categories, opposed to symmetry, neutralization of contradiction, and closure. McBride on the figure of chiasmus sounds like Kugel on biblical
parallelism: both oppose "exchangist" readings, which would reduce
parallelism and chiasmus to synonymity.[17] McBride reads Haman's attempted genocide as a wish "to eradicate . . . difference," and insofar
as readers of Esther tend to purge the book's chiastic difference they
are Haman-like. Asserting that a "totalizing, homogenizing effect is
characteristic of . . . tyranny," he demonstrates the disturbingly powerful
centripetal force of Xerxes's Persian empire, which obliterates the
"other" as it pulls it inside its own orbit.

In a very different way, Sanders suggests a similar morality in difference when, for example, he writes that the two creation accounts in
Genesis 1 and 2 make "a uniquely poignant statement that could not
be made otherwise, either by one of the chapters alone or by a homogeneous blend of both," and his argument to us even implies disturbingly
that those form-historical critics who locate "authority only [at] the earliest levels" are akin to biblical fundamentalists who "refuse honestly to
admit biblical pluralism out of fear of loss of the kind of authority they
think the Bible gives them."

Interpretive tension thus endures both within the biblical text, between readers, and between text and reader—and the reader's need
to reduce or eradicate it crosses specific interpretive traditions, perhaps
most strikingly from form-historical to fundamentalist. The necessary
historical specificity of diachrony, issuing in pluralism, must be set

against the strong human need to achieve synchrony by finding some permanent relevance in the texts of the past. That need lies at the heart of midrash, and at the heart of what is perhaps the most powerful concept now available to any consciously modern biblical hermeneutics of accommodation, Gadamer's "fusion of horizons." Like midrash, it seeks to reduce this tension by incorporating both the claims of the modern reader and those of the past text, rather than one to the exclusion of the other. For Gadamer, the horizons of author/text and reader/interpreter are by definition not identical; the process of interpretation consists in the interpreter's perhaps growing awareness of the relations possible between the two, leading ideally (our word) to a fusion of the two horizons. "Every encounter with tradition that takes place within historical consciousness involves the experience of the tension between the text and the present. The hermeneutic task consists in not covering up this tension by attempting a naive assimilation but consciously bringing it out." For Gadamer, however, this interpretive tension is transitory because "historical consciousness," he argues, is "only something laid over a continuing tradition, and hence it immediately recombines with what it has distinguished [that is, past from present] in order, in the unity of the historical horizon that it thus acquires, to become again one with itself"—"a real fusing of horizons."[18] So that, for example, the modern reader, perplexed as Drury argues by all of Mark's numbers, can approximate a first-century Christian reader by attending to the text (Mark and his alluded-to antecedents), and can thereby make some sense of those numbers—that is, the modern reader's horizon is altered and expanded. Correspondingly, Mark in this process becomes like a postmodern "gapped" text—that is, the text's horizon is altered and expanded by being placed next to that of the modern reader (with his or her experience of modern texts).

But it is hard for us to see why "fusion" is necessarily the inevitable ending to this process—or that fusion is the only alternative to its other extreme, the indifference or irrelevance of the two to each other, which is effectively the death of the text as culturally relevant, or of the reader as "cultured." We may instead remain in between these two poles, uncomfortably aware that our horizon (which after all we do not know so very well) is not the text's, and that there can be at most a partial, even temporally finite, intersection between the two—sometimes longer than but akin to Frank Kermode's "perception of a momentary radiance, before the door of disappointment is finally shut on us."[19] This may be interpretive tension with a vengeance; like it or not, for many of us it is the condition of cultural life.[20] Our argument here has been that it is obliquely reflected in the biblical text itself, and also in the present collection of essays.

The readers in this volume may seem not to reflect this tension. If we read their biblical interpretations as they read the Bible itself, looking for rhetorical and structural evidence of coherence and purpose, we find that—whatever their disagreements—they are fairly confident about their roles as coherent, purposeful readers able to discover truths about the text, however conflicting those truths may be. And yet they are concerned indirectly, or in different terms, with this issue. Alter's opposition between literary play and religious dogma might be seen as a tension between forms of uncertainty and certainty. (Elsewhere he has opposed "literary" to psychoanalytic, deconstructive, and feminist reading, by implication incorporating them as dogmatic in their certainty.)[21] Drury ultimately argues for the reader's "intelligent charity" as the intellectually and ethically proper response to the otherness of Mark's text and its early readers. And Sanders finds that the Bible pluralizes monotheism in the sense that its intertextual presentations of God, however overlapping, are sufficiently conflictual to prevent God's being captured by any unified human conception. On the other hand, Trible starkly juxtaposes an orthodox, patriarchal reading of Abraham and Isaac in Genesis 22 to an unorthodox, feminist reading of Sarah's absence from that text. And Schwartz unhesitatingly rejects unified "traditional history" in favor of the disruption and discontinuity of Foucault's "effective history."

Perhaps the next movement in literary biblical interpretation will be a return to the fundamental hermeneutic problem of text and reader, with the heightened respect for the complexities of the former shown to us by the kind of readings included here. For now, if we can accept that our own complexity as readers might parallel the sometimes irreducible complexity of narrators, we may be on the way to appreciating the diversity of the biblical readings in this collection—not for diversity's own sake, but because this particular diversity can tell us something about ourselves, and enable us to see some value in, if not resolve, our own interpretive uncertainties.

BIBLICAL IMPERATIVES
AND LITERARY PLAY

Robert Alter

For many readers, it has been something of an embarrassment that there should be literature in the Bible, or that the Bible should ever be thought of as literature. If it is revealed truth, if it is meant as a guide to the moral life and a source of theological principle, if it is the authoritative account of the first and last things, what, after all, does it have to do with literature? Let me hasten to say that one doesn't have to be a Bible Belt fundamentalist to entertain such views. T. S. Eliot, in the years after his conversion to Anglicanism, several times publicly reproved those who read the Bible for its poetry instead of for its religious truth. More recently, much the same argument, couched in slightly different terms, has been made by the eminent Bible scholar James Barr and by the distinguished critic and poet, Donald Davie. Readers as subtle as these hardly want to deny the presence of remarkable literary qualities in the Bible, but they prefer to regard them as accidental by-products, or at best as felicitous embellishments, of the imperative religious concerns that are the heart of Scripture.

This way of seeing Scripture is continuous with the consensus of two millennia of Jewish and Christian interpretive tradition, and over the past two centuries it has been oddly reinforced by the dominant emphasis of academic biblical studies. The critical-historical investigation of Scripture, in the process of providing genuine illumination for much that was long obscure, has tacitly assumed a kind of Lockean distinction between primary and secondary qualities of the Bible. The former, deemed susceptible of scientific inquiry, include the philological constituents of the text, variously accessible through comparative Semitic studies; the sundry elements of historical context reflected in the text, often clarified by archeological or other extrabiblical evidence; and the conjectured stages of evolving traditions that produced the text. The literary features of the text, on the other hand, have by and large been relegated to the status of secondary qualities, mainly suitable for discussion in the effusive appreciations of aesthetes and amateurs, but hardly worthy as objects of serious scholarship.

13

This marginalization of the Bible's literary characteristics presupposes a peculiarly limited notion of literature—a notion, one suspects, especially congenial to German professors of the previous century who wrote sentimental verse at the age of eighteen and afterward scrupulously devoted themselves to the pursuit of graver matters. The idea of literature as a kind of elevated hobby for sensitive souls, an appurtenance to life's more urgent enterprises, leaves scant room not only for Dante, Dostoevsky, and Blake, but also for Shakespeare, Stendhal, Tolstoy, Joyce, and Faulkner. Gabriel Josipovici, in a recent book called *The Book of God* that is a kind of long and bold meditation on the status of the Bible as literature and its relation to later ideas of literature, aptly proposes that the Bible stands with a whole family of literary texts that seek—fiercely and in the end futilely—to transcend their own status as literature through necessarily literary means. Among writers of our own century, he mentions Proust, Kafka, Beckett, and Celan as figures who share with the creators of the Bible an aspiration to "produce something which is other than literature, something essentially truer and more necessary than literature could ever be."[1] This dream of self-transcendence, I would suggest, merely reproduces at the level of moral or spiritual expression a dynamic intrinsic to the evolution of all literature, however worldly or secular, which is constantly to reshape inherited conventions and genres in some fashion that will seem to go beyond their manifest artificiality. Thus, as Harry Levin has observed of the history of realism in the novel, writers from Cervantes to Flaubert to Joyce achieve an illusion of reality by incorporating in their fiction through allusion and parody the contrastive instances of earlier, more patently artificial fiction.[2]

It remains a question whether the Bible does something absolutely distinctive with literature, or with the use of literary means to transcend literature. Meir Sternberg's work, and, on a more modest scale, my own as well, has sought to uncover a distinctive poetics of biblical narrative fashioned for the special ends of the Bible's new monotheistic understanding of history and human nature. Northrop Frye, in an imaginative refurbishing of Christian typology, has offered an account of Old Testament and New as a beautifully interlocked system of symmetrically arranged archetypes, but this proves to be only an extreme and exemplary instance of literature in general as Frye had long perceived it. In quite another direction, a recent study by David Damrosch boldly attempts to synthesize a literary perspective with a critical-historical one by analyzing biblical narrative as a distinctive form that works through the interaction of the various historical strata it comprises.[3] (Damrosch properly admonishes all of us new literary students of the Bible for neglecting the background of ancient Near Eastern genres and the peculiar historical circumstances in which biblical literature evolved by uneven stages, but he is stuck with the opposite quandary of basing an analysis on scholarship's conjectural identification of discrete strata in the texts and on the still shakier dating of the proposed strata.)

Perhaps the most powerful of all the recent attempts to render an account of the Bible's distinctive literary character is Harold Fisch's new book, *Poetry With a Purpose*.[4] I would like to reflect on Fisch's challenging argument because it illustrates so instructively the essential difficulty of talking about this subject. It is in some ways very helpful, in others misconceived, and the distance between the former and the latter is roughly marked by the way Fisch's position slides from one like that of Gabriel Josipovici to one like that of T. S. Eliot. Let me isolate what I think are the three essential points in Fisch's conception of biblical literature. I will list them in descending order of plausibility.

A great deal of biblical poetry, Fisch argues, is informed by what he suggestively describes as "a poetics of violence." The poetry of the Prophets and, again, the poetry of the Song of Moses (for which he provides a splendid analysis) do not read like the tradition of verse derived from Greco-Roman origins. Fisch notes the prominence in poetic texts of the Hebrew verb *hpk*, "to overthrow," and proposes that "as against the rhythm of the natural world, we have a different rhythm, one that carries with it the ever-present potentiality of divine interventions."[5] Commenting on Hosea and the other Prophets, he develops, like Herbert Schneidau before him, the notion of a biblical swerve from myth to history and covenant, away from "roundedness and closure" and toward "discontinuity and violence."[6] Coupled with this notion of a poetics of violence is the assumption that God in the inscrutability of his absolute purposes is implicit in all biblical texts, beyond beauty and artifice, ultimately negating any such secular or merely literary values. At first glance, this seems an unexceptional application of orthodox principle to literary analysis, but, as we shall see in a moment, it becomes problematic when it is applied even to texts like Esther and the Song of Songs that do not mention God.

The most ingenious and the least persuasive of Fisch's main theses is that biblical literature as a whole represents a subversion of poetic genres in the interests of its monotheistic "purpose." Thus, Deuteronomy 32, the Song of Moses, subverts the pastoral; a passage in Lamentations "reads like a veritable confrontation between pastoral and antipastoral";[7] tragedy is deflected and subverted in Job, lyric in Psalms, "pagan epic" in Esther, carnal love poetry in the Song of Songs. What we have here is essentially an application to the Bible of Stanley Fish's notion of the "self-consuming artifact" originally developed as an account of Protestant English literature of the seventeenth century,[8] and

I find it too Protestant by half. The most salient difficulty is that Harold Fisch's superimposition of the idea on the Bible is ahistorical. There was no ancient Near Eastern Theocritus and there is scant evidence of a pastoral genre in this region during this era that the poet of Deuteronomy 32 would have been aware of as something to subvert. (Juxtaposing two generic models out of historical context may have its own validity, but Fisch makes larger claims for his argument.) Again, one may question whether there was any real equivalent of a Greek lyric genre in the ancient Near East, and Fisch is compelled to date the Book of Job at least a century later than scholarly consensus will allow in order to see in it a Hebrew response to Aeschylus and thus a subversion of tragedy.

The supposed undoing of pagan genres in the Bible need detain us no further, but the overarching idea with which it is linked—that God's imperative presence in these poems and stories is pervasive and absolute —must be seriously confronted. For if the commanding God of creation, covenant, and history is everywhere, can there be any place for the play of literary invention except in the insistent service of his purposes? The Book of Esther, where there is no actual reference to God, is an instructive test-case. Superficially, it looks like an antithesis to that stark Hebrew narrative fraught with background that Erich Auerbach described so memorably in his classic discussion of the Binding of Isaac.[9] But Fisch proposes intriguingly that Esther's ornate tale of imperial glitter is contrived to be undermined by a very different, urgent, God-haunted story submerged within it: "Thus, in the book of Esther is embedded a Hebrew type of narrative, marked by a realism in which nothing is on the surface, everything standing out against the darkness of its own background. Mordecai is the sign of this other narrative, Mordecai shrouded in darkness beyond the gate of the palace while the feasting goes on within, a feasting to which he is totally indifferent and from which he is totally cut off."[10] This reading, inspired by Auerbach, is imaginative, and evocatively expressed, but is it convincing? At an early moment of the plot, and in part as a necessity of the plot, Mordecai does stand outside the palace gates, but it is strange to say that he is cut off from the feasting, for the plot is contrived to bring him into the center of the world of feasting and regal pomp and circumstance. In fact, the story of Esther is a vehicle *for instituting* a feast, and Mordecai's grand gesture at the end as newly appointed viceroy is to enjoin an annual obligation of feasting on his fellow Jews—"that they should make them days of feasting and joy, and of sending portions one to another, and gifts to the poor" (9:22). To evoke an abstemious Mordecai swathed in darkness is to play the role of a critical Malvolio objecting to cakes and ale in a story where cakes and ale are paramount. The

Book of Esther illustrates how hard it is to sustain generalizations about a biblical narrative style or even a biblical outlook because this particular text vividly expresses a festive, perhaps even saturnalian, view of life. There is abundant comedy here of a sort that would scarcely be allowed by the usual preconceptions about biblical gravity, and if it seems an exception to the rule, it may well exemplify the rabbinic interpretive principle of "the exception that comes to teach us about the rule." Feasting in Esther is intimately associated with sexual comedy, and the inventive deployment of sexual comedy in the story is not readily reconciled with the sober purposes of covenantal faith.

The tale begins, one recalls, by offering an account of a royal feast with all its sumptuous trappings at which Queen Vashti is summoned to display her beauty before the eyes of the wine-befuddled male guests. What is implicitly stressed at the beginning is the physical separation between harem and king, women and men. Whether or not the original idea was for Vashti to display herself naked, as some medieval commentators proposed, the obvious implication of Ahasuerus's summons is his pride of sexual possession. It is not altogether clear if that possession is more than titular, a matter of mere display. In any case, after Vashti's grand refusal, the royal counselor Memucan sounds an alarm that unless Vashti is turned away, male dominance of wives throughout the empire will be undermined by this act of insubordination. The prelude to the main plot, then, strikes a note of male anxiety that points forward to the climax in which the ever malleable Ahasuerus will be manipulated by his new consort Esther to do exactly what she requires of him.

The sequel to the prelude is a delicate dance of teasing possibilities that invites a reconsideration of conventional assumptions about Scripture, for the Bible is surely not supposed to tease. The most beautiful virgins available are brought to the capital from the length and breadth of the kingdom, and after each spends six months dunking in oil of myrrh and another six months in assorted perfumes and unguents, she is led to the royal bed for a night of amorous trial. If one may address a practical question to a fairy-tale fantasy, trial of what? The young women are all equally fragrant and lubricated, and being virgins, none has any sexual expertise by which she might plausibly offer the king some unexpected pleasure. Ahasuerus himself, hardly an energetic or assertive man, seems an unlikely figure to be up to this strenuous regimen of nightly erotic exercises. Is it conceivable that the reason he is said to "love" Esther above all the other women and choose her as queen is that with her alone he is able to perform the act? (The subsequent narrative, after all, shows that Esther is not only beautiful and loyal but patient and quietly reassuring.) I am of course not suggesting that the text ever explicitly mentions royal impotence, but the comic specter

of the idea may well be raised, and then brought closer to the surface
in the revelation in chapters 4 and 5 of a hitherto unreported ritual
of separation between harem and throne: anyone who appears uninvited before the king, including even his supposedly beloved queen,
will be forthwith put to death unless the king responds to the appearance
by holding out his golden scepter. Whether or not this corresponds to
any actual court practice in the Persian period, it surely confirms our
double sense of Ahasuerus as a man with a shaky scepter. Fortunately,
Esther survives the trial in which her life hangs in the balance just as
she alone survived the nocturnal trial of selection. Her uninvited appearance before the king is followed by a party *à trois* on two successive
days to which she invites him together with Haman. At the climactic
moment of the second party, when she has announced that Haman intends to destroy her and all her people, the king walks out onto the
terrace in a fit of wrath and consternation. At this point, the teasing
possibilities of sexual undermeaning that I have traced are made entirely
explicit: Haman, in desperation, flings himself on the couch where Esther is reclining in order to plead for his life; the king, turning back
into the room and seeing Haman "fallen on the couch," cries out in
royal indignation, "Does he intend to ravish the queen before me in
my own house?" and Haman pales in terror (7:8). It is quite likely that
a common ancient Near Eastern political rite is being invoked here:
to take sexual possession of the king's consort or concubines (as Absalom
did when he usurped his father's throne) was to proclaim legal possession of his political power. If Ahasuerus's momentary misperception
of Haman as would-be rapist exposes the plotting vizier as a potential
usurper, it also jibes with the sundry intimations from chapter 1 onward
of the king's rather uncertain dominion over the female sex: at the moment of the villain's unmasking, in a piece of comic invention by no
means necessary to the plot, Ahasuerus imagines Haman assaulting the
lovely woman he himself has possessed only intermittently, and perhaps
precariously.

Not all Hebrew narrative is a version of the Binding of Isaac, with
its stark conjunction of fire, wood, knife, and impending sacrifice, its
breathtaking violation of human conceptions in man's terrible exposure
before God. To be sure, Esther is a late text that gives us Hebrew narrative in a holiday mood, and the holiday mood is rare in the Bible. The
mere fact of its presence, however, is instructive. Although it is evident
that the biblical writers did not generally conceive themselves as enter-
tainers and that they were intent on conveying through narrative and
poetry God's plan in creation and in the history of Israel, the literary
art they exercised so splendidly was not always, or not entirely, subservi-
ent to religious ends. I realize that what I am saying may sound blasphe-

mous, or at least excessively modernizing, to some, and so I want to put in due perspective the claim I will proceed to spell out. The Hebrew writers do of course keep in steady focus God and Israel, creation, covenant, and commandments (though not very noticeably, I think, in Esther), and from moment to moment all the subtleties of their literary art are exploited to make palpable their God-driven vision of reality together with the individual and collective obligations dictated by it. This is virtually a truism, and I think it requires the following modest but important qualification: no writer, not even the most intently religious one, can ever quite escape the momentum of the medium in which he works. The making of literature everywhere involves a free play of the imagination with language, inventively using such elements as rhythm, repetition, musicality, imagery, character, scene, act, and symbol, even when the writer's aim is to produce "something essentially truer and more necessary than literature." If virtually every utterance of biblical narrative points toward the imperative concerns of covenantal faith, it is also demonstrably evident that virtually every utterance of biblical narrative reveals the presence of writers who relished the words and the materials of storytelling with which they worked, who delighted, because after all they were writers, in pleasing cadences and surprising deflections of syntax, in complex echoing effects among words, in the kind of speech they could fashion for the characters and how the self-same words could be ingeniously transformed as they were passed from narrator to character, or from one character to another.

Let us consider the presence of this sense of writerly delight in two passages from more historically urgent texts than Esther, belonging to the classic age of Hebrew narrative that produced the chain of masterworks from Genesis to Kings. Now, a prominent and, I think, distinctive convention of this body of classic Hebrew narrative, which has been analyzed by Meir Sternberg, George Savran, and by me, is the modification of dialogue in near-verbatim repetition in order to indicate the attitudinal angle, the changed audience, or even the downright mendacity of the speaker who repeats someone else's already cited words.[11] Understandably, most of the examples of the technique that have been discussed—and it is used pervasively in this corpus of narratives—are cases in which the moral or psychological or thematic definition of character is sharpened or somehow subtly advanced by the changes the character introduces in someone else's words. Thus, in 1 Kings 21, the false witnesses report to Jezebel that Naboth has been stoned to death, their words echoing the narrator's statement of that fact, but when Jezebel passes on this news to Ahab, she quietly deletes the unpleasant detail of stoning and prefaces the report of Naboth's death by telling Ahab he can now go ahead and take possession of the coveted vineyard. Not all occurrences, however, of such "editing" by a character of another character's speech are so evidently instrumental. A piquant case in point is the triangular relation of narrator, Sarah, and the angel in Genesis 18 at the annunciation of the birth of Isaac. In this instance, as we shall see in a moment, the repeated bit of direct discourse is something thought, not audible speech:

> And Abraham and Sarah were old, advanced in years, Sarah no longer had her woman's flow. And Sarah laughed inwardly, saying, "After being shriveled, shall I have pleasure, my husband being old?" And the Lord said to Abraham, "Why is it that Sarah laughed, saying, 'Shall I really give birth, I being old?'" (Gen. 18:11–13)

We have in rapid sequence three statements about the advanced age of the future parents of Isaac—the narrator's, Sarah's, and the angel's version of Sarah's statement (he is referred to simply as the Lord, YHWH, in keeping with a frequent usage in Genesis). The narrator's authoritative report is balanced, emphatic, and in a sense neutral. There are three brief clauses: the first flatly tells us that both Abraham and Sarah are old; the second underscores the initial information by reiterating it synonymously; the third spells out Sarah's condition of menopause, thus capping the couple's great age before procreation with the one biological fact that should make procreation an impossibility. The next sentence is devoted to Sarah's review of this same narrative datum in a brief interior monologue. It is introduced by the term "saying" (*le'mor*) that is regularly used to introduce direct discourse, whether spoken or unspoken, throughout the Bible. What is peculiar, and thematically weighted as we move toward the birth of Isaac, "he-who-laughs," is that *le'mor* is preceded not, as convention dictates, by a verb of speech, but by "laughed," adverbially qualified by "inwardly" (*beqirbah*). Sarah, like the narrator, reflects that both she and her husband are old, but she crucially modifies the human meaning of this information through the new terms she chooses for it and the new syntactic order in which she conveys it. She begins with her own condition, which is now manifestly a plight, the subject of a complaint. She is not simply old but "shriveled" (the Hebrew root *blh* means worn out or in rags when applied to garments, evidently the primary meaning of the term, and wasted or shriveled when applied to flesh), and she cannot imagine that she will again experience pleasure. Though the immediate context, the promise of the birth of a son overheard by Sarah, could mean that the pleasure in question is the pleasure of maternity, the root of the word she uses, *'ednah* (cognate with Eden), has connotations of sensual delight, and so it is likely that Sarah is referring to sexual pleasure, or perhaps even, in a double-edged usage, to sexual pleasure leading to the joy of motherhood. (The conclusion of some philologists that *'ednah* means "abundant moisture" would make the word point even more directly to sexual physiology.) The fact of menopause, though obviously implied, is not actually mentioned but instead displaced into Sarah's brooding over her withered body and her removal from conjugal gratification. Her husband's old age is invoked in a tacked-on clause at the end, the syntax yielding a progression of thought along the following lines: I am hopelessly ancient, besides which, my husband is old, too. The three phrasal components of Sarah's interior monologue create a certain ambiguity of causal attribution quite typical of biblical characterization. Is Sarah beyond hope of pleasure because she is shriveled, as we initially suppose, or because she is stuck with an aged husband? The biblical writer's ability to produce complexities through the starkest economy of means is breathtaking. The objective data given in the narrator's report of a postmenopausal matriarch and an elderly patriarch are converted in her interior monologue into a woman's emotionally fraught statement of her biological predicament that might at the same time carry a hint of sexual resentment toward her aged husband.

When the Lord, or his emissary, reports Sarah's inward "laughing" to Abraham, a whole new set of transformations is introduced. Exercising as divine being the auditory equivalent of clairvoyance, he has obviously heard the unspoken words of disbelief of Sarah's interior speech, but what he chooses to report to Abraham is another matter. The most prominent change was noted long ago by the great medieval exegete Rashi—the deletion of any reference to Abraham's old age. Rashi phrases this touchingly: "Scripture made a change in the interests of domestic harmony [*mipney hashalom*], for she had said, 'My husband is old.'" Always a keen reader, Rashi is acute in observing the difference in the repetition, but it is noteworthy that he motivates it on implicitly didactic grounds: Scripture is eager to teach us through this example of divine speech that for the sake of domestic tranquility it is important to exercise diplomacy. But the angel's version of Sarah's words is impelled by something other than didacticism, as may become clearer in attending to the other alterations he makes. The angel not only omits the reference to Abraham's old age shared by Sarah and the narrator, but he also edits out all mention of female biology associated with Sarah's old age: his words to Abraham say nothing of the absent menses in the narrator's report or the shriveling and the deprivation of pleasure in Sarah's interior monologue; in his version, she expresses incredulity only over the simple fact that she could give birth.

The interesting question is why this whole set of changes should have been introduced. The narrative has come to a moment of high solemnity,

when the seemingly impossible covenantal promise of progeny and future national greatness is repeated one last, climactic time. It is far from
clear how the intricate triangular game of variation in repetition that
we have been following contributes to this grand historical theme, or
how it illuminates any of the spiritual imperatives that are the very purpose of Scripture. Why didn't the writer simply transpose the narrator's
words into the first person without further change for Sarah's interior
monologue, and then allow the angel to quote her words verbatim in
addressing Abraham? One can hardly say that he simply wanted to avoid
the tedium of exact repetition, because the Bible abounds in examples
of exact repetition, or at least much closer approximations of it than
we have here. In my view, the only plausible explanation is that the
writer, for all the seriousness of his purpose to render the history of
Israel as the history of the beginnings of redemption, was imagining
Sarah, Abraham, and the angel (despite himself?—we shall never know)
as *characters*. Among my own past sins, I have managed to vex a number
of critics by applying the term "fiction" to biblical narrative, though
I did try to make clear that at least in my usage there was no contradiction between fiction and the intent effort of historical truth-telling. The
angel eavesdropping on the interior speech of the eavesdropping Sarah
on the other side of the tent-flap is a nice microscopic illustration of
the operation of the fictional impulse in Scripture. The writer is not
content merely to report the essential data of covenantal history with
the strictest efficiency or the optimal thematic emphasis. What he has
done here is to imagine himself into Sarah, and then into the angel
addressing her aged husband. The extraordinary economy of means
employed in no way precludes a richness of imaginative identification.
In seven scant Hebrew words of interior monologue, Sarah is revealed
not simply as emblematic matriarch in a divine scheme but as a woman
struggling under the load of a particular life-experience, hyperconscious
of her own withered flesh, resentful of her estrangement from the pleasures of the body, whether in maternity or sexuality or both, and perhaps resentful as well of her aged husband. The divinity who overhears
all of this deems it unsuitable for the ears of Abraham, who may have
his own vulnerability as a man in his declining years never able to beget
a child with the wife of his youth; who presumably has long since given
up trying; and who ought not to be confronted with the biological details
of his wife's geriatric condition—especially since the divine plan now
requires him to feel the urge to cohabit with her.

Literary style, I have argued elsewhere, is an exercise of the expressive
resources of language that seeks a nuanced precision beyond the reach
of ordinary usage and at the same time exhibits a repeated delight in

the sheer shaping of its materials which is in fine excess of the occasion of communication.[12] Because this sense of writerly pleasure, in which the alert reader is invited to join, is manifest even in the darkest and most urgent of literary works, from *King Lear* to *The Brothers Karamazov* to *The Trial*, I have described it, perhaps a little provocatively, as "the high fun of the act of literary communication." There is evidence of its presence in almost every line of biblical narrative, and though the biblical writers are of course concerned with conveying "messages"— credal, moral, historical, ideological—the lively inventiveness with which they constantly deploy the resources of their narrative medium repeatedly exceeds the needs of the message, though it often also deepens and complicates the nature of the message. The excess of which I speak is not at all like the supposed "supplement" in Deconstructionist parlance that is produced by an endless sense of lack in the act of communication. On the contrary, it emerges from the writer's vivid intuition of a superabundance of possibilities suggested by the creative associations of his literary medium.

We began with a highly exceptional festive narrative where the free play of literary invention should hardly surprise us, and now we have encountered it operating on a more restricted scale, but nevertheless strikingly, in the Patriarchal history of national origins. My concluding example, as a kind of limit-case for my thesis, will be a text in which the manipulation of style seems very much subordinate to thematic ends. Even in such an instance, however, the handling of narratorial report and dialogue pushes beyond the boundaries of thematic utility, hints at that collusive game between writer and audience which is the hallmark of literary narrative. I shall quote the very beginning of the story of Deborah (Judg. 4:4–5) in a flagrantly literal translation because the Hebrew here has a certain purposeful awkwardness that is smoothed over in all the conventional English versions: "And Deborah, a prophetwoman ['ishah nevi'ah], Lapidoth's woman, she was judging Israel at that time. And she would sit under the palm tree of Deborah. . . ." What is odd about these initial expository clauses in the Deborah story is the obtrusion of feminine gender and of the term "woman." Since all Hebrew nouns are either masculine or feminine, the moment you hear *nevi'ah* and not *navi'* you realize that you are dealing with a prophetess, not a prophet. The superfluous "woman" in apposition with "prophetess" is immediately picked up in "Lapidoth's woman"(like the French *femme*, the same term means wife or woman). This foregrounding of the feminine is then reinforced by the introduction of an easily dispensable pronoun: "Deborah, . . . *she* was judging Israel." The use of the participial form at the beginning of the next verse (my translation ren-

ders it as an iterative verb) is the occasion for immediately repeating
the feminine pronoun: "And *she* would sit" (*wehi' yoshevet*; an imperfect
verb, *wateshev*, would have required no pronoun).

Let me suggest that the quality of stylistic bumpiness at the beginning
of the story is intended precisely to bump our sensibility as audience.
It is the rare exception and not the rule to have a prophetess rather
than a prophet, a female rather than a male judge. A reversal of roles
between woman and man, *'ishah* and *'ish*, will be at the heart of the
story, with Deborah's role as commander perfectly complemented by
Jael's role at the end as assassin of the enemy general: the reiteration
of the thematic term in the Song of Deborah is noteworthy—"May Jael
be blessed above women,/woman of Heber the Kenite,/above women
in tents may she be blessed" (5:24). The first episode of the story is
then a dialogue between a very hesitant male field-commander, Barak,
and the firmly insistent Deborah. Her initial words to him seem to assume a prior communication to which he has been unwilling to respond:
"Has not the Lord commanded you . . ." and the very first word of
the Lord's message to Barak which she quotes is the masculine imperative verb, *lekh*, "go." What happens to that verb in the immediately subsequent exchange between Barak and Deborah is almost comic. He says:
"If you will go with me, I will go, and if you won't go with me, I won't
go," and she answers, "Go, I will go [*halokh 'elekh*] with you, but it will
not be your glory on the way you are going, for by the hand of a woman
will the Lord deliver Sisera" (4:8–9). Literary students of the Bible have
drawn abundant attention to what Buber and Rosenzweig first described
as *Leitwörter*, "leading words," or thematic key-words, by which the
meanings of the narrative are progressively complicated through repetition. In this instance, the technique is pushed so far that it verges on
self-parody. Barak, in a paroxysm of hesitation, releases a stammering
chain of "go's," his going repeatedly conditional on Deborah's going,
on her leading him along the way by the hand. This last idiom, which
is not stated though perhaps implied, surfaces in another sense, with
proleptic irony, in her reply to him. When she says that the Lord will
deliver the Canaanite commander "by the hand of a woman," she is
using what amounts to a lexicalized metaphor, with the sense of "by
the power of," "through the agency of," and which is a recurrent idiom
in the frame-narratives of Judges (the Lord delivers X in or by the
hands of Y). The subsequent narrative and poem then shockingly litera-
lize the metaphor as Jael is seen with right hand on the hammer, left
hand on the tent-peg that she drives into Sisera's temples.

I don't mean to suggest that the author of the Deborah story is making
some sort of programmatic feminist statement about the reversal of sex
roles. On the contrary, whatever musings about such reversal may be

raised by the story (and it is not alone in the Book of Judges in its concern with ambiguous gender relations) belong precisely to the realm of teasing possibility that is separable from the explicit ideological messages of the narrative, which involve a plea for national solidarity, a responsiveness to divine imperatives, and—beyond the frame of this story—a polemic against idolatrous backsliding. The piquant idea of the woman of manly courage and the pusillanimous man (Barak at the beginning) or the man of childlike helplessness (Sisera in Jael's tent) was appropriate for the writer to explore without explicit thematic assertion in the dialogue's play of *Leitwörter* and in the narrator's small deformations of idiom and syntax. Did he do this because he wanted to introduce a note of satiric rebuke to an Israelite nation unwilling to exercise requisite martial virtue (an idea that might have had some practical urgency for the original writer as against his later Deuteronomistic editor), or simply because he discovered an intrinsic allure in this surprising turn-around of sex roles? What makes this narrative, like all literary narratives, interesting is that there is no way of simple accounting either for the writer's motives or for the range of implications to which his work points. The flickering presence of a perhaps gratuitous theme producing a hint of comic by-play in the midst of a presumably historical report of military triumph over Israel's enemies and the Lord's is an instance of that fine excess of the ostensible occasion of communication toward which the literary imagination constantly moves. Language, straining against the decorum of ordinary usage, is fashioned to intimate perspectives the writer would rather not spell out, and invites our complicitous delight in the ingenuity of the fashioning.

The distinction I have tried to indicate is by no means one between form and content, or message and embellishment. Everything in the story contributes to an encompassing vision of history, social institution, human nature, individual character, and, of course, God. Part of this vision is a core of consciously held intentions to provide informational and moral instruction—intentions that either address a national consensus or, perhaps more often, seek to create one. The wavering character of the consensus is reflected in the fact that it contains at least some different items of concern, sometimes conflicting ones, for different writers and in different periods. But one measure of the greatness of biblical literature is that the energy of its literary imagination led to a probing—at once playful and serious—of the borders of consensus and what lay beyond it even as the consensus was being forged through narrative.

It will be noted that all three of my examples involve the power or plight of women in what is generally presumed, with good warrant, to be a set of narratives dominated by men. These instances seem to me especially instructive because they show the literary imagination—perhaps inadvertently—testing the limits of biblical ideology. Such imaginative exploration of what lies beyond received values is characteristic of the dynamic of literary expression everywhere. Ideology tends to draw lines, insist on norms, in the interests of a particular system of governance and social relations. Literary invention, to a large extent because it involves the kind of free play of the imagination with a verbal and fictional medium that we have been following, often has the effect of calling ideological assumptions into question, or qualifying them ironically, or at any rate raising certain teasing possibilities counter to the accepted ideology. It may well be that the relation between the sexes, which is at issue in all the examples I have chosen, is a realm of experience that in most cultures offers an especially potent invitation for the literary artist to conjure with notions that run counter to established views. Two of the three texts we have considered involve not just gender roles but sexuality, a sphere every culture tries to police in various ways but which stubbornly persists in the privacy of its enactment as a zone of freedom, a perennial outlet of free play for the body, and perhaps for the spirit as well.

The literary imagination qualifies or challenges prevalent ideological assumptions not necessarily—in fact, not usually—because it has an ideological program of its own, but on the contrary, because its inventive, associative, and even formal engagement with its own verbal, narrative, and referential materials leads it to peer over the other side, or at the underside, of things as they are ordinarily seen. "The artist," as Leo Lowenthal has aptly put it, "is no Cartesian but rather a dialectician focusing on the idiosyncratic, on that which does not fit into the system. In short, he is concerned with human costs and thus becomes an ally of . . . the critical perspective."[13] Hence these remarkable moments in the notoriously patriarchal Bible when a woman's predicament or her ability to act forcefully is brought to the fore.

All this does not mean that the Bible is just like any other body of literature. On the contrary, its distinctive traits are so striking that one hardly needs to argue for their presence. The ancient writers, as Fisch, Josipovici, and countless others before them have observed, steadily seek to realize through the medium of literature an order of truth that utterly transcends literature. The anonymity and the collective viewpoint of biblical writing are tokens of this aspiration—no place is allowed for the self-promoting identity of the individual writer or for the ephemerality of merely private experience. The implicit drive, moreover, of the sundry biblical texts toward forming an overarching unity of statement about God, history, and creation also sets Scripture apart: Genesis, Judges, and Kings are not just literary works by different hands related through genre, like the novels of Dickens and Trollope, but complementary voices, harmonized by later editors, in an authoritative chorus of collective destiny. Even the dimension of imaginative free play that I have described is at least partly realized in distinctive ways because the drastic economy of biblical narrative usually means that the elements of fine excess are manifested at a more microscopic level of the text than is common in other literary traditions. Such manifestations are nevertheless abundantly evident throughout biblical narrative, and are often as brilliantly inventive, sometimes even as playful, as anything to be encountered in secular literature. For the covenantal urgency of the biblical authors impelled them on a bold and finally impossible project: they sought to use literature to go irrevocably beyond itself, but, being writers of genius enamoured, as writers always are, with how they could tap the endless resources of their medium, they could not avoid producing in their work an enchanting affirmation of the free-playing logic of literary expression.

DOUBLE CAVE, DOUBLE TALK: THE INDIRECTIONS OF BIBLICAL DIALOGUE

Meir Sternberg

Literary dialogue entails indirection by its very form, because in staging it the artist communicates with the audience *through* the communication held among his speaking characters, the dialogists. Itself silent or silenced, the frame then quotes a vocal inset. This is even more perceptible in narrative than in drama, because the narrator could always do otherwise. Free to speak in his own voice and to his own addressee, he could tell us everything straight: what happens, why it happens, where the sense and the point of the happening lie. Instead, in the role of dialogue- maker he withdraws behind the scenes to leave the floor to the dialogists themselves—but without surrendering for a moment his privileged viewpoint on what they say and do. After all, he brings them on for a purpose. As scriptwriter and stage manager rolled into one, even if he speaks in voices other than his own, he still speaks through voices and words and obliquities of his own devising. Hence every piece of dialogue enacts no less than a double message: two levels of communication, two pairs of communicators, each having its peculiar sphere, norms, horizons, intentions, rhetoric, but with the artistic one always overlaid or *mediated* by the lifelike.[1]

From the reader's side, of course, everything works in reverse. A double message calls for a double reading; indirect communication means twofold interpretation that relates the overt to the hidden speaker, the immediate words uttered on stage to the mediate and disembodied perspective behind them. If, in short, the artist knows his own mind, including the reasons for modulating into dialogue, we must read his mind by making sense of the discourse he has assigned to the characters. This is a land of trial and error, as we have all learnt from experience.

But the indirection built into the form of dialogue as mediated discourse may in effect prove easier or harder to straighten out according to a number of variables. Some depend on whether the narrator opts

28

for concealing or for revealing his own voice before, after, or during the framed dramatic interchange. Does he, for instance, choose or refuse to share with the reader his privileges: his goals, his value system, his knowledge of action and psychology, his views on art in relation to life?

Other variables bear on the speakers and the speeches dramatized, especially as regards plain speaking. "As I detest the doorways of death, I detest that man who hides one thing in the depths of his heart and speaks forth another": thus Homer's Achilles, in reference to that arch deceiver Odysseus. Yet despite thunderings right and left, not least from Scripture, duplicity still prospers in real-life conversation and in its artistic imaging as dialogue. Morality apart, such two-facedness on the part of a speaker complicates matters for his conversational partner-and-interpreter within the dialogue, and even more for us eavesdroppers on the dialogue, already confronted by a hidden, possibly ironic teller behind the speaker. But then, once the speaker himself "hides one thing in the depths of his heart and speaks forth another," morality will not be kept apart from the general entanglements. On the contrary, the double-talk starts a chain reaction whereby the moral aspect of the text gets doubled, too, branching out into the ethics of world and discourse, of the matter spoken about and the manner of speaking. Ethical imperatives, rights and wrongs, come to bear in force on communication as well as on nonverbal (inter)action. But are they universal or culture-dependent, and if the latter, fixed or variable according to, say, genre or register or circumstance? How do the relevant norms manifest and suggest themselves? How do they stand to other normative scales—practical, social, ideological, artistic? Again, how do those governing the matter of discourse relate to the manner? Do the two sets bear the same relation for the narrator as for his dramatis personae, and to what effect? Such value-laden questions are always formidable and unavoidable, yet never more so than in structures of communicative duplicity that involve the characters themselves: the difficulty of making sense then redoubles along with the pressure for exercising judgment. As if one barrier of indirection were not enough, readers find themselves at a still further remove from the narrator, with another façade to pierce and explain and assess in interpretation.

At its most problematic, therefore, a dialogue will compound the enigmas of mediacy with silence from the mediated voice and double-talk from the mediating agents. This combination is a favorite of biblical narrative, and I would like to exemplify its means and its ends, its reasons and workings and consequences, through a deceptively simple tale: Abraham's purchase of Machpelah from his Hittite neighbors in Genesis 23.

(2) Sarah died in Kiriath-arba (that is, Hebron) in the land of Canaan;
and Abraham came to mourn for Sarah and to weep for her. (3) Then
Abraham rose up from before his dead, and spoke to the Hittites, saying: (4) I am an alien and a resident with you. Give me a holding for a
burial ground with you, and I will bury my dead out of my sight. (5) The
Hittites answered Abraham, saying to him: (6) Hear us, my lord. Thou
art a great [Elohim] prince amidst us. Bury thy dead in our choicest
burial grounds. No man of us will deny thee his burial ground to bury
thy dead.

To readers who run as they read, this initial exchange may well look
friendly and harmonious. No sooner has Abraham expressed his need,
invoking and socializing the prime moral imperative of burial, than the
Hittites respond with hearty goodwill. In effusive compliance with his
request to "bury my dead," they echo it twice: "Bury thy dead. . . .
bury thy dead." They likewise extend their undertaking, and his range
of choice, to the entire community: "No man of us will deny thee."
The only thing they will not grant is Abraham's self-portrait. As if
shocked at such a failure to do oneself justice, they hasten to contest
this self-deprecation point by point, from premise to conclusion, so as
to set right at once his footing and deserts. *You* "an alien and a resident
with" us? they protest. "Thou art a great prince amidst us." You relegated to an ordinary "burial ground"? "Bury thy dead in our choicest
burial grounds," for nobody will deny himself such honor. All along
the line of response, it seems, the Hittites volunteer more than Abraham
asks for: their manner of speaking goes even beyond the demands of
the matter spoken about, the ethical obligation to the departed.

But if so, one wonders, why does not the dialogue end right here
on this cooperative note? In the circumstances, even if the characters
still have arrangements to make, they are hardly of such interest as
to need reporting, far less dramatizing, least of all within the Bible's
rigorous narrative economy. Why, then, drag out the scene for another
two rounds—why indeed stage it at all, instead of burying Sarah in
decent silence? Retrospectively, the answer grows plainer and plainer
with each bend in the corridor of dialogue. Whatever the appearance
of harmony, that is, no resolution has yet been achieved, because the
Hittites do not speak their minds but still convey quite enough to leave
everything suspended: Abraham's emergency therefore continues, and
with it his need to push for an agreement.

Sooner or later, this inference about the true state of affairs will force
itself on the most careless or credulous reader. But the truth suggests
itself as early as the opening round, complete with the questions why
the Hittites protest so much and why the gap dividing their protestations

from their intentions. Here, as throughout the dialogue and other narratives, the clues lurk mainly in the Bible's poetics of repetition with variation. In a sense, this key to secret thought beckons us through the overt words themselves, for the Hittites go out of their way to differ with Abraham (e.g., regarding his self-image) even amidst concurrence ("Bury thy dead"). Once the disparities between request and response, speech and counterspeech, leap into prominence under the pressure of Hittite disclaimer and amendment and superlative, they invite a closer inspection and assume a much less favorable meaning—one not nearly so ethical, let alone noble, regarding the matter and the manner alike. In the process of comparing the speeches, even what appears to recur verbatim may come to signal a divergence; the least divergence in wording often hides and implies a clash of perspectives; the very changes for the better reveal another face as changes for the worse.

Those signals of friction, like the inside views or messages that each transmits by itself, are many and diverse. Yet they do compose a network of indirection spread for a purpose below the official response—in short, they cohere into a pattern of doubletalk that makes for a double reading. This is because all the pointers have one feature in common and an ominously negative feature at that. Whatever the Hittite answer professes, its repetitions and variations manage among them to evade the heart of Abraham's appeal, "Give me a holding for a burial ground with you." In biblical idiom, "holding" (*akhuzzah*) unequivocally refers to possession, as distinct from all other forms of occupying land. The patriarch will not bury his wife, any more than in the next chapter he will marry his son, among the people of Canaan. The follow-up phrase "with you" then softens a bit the impact of this stipulation by redressing or reaffirming the balance of social coexistence. Bringing together the ideas of contact and separateness, this phrase assures the Hittite audience that the would-be landholder means to adjoin rather than join the native citizenry, to remain on the fringe yet under authority as ever. Nothing will change. In status as well as in wording, burial "with you" follows the humble self-introduction "an alien and a resident with you." It is fitting, Abraham tacitly argues, that we outsiders should rest the way we have lived: in relative apartness, or *with*drawal.

But this appeal gets a reception that is not nearly so outspoken, let alone favorable. Shorn of its trappings and considered in practical terms, what the Hittites say amounts to very little. All appearances to the contrary prove illusory, hollow, deliberately two-faced. The very plural form given to the declarations, instead of multiplying their strength for extra security, actually renders them indefinite and inoperative. Thus the extravagant offer of "our choicest burial grounds" is reminiscent of the fake countess in Balzac's *Père Goriot*, who gives herself

away by boasting of her husband's death "on the *fields* of battle" ("sur
les champs de bataille"). In each context, the plural sounds impressive
but jars against the humdrum fact that one usually neither dies nor
rests in more than a single place. Therefore, to direct the mourner
in quest of "a burial ground" to "our choicest burial grounds" is to
leave him with the corpse on his hands. Further, to meet Abraham's
affirmative "Give me" with the double negative "No man of us will deny
thee"[2] is to promise even less than would the sweeping engagement
"Every man of us will give." A plurality or community of non-deniers
does not yet make a single giver.

Worst of all, the promise of not denying is itself an act of denial since
it ignores, and by implication disfavors, Abraham's request for a family
vault of his own. Note the care taken to distribute the possessive particles
in a symmetrical fashion, whereby "burial ground" twice attaches to
the Hittite speaker ("our . . . his") and the "dead" to the Hebrew addressee ("thy . . . thy"). By this mock division of rights, they give Abraham to understand that the land must remain their property, though
of course without prejudice to his claim to the dust below.

While as good as a rebuff, however, the legalistic touch yet enables
the double-talkers not only to preserve their façade of goodwill but even
to embroider it with a special mark of honor. To this end, two otherwise
unrelated variations come together: the line drawn by the possessives
finds its blurring *and* its excuse in the switch from "with you" to "amidst
us." By "with you," we recall, Abraham hoped to strike such a balance
between withdrawal and contact, outsidership and insidership, as would
work an arrangement of relative apartness ("my holding, your control").
But in changing the preposition, the Hittites upset this delicate balance,
apparently for the better, as if "with you" were a synonym or an over-
modest euphemism for "amidst you." Whether they choose to take or
to substitute Abraham's phrase for one of togetherness, the shift lends
color to their pretense of well-disposed and complimentary reasoning.
If he is living (and as "a great prince") among them, it follows that
he must also want to be buried among them.[3]

Once read against the play of variant repetition in the dialogue, then,
the compliance that professes to go beyond the request actually falls
much short of it; not for the last time, the appearance of excess overlies
a deficiency. Far from assigning Abraham a lot of his own, the Hittites
do not even direct him to one of theirs, so that the funeral remains
quite in the air.

Amid the light shed on the response, however, a core of darkness
remains. The fuller our tracing of the Hittite network of indirection,
the deeper our perplexity about the motive behind it. Why perform
such acrobatics? The code of politeness at once suggests itself, especially

in opposition to Abraham's blunt approach, which may really have shocked those Orientals. But this does not so much resolve the enigma as invite further digging for resolution. For politeness itself grows such a thick and flowery surface only in answer to a need to wrap up some deeper unwillingness to comply or commit oneself. So what in turn lies behind their reluctance? What motivates the public motivation?

At this level of double reading, again, the hypothesis that comes readily to mind accounts for some of the facts but leaves others unobserved, incoherent, pointing further down. Interpreters ancient and modern have recognized the sociopolitical dimension of the tale. As a foreign settler, Abraham the Hebrew does not enjoy the citizen's right to own ("hold") land. In law as well as in origin, he is an *out*lander. Strictly explicated, his coordinate sentence means not "Because" but "Although I am an alien and a resident, give me a holding": his opening clause has the force of a concessive, because it is precisely a concession that he seeks. This context, no doubt, throws light or at least emphasis on various points in the text. It explains, for instance, why the patriarch —so blessed with everything else—never attempts to acquire land except in the emergency of bereavement. (Observe, moreover, how the exposition's grim advance from "Sarah died" through "Abraham came to mourn" to "rose up from before his dead, and spoke" anticipates any possible suspicion that he may now be trading on his loss: the emergency forced rather than enabled him to seek a piece of ground, and the bare minimum at that, by appeal to the highest moral obligation.) It also explains why, once reduced to throwing himself on the common sense of duty, he does not immediately address some individual landowner but first applies to the community for approval in principle. In the form of that application, it also coheres with the humble exordium, with the pointedness of "a holding," with the explicit reference to "my dead" by way of *force majeure*, not least with the strings attached to the "with you's," which the egalitarian "amidst us" later challenges as a flower of speech alone. And of course, it helps to make legal and political sense of the Hittites shying at a request that would have them change the status quo in favor of an alien. Words cost nothing, but law and land are serious matters.

So far, so good, or, from Abraham's viewpoint and the implied reader's, bad. The trouble is that such a gap-filling would by itself leave certain nicer features of the dialogue out of sight and pattern, unexplained if not downright resistant. For one thing, the Hittite counterspeech makes a counterproposal rather than a flat rejection of Abraham's own proposal, which is accordingly still negotiable (and indeed successfully negotiated) across the barrier of citizen rights. And if a deal remains in the cards, then maintenance of the status quo can hardly have been the overriding, far less the exclusive, concern below the fine talk. Politics can at most account for the reluctance to say Yes, not for the avoidance of a civil but firm No. For another thing, the counterproposal itself stops short of absolute commitment. "Our choicest burial grounds" names no place and "No man of us will deny" no person—in the guise of extending the range to all—as if to invite or in fact to compel Abraham to nail things down by making an offer. And, again, what has the outlander to offer in exchange for a share in a burial site (or "a holding") except a slice of his evident wealth?

For yet another thing, the suspicion that the Hittites literally mean business aligns and focuses some new elements in the language of dialogue, variations included. To a businessman speaking for a community, the negative circumlocution "No man of us will deny thee" has more than the virtue of binding nobody in particular under the attractive cover of binding everybody. It also markedly avoids and indeed probes Abraham's "Give me," ruling out the idea of a free gift as distinct from a negotiated give-and-take. To be sure, the patriarch had no such idea in mind. Chapter 14 having shown him turn down a fortune that he had earned, "lest thou shouldst say, I have made Abram rich" (14:21-24), we know that he would never trade on another's generosity and that his "Give" must be a shorthand for "Give me permission to acquire or to proceed."[4] But the Hittites do not know and will not take any chances. Why should they commit themselves to anything definite when they can afford to wait for the other party to do so first? The variation in wording (un)covers an opposition of perspectives, whereby readers find themselves allied with Abraham against the unknowing as well as unobliging Hittites, but only to gain a new, ironic sense of how the dialogists themselves converge toward a deal.

No single hypothesis, therefore, can explain the response as given, ambiguities and all, nor will a simple addition of alternatives do. We readers have to infer and coordinate a set of three Hittite motives, or rather three levels or layers of motive, one atop the other: Politeness, Politics, and Profits. These three P's—all secretly alien, if not opposed, to the imperative of burial—mark a descending order along various related scales. A scale of transparence, to begin with, for each veils the next in depth. The politeness is manifest to the point of extravagance; the politics, built into the situation and unmistakable even in disclaimer; the greed shows only through the fractures and loopholes left above. But then such veiling is deemed necessary, by the Hittites themselves as well as by the narrator, because the three motives also descend in seemliness. After all, politeness is a boon of social intercourse, certainly when going from superior to inferior; politics imposes cruel laws and inequalities, alas, but such is life; making money, and out of a

mourner in distress at that, requires the thickest cover short of impene-
trability. It is extremely revealing that this descent in the seemliness
of the speaker's intentions has a parallel in the three biblical senses of
the "Hear us, my lord" demanded of the listener: "hear" as a call for
attention, for obedience, for understanding. The uglier the message behind the speaking, the larger the role played by the "hearing."[5]

Again, the three motives provide an orderly line of retreat: if pressed
to the limits of decorum, the Hittites can always fall back on political
constraint—"Sorry, but . . ."—and then, if favorably *im*pressed, they may
abandon the *status quo* for a *quid pro quo*. It's all a question of price:
they need not even have made up their mind but keep it open, along
with the set of options, and let the other side make the running. Indeed,
why hurry when, apart from everything, their line of retreat doubles
as an offensive weapon ready to hand—political muscle (e.g.) supplying
the ideal leverage for business as well as the best insurance for the flour-
ishes of courtesy?[6] Finally, the three layers of motive trace a descending
order of certainty in inference. The deeper one goes in pursuit of the
motive, the less certain one's understanding of it—which is exactly as
the pair of indirection-makers would have it, each within his own sphere
and for his own reasons and at the expense of his own interpreter. Only,
as always, the characters' reasons (belonging to the inset exchange) dis-
guise and justify in lifelike terms the poetic reasons that lead the artist
(operating from the frame) to devise such an obstacle course for the
reader. If the Hittites play a waiting game because it pays, then we readers must wait and see (with Abraham) because it suits the all-knowing
narrator to keep us guessing at what he could unfold in advance.

The first thing to see is what Abraham himself makes of his reception:

> (7)Abraham rose and bowed to the people of the land, the Hittites.
> (8) And he spoke to them, saying: If you wish to bury my dead out
> of my sight, hear me and intercede for me with Ephron son of Zokhar,
> (9) that he will give me the cave of Machpelah, which is his, which
> is at the edge of his field; at the full price let him give it to me, amidst
> you, as a holding for a burial ground. (10) Ephron was sitting amidst
> the Hittites. And Ephron the Hittite answered Abraham in the hear-
> ing of the Hittites, of all who came in at the gate of his city, saying:
> (11), No, my lord, hear me. The field I have given thee, and the cave
> that is in it I have given thee; before the eyes of my people I have
> given it to thee. Bury thy dead.

As so often in dialogue, especially of the opaque kind, Abraham's new
move not only calls for interpretation but itself embodies and reflects
an interpretation of the earlier turn to which it responds. Having just
pieced together the Hittite attitude and tactics, we must now infer on

top of everything else what the patriarch inferred from the same bland surface. Since the narrative keeps his mind as closed to us as that of the opposition, to make sense of his discourse is largely to find out what sense he has made of theirs. Hence the need for gap filling within gap filling, for "hearing" behind hearing, for our reading of Abraham's reading of the Hittite viewpoint. What does *he* take them to mean? Further, has he understood their (mis)understanding, deliberate and otherwise, of his initial speech? And how does he hope to clarify and wind up matters? As it turns out, Abraham's reading fully corresponds to ours, with the result that we gain not only a welcome confirmation but a sense of solidarity: literature runs so parallel to life, as it were, that we go through the ordeal imposed by the double-talkers in the company of a worthy and like-minded interpreter.[7]

Clearly, Abraham has taken the hint and, at whatever cost to natural feeling, begins to play the game by the rules of indirection, Hittite style. Manner and matter alike convey this adjustment, through changes that amount to a reversal of front. Regarding manner, notice how the ceremonial "bowed to the people of the land, the Hittites" contrasts with the total absence of preliminaries to Abraham's first turn, "spoke[n] to the Hittites" with a directness befitting one who "rose up from before his dead." As with the novel formality of gesture, so with the forms of language, most notably the syntax. Gone is the simplicity of the earlier parataxis, "I am an alien and a resident with you. Give me a holding for a burial ground with you, and I will bury my dead out of my sight" —all sentences loosely but lucidly juxtaposed, as though the speaker has neither relish nor thought for any finesse beyond the barest coordination. Parataxis now gives way to the hypotactic syntax of "If . . . then": the conditional clause leads into a tortuous main clause, which increasingly multiplies repetitions, oppositions, qualifications, parentheses.

Whether nonverbal or verbal, all these novelties in the form of Abraham's request are part of a new and newly intricate style of communication. Thus the shift from abrupt to bowed-in utterance not only marks the change from the spontaneity of the mourner to the deliberation of the negotiator, assumed for rhetorical effect and time gaining. It also goes with a shift in the terms whereby the narrative refers to the addressed assembly. Instead of the bald proper noun "the Hittites" comes now the expanded "the people of the land, the Hittites," whose redundancy underlines *afresh* the inequality in status between the speaker below and the audience on top. Afresh, because the new term of reference attached to the bow interprets it as suggesting what the earlier round began by spelling out, "I am an alien and a resident with you." Same meaning, same relation in the world, same position and priority in the discourse, only in a different medium. The hierarchy exists, no matter how vocally the Hittites brush it aside, or even turn it upside down, by their "my lord" and "great prince." So in reintroducing it by way of silent gesture, Abraham lets his hearers (and the reader) know that he has taken the point: for the negotiations to go on, the demands of etiquette and realpolitik need to be fused into a harmonious surface of expression, without being for a moment *con*fused.

In fact, the bow itself inaugurates as well as accepts this rule of two-level, two-faced discourse. For it conveys the inferior's submission to authority, down to matters of form (as in Gen. 22:5), under cover of the petitioner's gratitude for a favor done (as in Gen. 24:26–27). His request having been granted in essence, he pretends, it only remains to settle the details.

Nor does Abraham's ensuing speech betray the least awareness, far less resentment, of the equivocation and power play just exercised on him. On the contrary, as if the first round has produced nothing but accord, he invokes the assembly's good offices in approaching the next in line: "If you wish to bury my dead out of my sight, hear me and intercede for me with Ephron son of Zokhar." Apparently a simple transition from the general to the particular, this move demands close "hearing," of an order that it no doubt received from the audience. With all moot points glossed over, what Abraham's opening does voice gives a boomerang effect to the Hittite words and tricks. Not that Abraham really hopes to force a deal this way, but that in rhetorical as in physical combat the weaker party must seize every advantage, and his only chance often lies in turning, if necessary twisting, the opponent's very strength against him.

Accordingly, whatever the Hittites' secret reasons for preferring a blur to a straight answer, Abraham publicly translates their effusions into a Yes. His conditional clause even treats their good offices from now onward as an index of goodwill, if not a test of good faith. And the loaded phrasing of that clause makes it virtually impossible for them to retreat or demur. Like other skillful rhetoricians—including his own servant in the next chapter, 24:49—Abraham does not settle for the pale "If you agree"; he rather opts for a conditional that is equivalent in sense but incomparably superior in deterrent force, one that stigmatizes any noncompliance or quibbling as inhuman. Wince as they might at the intentions and commitments ascribed to them, how can the Hittites have the face to deny the wish "to bury my dead out of my sight"— especially considering that the phrase takes them at their word, "Bury thy dead. . . . bury thy dead"? (Observe that they find themselves burdened with the entire responsibility, "If *you* wish to bury my dead," not, as careless or timid translators would have it, with the halfway "If you wish *me* to bury.")

While the Hittites are still squirming under the point given to their empty offers, the mention of Ephron follows to trap them in their wily silence as well. Had they earlier referred Abraham to a specific person or place, however undesirable from his viewpoint, it would have become extremely awkward for him to turn elsewhere. Beggars can't be choosers and you don't look a gift horse in the mouth. Yet in their eagerness to leave all the options open, to give nothing away but wait and see, they have named no names; with the result that they have overreached themselves, because their vagueness enables Abraham to spring his own choices. "'No man of us will deny thee,' you said? Well, the man I have in mind is Ephron, owner of the Machpelah."[8] It is now they who would find it awkward to cavil at the person or the place named.

For all this maneuvering, to be sure, the Hittites could still block the way to a deal with no more breach of commitment than of politeness, simply by adhering to burial "amidst" them. After all, on the most liberal interpretation, they have never agreed to a transfer of property ("holding"). But then, nor have they vetoed the idea, and Abraham hastens to turn this loophole to psychological account. Having correctly read their evasiveness as a green light for negotiation, he even pretends to applaud it as a mark of support, as official blessing to private dealing. That is also why he does not directly address his offer to the prospective seller, Ephron, but to the community at large—appealing as it were to the voice of public opinion behind him to intercede with a possibly recalcitrant individual. They who have shouldered the responsibility "to bury my dead" must work for its fulfillment. Except as a figure of rhetoric, needless to say, public opinion hardly stands behind Abraham vis-à-vis Ephron. Quite the other way round: it is Ephron's cooperation alone that can swing official policy in favor of business and thus "intercede for" Abraham.

This reveals the body of Abraham's proposal in verse 9 to be a multiple message par excellence, with a double audience and goal as well as a complex of double meanings. He must negotiate on two levels at once—to secure Hittite approval for the transaction in and through the arrangement of its terms with a particular Hittite—and without giving away so much as the activity of negotiating. This need for persuasive polyphony explains the structure and the detail of the address, both highlighted by the Bible's artful aids to intelligibility. Observe, again, the play of repetition and variation vis-à-vis the original gambit:

> verse 4: Give me a holding for a burial ground with you
> verse 9: he will give me the cave of Machpelah, which is his, which
> is at the edge of his field; at the full price let him give it
> to me, amidst you, as a holding for a burial ground.

The recurrence goes far beyond the propositional content. It also carries over the nuclear syntactic form (subject, verb, indirect object, direct object) and all the operational wording: "You/He give me . . . a holding for a burial ground." From semantics to grammar to lexis, the self-repetition works both to reassure and to press the audience by driving home the speaker's consistency. For consistency inspires confidence: having gained a point, the man does not change so much as his language, with an eye to further concessions. At the same time, consistency signals a determination to have one's own way in establishing a frame of reference for the bargaining. Anything other than "a holding," on whatever terms, is out of the question. Naturally, Abraham speaks as though such common ground already unites the parties—except for Ephron maybe—yet he knows that it does not. So, ignoring and in effect dismissing the in-between Hittite acrobatics, he reverts to his original formulation, as if to say: "My proposal stands, and I cannot settle for less."

Here, indeed, variation joins forces with repetition to novel and striking effect. The most creative explorer of this device in literary history, the Bible shows how widely replay in dialogue may differ from *self*-replay; how, in short, the same form of indirection may work to opposed ends, depending on the speaker's voice and interests. Thus, when the Hittites echoed Abraham's plea, their variations masqueraded as the repetitions of compliance or even overcompliance, while underground sharpening into dissent. On the other hand, so far from contradicting the original request, Abraham's self-variants reinforce it by way of specification and pinpointing. Such is evidently the case with the wholesale shift from the plural (*t'nu li*) to the singular (*yitten li*) "give." Taken together, this repetition and variation give a sense of continuity while marking the coming down to brass tacks; they also fuse the two addresses into a kind of dialogic montage, which suggests that the Hittite addressees are really one and at one, while keeping them formally apart in number, person, posture, and rhetoric.

The component shifts are even more notable. From start to finish the elaboration amounts to an act of self-interpretation on Abraham's part, where the repeated appeal figures as text and the variants as glosses. (By something like an iconic image of this meaning-bond, the repetition physically encases the variations.) Moreover, each "gloss" promotes the "text" by its double-edged effect, combining hardness and softness, tenacity and conciliation, give and take. Thus, *the cave of Machpelah* harps anew on the distinctness and *at the edge of his field* on the apartness of the site, in the guise of pleading its smallness, uselessness, out-of-the-wayness. *At the full price let him give*, again, bargains for an outright sale while playing on the seller's greed *and* saving his face

through the avoidance of the ugly word "sell."[9] Instead of changing
the operative verb, Abraham repeats it with a gloss designed to correct
a possible (or probable) misapprehension: "When I said 'give,' I hope
you did not understand me to have in mind a present or even a token
payment. At the full price, it would still remain a gift from a kind donor
to a grateful recipient." *Amidst you*: "I myself said 'with you' and I still
mean to remain 'at the edge' culturally as well as topographically; but
since you insist, let us put it your way."[10] *As a holding for a burial ground*,
finally, repeats the earlier legalistic formula with the extra stress of closure but also with the addition of "as," implying a practical or even
a political waiver. The land transferred, that is, shall serve no other
purpose, so that the restriction of use ("burial") compensates for the
absoluteness of possession ("holding"). Under the constraints imposed
by the plurality of norm and audience, repetition thus dovetails with
variation to make things plain. Abraham will not give way in the one
essential but, if anything, he actually asks for less than "the people of
the land" might suppose and offers more in return. Why, then, not
talk or at least do business?

But Ephron, it seems, will not hear of business. "I have given . . .
I have given . . . I have given," he exclaims, without even waiting for
either intercession or direct appeal. This certainly sounds better. The
verb chosen, "give," abandons the Hittite double negative "will not
deny" for Abraham's straight and binding positive. Its triple iteration
makes for emphasis. Its perfective form in the Hebrew (*natatti*, "have
given,"[11] as against Abraham's future *yitten*, "will give") treats the act
of giving as an accomplished fact ("it's all done already"). So, more delicately yet, does the removal of the possessives hammered in by Abraham
as well as the Hittites. For Abraham's "the cave of Machpelah, which
is *his*, which is at the edge of *his* field," the owner himself substitutes
the neutral reference "*the* field . . . and *the* cave," as if the places no
longer belonged to him. And the modulation of the verb's final occurrence by "before the eyes of my people" seals the transfer with a public
commitment. Ephron's only concern is to get the dead buried.

Have we (with Abraham) done injustice to the Hittites, after all, or
at least to this one Hittite? Have we (mis)taken an excess of pious and
neighborly zeal for political and commercial jockeying, double courtesy
for double talk? A sorry reorientation would appear due, were it not
for the earlier lesson in deciphering Hittite compounded by a new set
of dissonant notes. That this dissonance is anything but loud makes
it all the more suggestive, because it owes its force to the contextual
encoding and loading of clues which is integral to the Bible's poetics,
in and out of dialogue. As an art of indirection, the Bible's is an art
of relations.

What first puts us on our guard, even before the talk resumes, is an otherwise innocent and casual detail in the narrator's stage directions, which introduce Ephron as "sitting amidst the Hittites": he is truly and literally (not, like Abraham, by hollow courtesy) one of them. Ephron's link with his circle soon tightens through the symmetry between the endpoints of their utterances. Each opens with the telltale "Hear us/ me, my lord" and finishes with "bury thy dead." It is not really surprising, therefore, that what comes in-between should sound as benevolent and prove no less tough.

Surely, if the townspeople offered too little, Ephron now offers too much. For him to present a stranger with the cave "at the edge of his field," in disregard for self and society, would make an extraordinary act of generosity; but that the entire field should be thrown in for good measure is incredible. It is also self-defeating, for the very standard of magnanimity set by the "giver" must deter the recipient on pain of a complete loss of face. The excess makes the gift as untouchable as would a refusal—which, one begins to suspect, is precisely the catch that Ephron (like the overstating spokesman before him) relies on. He can safely relinquish what nobody can afford to take over; and in the remote contingency that Abraham does venture to take him at his word, Ephron need no longer scruple about holding him in turn to his own definition of "giving . . . at the full price." The offer is airtight.

But this still leaves a gap in our understanding of Ephron's motivation. Does he want to play with the stranger? To humiliate or discourage him by overgenerosity? Most likely, because most in tribal character, he means to drive a hard bargain by raising the sale from a cave to the field that encloses it. In this he runs true to Hittite form all along the line. As before, the façade of piety and courtesy lifts to reveal the politician with a vested interest: "I would rather give you the land than the privileges that go with its sale." But the *over*giving points further back to disclose in turn the man of affairs exerting his leverage to the full. A mere cave, Ephron implies, is beneath discussion: a breach of principle does not come so cheap, and if I am to adjust the status quo for your benefit, you must make it worth my while. The three-layered pattern is complete.

On this reading of motive, the language bristles with equivocations, whose attractive aspect reverses between the lines. By a nice escalation of ambiguities-by-insincerity, if the Hittites did not say what they meant, Ephron does not mean what he says. The family resemblance presents itself as early as the correspondence between the respective openings:

(5) The Hittites answered Abraham, saying to him: (6) Hear us, my lord

(10) Ephron the Hittite answered Abraham . . . , saying: No, my lord, hear me.

The correspondence is even closer in the Hebrew original, where the pocket of diversity rendered above as "saying to him" vs. "saying: No" shrinks to a minimum, given the sound-equivalence of "saying *lo*"/"saying: *lo*." Unfortunately, the loss to homonymity (or, strictly, homophony) entailed by translation has often been compounded by interpretive tampering with the received text on the part of translators and critics. Their irritant is the first *lo*—supposedly redundant here, as well as in verse 14 below—and its doctoring goes in two opposite directions. According to one treatment, which begins with the Septuagint, the *lo* ("to him") framing the Hittite answer should be respelled (and accordingly relexicalized and relocated within the inset of the next verse) as *lo* ("No") to equal Ephron's. If this pushes the homonymity into full identity, a more popular line draws the members apart by excising the first *lo* altogether (e.g. Vulgate, RSV) or, most often, repointing it into the desiderative *lu* ("please," again with relocation forward to the inset). So both emendations would replace the Masoretic complex of phonemics/orthography, lexis, syntax, verse and discourse segmentation (as well as interdialogic linkage) by some substitute of their own devising, which allegedly recovers the consonantal text.

Gratuitousness apart, however, this is all Low Criticism with a vengeance: literally blind and deaf to the narrative's long-range play of sound and sense—one that moreover involves a shifting balance between deep and surface punning, between reiteration for continuity and variation for dynamism. A thematic element within the tale as a whole, the Hittite "No" actually makes an appearance on either occasion, only in a (dis)guise proper to the speaker and the stage.

In the first round, as befits the Hittite Yes/No prevarications about the very idea of making over land, the negative both is and isn't there. It is there, between the lines, and not only because it fits: the very rarity and redundance of that *lo* as a complement to "saying" invite its alternative reading as a standard prelude to a refusal. But it is not there, or not yet, on a footing of equality. Rather, the negative lurks underground by homonymic and contextual association with the manifest *lo* ("to him"), whose grammar, verse-and-discourse placement, as well as meaning, supply deep cover—so deep that the less favorable alternative may pass unnoticed, for a time at least. Whether out of sight or temporarily also out of the reader's mind, however, the homonymic alternativity remains appropriate and will sooner or later take effect: the sound is an echo, or an icon, of the elusive sense.

The original *lo* must therefore be trimmed neither into explicitness nor out of existence, on pain of upsetting the in-between balance of implication by wordplay and the adjustments to come. That balance indeed gets disturbed by the tale itself, but not before the second round, where retrospective illumination combines with forward movement to produce a new, heightened equilibrium of duplicity. By way of disclosure, Ephron's outspoken "No" looks back to his fellow Hittites' *lo*, as part of a larger correspondence, and (re)charges it with its own force all along the line—including the transfer from the narrator's frame to the body of the inset. By way of development, once it stands repatterned and revealed, the community's answer in turn helps to pinpoint the individual's variance amidst family likeness, hence the onward march of the negotiations. Things are showing progress, if only in (or in the guise of) formal resistance to Abraham's business talk. Either way, as early as the common preamble, the negative buried in the Hittites' "saying to him [*lo*]: 'My lord, hear us'" rises to the surface in and through Ephron's "saying: 'No [*lo*], my lord, hear me.'"

As it assumes formality, however, the negative by no means sheds but rather sharpens its duality. Before, in keeping with the assembly's entire response, their uncertain No mildly wavered underground between token objection to Abraham's self-image and tentative objection to his "holding," between counterportrait and counterproposal. But what does Ephron's overt "No, my lord" bear on?[12] From a principled No to Abraham's reference to payment—as well as to intercessors—its meaning veers round to a mercenary No to the smallness of the transaction, hence of the amount to be paid. "No money," in short, becomes "Not nearly enough money." Under cover of magnanimity, Ephron actually issues an ultimatum: all or nothing, take what "I have given" or leave it.

Nor is Ephron's ordering of gifts, whereby the volunteered "field" gets mentioned before the required "cave," an accident but a condition. So is his reference to the cave as being "in" (as against Abraham's "at the edge of") the field: the two inextricably go together. Likewise, "give" defines itself as a euphemism for "sell," in contrast to the plain sense of "giving" that it flaunts, and barbed with the sting of "give" as permission to deal. The calling of the people to witness, finally, turns from a commitment made to a friendless beneficiary into a reminder of the strength of his own position in this seller's market. "Sitting amidst," then speaking "in the hearing," then making gestures "before the eyes" of the Hittites, Ephron dictates terms as he thinks fit; and these three glances at the balance of power seem calculated to ironize the three solemn *give*'s that are difficult to take except as an order to deliver. Politeness, Politics, Profits: all recur in due order of depth, but in a stronger combination, as one might expect of a second round.[13]

Any lingering doubts about the incongruity between word and thought vanish with the final exchange.

> (12) Abraham bowed before the people of the land. (13) And he spoke to Ephron in the hearing of the people of the land, saying: If thou wilt only hear me. I have given the price of the field; take it from me, and I will bury my dead there. (14) Ephron answered Abraham, saying to him: (15) Hear me, my lord. A piece of land worth [lit., Land of] four hundred silver shekels—what is that between me and thee? Bury thy dead. (16) Abraham listened to [lit., heard] Ephron, and Abraham weighed out for Ephron the silver that he had named in the hearing of the Hittites, four hundred shekels of silver, according to the rate current among the merchants. (17) So the field of Ephron in Machpelah east of Mamre, the field and the cave which is in it and all the trees in the field in all the borders round about, (18) was made over to Abraham as his possession before the eyes of the Hittites, all who came in at the gate of his city. (19) Then Abraham buried Sarah his wife in the cave of the field of Machpelah, east of Mamre (that is, Hebron) in the land of Canaan. (20) The field and the cave which is in it were made over to Abraham as a holding for a burial ground by the Hittites.

Once Abraham speaks of "the field" (with no possessive either), rather than "the cave . . . at the edge of his field," we know for sure that we continue on the right track and in the right company. As in the second round, however, the double perspective on Ephron gains support from our fellow-interpreter within the dialogue even before he opens his lips. "Abraham bowed before the people of the land": the narrator's stage direction again encodes a reading directive. For all its external and neutral look, it communicates an inside view of the bower together with a judgment of his audience. The new bow not only makes for continuity—another round, familiar undercurrents—but also gives a sense of progression: less choice, more surrender, growing discordance between show and reality.

All this movement lurks in two small variants in the language of stage direction: one concerning the name and the other the identity of Abraham's audience. Called *the Hittites* in the first round and *the people of the land, the Hittites* in the second, they now appear (twice) as *the people of the land*. On the face of it, or in a purely linguistic view, the narrative just shifts from a proper noun, through a definite phrase on which the proper noun follows in apposition, to the definite phrase by itself. In poetic context, however, the fact that the referent stays constant does not yet make the referring expressions equivalent, nor their changes random or even merely "elegant." For the variations escalate from (1) an opaque tribal name, through (2) a redundancy where that name coexists with a descriptive term geared to the status of its bearers, to (3) a shortened form where the status-term replaces the name altogether, as if crowding it out. Accordingly, the three designations parallel the three rounds in more than number. The shifts among them fall into a dynamics of reference that miniaturizes and elucidates the dynamics of the dialogue as a whole: they reflect a steady rise in political implication and constraint from one round to another, an increasingly marked bearing on the imbalance of power. Abraham bows to the inevitable.

But this elucidation goes with ambiguity, because as the receiver of the bow looms larger, his identity grows darker. To whom does Abraham now direct this gesture? He no longer bows "to" but "before the people of the land," so that it is hard to tell whether the novel preposition bears the same meaning and indicates the same addressee as the old. Does the obeisance again go *to* the Hittites at large—"before" as in 2 Kings 18:22—and if so, why? Or does it this time change direction to Ephron *in the presence of* the others—"before" as in Gen. 18:22—and if so, why omit the recipient's name in favor of the witnesses?

Contrary to the choices made by translators and exegetes one way *or* the other, the wording defies resolution to suggestive effect. Abraham's bow covers the two addressees at once because both are in the picture and the individual cannot really be told apart from the collective. Given the situational context—which the pressure of ambiguity brings back to mind—they are even literally inseparable. For Ephron remains "sitting amidst the Hittites": a physical placement that now focuses afresh a position of strength. So does the immediate sequel, "he spoke to Ephron in the hearing of the people of the land," which formally switches the roles of direct and indirect listener assigned in Abraham's earlier speech, but without truly changing the relations. In bowing as in speaking, the nominal receiver makes very little difference. The show includes a make-believe of a three- rather than two-party dialogue; and the show must of course go on, now appearing to modulate with the shift of partners into a man-to-man encounter. Yet the realities of power cut across all dialogic movement to pit an outsider in straits against a citizen with his people solidly around and behind him.

Again, the two-directionality of the bow not only preserves but redoubles the twofold meaning and message it assumed in the earlier round. By the gratitude overtly expressed, the gesture pretends to thank Ephron for acceding to (if not exceeding) the request and the townspeople for exerting their influence in mediation. At the same time, the obedience tacitly conveyed bows to Ephron's ultimatum and to the town's power to enforce it. In Abraham's hands as well as the narrator's, therefore, the fiction and the reality of the signal are each so doubled as to heighten their polar incongruity. This proportionally sharpens the judgment on the Hittites, who must be no less alive to this irony than their interlocutor himself or for that matter the reader aligned with him. But then the Hittites do not mind, to say the least, as long as appearances are kept up.

In Abraham's ensuing speech, the ambiguities packed into this dumb sign have their vocal counterpart and development. Judging by his professions, one might think him too deaf and dense to notice that the terms of the deal have been altered, let alone dictated. The burial site at last within reach, he will not make the slightest difficulty about the forms or the conditions of transfer. Rather, having bowed his thanks, he proceeds to slip in an assenting reference to "the field," as though this were the point at issue all along. Where else would he want to "bury my dead" if not "there"? As a matter of grammatical fact, this all-important reference even appears in a lowly genitive role—"the price *of* the field"—with the money fronting as topic, the only one that still needs discussing, as it were.

Not that Ephron himself has ever introduced this sordid topic. By another twist of the grotesque fiction, Abraham having been coerced into making a bid for a site beyond his requirements, he must now press the urbane blackmailer to accept the ransom as a personal favor. "Don't embarrass me by your liberality in front of all our neighbors, but let me reciprocate." *If thou wilt only hear me,* Abraham begins his mock pleading, amidst ironic echoes and collisions of sense.[14] "Please hear me as I have 'heard' you." *I have given the price of the field; take it from me* asks anew for a balance of honor, with mutual give and take. Abraham's "I have given" replicates Ephron's completely—in tense as well as in person and root—to suggest that if the one act of voluntary giving is an accomplished fact, so is the other. It now remains for either party to do the taking. *And I will bury my dead there*: if Ephron does not lead the way in taking—Abraham ends with a polite threat implicit in the order of actions—there will be no burial. Under the veil of saving his own face, Abraham thus saves Ephron's.

But even in face of this argument, unexceptionable by any standards of tactful obliquity, Ephron will not yet call it a day. Really, he counters, what is a lot "worth four hundred silver shekels" between us? This protest must ring false to the most innocent ear, but it is not so easy to say precisely where and why, because Ephron still covers his tracks.

For the record, after all, he adheres to the letter as well as to the spirit of his original offer. The opening and closing formulas repeat themselves almost verbatim, and the in-between rhetorical question makes an expressive, heightened, sentence-length parallel to the insistence on "giving." This continuity even extends to the choice of topic, since Ephron persists in foregrounding the property ("field" and "cave" before, "a piece of land" now) at the expense of the money. In the Hebrew, this topical emphasis or scaling finds a precise linguistic reflex in the inversion of a two-noun group—one noun in the construct state, the other in the genitive—with the change of speakers: Abraham's speech refers to "the price of the field," Ephron's counterspeech to "land of four hundred silver shekels." *X of Y* becomes *Y of X*. Consistently, then, this inversion meets Abraham's plea for reciprocity by shrugging off the favor done—or at least the idea of making such an ado about it in the present company ("between me and thee")—and putting the priorities right. The main thing is to "bury thy dead."

And yet Ephron's mask is of course slipping, the gap between word and will far more perceptible than before. But how to pinpoint this false ring, how to trace the effect of insincerity back to its causes? Even here, it is not enough to scrutinize the language by itself, as a modern close reader might be tempted to do. Out of context, the hardest digging into Ephron's words and speech patterns will scratch but not break through the surface of duplicity. Language in real-life or artistic action must always take its reference from the world. And realistic as ever, the Bible indeed anchors the decisive clue in the way of the world, especially the brute facts of commerce in relation to the probabilities of human nature. On top of the earlier incongruity between the cave requested and the field given, we now have that between the money due (indeed "given") in exchange and the money refused. Above all, what lays bare Ephron's mind is the site's valuation in the process—if not the very naming then certainly the largeness of the sum he ostentatiously dismisses.[15] It is a strange donor who will put a price-tag on his gift; how much stranger to meet one who jacks up the figure in explaining why he gives it away. And the figure is, literally, extortionate, as the narrative expects the reader to grasp on the spot along with the parties themselves. Just look at a few comparable transactions. Many centuries later, and in a scene modeled on ours, David paid Araunah the Jebusite fifty shekels for the site of the Jerusalem Temple, including cattle for sacrifice (2 Sam. 24:24). Jeremiah bought his cousin's field at Anatot for only seventeen shekels (Jer. 32:9). Again, Omri gave six thousand shekels ("two silver talents") for the whole area of his future capital Samaria (1 Kings 16:24). Devaluation over the centuries apart, then, the valuation at four hundred shekels must have come as a staggering blow, its very exorbitance making the valuer's show of magnanimity yet seemlier *and* safer than the expansion from cave to field.

Ephron prolongs the dialogue, then, not because his honor but because his greed is still unsatisfied. His assessment does not even reflect any fear of being shortchanged by Abraham, who stands committed to buying "at the full price." On the contrary, Ephron's fear is exactly that, if he agrees to "take" the money "of the field" already "given," he will receive no more than the going ("full") value. And to prevent this fair exchange, he reverts to his old trick of dictating terms. Just as the earlier insistence on "giving" served as a cover for maximizing the property negotiable, so does the waving aside of the money actually set the price.

Once the facts and figures expose Ephron's high-mindedness as high-handedness, the language follows suit down to the minutest details. Generally, like Abraham's own last speech, the relative shortness of the counterspeech marks a getting down to business—hence a concern to wrap the deal up less in the ceremonial than in the operational sense. No rehearsals, no self-explications, no mock appeals to the silent gallery. With the padding reduced to a minimum, statement draws closer to suggestion, and ambiguity between exterior and interior gets much easier to resolve. The less distance, the more dissonance and transparence.

Thus the very opening, "Ephron answered Abraham saying to him [*lo*]: My lord, hear me," rings yet another change on the *lo* wordplay between "to him" and "no." At this late point, however, the variation is not only more expected than in the two earlier rounds (as is also its traditional emendation into *lu*) but also more salient and revealing. For Ephron's "*lo*," which in his previous response (vv. 10–11) departed from his tribe's (vv. 5–6) in configuration and sense, now falls back into line: it changes position from quoted inset ("saying: *lo*") to narrative frame ("saying *lo*: . . .") along with overt meaning from "No" to "to him." This full realignment with the community, down to the twofold (re)suppression or (re)submergence of the negative, may appear to signal a change for the better. But as elsewhere, only more so, the favorable appearance reverses to ironic effect. In context, the homonymity among all three Hittite exordiums now reflects in small compass a decreasing thought for appearances relative to both Ephron's own earlier posture, from which he now varies, and that of the Hittites, into which he now varies by way of seeming return to the outset. Except for sound play and related indirections, after all, they didn't say No to a holding, while he no longer says No to the money.

Next, in "land worth four hundred silver shekels—what is it between me and thee?" the fact of Ephron's departure from his "the field I have given thee" is evident, and its message by now transparent. But this variation also has its finer points, mainly pressure points, that still await decoding. Note how the replacement of the specific term "field" by the all-inclusive "land" brings the judicial context to the fore, wielding the citizen rights vested in "the people of the land" as stick and carrot at once. Note likewise the diametric opposition that separates the manifest from the latent sense of "between me and thee": "between friends" (if not "between an ordinary Hittite and 'a great prince'") vs. "between superior and (rich) dependent." The figure named and disclaimed at the heart of the sentence thus enjoys the protection, as it were, of unspoken threats coming from either flank.

Perhaps most underhanded of all is the question form into which the sentence as a whole transposes. Even if taken at face (or face- saving) value as a rhetorical question, the interrogative would weaken any commitment to altruism made by the declarative "I have given." And below the surface, the force of commitment evaporates altogether. Considering the removal of the negative (*lo*) from the preamble, the question need not amount to anything beyond a statement of credit, i.e., "There's no hurry about the payment, but first bury your wife; what is such a debt between parties who trust each other?" But even the disparity between "I have given" and "I will give on account" still lends itself to further widening toward polarity. For by another indirection typical of biblical dialogue, the rhetorical query may always imply or receive an answer different, at times contrary, to the one it appears to assume. Accordingly, given the proper "hearing" demanded again in advance, the answer to "four hundred silver shekels—what is it?" turns all the way from the pretended "Nothing" into the intended "Everything": this sum alone will make the difference between clinching and calling off the deal. (Or indeed, with the tail-end as sting, "Nothing between our two selves, whatever the case between equals.")

On this interpretation, the ugliest but also the likeliest of all, Ephron does not extend to Abraham so much as credit. Instead, he finishes his call for money by repeating the same ploy whereby he fixed the size of the property: ultimatum through word sequence. Converting in the process Abraham's polite threat against himself ("take . . . and I will bury") into a practical scenario, Ephron so orders his sentences as to lay down the order of events: first payment, then burial. Cash on the barrel-head, indeed on the barrow-head.

In fact, whether or not the reader "hears" Ephron right, Abraham certainly does: the shift from the hitherto transitive to the intransitive form of the key-verb ("listened *to*") in the ensuing sentence even stresses the aspect of forced obedience. Hence also the marked equivalence (especially in the Hebrew) of the two sentences "Abraham listened to Ephron and Abraham weighed out to [for] Ephron," which implies a tight causal sequence: what Abraham heard behind the utterance he at once performed, doing as he was bidden rather than as he saw fit despite the bidding to the contrary. This implication draws yet further support from the etymological link, actualized in context, between *va-yishkol* ("weighed out") and *shekel*: having heard the reference to the shekels, he shekels them out, so to speak. All the more so considering that the money has been "named in the hearing of the Hittites"—formally claimed, that is, not disclaimed. And the silver thus named and paid out comes at the fullest rate, or in the narrative's own idiom, again quietly realized for irony, at "the rate current among the merchants."

By now, to miss the implications of as well as on top of the plain facts themselves, one must be blind and deaf:[16] blind to the doings, deaf to all that the protagonist hears and that the text even re-sounds through such exact echoes as the literal "four hundred silver shekels" or the literalized *va-yishkol*. Beyond the echoes, however, there no longer remains anything on which to exercise our sense of hearing, for the dialogue has abruptly turned into dumb show. Everything now happens in complete silence between the parties, watched by the assembly that has long reduced itself to a collective ear and eye. Abraham makes no objection to the price, nor does Ephron utter a single word of protest against the payment or even against its promptness. Abrupt and discordant, the silence is also drawn out. In the verse just considered, note the iconic manner whereby the sheer length of the discourse mirrors the slowness and extension of the weighing process in the world. Yet the very perceptibility of this shift, again miniaturized in the dynamizing of the noun "shekel" into the verb "va-yishkol," suggests not only how but why utterance gives way to action: the time for words has passed. The sounds made thus far having concealed the sense, their absence now reveals it.

But as the characters fall into silence, the narrator grows wonderfully vocal all at once. This change of speaking parts between inset and frame appears strange for its inconsistency and its consistency alike. On the one hand, the narrator breaks pattern: having earlier limited himself to barely introducing the turns of others in his role as quoter, he now assumes a monopoly on voice, addressing to the reader in his own person what is for the tale (and the Bible) an enormous stretch of five verses (16–20). On the other hand, he reverses the pattern of speech versus silence only to overwhelm us with a torrent of ostensibly technical as well as repetitious details concerning the externals of the transaction, instead of unfolding at long last the essentials of thought, motive, value judgment. Combined, the two choices jar with each other's oddity. Why the pointed reticence before, and why now the pointless loquacity amounting to continued reticence?

As the example of verse 16 indicates, however, the dialogue-maker's sudden speaking works to much the same effect as the dialogists' lapse into silence: final exposure, though still by indirection. Thus, the very bulk of this ending has its significance. Just as verse 16 enacts by slow motion the length of the weighing, hence the quantity of the silver paid, so does the rest mime the deliberateness of the following procedures of transfer. Contrary to the pretense of cavalier treatment, every specification counts along with the counting of every shekel. Nor, this time, is the reflection—discourse tempo and extent mirroring the plot's own —just iconic but properly mimetic. For if these verses sound like a bill of sale—and historians have indeed documented a close adherence to contemporary forms[17]—then the pattern has not really broken, after all. The characters have only modulated from speech to writing, and the narrator accordingly quotes their finished written contract, small print included, just as he reported their oral dealing and double dealing. To clinch this effect, the phraseology and arrangement of the writing again glance back at the speaking. For echoes of the dialogue continue to reverberate in force throughout—"the field of Ephron in Machpelah . . . the field and the cave which is in it . . . before the eyes of the Hittites, all who came in at the gate of his city. . . . in the cave of the field of Machpelah. . . . the field and the cave which is in it . . . as a holding for a burial ground"—but now explicated and fixed in their due contractual register. (As always, repetition goes with variation, if only in stylistic context and intelligibility.) Likewise with the arrangement of the block as a whole. Observe the recurrence (and confirmation) in enactment of the order of events projected earlier by way of an ambiguously extortionate scenario: first payment and transfer, "*then* Abraham buried Sarah his wife." It is even possible that the sequence of verses reflects an ascending sequence of possession: first the commercial give-and-take between the individual parties, "before the eyes of the Hittites" as witnesses, then the burial and with it the sealing of the title to "a holding for a burial ground by [lit., from] the Hittites" as a political body. At any rate, what has begun with a smokescreen of civilities ends with an array of hard legalisms. The show is over.

Evidently, this narrative makes heavy demands on its readers—if only because it places us at no less than three sizable removes from the narrator with whom we are supposed to keep in touch. Over and above the indirections built into dialogue as such, we must unravel the indirections of double-talk contrived by the speakers locked in silent battle, all expert rhetoricians and all but one accomplished hypocrites as well. In turn, the double-talk itself multiplies on either side of the dialogic fence. With the Hittites, the layers of indirection follow an order of decorum: a surface of politeness, a subtext of legalistic leverage, and a bedrock of naked greed. On Abraham's side, communication must first be quietly established with Ephron through the assembly, then maintained with the assembly through Ephron, so as to operate on the private and the public front at once. Wheels within wheels within wheels: even for the Bible, this pushes complication and hence comprehension to an extreme.

So, as if to give the screw yet another turn, does the narrator's reticence throughout. Instead of using his privileges to make up for the extra distance and load imposed on the reader, the narrator withholds all overt guidance. As an omniscient, he could at any point expose for our benefit the busy minds of the speakers, but he leaves them opaque. As the supreme ideological authority, he might tell us what to think and how to judge, but he prefers to refrain from evaluation too. As the master of his tale, he is in the best position to elucidate for us why he tells it, and why in this of all ways, but again he doesn't. His withdrawal from the scene where the characters negotiate is complete, except for a supply of bare factual data: the briefest exposition to the dialogue, stage directions between turns, closure. As a maker of dialogue outside drama, in short, the narrator could freely communicate with us in his own voice, yet he chooses to play, indeed to outplay, the dramatist. For he keeps back even the kind of aids and shortcuts to understanding granted by dramatic license. No Greek chorus, no aside or soliloquy, not so much as a change of scene to adjust perspective. The dialogists are left to their own devices, and with them the reader.

But the heavier the load and the higher the premium that the narrative puts on interpretation, the sharper the wonder about the point of it all. If we find ourselves driven to assign a role to parts that look superfluous, such as repeats within and across turns, how much more so regarding the whole. To what end does the Bible narrate this tale, and why in this of all modes of narration? If the characters turn their indirections to such account, then what does the storyteller wish to say and achieve through his, which include and radicalize as well as frame theirs? It would be strange to find the dialogue-maker less purposive in communication (or, figuratively, less profit-minded) than his own dialogists.

Of course, the pleasure and excitement and sheer challenge to ingenuity given by the drama of reading are their own recommendation, especially when so multifold and of such a high order. Where, if not in art, is the play the thing? However true—and I would be the last to deny it—this answer fails to explain why the drama of reading should be enacted and experienced on the particular ground of Machpelah. Given that the art of indirection (implication, silence, difficult coherence) is the Bible's rule, it would yet seem a waste of energy to exercise this art at its most demanding on the purchase of a mere cave—and in a book like Genesis, too, which skips or skimps landmarks in universal and patriarchal history. If the tale of Machpelah is tellable, others are even more so that remain untold.

This problem of overall relevance—or, the other way about, redundancy—grows even more troublesome from other directions. In the eyes of Hebrew ideology, for example, the tale may appear not just light-weight and as such unworthy of notice, but objectionable, decidedly to be avoided. For the Bible normally suppresses (or minimizes) whatever is liable to promote the cult of the dead, in line with its war against idolatry. Recall how the Deuteronomist pretends ignorance as to the whereabouts of the grave of Moses himself; and indeed, not a single mention of Machpelah occurs beyond Genesis. In genetic terms, again, source criticism usually attributes this narrative to the Priestly writer, notorious for the limitations of his horizons and interests: figures, lists, genealogies, statistics, divine control of events. If so, why should this dry chronicler—who begins by recording Sarah's lifespan down to the last year (23:1)—suddenly break into rich and crafty dialogue? And why should the God-centered moralist silently elaborate a drama fought out by men?

No wonder this tale has always puzzled commentators of the most various stripes. In fact, the main lines of explanation go so far back as the rabbis, and none really covers the facts to be explained. According to one line, the narrative celebrates the first step in the fulfillment of God's promise to confer the land of Canaan upon Abraham and his descendants. According to a contrary, and in my view better line, the chapter rather marks the distance from such a happy state. A third line appears in a famous midrash: "This is one of the three places out of which the nations of the world cannot cheat Israel, saying, 'You hold them by robbery.' These are they: the cave of Machpelah, the Temple, and Joseph's burial site. The cave of Machpelah, for it is written: 'Abraham listened to Ephron and Abraham weighed out for Ephron the silver that he had named.' The Temple, for it is written: 'David gave Ornan six hundred gold shekels for the site.'[18] And Joseph's burial site, for it is said: 'He [Jacob] bought for a hundred qesitah the piece of land on which he had pitched his tent from the sons of Hamor, Shechem's father'" (*Bereshit Rabba* 79:7). This last attempt at resolution does not even account for the space allotted to the Purchase of Machpelah but rather focuses its oddity by association: the bracketing with Jacob's purchase of the encampment, which receives just the one verse quoted by the Midrash as title deed.[19] But none of the three answers makes any sense of the tale's narrative structure, leaving its indirections an expense of spirit on the Bible's part and the reader's. If the moral could be pointed any way, then the way chosen becomes less than pointless.

It would therefore seem best to pursue the consequences of those indirections beyond the play of inference as such. What difference does the strategy of storytelling make to the overall impact of the story-stuff, namely, to the basic facts that must go into any version, from the least to the most artful? The strategy chosen will doubtless have a crucial, yet typically two-edged, effect on our attitude toward the participants in the dialogue. On the one hand, the simpler or more transparent the narration, the more automatic the polarization of values (emotional, ethical, theological) between Abraham and the Hittites. Given the conflict, the implied reader's sympathy as well as loyalty go out to Abraham —patriarch, old man, newly bereaved, solitary, underdog, victim—and it would be only too easy for our disapproval of his grasping antagonists to kindle into hot rage and outrage. The situation has all the makings of melodrama, complete with sentimentality, stock response, black-and-white portraiture. In its contempt for this line of least resistance, therefore, the Bible typically plays off narrative manner against narrated matter. The storytelling balances and brakes, distances and disciplines the story-stuff by enveloping it in all the ambiguities—silence, darkness, oscillation—that make up the favorite posture of irony.

As a result, we are not just kept too busy making sense of what happens to cultivate our grievances about it. The reader must grope his way to the judgments, along with the facts and motives, that a transparent narration would establish from the start. The loaded normative opposition between the camps is still there to affect us, but as an inference that leaves room for doubt *and* the benefit of doubt almost to the end, rather than as a given whose outrageousness escalates with each further speech. (In fact, the gaps about motive and tactics are *never* overtly closed nor judgment passed, even when they have in effect been resolved beyond doubt.) The protagonist comes on stage as such, but whether and how and to what extent the antagonist deserves the name remains to be discovered. And by the time the process of discovery has run its course, the crisis is over and Abraham in firm possession of his object. In this regard, the workings of indirection are governed by a poetic rationale that seeks to align the plot with the rhetoric, to control our sentiments and evaluations by twisting our route to comprehension. As well as forming an end in itself, the ordeal of understanding is also a means to the desired response that evolves together with it along the reading process.

On the other hand, this desired response aims for a sense of contrast that is ironic and developing but on the whole not much softer relative to straightforward narration; and the services rendered by the means adjust themselves accordingly. To go by the surface, the parties are equally opaque and therefore equally distanced. But this is only an impression generated by the dialogue's art, and probably deepened by the widespread theoretical illusion that dialogue in or out of drama entails an objective point of view. Actually, the narrative allies the reader throughout with Abraham's perspective against the Hittites, and regarding not only belief system but also information and interpretation. Of the two sides, he alone is the known quantity. From our earlier encounters with him, we know that he would not dream of mixing his family's dust with the Canaanites', or of accepting, let alone expecting material favors. We also know him to be a righteous man, who will deal straight with his neighbors, as indeed he tries to do here, unless forced into playing the game. Even then, he knows his own mind, while the other parties seem to be making theirs up as they go along. In effect if not in form, therefore, Abraham becomes relatively transparent—a focus and a fellow in the ordeal of reading the Hittite double-talk. If not a subject of narration or consciousness in the modern manner, he certainly establishes himself as our man in the dialogue—with a further lessening of distance and increase of sympathy to match. Here, then, the dynamics of plot disclosure or discovery and the dynamics of judgment come together again. The difficulties of comprehension operate to goad as well as to rein evaluation, dovetailing the artistic pressure for obliquity with the ideological imperative of polarity.

Further, as with art and ideology so with large-scale composition. The more first-hand our experience of the trouble in which Sarah's burial landed Abraham, the sharper our insight into its continuity and discontinuity with the wider pattern of his history as a whole. Continuity, because Abraham's life extends as a long series of ordeals, the most terrible of which unfolded as recently as the previous chapter, the Binding of Isaac. And also discontinuity, because the scene contradicts God's repeated promise to the Patriarch. The narrative even seems to go out of its way to nail down the contradiction in the language itself. At the earliest opportunity, Abraham's role and deserts are brought to mind through the backstairs of literalized meaning. The Hittites title him *nesi Elohim*, which they probably (and falsely) use as an idiom for "great prince" but which we know to be the simple truth: "prince (or elect) of God." And as if to rub in the incongruity, the key words of the dialogue fall into ironic rhyme with the divine words of promise, starting from Abraham's call. For example, after the parting from Lot: "All the *land* that thou seest I will *give* to thee and to thy descendants forever. . . . Arise, walk through the breadth and the length of the *land*, for to thee will I *give* it" (13:15–17). Then, in terms of official covenant, "I . . . have brought thee out of Ur of the Chaldeans, to give thee this *land* to possess. . . . To thy descendants *I have given* this land, from the river of Egypt to the great river, the river of Euphrates, the land of the Kenites, the Kenizzites, the Kadmonites, the *Hittites*. . . ." (15: 7, 18–19). Again, before Isaac's birth: "*I have given* to thee, and to thy descendants after thee, the *land* of thy *alienness*, all the *land* of Canaan, for an eternal *holding*" (17:8). Or consider the ultimate rhyming of the "four hundred silver shekels" with the "four hundred years" (or "the fourth generation") in which Abraham's descendants are supposed to come into their own (15:13–15), including the City of the Four, "Kiryat-Arba (that is, Hebron)."

Land, give, Hittite, alien, holding, numbering: the echoes (down to verbal forms) are exact, manifold, cumulative, and proportionally discordant. If within the episode itself the structure of repetition always involves variance, then in interepisodic perspective variance goes to the limit of flat opposition. And if men play with words to make their bargain, God does not appear to keep his at all. Duplicity again, if you will, with a vengeance.

It would therefore be absurd to explain the tale as a celebration of the beginning of fulfillment. Rather, the text joins forces with the context to radicalize the sense of nonfulfillment, bringing into full view the patriarch urged for decades to regard the breadth and the length of Canaan as *his* possession[20] yet driven to beg "the people of the land" for a cave at the edge of a field in which to bury the matriarch. Not to speak of the multiple price—emotional, spiritual, financial, inferential, all at their highest—exacted by those dealings. Here, as in other respects, the fuller our view of externals the more intriguing the darkness thrown about the secret self. The reader, from his vantage point in history, cannot help wondering how the hero himself inwardly squares past commitment with present straits and the question mark about the future. If we know that what sounds like cumulative divine duplicity will resolve itself in its own good time, our fellow interpreter enjoys no hindsight. From his perspective, amidst the human duplicity heard and countered at Kiryat-Arba's city gate, the doubts arising about the Promise must be formidable; but does he still find a loophole for faith and hope? Take the link between four hundred shekels and four hundred years, the Fourth Generation and the City of Four. Does Abraham view the reappearance of the numbers of the Promise as a mockery or, quite the opposite, as a sign of divine order and control in apparent coincidence? Does he now envisage a disheartening continuity between the plight indicated by the four hundred shekels and the four centuries of suffering ahead—"thy descendants will be aliens in a land that is not theirs, and they will be oppressed for four hundred years"—oppression in exile following on oppression at home, the hardship of servitude long and certain but deliverance and inheritance all the more questionable? Or does he draw comfort from the analogy with the scenario of oppression-as-a-prelude-to-deliverance in Egypt, of "alienness" and "servitude" before "great possessions," of judgment overtaking the Canaanite oppressor ("for the iniquity of the Amorites is not yet complete") as well as the Egyptian ("the nation which they will serve") in the ripeness of time—with the money extorted now forming a kind of earnest or limit, shekel per year? Does he see the numerology, in short, as a contradiction or as a confirmation of the Covenant? Or does he oscillate, here as with other echoes, between fear and hope?

We simply cannot tell. For the patriarch neither reveals his thoughts nor has them revealed for him by the narrative, not even through the indirections that go behind his dialogue with the Hittites. There are gaps and gaps, and this one, surely the most crucial, remains permanent for contrast. It is as if on this puzzle Abraham simply *has* no thoughts —as if, amid strenuous and expert reading of the minds of his fellow men, he withstands every temptation to read God's. In such light, the midrashic term of praise for him who "does not reflect after" God's ways (e.g., *Shemot Rabbah* 6:4, *Baba Batra* 15b) indeed applies, in the double sense of no more venturing to entertain than to cast a reflection, or of suspending judgment by suppressing thought on divine mysteries.

This incongruity between God's promise and performance also disables the attempt to relegate our chapter to a grab bag of "final experiences, testamentary steps and procedures" that bow Abraham out as soon as his history has reached its climax and closure in the foregoing chapter, the Binding of Isaac.[21] On the contrary, the narrative furthers the thrust of the book, notably the twofold concern with seed and land, both promised only to be long withheld and finally given in the shortest measure, except for pain. So far from an appendix, it makes not just a sequel but a companion piece to the Binding of Isaac. Not for nothing are the two stories juxtaposed. Each focuses and problematizes a member of the natural pair "life versus death"—the one threatening Isaac with untimely departure, the other Sarah with unseemly rest. Each brings to a crisis one of the grand elements of the Promise. Each shows the Patriarch heroically rising to the challenge, doing what he must without a murmur on his lips and with a heart closed to impertinent questions, his own apparently included. And if the crisis about the land pales beside the threat to the line, or rather shows its lighter side in the telling, it still remains ideologically as weighty. Again, it requires less than the supreme sacrifice but also more than straightforward action: a peculiar effort to make sense and not to make sense at once, to keep interpreting the scene at Hebron in isolation from its causes or consequences in heaven, to double-think in a way as well as to double-talk. And for further balance, Isaac survives, yet the issue of Canaan is left all the more perceptibly unresolved outside the burial-ground; nor will it be resolved by the time the husband joins his wife there. The theme of the Purchase of Machpelah thus defines itself in relation to the whole as the last, and the most lasting, of Abraham's trials.

PRINCELY CHARACTERS

James C. Nohrnberg

"Who am I, Lord Yahweh, and what is my House, that you have
led me as far as this?" (David in 2 Sam. 7:18b)

"Do you not know that in Israel a prince, a great man, has fallen
today?" (David on Abner, 2 Sam. 3:38)

I

In the following paper I wish to consider an analogy that has been suggested to me in the course of trying to expound the books of Robert
Alter and Meir Sternberg. This is the analogy between the biblical characters of Joseph and David. Both Alter and Sternberg suggest that the
formation of these particular characters equates with something like
the literary formation of character itself,[1] and both authors have demonstrated that in the stories of Joseph and David "the inward turn of narrative" can be pursued rather further than with any other of the biblical
characters.[2] Sternberg in particular traces such a path through the
Davidic imbroglio or morass by means of a pioneering analysis of what
we could know of David the schemer. We can never know the identity
of the anonymous Deep Throat of the Davidic Watergate,[3] but we can
see every twist of David's manipulations, as Bathshebagate begets
Uriahgate, and Uriahgate begets Rabbahgate. Similarly, we can never
know exactly what became of Joseph from the time he was abandoned
by his brothers to the time he is found in Egypt, but we can hardly
escape the fact that his brothers did not want to know, and that Joseph
is determined to know how much they did not want to know.[4]

The question is, why do such questions, with their epistemological
overtones, belong to Joseph's and David's stories in such eminence? Furthermore, why are these characters the Bible's two "egoists," even if they
are also the two characters who can be shown to have the ability to
put their egos on hold in the presence of others? As such questions
suggest, these two characters make an immediate appeal to novelistic
analysis: they are "characters" in narrower senses of the term, distinc-

tively "modern" and hence "worldly" within the context from which they emerge. They have "lives" in the special Plutarchian sense of a distinctively careerist mode, and these lives are shown by means of the interface of public personage and private person. Furthermore, these characters are found in the domestic setting for which the frequent novelistic concomitant is leisure-class adultery. These lives strike us as material that could be recycled for the consumers of fiction and "literature," as it has been, by authors as different as Henry Fielding and Mario Puzo.[5]

If we had to characterize these lives as lives, we would say that their common feature is adversity: the doubling of each character's particular jeopardy. And both characters are jeopardized in another "house." Ignored at home, David the musician earns enmity in the house of Saul; cast out by his brothers, Joseph the servant becomes a victim in the house of Potiphar. Both have to flee from the interior space of their master, and both are under suspicion of having seduced the second person of the house.

Though our questions about the stories of these parallel characters ask themselves without much prompting, they nonetheless cannot be asked except through a contrast with biblical characterization in general. It is the purpose of this essay to consider what these lives have in common, and to explain what kind of exception or conformity they exhibit in regard to the biblical rule. The apparent uniqueness of the narratives belonging to Joseph and David, I will be arguing, conforms to some deeper logic inherent in the major biblical narrative taken as a whole.

II

A modern literary critic will love the Bible for all its characters, and for the incidents that dramatize character. Like Shakespeare, Chaucer, and Dante, the Creator did not repeat himself as to character, or limit himself as to its variety. God's resolve to convoke Israel as a morally answerable corporate individual suggests both why character matters so much in the Old Testament, and why none of its characters are to be understood without incorporating them into their national experience or incorporating it into them. But the regularly jeopardized history of Israel as a whole, from the selfish gene of Genesis to the selfless Suffering Servant and deracinated national remnant of deutero-Isaiah, can give this national character only an episodic purchase on itself, not to mention an even less secure self-possession accorded to the individual. Thus Moses cannot enter the Promised Land, Samson's ruin makes a greater figure than his life, and Elijah is spirited away beyond Jordan; the Lord giveth and the Lord taketh away. Character in the Bible is thus something rather ecstatic, and like the breath of life breathed into

Adam, subject to exhaustion. Or like Eve, fashioned secondarily, in the image of dependency and contingency. Or like the stricken Job, tremendously overshadowed by the only character in the Bible whose character is genuinely autonomous. All other characters—that is, other than God —have their lives and substance on loan.

The recurrent idea that the reader's main access to the minds of biblical characters comes from observing their responses—Gunkel's idea[6] —does not stand up to Sternberg's evidence for both free indirect thought and mentation as dramatized by dialogue. And when the Bible is silent or opaque about what a character has for an inner life, the alternatives open to him usually speak for themselves; and the de´nouement can also speak for an otherwise laconic agent. But if the Bible anticipates "the inward turn of narrative," it nonetheless never turns away from human activity being made public and visible. The heart that is inscrutable exists in an interpretive relation to the heart that is worn on the sleeve; in the story of David, in particular, they are the same heart. And despite the reserve of the narrator himself, it is generally shown that God, in the narrator's place, knows the other characters' minds. Given the "givenness" of biblical character,[7] it is precisely to this all-knowing God that such a vast variety of human individualities must be referred. Persons in the Bible do not owe their character to their own casting, like the princely individualists in Shakespeare; nor do they owe it to their habits, like the reiterative sinners in Dante; nor do they owe it to their stars, like the earthbound types in Chaucer. They owe their character to an exceptionality that finally comes from the God who has determined upon nothing less wondrous and variegated. Yet they do not owe their character to anything like an utter personal distinctiveness, because they are always constrained by their election to their role: vocation, mission, station, office or duty. In the Bible the outward expression of a character in the world of other people checks and qualifies the inward turn of narrative well before any character might follow himself into the recesses of an idiosyncrasy that would render the public world irrelevant to him or render him unaccountable to it. No character is ever dehistoricized or personalized in this quixotic way, unless Nebuchadnezzar and Job be counted as exceptions. Both the Creator and the tellers rehabilitate—or restore to public function —even these examples. Apart from Job, a character's personal passion is not studied for its own sake, that is, for the sake of the figure his story might make apart from the place it will have in the ongoing collective destiny, represented at the outset by the continuity of the genealogies.

Along with the collective destiny, the Bible also emphasizes that the possession of their various individualities is itself part of what members of the human species have in common. Though a man's good may turn to evil or his evil be turned to good, and though he may be either a surprise or a disappointment, the matter is there to be tested, and so there is also character to be tested or summoned forth. In particular Sternberg has shown that although such character may be temporarily identified by externals, it is finally defined by an inquiry into internals.[8] For the Bible offers us no characterological "package deals." The truth about a character emerges from gaps and ratios between what he or she is in the abstract—say a father, or a judge—and in particular— say very elderly, or left-handed. The Judges are a case in point: on the one hand, they were all judges; on the other hand, they were all oddballs.

The Bible necessarily insists on individualizing characters, in the very process of bringing them to judgment. Solomon devises his famous test for distinguishing between a kidnapper and a kinsman. The duodeca- logue of Deuteronomy 27 makes the long arm of Yahweh's curse answer- able for the discernment of such secret crime, in the confidence that Yahweh will know, but in the narrative proper it is all the Lord's readers who are to be made prophets. Daniel divines the sexual idiosyncrasies of the two accusers of Susannah, and Jesus exposes the secret sinfulness of each of the individuals banded together to collectivize the casting of the first stone. Jesus does not mean that everyone in his audience has a sexual sin on his conscience, but that they all have consciences and knowledge of sin in the biblical sense, therefore they all have a realizable guilt. But the earlier story of Daniel also suggests that charac- ters could have something we may call "subjectivity" as one of their defining characteristics: each has a personal idea about the best auspices for the sexual act.

We tend to think of the possession of subjectivity as the possession of a self. Apart from their each having a somewhat fixed point of view, we should note that the Bible does not credit its persons with a perma- nent possession of much of anything, and a given character is much more likely to think of himself or herself as possessing a relative than either a "self" or a personal consciousness. At the end of Shakespeare's *Othello*, Iago refuses to explain himself, while the alienated protagonist whom he has ruined eloquently clings to something from his personal past that he regards as inalienably his—"a poor thing, and yet mine own," as another Shakespearean character says of the mate from his class. From our present point of view, Iago's and Othello's and Touch- stone's reactions are all more or less the same "egotistical" and "idiosyn- cratic" one, and, as such, are more or less unimaginable within the Bible. Thus our feeling that Joseph and David are "egoists" in some special sense or other is quite remarkable, and is only possible, one might argue, because their privilege is one directly extended to them from God— for God is the Bible's only true "I am." Everyone else is someone else's, and Cain's protest, "Am I my brother's keeper?" goes very deep, i.e., very deeply against the grain of the Bible's theory as a whole.

At the outset the Bible's human characters are solely Adam and Eve, and what is said of them may well be true for all their progeny. As we have said, their character is to be conceived of as transient, ecstatic, and contingent. Abel's name means "puff," Seth's means "substitute," Enosh's means "mortal."

Adam and Eve, however, certainly have "human consciousness" as part of their character. Indeed, the memory of what has happened to this primal pair is part of our inheritance from them. This memory includes their own foreknowledge of what is to happen to them: they are to die, as it were, on behalf of all of us. Human prescience is indissociable from the human retention of happy or unhappy but in any case previous experience. Now this theme of the human subject's immersion in time-consciousness is found throughout Genesis—which is, after all, the story of the genesis of a particularly strongly remembered historical future. Having a character, in the Bible, means having a place in the elongate ethnic history. But the effect of having such a place, namely the conscription of the character by the history, makes any one character that much less self-sovereign or centered on his own identity.

Thus the story of an indelibly personal isolation that throws the human character into high relief precisely because of his or her lack of communal protections or affiliations, belongs only to characters like the excommunicated Cain and Hagar, and to the kidnapped Joseph, and it belongs to them only temporarily. Reuben, after discovering that Joseph is missing from the pit in which his brothers have exposed him, speaks in the accents of the despairing manslayer Cain; thus Reuben's were originally the accents of a man without a kinsman. And where is Joseph? Significantly, he has since been sold to Ishmaelites; that is, he has been sold to a band that is descended from the ostracized bondwoman Hagar, the Ishmaelites now being a clan that traffics in chattels such as Hagar herself once was. What goes around, comes around, as the current phrase has it. Similarly, Lot offers his nameless daughters to the Sodomites for rape; he is raped in turn by his daughters, whose offspring do not know their true father's name. They are Ammonites and Moabites, and not the Lot-ites they should be, or could have been.[9] Yet all have found their communal future.

Literary character implies possession of a distinctive, nameable self, shadowed by loneliness, and possession of a distinctive personal story, shadowed by adversity. Character is fate insofar as the personal story is teleological, but character is individual only insofar as the fate is not collective. In the Bible much of the fate is collective. Individual fulfillment of a personal destiny is short-changed. Isaac's story is that he is the weak son of a strong father and the weak father of a strong son. He is overshadowed by the collective destinies of those widely dispersed peoples who call Abraham their father and those narrowly ethnic tribes who call themselves the sons of Jacob. The chain is only as strong as its weakest link, but not to worry: that link is not really Isaac himself, but Rebekah his wife. It is really Rebekah who answers the call of Abraham to pass on the blessing of Abraham—on to Jacob.[10]

III

As I have implied, the most provocative recent analyses of biblical character attach to the stories surrounding the princely Joseph and the royal David. Theirs are the best stories, theirs the most complex yet integrated characterizations. Why might these stories tell *our* kind of story best, the story of the orientation of biblical narrative on the publication of the "inner life" of character? Is this only because both Joseph and David, since they each act covertly, bring out the detective in the Jamesian reader? The biblical inner life is less than directly available, and so these stories do offer us models for the reader's and other characters' penetration to that life. But is it entirely accidental that these two exceptional characters seem prominently and analogously located at critical junctures of the biblical narrative taken as a whole? The House of Joseph is to be associated with the Northern Kingdom and the House of David with the Southern Kingship. Furthermore, these two characters are at the respective centers of the histories from Adam to Joshua, and from the first of the Judges to the last of the Kings. Moreover, Joseph stands between the pre-Israel of the patriarchal guest-in-the-land, and the pre-Israel of the constitutional generation in the wilderness. Similarly, David stands between the tribal-confederate Israel of the Judges and Saul, and the statist Israel of Solomon and the Kings. Thus it is in just these characters' stories that private stories are made disgracefully public, as if the indictment of personal integrity loomed very large in the historical interval—or as if "character" were being reconceived there, along with the novelistic and biographic means for redescribing it.

IV

On the basis of our two criteria—personal distinctiveness and biographical closure (i.e., a "story")—Joseph can claim to be the preeminent human character in Genesis. But the story also identifies Joseph, in some sense or other, as a "prince." Joseph's character is distinctive, yet it is not finally purely idiosyncratic—Joseph is to be included in his society in a unique way, by coming to its fore. This motif of social promotion differs from the givenness of the patriarchal future belonging to Joseph's forebears, since the homage Joseph receives is made to come directly from contemporaries, not descendants. Similarly, the preeminence of the princely David, which is personal, differs from the divine sponsorship of the Israelite kingship in general: David's relation with Yahweh is such an immediate or internalized one that it is most evident in the situations that appear to be the most godforsaken.

In explaining the uniqueness of David and Joseph we also have to explain the particular "worldliness" of our two princely characters. Each of them is shown "operating in the world," attaching himself to other such operants in exchange for help, sponsorship, and support. Both characters are shown in the employ of others who are decidedly in the world: Potiphar and Pharaoh in the case of Joseph, Saul and the Philistines in that of David. They are also shown as individuals very much at the mercy of others, both foreigners and family members. Yet they are worldly operators: David between Saul and Solomon, Joseph between his kinsmen and his Egyptian overlord. As this way of putting it shows, Joseph and David in fact operate between two worlds: a more feudal one, from which they come, and a more statist one, into which they are leading their societies.

Thus Joseph and David may be the Hebrew Bible's most absorbing characters because they are each found at the confluence of those forces making for a personal character and for a public figure in a single compound. It is no accident that the story of how an exposed Joseph got into Egypt—and got "Jacob" there—is locked into the story of how an exposed Moses came out from there, and got "Israel" out. The beneficence of the evil Joseph's brothers meant toward him is kindly explained by Joseph to his brothers as making their salvation and indeed the exodus possible (Gen. 45:5, 50:20). "Shalt thou indeed reign over us? or shalt thou indeed have dominion over us?" (Gen. 37:8a), Joseph is asked by his brothers at the outset, and the question accordingly echoes in both early and late Israelite reactions to the ministry of Moses ("Who made thee a prince and a judge over us?" Exod. 2:14; "Is it a small thing that thou hast brought us up out of a land that floweth with milk and honey, to kill us in the wilderness, except thou make thyself altogether a prince over us?" Num. 16:13).

David, who turns Saul's evil toward him to good, is a similar beneficiary of evil, and a similar link to the future. "Be strong," Moses tells Joshua (="Yah saves") at the borders of the Promised Land (Deut. 31: 7, 23), and the advice is accordingly echoed in the final commission David gives to Solomon (1 Kings 2:2–3; cf. Josh. 1:6–9, 17f for the link). The kingship was supposed to be God's instrument for delivering Israel, but Saul dies battling the Philistines whom only David will be strong enough to defeat consistently. David succeeds in delivering the kingship from itself, that is, from the disasters of Saul: delivering it for Israel. And he succeeds in preserving it, from an in-house revolution, for Solomon. Thus the princely characters function as a saving bridge between the father-figures of Jacob and Samuel, and the founder-figures of Moses and Solomon—and between their respective dispensations.

Clearly we need some way of describing the privileged status of such characters, if only to understand the story's investment in persons who are not only in some way historical, but who also derive an authority from texts that typically understand themselves—and that therefore can come to appropriate themselves—as institutions. The conservation of the biblical text in general is of course underwritten by the existence and survival and preservation and memorial of the more authoritative characters within it. And of course the literary remains of our two characters—Joseph's dreams and David's three elegies (over Saul, Jonathan, and Abner)—point to such a motif of personal and textual survival, otherwise epitomized by the embalmed remains of Joseph, and by David's accumulation of materials for the temple built in the reign of his son Solomon. In these remains one history comes to an end and another is begun, a sort of "ecclesiastical history of the polity." Joseph's bones accompany the Mosaic tent or tabernacle in the wilderness; the ark that David brings into Jerusalem adorns the Solomonic temple. But it is Moses and Solomon, not Joseph and David, who specifically appear as the conservators of texts.

Thus both Joseph and David come between two histories, and each is the hinge for that particular two-part history in which he is situated. Furthermore, the "saving history" has been hinged not only on characters whose stories constitute critical installments in it, but on characters who allow us to see a given history's earlier themes becoming its later themes. The Josephic and Davidic motifs of social promotion come at the crucial historical points that cross the space between inherited functions in family-like or tribal social structures, and elective or appointive functions in civic organizations: from being the son of a sojourning rancher, Joseph becomes a high office-holder in the Egyptian state; from being an armor-bearer to a tribal chieftain, David becomes the administrative head of state, a state with a professional army. However unlikely these promotions seem as matters of historical fact, they are plausible representations of the social change otherwise apparent in the transition from Patriarchal to Mosaic Israel by way of "the house of Joseph," and from the tribal federation to the royalist state by way of "the house of David."

But what are the two histories? The proto-saving history extends from Abraham to Moses, but its fuller form expands backward to Adam and forward to Joshua. It is this expansion that seems to have caused Joseph to come into place between Jacob and Moses, as Noah has come into place between Adam and Abraham, and as the primeval history has come into place between the Creation and Abraham, and as the Joseph novella itself has come into place between the "Patriarchal marriage-saga" and the Israelite exodus from Egypt. The Joseph-Moses interface is given to us through the mutual interference of the literary motifs belonging to the two story patterns of their careers (roughly "riches-to-rags-to-riches"),[11] just as the Saul-David interface is given to us through a dynastic interference of two houses. But the analogy extends back to Jacob in the first case, and forward to Solomon in the second. Jacob and Saul are alike in being problematic personalities, against whom Joseph and David are evaluated as independent persons. Moses and Solomon are alike in representing the settling of the institutional order, against whom Joseph and David are evaluated as officers. There is also the further analogy implicit in the history covered by the two installments, between the deeding of the earlier historical leadership of the people over from Jacob-Joseph to Moses-Joshua, and the deeding of the later historical leadership of the state over from Samuel-Saul to David-Solomon. We may diagram the pattern thusly:

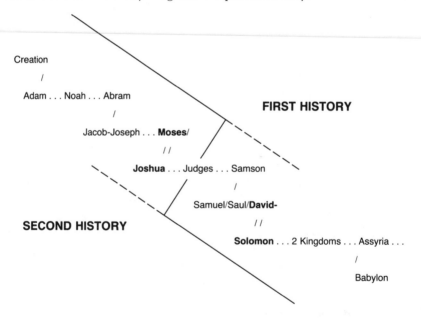

Placed where they are, the stories of Joseph and David both involve a critical theme of a new public accountability of private persons. Joseph calls his brothers to account while he is in the court of Pharaoh; Nathan calls David to account as the public adversary of the king. (Saul begs

Samuel to keep his disgrace a secret, and Samuel accedes to keeping up the appearance of Samuel's support for Saul, at 1 Sam. 15:30f.) In the divulgement of in-house scandals the tribal confederation "Israel" and the kingship are also called to some larger account. For the brothers' crime against kin goes back to Cain's crime against Abel. And the king's crime against citizen Uriah, for his wife, as portrayed in Nathan's parable (where Bathsheba is a poor man's lamb), goes forward to Ahab's crime against citizen Naboth, for his vineyard.

Since the scandals do not seem to want to die, we feel in these particular stories the institution of publicity. A good example of the new institution is the campaign of Absalom for the kingship. Absalom gets a chariot with horses and fifty men to go before him, and succeeds because of his mastery of a symbolism that makes for effective publicity. Joseph's clothing and his divining cup likewise conduce to a symbolic knowledge or acknowledging of Joseph: they are part of the celebrity or gravity of his person—his regalia, as it were.

It is significant that Absalom, with his fifty heralds and his glad hand, exploits the complaint that David's administration has become remote from the people (2 Sam. 15:1–6). Joseph's brothers likewise imply that the Egyptian vizier is a hard man to deal with (Gen. 43:3, 7, 18). The criticisms, like the regalia, accompany two major changes in the history of the Israelite institutions generally, the change from Patriarchal to Mosaic leadership, and the change from military to royal leadership. Joseph is found between the forefather Jacob and the bureaucrat Moses: he is at once the princely father of the tribe of Joseph, and the able bureaucrat of the Egyptian Pharaoh. The House of Jacob, or "Israel," has its greatest component in the double House of Joseph. David is found after Samuel and Saul, the last of the Judges and the first of Israel's kings, and before Solomon, Solomon being the second Judaic king and the literalizer of the House of David as Solomon's House. (Insofar as a "house" is bigenerational, David has no royal house until his son's succession to the throne is secured: only children can build up a house.)

The House of Joseph and the House of David are the two great houses that emerge in Israel as a whole, corresponding to the Northern Kingdom and the Southern Kingship respectively. Joseph comes between patriarchal and Mosaic Israel, David between confederated and bureaucratized Israel. Each character is situated between the tribe and the state —Joseph between clan and constitution; David between militia and army, ad hoc and dynastic rulership. The predecessors Jacob and Saul, as personalities, are problematic, and haunted by doubles and rivals (Samuel is a kind of double for Saul, Esau for Jacob). Jacob and Saul experience "ecstatic" self-displacement, and spectral visitations (Saul is found among the prophets and communes with the ghost of Samuel; Jacob wrestles with an angel). Even the names they bear are doubled. This is also true of the names of the respective successors, Joshua and Solomon. Joseph and David, on the contrary, are whole, and through them passes the relation of a person to a specific institution that is absent from the predecessor's original experience, namely, the court.

Both Joseph and David are preferred at court, and both arrive to change that court: the career there throws these two characters' answerability to others into notable public view. The career's location at court is important because the court is the locus of authority these characters appropriate to themselves, on the one hand, and appropriate for the future establishment itself, on the other. Without Joseph the indicter of his brothers, there would be no Moses the lawgiver of his people; without David the Yahweh-beloved warrior-king, there would be no kingship in Israel. Joseph accomplishes the economic and imperial unity of Pharaoh's Egypt, David the hegemony and royalizing of Jerusalem.

The self-sovereignty of the two princely characters, as we may call it, is unique and privileged by the place in which they find themselves, mediating between dispensations. This self-sovereignty is impossible to Jacob and Moses, or Saul and Solomon. It is impossible to Jacob, if only because Jacob is a twin, to Moses, because God is sovereign in his reaction to the sovereign pretensions of Pharaoh and because Moses exists to delegate a host of Mosaic functions that make the Mosaic office itself a kind of clearing-house for all other offices—those of Joshua, Hur, Phinehas, Aaron, and the Seventy Elders. Self-sovereignty is impossible to Saul, because God alone is sovereign in the demands made upon the kingship, and because the kingship is at odds with the priesthood; and it is impossible to Solomon, because Solomon is shown carrying out the will of David. The self-sovereign character is virtually an anomaly in the Old Testament story, and therefore other characters that we have mentioned are doubled. Moses the Egyptian with Aaron the Israelite, Saul with Samuel, Jacob/Israel with Esau, and Solomon/Jedidiah (2 Sam. 12:25) with Adonijah. These doublings can express the collective and—at the same time—the divisible nature of the various polities in question. Or they can express the collective nature of a leadership shared with God, or the collective character of any personage and personality that is shared with the personage and personality of a people as a whole.

V

Now, what stories necessarily attach to the change in status passing through the so-called princely characters? With Joseph, the Genesis motif that I have elsewhere called the keeping of Nahor,[12] namely the maintenance of tribal kinship and ethnicity genetically, becomes the keeping of brotherhood, namely the contractual maintenance of political alliance legally and culturally. The kidnapped Joseph returns to spy on the consciences of the reformed man-stealers, and to compel them into something like a courtroom acknowledgment of their liability and personal responsibility for the life of their father's missing favorite. Thus the youthful victim of kidnapping at the internecine level—the level of man-stealing between the tribes—in turn becomes the taker of hostages among the nations, at the international level. With David, the leadership motif we may call the troubles of the land becomes specified as the motif of the troubles of the royal house. The result is that, when David acts like the womanizing Samson and does what is right in his own eyes, this is not at all right in the eyes of the Lord, for the king is also commandeering a poor man's life and property as Ahab did Naboth's life and vineyard. Therefore the king's sin is published for the eyes of all Israel when the king's own usurping son makes public use of the king's harem on the rooftop from which David first spied on the bathing Bathsheba.

These descriptions show the inner life of character being made visible in just those characters who act covertly, and so polarize the publicity that reveals character. Since the inner life of character in the Bible is typically less than directly available, an insider's access to it appears in both stories, in the form of Joseph's trying and knowing of his brothers in court, and in the form of the narrator's knowledge of the schemes of David—the results of which Nathan the prophet comes to court to expose. The brothers are punished in the shape in which they have sinned, by having to go back before their father and disclose the silver secreted in their grain-sacks. The father now sees the unspeakable money as he once saw the bloodstained coat, as Sternberg has observed. The money is thus identified as blood-money, the price got for selling off yet another brother.[13] Jacob has perhaps seen deeper than the brothers themselves, who do not know that Joseph has been sold more than once. The brothers nonetheless willingly suffer incrimination for the alleged crime of the innocent Benjamin, from whose sack the vizier reclaims his missing cup: this divination device is the external symbol of the brothers' failure to acknowledge Joseph and his dreams. They cannot steal the knowledge of what has happened to him from their brother, even if they have tried to steal it from his father and from themselves. Thus Joseph is compelled to restage and revisit the traumatic scene of the crime against him, namely the scene of his brothers' counsels over the fate of a Rachelite brother. While Joseph accuses his brothers of spying on the nakedness of the land, he himself is spying on the nakedness of kin—that is, their consciences.[14]

Scholars suggest that the doublets and conflations in the Joseph story result from the joining of two separate versions of the narrative. But one has to fudge a little in order to make them out in the case of the disposal of Joseph. The story (or stories) is (or are) as follows: Joseph is proposed to be slain and (presumably his body) to be cast (presumably dead) into a pit; his life is spoken for by Reuben, who proposes Joseph be cast (presumably alive) into a pit; *his life is spoken for by Judah, who proposes Joseph be sold to passing Ishmaelites—this is agreed upon (and presumably he is sold)*; he is rescued by Midianites from the pit (and presumably sold by them for silver to Ishmaelites, and *the Ishmaelites bring him to Egypt [and presumably resell him]*); he is discovered missing from the pit, and presumed to be as good as dead by the distraught Reuben and to be dead by his distraught father at the persuasion of his sons; he is sold by (the) Midianites into Egypt, to Potiphar.

If the information in this account cannot be fully reconciled with itself, neither can it be fully discriminated into two neatly divided alternatives: for the Joseph-buying Ishmaelites from the Judah-favoring strand —here italicized—also appear as second buyers in the Reuben-favoring strand, yet the Midianites from the Reuben-favoring strand then reappear, in what seems to be the same strand, where they are discovered selling their find *for a second time*. Alter says that the compound story of the exposing and/or selling of Joseph pointedly equates slave-trading with murder (for which we can substitute man-stealing and murderous intent, since they are the preludes to the crimes in question). Such a point would be close to the spirit of the opening of the Exodus, where enslavement does contradictory double-duty with genocide. And it is true that the story's doubleness serves to emphasize the uncertain fate of chattel and kidnap-victim alike: God only knows where they are, or what has been done with them—or *to* them.

We can go further. The compound text makes Judah and Reuben rivals in trying to extricate themselves from complicity in a murder, "Southern" Judah relying on the Ishmaelites, and thus Egypt, "Northern" Reuben relying on Joseph and on himself. The strands maintain a quarrel of the brothers over preeminence to this day. And since the story turns on second thoughts and recriminations and self-division among the coconspirators, it is important that these not be unanticipated or unprecedented by the things originally done for and against Joseph. Joseph must discover that his brothers are capable of compassion, because that is how he will discover the same thing about himself.

As it stands, the story is only consistent if Joseph is sold and rescued as many as four times. Joseph is subject to a double jeopardy consistent with a double blessing—for his house will be a double one. Joseph himself explains the import of an analogous mechanism: "the dream was doubled unto Pharaoh twice: it is because the thing is established by God" (Gen. 41:42). But in the case of Joseph's disposal, the right hand does not know what the left one is doing: characters are not in touch with their whole moral beings, the brothers refuse to know what might happen to Joseph, they are guilty of a Sartrean "bad faith," and they let Jacob draw his own conclusions (from the blood they have put on Joseph's coat), as a way of disowning what they have done (even while their bloodying of the coat must confront them with the probable result —blood-guiltiness—of abandoning Joseph in a pit). Jacob may agree to the "wild animal" explanation, rather than admit a worse one. The compound text thus reflects these characters' own double-mindedness, and their willful ignorance about the fate of the one they have cast out from among them. In the repeated scenes with the grainsacks, the brothers must replay a scene that implies an incrimination from which they would gladly dissociate themselves, even while they experience the intervention of God. Without this experience of God's hand, there might be no final recovery for them from their subsequent conviction by their father. Yet they are already being convicted by conscience. The brothers want to show their father that they did not know that the money was in their sacks. They do not look in the other sacks—perhaps they think the other shoe will not drop, perhaps they think it will be easier to pretend they have not looked in *any* sacks if they have only looked in *one*. But their replaying of the scene only dramatizes what this action would deny, namely their incrimination's already being in effect. The one father looking at nine guilty sacks and nine sons cannot be more comfortable than the experience of nine brothers looking at one guilty sack and each other.

By reopening their sacks in front of their father, the brothers subject themselves to reexperiencing alienation before another, in the hope of taking possession of themselves again, and in the hope of somehow being forgiven. They hope to be forgiven for what they might honestly deny, wrongdoing regarding the acquisition of *this* money, in lieu of being forgiven for what they are actually guilty of (disposing of a brother, for Ishmaelite money). But the *krisis* (or "judgment") has surely not gone away: another brother is missing, and moreover the remaining brothers are obliged to propose carrying off yet a third of their number, if they are to have any further dealings with the "keeper" of the second. Willy-nilly, both Joseph and his brothers have become their brother's keeper. The story shows how inextricably the keeping of a brother, or of his memory, is entailed in the keeping of one's own moral self-possession—and in the possibility of moral self-discovery as well.

The portrayal of David's strong feelings for the many characters who either come under his charge, or fall into his power, repeatedly makes the same point. The story tells us that David can take his responsibility to others very seriously, precisely because he would not be either his own man or a whole man if he could not. Thus the portrayal, when it shows him compromised by his own worst tendencies, also shows him confronted by their evil effects. A man who fobs his murder-plots off on others is not a strong man: Joab, the agent he tries to stick with the dirty work, makes a fool of David. A man who tries to father off his child on someone else is not a whole man: and the child sickens and dies.

Significantly for the existence of the Bible, Joseph is a tale-teller: Jacob or Israel has heard the tale of Reuben's sexual sin with his father's concubine, and thus it is through a Joseph that such stories have been preserved in any latter-day Israel. The brothers standing before Joseph-in-disguise never wholly confess their crime against their brother, yet their guilty assumption of responsibility for things they have not done as much as confesses their crime for them. David likewise is brought to acknowledge his sin against Uriah and humbly to accept the mortality of his sin's first fruits.

It is as if the integrity and disgrace of personal character loom very large in the historical juncture mediated by the Bible's apparently freest agents. Michal, for example, sees her husband David dancing naked and suggestively among the bimbos, and despises him as a vulgarian. Michal's reaction is important because it shows the generation of scandal as a determinative element in the narratives about David. The same observation applies to Jacob's terminal invocation of the offenses of Reuben, Simeon, and Levi, in the "blessings of Jacob" on his deathbed, at the conclusion to the Joseph novella.

Thus each story itself amounts to a kind of scandal: what is secret will be revealed, the stories tell us, but they also suggest that the revealed secret is virtually nationalized. Thus Joseph's brothers are seated at the table according to both tribal *and* diplomatic protocol, that is, according to the order of their birth. This tabulation can hardly help calling attention to the absence of the One Who Is No More, the one whose preferment by Jacob originally threatened the just expectations of the first-born. Deut. 21:15–17 provides the double portion for the firstborn even though his mother was not the favored wife, and in the presence of his brothers Joseph—deliberately ignoring the rule—awards this same double portion to the last-born Benjamin, as if awarding it to himself. The house of Joseph will be a double one.

Bathsheba's original paternity suit likewise contributes to the institutions of Israel. The child of David's sin sickens, and David's mourning for it before it is dead seems to be a part of the mourning for Jonathan,

Abner, and Absalom, who are all part of the high historical price David
must pay for there to be a reign of David. Yet the second fruit of David's
union with Bathsheba will be Solomon, the son of David whose succession to the throne will confirm the actuality of David's House as it prevails over its own disastrous inner history. Bathsheba will become the
first of the Judaic queen mothers.

The Joseph story and the David story have a certain unity as stories
that belongs to their construction as a cycle of events, but also to their
telling as a mode of *knowledge*, and as a mode of *coherence*. But while
one may speak of scandal as a mode of knowledge common to the two
stories, we are talking about two very different kinds of coherence.

The coherence of the Joseph story is novelistic and dramatic, for the
narrator observes the rule of the unity of action: the drama-like
recognition-scene would have no force without it. Joseph begins his career as a kind of tattletale or scandal-monger, and then returns to his
brothers innocent of scandal himself, to put his creatures through a
therapeutic reenactment of what they have done and been. But even
while Joseph seems to be stage-managing a dress rehearsal for the creature's ultimate meeting with his maker, the technique of repetition (very
notable in the brothers' doubled discovery of the money in the grain-
sacks) insists on catechizing the parties to the story in the story,
which the brothers must keep telling to Jacob and Joseph-in-disguise.
This story will be told in Israel because it is already structured as a
kind of "tell-it-again" story: the story of how "Israel" treated "Joseph,"
and how "Joseph" in turn and in kind treated "Israel." Such a story
must needs be acknowledged and repeated as a communal story to prevent its ignorant perpetuation as an internecine history.

The Joseph novella provides a fictional interlude between the patriarchal and Mosaic "histories." It is framed by the jeopardy of a Patriarch's
son and by the son's repatriation to "Israel" (the restoration of the son
to the father and to the land): these are motifs from the overall patriarchal saga that maintain its premise of the protohistorical continuity of
the collective identity.

The ratio of fiction-making to history-recording is reversed in the
David story, for the coherence of the David story is not fictional, but
historiographic: in place of the rule of the unity of action, the narrator
observes the rule of the circle of relevance. That is, what is told is told
insofar as it is relevant to the course of events leading from Saul through
David to Solomon. Even while he supplies names that there is no reason
for knowing except that they are factual and historical, the teller permits
himself the invention of any scenes and dialogue that are possible and
probable, given the main course of events: such inventions belong to
the historian and the storyteller alike. Thus the childlessness of David's

marriage to Michal has as its logical antecedent a scene of rebuke, or a falling out between the marriage partners, which we duly hear about.

Just as Joseph's treatment reveals the potential for scandal in Israel, so David's story is public property because it concerns the sword, the court, and the throne as they are established in his reign. Communications and the transmittal of information seem very important in the history of this regime—the figure of the courier is prominent. The storyteller provides an inner access to the events of the story, but he also reports, regarding the events leading to Bathsheba's espousal by the king, that "the thing became known." In the story itself the thing becomes known not through Joseph's kind of dramatization and fictionalizing, but through Nathan's publication of his parable. The narrator himself relies on a quasidocumentary or journalistic presentation of actual communications—advisements, information, communiques, announcements, reports, petitions, negotiations—among parties to the events. The importance of such communications and reactions to them, and their comparison for agreement and discrepancy, appears in many apparently minor episodes, such as the news of the victory of David's generals over David's son Absalom: how uncomely on the mountain the feet of one who brings bad news. The documents are presumably constructions not only by characters within the narrative, but outside it, on the part of the inspired author.[15]

As the prophet Nathan's own parable tends to show, publicity, and not prophecy, is the important medium in the David story. But throughout the rest of the narrative of the kings this is not so: public reaction more or less drops out, and the prophets' reactions take its place. The historiographic norm is therefore different. Knowledge of the course of events for its own sake is reduced to a dismissive "the deeds of King So-and-so," and the major event within the narrative accordingly becomes the adversarial encounter of the king with the man of God, going back to the story of Saul and Samuel. Thus both the Joseph story and the David-Solomon story take exception to the larger narratives that are their context. They give us plot, intrigue, and discovery. Such things are the products of a complex mind, which is why these stories illustrate Joseph and David themselves, insofar as these are the two biblical characters who are singularly able to pursue their purposes on more than one front.

VI

Now, what is the relation of the history of David to the second installment of the history of Israel, from the death of Joshua to the Babylonian exile? And what is the relation of the novella about Joseph to the saga of the Israelites, the first installment, from the removal of certain Sethite Shemites from "Nahor" in the East, to the occupation of the Promised Land by the descendants of the Abrahamic sons of Jacob? We divide the overall history with the burial of Joshua, for the burial of Joshua is accompanied by the final burial of the remains of Joseph. And this evidence of mortality goes all the way back to the beginning, back before Joseph himself, to the original taking of Adam out of the ground, and the taking of Eve out of Adam. For the creation of man and woman is nothing less than the Israelite version of the Egyptian pretension to embalm the dead in preparation for immortality: the removal of the organs, the filling up of the body cavity, the sealing of the incisions, and the in-breathing of the soul—these are all allusively rendered in the resuscitation-like administration to Adam in his creation and in the procedures pertaining to the extraction of Eve. The remains of a sufficiently inspired prophet, the burial of Elisha tells us, could bring the dead back to life. No such story attaches to the remains of Joseph, but the conservation of Joseph's relics is nonetheless one with the conservation of his memory, and the conservation of his memory is essential to bridging the gap between patriarchal and Mosaic Israel. For the more abbreviated psalmic accounts of the saving history seem to know nothing of the very story that brought Israel into Egypt in the first place and that announced the role of Moses in interpreting meteorological disaster to Pharaoh: in these accounts Joseph is still, so to speak, "the one who is not." And so also, for that matter, are the generations before the Patriarchs, as of course is Adam himself. Thus the addition or annexation of Adam to the saving history takes place in the form that Joseph's remains are conserved, precisely because the fuller text of the history is created by a supplementation that analogizes the restoration and reconstitution of Israel in Egypt to the original creation of man in the East. Deriving the pre-Israel from the Creation means that the story of the taking of one people out of the midst of another people began from the taking of Eve out of Adam's side. God did this so Adam could marry Eve—like his removing Abraham from the East so that the two post-Abrahamic Patriarchs Isaac and Jacob could marry back into the stock Abraham left behind.

VII

The honoring of Joseph in post-occupation Israel, by means of his tomb or memorial, "remembers Joseph," as the Pharaoh four generations from him pointedly did *not* do, and as Pharaoh's butler originally forgot to do when Joseph was in prison. But the burial also signifies the remembering of Israel by Joseph, the Joseph who named one of his two Egyptian sons after his forgetfulness of his treatment in the Promised Land, yet who eventually arranges for his bodily remains to be repatriated there. Thus the burial both remembers and terminates Israel's "Egyptianization," for Joseph is ultimately buried in the half-Egyptian sons' inheritance in Israel. Significantly, Joseph is buried in the land of the son whose name means Fruitfulness (Ephraim), rather than the one whose name means Forgetfulness (Manasseh). Going to go the way of all the earth in Egypt, Jacob, on his deathbed, blessed these two sons of Joseph with crossed arms over the objections of their father—a peculiar gesture that, it gives one a start to remember, is the way the arms of the embalmed in Egypt are typically folded in death.

There came a time, the narrator of Judges reports (2:10), when Israel forgot all that the Lord had done for it. This is much like the information that there arose a Pharaoh who knew not Joseph, the one who was not.[16] The lapsing of the saving history is a motif within Judges itself, in the questions that Gideon puts to Yahweh at Judg. 6:13:"Pray, sir, if the Lord is with us, why then has all this befallen us? And where are all His wonderful deeds which our fathers recounted to us saying, 'Did not the Lord bring us up from Egypt?'" Judg. 2:10 implies that such questions date from the death of Joshua and all of his generation: significantly, this is the time of the burial of Joseph's remains (Judg. 2:8–10, with Josh. 24:29–32). Thus the creation of the first mortals and the burial of Joseph mark the two termini of the first great installment of which we have spoken.

Yet, as Chronicles shows, the framework stretching from Adam only ends with Cyrus the conqueror of Babylon. Within this framework the two installments are mutually entailed by virtue of the very activity of the scribal establishment in Jerusalem: in Chronicles' own concentrated formulation, "So all Israel were reckoned by genealogies; and behold, they were written in the book of the kings of Israel and Judah, who were carried away to Babylon for their transgression" (1 Chron. 9:1). With them went the Temple vessels (Jer. 27:22).

And is the remaining installment as carefully and distinctly marked as the first one? The first installment (Genesis through Joshua) is characterized at the outset by the genetic continuity of the pre-Israel from Adam, and it ends at the grave. In the second installment (Judges through Kings), the analogous jurisdictional history of the leadership in the land is characterized, in the dénouement, by the dismantling of the Jerusalem temple and the exile of the last of the Judahite kings to Babylon. The kingship is postscripted with this king of Judah being taken out of prison in Babylon and being given an honorable pension at the dinner table of the Babylonian monarch.

So what does this history begin with? It begins with a Judahite victory over a Canaanite king. Thus essential commentary upon the ignoble conclusion for the throne of David is offered by the initial tale in Judges, which starts from the divine initiative toward the tribe of Judah:

> After the death of Joshua, the people of Israel inquired of the Lord, "Who shall go up first for us against the Canaanites, to fight against them?" The Lord said, "Judah shall go up; behold, I have given the land into his hand." . . . Then Judah went up . . . and they defeated ten thousand of them at Bezek. They came upon Adoni-bezek at Bezek and fought against him. . . . Adoni-bezek fled; but they pursued him, and caught him, and cut off his thumbs and his great toes. And Adoni-bezek said, "Seventy kings with their thumbs and their great toes cut off used to pick up scraps under my table; as I have done, so God has done to me." And they brought him to Jerusalem, and he died there. (Judg. 1:1–7, RSV)

Thus the end of the kingship is found inscribed in the beginning of Israel's jurisdiction within the land. Furthermore this incapacitation of royal blood is found in the kingship itself, in the expropriation of one dynasty by another. And that process is most fully set out in the relation between the House of David and the House of Saul. The figure of the maimed royal pensioner at the table of the reigning monarch in Jerusalem is of course the figure of Jonathan's lame son, privileged to sit at the table of King David throughout his days (2 Sam. 9). As others did to Adoni-bezek, so history has done to the House of Saul. The Saulides as a whole fare less well than the lame son of Jonathan, for they are exposed to a scapegoat's death on trees. But since an analogous death overtakes Absalom, we may say that as David has done to the Saulides, so Joab will do to David's own son.

The fate of the kingship is tied to the name Jeconiah by an odd detail from the overall frame. At the time when the kingship was being instituted, the ark and its keeping emerged as a symbol of the beset Israelite leadership. When she hears that the ark is lost, Eli's daughter-in-law dies giving birth to a child she names "Where is the Glory?" (1 Sam. 4:19–22). David is able to bring this ark into Jerusalem, and thereafter refuses to move it from there; Solomon was able to draw the glory down upon the temple housing it; but at the exile into Babylon, the glory removes with the dismantling of the temple. And thus it is significant, in the early history, that when the ark, returned by the Philistines, came back to Israel, either seventy or fifty thousand Jeconiahites all died, be-

cause they did not rejoice at its coming among the men of Beth-shemesh
(1 Sam. 6:19). We know nothing else about this particular clan, but its
numbers, both being wholes, speak for the death of Jeconiah's whole
house, prefatory to the history of the kingship.[17] For this is how the
house of an evil king might die, witness the seventy sons of his father
killed by Abimelech, in Judges 9, and the seventy sons of Ahab killed
by Jehu, in 2 Kings 10. We conclude that the first Jeconiah suffers something like the proleptic destruction of all the kings that failed to hallow
God's presence among them.

As 1 Chronicles says: "So all Israel were reckoned by genealogies,
and behold, they were written in the book of the kings of Israel and
Judah, who were carried away to Babylon for their transgression."

VIII

The general effect of the Bible's incorporation of the norms of the Israelite experience into the individual lives that make it up is to mortgage
those lives to a history that is not altogether the character's own. With
Adam, King Saul is guilty of disobedience to God; with Cain, King David
is guilty of murder; with the builders of Babel, King Solomon is guilty
of a cultural imperialism and pluralism that cannot hold the kingdom
together.[18] It is as if the early history of the kingship has been borrowed
for the early history of sin, though it is the other way round, typologi-
cally speaking.

David is not shown summoning any of this to consciousness—the primeval hamartiology is, so to speak, a parallel that David can never meet,
insofar as it belongs to the other installment. David's history would
rather have to remember the stories of Saul and the Judges Jepthah
and Abimelech and the widow Ruth, as Ahab's story remembers that
of Saul and David, or as the life of Moses, in the first installment, recycles
the Egyptian-Israelite duality from the career of Joseph.

The question is, what does the Joseph story recycle from the patriarchal cycle, in the way that David's story recycles the judges', or in the
way that Moses's story will recycle Joseph's? Joseph is the master of the
historical interval between Patriarchy and Polity, Jacob at the end of
Patriarchy and Moses at the beginning of Polity, yet it is not exactly
history proper that Joseph mediates—unlike Moses, who creates a prehistory and a liturgy out of Pharaoh's repeated resistance to Israel's
claim on history. Rather, Joseph mediates dreams. Dreams are the links
across the intervals or lapses of consciousness between events: dreams
recall or anticipate events in the absence of events themselves. Thus
the dream of Joseph's brothers bowing down to him crosses a time from

which he is missing to them, to the time when they are brought into Joseph's presence in Egypt. As his dreams stand in place of the missing Joseph, so his novella stands in place of the missing record of Israel's four hundred and thirty years in Egypt. In the absence of this record, we must ask how the dreams themselves might establish the continuity of the history.

Joseph deals with three sets of paired dreams. The first pair of dreams is Joseph's own, yet everyone is able to interpret them, presumably because either their content, or Joseph's recital of it, is clairvoyant: thus the narrator has no reason to retell the dreams, and they are reported but once. The brothers repine at the obvious interpretation, which does not favor them. But why should any interpretation be obvious? How does one know that the obeisant eleven stars are the eleven brothers? Because the two dreams are cognate, and can be used to interpret each other. The obeisant sheaves are the brothers', the princely sheaf is Joseph's. The brothers know their class when they see it, certainly when they see it *twice*.

The second set of dreams are those of Pharaoh's two imprisoned servants. These dreams get told twice, and they favor a cupbearer over a baker. Joseph alone offers to interpret the dreams, and he correctly divines that one dream favors its dreamer, and that the other does not.

Joseph's mixed fortune allows him to see fortune and misfortune in the two dreams. Things are better for the cupbearer than for the baker —bakers use yeast, and so Joseph may be divining the favor shown Israel on the night of the Passover, when it is the people who are eating unleavened bread who are spared. But this conjecture only suggests how history might eventually interpret the dreams, and not how the dreams can be used to interpret themselves. The dreamers are in the third year of their imprisonment (two years plus a "season"), and therefore the critical third in the second dream signals that the present year will be terminal for hope (not for dearth, as the burgeoning grapes suggested for the butler): for the birds pillage the "head" basket, and the head of a dead body is natural prey for carrion-eating birds. The dreams are told twice by the narrative, to give them the chance of being heard in this comparative way. The baker seems subject to a Joseph-like double jeopardy. The butler seems subject to a Joseph-like deliverance from adversity. In interpreting the two dreams, Joseph has become the interpreter of his own mixed fate, as reflected in the fate of others. He is no longer just the dreamer of his own importance, and of the relative unimportance of others.

The first set of dreams seems to go back to the Creation and to suggest homage to the Creator. Yet the eleven obeisant sheaves of grain also suggest the eleven sacks of grain later in the story, when the sheepherding sons of Israel become dependent on the agriculture of Egypt in time of famine. In the second set of dreams, the two offerings seem a little like those of Abel and Cain: one service is favored and one is not. The butler's offering is to be favored, decisively and arbitrarily over the baker's, by an almighty power. The fruits of the vine, identified by the Bible with the first successful farmer Noah, perhaps prevail, where the firstfruits of Cain's agriculture did not. (Because his farming may have been unsuccessful or his harvest partly devoured, the first farmer may have been unable to make a truly acceptable offering.)

Thus the second set of dreams seems to go back to ideas of election and diselection. But the third set of dreams can refer to the previous history of election in a much more definite way. This set of dreams gets repeated not once but twice, and thus we are in a position to compare the narrator's report, Pharaoh's report, and Joseph's report, and to see with Sternberg that Pharaoh's account is fuzzier, and that when Joseph retells the dreams he is able to restore the symmetry and equatability of the original integral duplex that Pharaoh's telling obscures.[19] Sternberg explains that the Hebrew "fat" properly belonging to cattle is found in the narrator's description of the corn because, although it is one thing that God speaks and two that the Psalmist hears, it is also two things that Pharaoh speaks and one that Joseph must hear.

But why is Pharaoh dreaming in Hebrew, and in the stuff of Hebrew thought-rhyme, or parallelism? Joseph is an interpreter, but his use of an interpreter in his interviews with his brothers is deliberately superfluous: it reminds us that Joseph's investigation of his brothers, insofar as it is like God's searching of hearts, really knows no language barrier. Still, we are also reminded that Joseph "knows" Hebrew, as he knows his brethren. Joseph can know Pharaoh's dreams insofar as they come from the Hebrew god, and insofar as their idiom is Hebraic.

The thirty-year-old Joseph has been called into Pharaoh's service on the third of Pharaoh's birthdays since Joseph was imprisoned. As Pharaoh's soon-to-be economic prognosticator (with a divining-cup), Joseph will know the signs of the times. And as "the President's Psychiatrist," so to speak, Joseph might well recognize in his impending favored status as "father to Pharaoh" the restoration of his past favored status, as son to Jacob. Joseph is in a unique position to make the transfer, from Jacob's dream-marked passage into and out of the old country, to Pharaoh's dreams of the cycles of economic history. For Joseph is himself the result of the dreams of his father: Jacob served two weeks of years abroad to win Joseph's mother from her father Laban: the seven easy years for Rachel, which earned Leah, followed by the seven hard years with Leah, which earned Rachel (Gen. 29:27f). For the first seven years were as a few days (Gen. 29:20), because they seemed to be for Rachel.

Yet they were not: from Jacob's point of view, he was no closer to possessing Rachel at the end of seven years than when he started. In the same
way, the lean cattle ate up the fat, and yet they seemed no fatter for
having done so.

Thus Joseph the interpreter can apply the tradition preserved within
the narrow circle of family immediacy to the forecast divinely published
to Pharaoh. He can find, in his long-lost father's old history of planning
for his estate, the interpretive key to his new master's recent dreams
of state-planning. For Pharaoh dreams not only about the good years
and the bad years, but also about the plan that bad years should feed
on the good.

Joseph's mastery of the dreams is followed by his new role in Egyptian
history. The kidnap victim within the internecine family has become
the taker of hostages between two different peoples: Joseph throws his
family into a prophetic mimesis of a situation where a whole nation
is held captive, hostage, or for ransom by another such nation, and
where God can prove the victim's situation to be divinely reversible.
Joseph has become the master of the historical interval that begins with
Jacob's Rachelite son hostage to his brothers and that will end with all
"the sons of Jacob" hostage to Egypt, when the Pharaoh has forgotten
Joseph.

The same mastery obtains for David, who finds himself between the
tribal federation and the bureaucratic state. But if Joseph is the master
of the dreams, what is the equivalent medium that David is the master
of? Narrowly speaking, David is the master of speech dictated by occasion. His documentary remains in literary form are not so much the
Psalms—though these figure in the carefully arranged archive ap-
pended to 2 Samuel—but the three laments over the fallen warriors:
Saul, Jonathan, and Abner. What these laments stand for is David's sure-
ness of touch in generously rendering to each man what is his due from
David. In the poems that see each warrior to his quietus, we hear not
only the mortification of something kinlike in David, but also the termi-
nation of those modes of military manhood that belong to the Judges
period and not to the Kings period. At the same time, the poems seem
to remember both a kind of scandal and something irreplaceable. David
is helpless in the face of Saulide deaths. Only the death of Joab will
make it possible for David to face Joab's victim Abner in the afterlife,
and it is with the death of Joab that David's story seems to come to
its postmortem end.

David is able to use these poems to reconstruct the facts. He says
that Abner has died as a fool dies, and he should not have—should
not have died betrayed by his trust in David, as Nabal the Fool died
betrayed by his trust in his wife Abigail. Abigail, in fact, trusts not in

Nabal her husband, but in David, her husband's churlishly treated suitor; and her trust is rewarded, not taken advantage of. By turning the question of Abner's death into a rhetorical one, David finesses his own responsibility for the activity of his agent Joab. With a similar disingenuous hopefulness, David says that Saul and Jonathan were not separated in death: David has hardly been a patron of the relation he presumes to memorialize.[20] The love of Jonathan for David (which the poem goes on to honor) has in fact opened a wide breach between Jonathan and his father. The common death of the king and his son, apart from David, might seem to have been the only engagement sufficient to repair this breach.

The dreams in the Joseph story are communications from the future, insofar as they conduce to the "teleology" of the story: that is, conduce to the founding of Joseph's house in Egypt. In a sense, the dreams are messages relayed through Joseph, and Joseph has been a go-between: at the outset Jacob sends Joseph in search of his brothers, to report back to him on their condition. On this occasion Joseph meets a man in the field who is able to point him toward the brothers' location: if the "man" is in fact an angel, then he is a messenger too, a kind of mirror of Joseph's own role in preparing the way into Egypt. On the same occasion the brothers say, "Behold, this dreamer cometh": they do not welcome the kind of message that Joseph comes to bring.

The corresponding phenomenon in the David story is the message which is a communication from the front, or from the place where the future is in the making. For David does seem to be in receipt of a remarkable number of communications. The message is frequently the one that catches David up: Jonathan's bowshot betokening the wrath of Saul, the Amalekite delivering the crown of Saul, Nathan announcing God's covenant with David, the message announcing Bathsheba's pregnancy, Joab's messenger dropping into his message the death of Uriah, Nathan informing David in court of Yahweh's displeasure, the messenger reporting the popular support for the conspiracy of Absalom, the maidservant and Ahimaz and Jonathan conveying the delay in Absalom's mobilization, the Cushite announcing the death of Absalom in the battle in the forest, Bathsheba and Nathan reporting the celebration of the kingship of Adonijah.

Like the dreams, the messages conduce to the teleology of the story, insofar as they promote the survival of David and the advent of Solomon. They also cast David as an interpreter on occasion. For example, the informant who announces the death of Saul—at the informant's own merciful hands—and then delivers David the royal insignia requires interpretation, because his account of Saul's death is at variance with the narrator's own: the informant seems badly informed. He has acquired Saul's relics, but according to the original account, such remains ought to have circulated among the Philistines and been enshrined in their temple. Yet here they are, returning to David—and not to the Saulide loyalists in Jabesh. The young man may have rescued Saul's honors, or he may be a trophy-taking bounty-hunter, a scavenger who is treating David as if he were just another Philistine. We cannot know if David is right to do so, but David punishes the messenger for complicity in creating the bad news he brings. It is, in any case, news that David does not wish to appear to profit by.

The messenger has interpolated himself between the death of Saul and the informing of David. David only hears about the actual disposal of Saul's remains after he has been made king over Judah by its men. It had long been predicted that David would be made king over Israel in place of Saul, but David wisely forbears accepting the crown with the news of Saul's death. Throughout his life, David understands that crowns are conferred, not appropriated, and he does not immediately retake possession of the crown after Absalom's death, but delicately sends inquiry after it. The place where the Amalekite fool jumped in is just the place where angels might fear to tread: David resists jumping the gun and closing the gap in storytelling that has created such a messenger, the gap across which a narrative pursued on two different fronts is coordinated and synchronized.[21]

For David, the gap between the death of Saul and the possession of the crown only opens on another one: between the crown in Judah and the crown in Israel. Like Joseph having to succeed with his Egyptian masters in several careerist installments, David crosses these gaps slowly and deliberately, one strategic step at a time; it is as if he divined that he might have to cross them more than once. He does not burn the bridge represented by Shimei, for example, when Abishai offers to cut the ill-wisher's head off. He says what Joseph comes to say, that God could mean this ill for good, that is, to repay it with good (2 Sam. 16: 5–13).

Indeed, Shimei also seems to invoke the intertribal conflict of the earlier story, for he identifies himself as "the first of all the House of Joseph" (2 Sam. 19:21)—the first representative of the opposed house to welcome the Judahite David back to Jerusalem—and David swears not to hold him guilty. But the phrase, "first of all the House of Joseph," bespeaks Shimei's pride in the midst of his humility, and David's promise only lasts until David's death, when the usefulness of Shimei's good will to David has been used up.

Thus Shimei's subsequent house arrest in Jerusalem is only ironically comparable to Joseph's generous establishing of the sons of Jacob in Goshen, when all that his brothers dare ask Joseph is that he take them as his slaves (Gen. 50:18). For Shimei owes nothing to Solomon, and therefore his presence in Jerusalem constitutes a danger to be circumscribed and watched. He dies for violating his parole, when he pursues two of his runaway slaves beyond the city to their Philistine refuge with Achish. Shimei seems to die, in other words, for a sin that may recall earlier harassments of David: both Shimei's own, and those of his fellow Benjaminite Saul, whom David escaped by serving with Achish. "The first of all the House of Joseph" finally wants that humility that inspires Joseph's repentant brothers and that prevails upon their judge; accordingly, David finally wants the feeling that "the rarer action is/In virtue than in vengeance," as Shakespeare's Prospero will say from a position analogous to Joseph's (e.g.: "they being penitent,/The sole drift of my purpose doth extend/Not a frown further"[22]). David does not distinguish between the virtuous purpose of securing the succession to the throne, and the bloody-mindedness of settling old scores.

IX

In the stories of David and Joseph we meet a public person whose life in public is defined as such by his also having a distinct—and structurally opposed—private life: thus we have both the "refuge" from war afforded David by his amour with Bathsheba while his armies are away at the front, and the converse fulfillment of Joseph in his public life in Egypt while he is away from the internecine conflict with his family. The sense of a mismatch between private and public selves, with which every truly conscious personality seems obliged to live, makes itself particularly visible in just these two characters' stories.

With the tension between public and private goes the sense of unfulfillment in either sphere. The political life of a judge was conceived mainly in terms of the leader's effectiveness in securing the land. Although some of the judges (Gideon, Jephthah, Samson) may have failed badly over the course of their lives, they usually have not failed in their more immediate calling: to exact from the enemy a toll corresponding to God's purpose in raising them up. David's elegies over the fallen may also do duty as elegies over this idea of fulfillment in a military commission. And at the same time these utterances are elegies over the kind of immediate personal bonds that will be ignored in the successful administration of the state. The fixtures of that state will be the Temple, the treasury, and the palace—all institutions unknown to Saul, not to mention the judges before him. Thus the execution of David's nephew Joab, at the beginning of the Books of Kings, spells an end to the kind of ad hoc leadership that had been the rule in the same motion that it secures Solomon the throne.

David's autonomy is suggested by his finally carrying himself intact through the vicissitudes of encounter with others. Yet the princely character's autonomy is entailed in the princely character's personal relatedness. The discernment of a character's interiority and subjectivity, paradoxically, requires an access to the character that reveals that an interior is "there"—this is an access provided by reactions to and of others. An apperception of relatedness is shown, for example, by the tears to which the two princely characters are brought by their own alienated kin.[23] Yet these same tears show our characters' ability to "stand apart" from kin.

The filial model looms large in the princely characters' relations to others. Both David and Joseph may be understood to project father-son relations onto those in positions of authority.[24] David acts the psychological part of a "son" not with his own father, but with Saul. And it is the part of an alienated son, David's alienation from Saul anticipating the rebellion of Absalom from David. We have already mentioned that David, in his elegy over Saul and Jonathan, insists upon the father's and son's ideal inseparability: but the ideal is perhaps belied by David's own rather negligible relations with Jesse. David wants to believe in a relation to Saul that he has both sought for himself and interrupted for Jonathan. But David appears, in respect first of Jesse, and then of Saul, a self-made man, that is, a man who has made himself respected in despite of slights from his elders and betters, in whose regard he seems to be an alienated or neglected son. To his eldest brother Eliab he is just a pest who does not belong on the battlefield; he should be back keeping the sheep (1 Sam. 17:8), which is just what Jesse had him doing when Samuel invited Jesse and his sons to the sacrifice where Samuel was about to anoint the next king of Israel (1 Sam. 16:1–11). David's stated policy of conferring equal honors on those who fight and those who remain behind with the baggage (1 Sam. 30:24) amends his own former treatment by his brothers, particularly Eliab—the son of Jesse who looked most like a king (1 Sam. 16:6).[25]

Joseph's treatment of Benjamin at court also insists on restoring rights to his own prior self. But with Joseph the parental relation is quite the opposite of David's. Nonetheless, separation from the father is the necessary precondition for the self-madeness of this son too. David's relations with his father-in-law and his sons are strained, which is what we should expect, if David's own father depreciated or distrusted David's abilities. Joseph's preferment by his masters Potiphar and Pharaoh is also what we should expect, given the filial approval he enjoys as Rachel's first-born. His sense of paternal election serves him well away from home: he becomes the trusted member of the staff of his master Potiphar's house, then a trusted member of the prisoners in the jailhouse, and finally a trusted member of the house of Pharaoh. Joseph's dream that his father, with the rest of his family, shall bow down to him, is balanced by his abiding concern over his father's welfare, and in the end he bows down to his father (Gen. 48:12). There is hardly any question of him sparing his father as there is in the case of David's sparing Saul. The coldness of the parentally alienated David is always alternating with the compassion of the parentally affected David: choosing Solomon means exposing the pretensions of Adonijah. The disaffected father in David sought to disown his first child by Bathsheba, and the disaffected son seems to disown the Moabite people who once provided sanctuary for his parents.[26] The affected son and the affected father in David harshly punishes the terminal agents of the defeat of the House of Saul: the Amalekite who claims to have dispatched the king dies as he said Saul died, and the two ruffians who beheaded Jonathan's son Ishbaal are treated similarly. In these reprisals we feel that the affected David is punishing the alienated one, namely the David who must disregard the fallen house that could not warm to him as heir to the kingdom. He is also punishing—or compensating for—the weak David, the David that is impotent to discipline the powerful Joab who has murdered Ishbaal's powerful general Abner, as opposed to the David who can easily punish the vulnerable Ishbaal's almost equally vulnerable murderers.

At the outset Joseph naively and solipsistically publishes his dreams to his brothers, with little concern for how obnoxious their revelation might be to others; and thus he sets in motion the train of events that will eventually realize the dreams' predictions—predictions of Joseph's eventual dominance and his brothers' eventual dependency. Jacob rebukes Joseph for his obtuseness, but he also keeps the thing in mind. What Jacob sees in Joseph is a superiority complex that threatens to alienate Joseph from his brothers. David is characterized in an almost opposite way, as a deliberately humble man who is concerned to distance himself from just that threatening superiority that proves so troublesome in his dealings with parties like the insecure Saul, the jealous Nabal, and the suspicious Philistines. Once he is apart from his family, David's reputation for prowess goes before him, like polls and flyers and media men in advance of a modern election. This is also somewhat true of Joseph's reputation in Egypt; his severity as a public official (though not as Joseph per se) is accordingly communicated back to Jacob in Israel.

Thus alienation from family seems a kind of prerequisite for the creation of the strong political man. In the creation of such men, the bond of the family itself is weakened, as the Joseph story itself seems to acknowledge when it has the brothers conjure up an oath allegedly taken at Jacob's deathbed, that Joseph would not engage in reprisals against the guilty members of his clan (Gen. 50:17). This weakening of the family bond is treated first sentimentally and then legalistically in the Joseph story. In the David story the weakening of the bond appears in the legalistic wrangling over David's wife and Saul's daughter, Michal, and in the sentimental and unsentimental executions of David's sons Absalom and Adonijah respectively. But with the weakening of the family bond goes a strengthening of the political one. Joseph's reverence for Jacob anticipates the reverence of Israel for the fathers *as the Patriarchs*: for while the Patriarchs are shown caring for their sons, the sons who are themselves Patriarchs (Isaac and Jacob) are not shown as attached to their fathers. Joseph is shown *remembering* his father, as Israel will remember the Patriarchs, which is the way that God in the exodus will "remember Abraham" (Gen. 19:29 with Exod. 2:24).[27] Similarly, David has reason to hate Saul as a man, but David never shows anything but reverence for Saul *as the Lord's anointed*, or king. David's reverence for Saul and his descendants through Jonathan asks for the honor that David will receive himself, and this is the honor that his own descendants might pray for. Thus the petition of Psalm 132:1a, 10:"Yahweh, remember David. . . . For the sake of your servant David,/do not reject your anointed." This is put in the mouth of Solomon, in 2 Chronicles, at the dedication of the Temple: "Yahweh God, do not rebuff your Anointed—/remember the faithful love [AV "mercies"] of your servant David" (6:42). The "love of David" is, so to speak, both subjective and objective genitive.

Joseph and David are understood to have made a great impression through great gifts. Attached to them are a unique strength of personality, history of preferment, competence in endeavor, and potential for celebrity. They are political men and their political influence seems to reach out to others even from beyond the grave; thus the estate or succession of both of our princely characters is settled with some concern for influencing another person's will in the matter of the settling of scores. Joseph's being recalled to the promise he may well never have made, supposedly over the dying Jacob, reminds us Joseph's will *was* shown as controlled by Jacob on one such occasion, when his father insisted on giving the blessing of his right hand to the later born of Joseph's two sons. Jacob also either swore Joseph (Gen. 24:2–6) or committed his sons generally to burying him in the Promised Land, or committed his sons to burying him with Abraham (49:29–32). Joseph subsequently reports this promise as an oath to bury Jacob in the grave Jacob has dug (50:4–6). Joseph, after seeing three generations of his sons, extracts the same promise from his brethren in Egypt (Gen. 50:23–24); the forgiving of the brothers, I might suggest, deserves the recompense of the conserving of the forgiver's bones. In the context of Genesis, these promises extend the oath Abraham originally required of

Isaac's guardian, at the death of Sarah and the purchase of the patriarchal family grave, the promise never to take Isaac back to the old country (Gen. 24:2–6 with 47:29–31).

The dying David is also recalled to an unspoken but understood commitment to support Solomon's claim to the throne (1 Kings 1:11–37). This claim, once David has sworn to it, is a potential death-warrant from David for the rival Adonijah, who is shortly put under house arrest. Uriah would not go down to his house, and so sponsor Bathsheba's pregnancy by David, and he dies. So Shimei will not stay in his house, and thus accede in Solomon's rule, and he dies too. Adonijah is told to go down to his house, but when he sues for the hand of David's widow Abishag he also effectively refuses to accede in the queen-motherhood of Bathsheba, and so he dies also.

Although both of our princely characters go the way of all the earth (and of the Old Testament narrations of life stories generally), both are moribund in a distinctively self-sovereign way: the impotent David sleeps with Abishag to keep warm, and the aged Joseph commissions his future burial in the Promised Land (and hence an embalmment and burial like the one he has given his father), which extends the interval between death and interment across four generations. Thus the power wielded by the princely characters includes an ability to preside over their own deaths by giving prescriptions for the future closure of their story.

Joseph divines nothing less than the Exodus, and stages a proto-Exodus in the funeral cortège for Jacob. David's commissioning of the judicial murder of Joab conduces to the same effect. Joab's hash must finally be settled not only because Abner must not have died as a fool or a captive dies, but because David himself must not die that way—must not die having been made a fool of by Joab, as Abner formerly was, or a prisoner of Joab, as David has often been throughout his kingship. For the dying David may well sense that he must finally go to Abner, even if Abner cannot be made to come back to him, in words like those that David uses concerning the dead child by Bathsheba (2 Sam. 13:23:"Now that he is dead, why should I fast? Can I bring him back again? I shall go to him but he cannot come back to me"). Behind David's fear of his not being square with Abner there may lie the greater fear of his having to go to Uriah, whom he repeatedly sent away from him, even when he was putting the future Solomon on the throne, by his getting Bathsheba with child.

The deaths of those who have crossed David, insofar as they are also the deaths of Solomon's adversaries, seem a little like the death of Uriah: the final result of the paternity suit leveled by Bathsheba against David.

"Daughter of an oath," the daughter of Eliam and mother of David's child, Bathsheba is sent by Nathan to collect as the mother of Solomon. The "textual" issue, then, is the casting of a legacy in binding form, and its conveyance beyond the present so that it may eventually be felt to have reached forward out of the past, to Moses in the case of Joseph, to Solomon in the case of David. The Josephic political legacy—deriving from Joseph's alleged pact not to turn on his brothers—is the federation of the tribes: the story teaches them the political confession, "We are twelve brothers, sons of one man" (see Gen. 42:13 with 42:32). The Davidic political legacy—deriving from David's alleged promise to Solomon—is the royal succession, the maintenance of God's promise not to let the throne go empty. Moses and Solomon themselves, however, not only mark out the ground for institutions—juridical, administrative, and ecclesiastical or religious—but sponsor the consolidation and codification of the collective experience in book form (Exod. 24:4, 34:27–28; 1 Kings 5:12; 2 Chron. 9:29; Prov. 1:1, 10:1, 25:1; Eccles. 1:1; Wisd. of Sol. 8:13; Ecclus. 47:15–17). But Solomon's sponsorship of wisdom is less important by itself than in conjunction with history writing, as implied at 1 Kings 11:41:"And the rest of the acts of King Solomon, and all that he did, and his wisdom, are they not written in the book of the acts of Solomon?" This first "Book of Acts" suggests what the text in which it occurs also suggests: the regime in the act of memorializing itself.

Judah's assumption of personal responsibility for Benjamin, and David's assumption of personal accountability for the evil census, dramatize a moral awareness that is subsequently bureaucratized and canonized, in the forms of Law and Wisdom. Moses's and Solomon's vocational consultations and negotiations with God presume the digestion of the earlier experiences, to the point where one can know the good and shun the evil, and make the right choices, by choosing Law and Wisdom. Therefore one can choose life—the life of hearkening—with the Deuteronomic Moses on the borders of the Promised Land, or pray the right prayers, with Solomon at the dedication of the Temple. Solomon's choice of wisdom is his choice of having a Deuteronomic power of informed choice, and Solomon's prayer, that God hearken unto the prayers uttered in contemplation of the Temple, cannot be prayed without God's having fulfilled his promises to Moses—the promises of "rest" and of a place for the worship of His Name—by means of the Temple itself. Therefore the Moses of Deuteronomy contemplates the establishment of Solomon's Temple in Jerusalem, and the Solomon of 1 Kings announces the fulfillment of Moses's commission in the Exodus (8:29, 56; 9:3).

X

What does the analogy between Joseph's and David's self- sovereignty have to tell us about the narrative as a whole? We began by saying that personal character in the Bible was ecstatic and on a kind of loan to its possessor, and that in this matter as in others the Lord giveth and the Lord taketh away. The more typical characters are those whose stories are in part dissolved in the history of the polity, as the history of the polity is dissolved in their stories—such as Moses in the wilderness or Samson in relation to the Philistines or Elijah in relation to the kingship. And we have shown that the more exceptional case of our two princely characters is indeed to be accounted for by the two kinds of history they connect.

Our two characters also happen to bridge two kinds of character— the dubious and insecure Jacob and Saul, and the authoritative and magisterial Moses and Solomon. Solomon, for example, solves the case of the two babies, but the story presents us with a hermetically sealed laboratory trial of the judge's wisdom, and nothing interferes with Solomon rationally establishing which woman is the mother to the living child and which its kidnapper, even though neither woman has a husband, or a witness, or a shred of evidence.[28] But Solomon's case is susceptible of a solution, and the women can be "known" by a wisdom sufficiently disinterested to devise the proper leverage. In the distance that is put between the parties at law and Solomon's own experience, this case remains somewhat theoretical. But elsewhere in the royal history, during a siege of Samaria in the time of Elisha, the Israelite king hears the story of two women in such desperate straits that they have agreed to eat their sons on successive days. One child has been eaten, and now the mother of this child cries out to the king, because the other woman has refused to keep her side of the bargain, and has hidden the remaining child. Here is a case meant to try a Davidic rather than a Solomonic king. The king tears his clothes in distress: "underneath he was wearing sackcloth next to his body" (2 Kings 6:30). Somewhat like the David who volunteers to fall into the hands of Yahweh rather than the hands of men (2 Sam. 24:14), this king suffers the sorrows of his subjects, as opposed to merely discriminating between their good and evil.

Like many of the "historical" characters in Shakespeare, Joseph and David get their story from being caught between "old kingdom" and "new state." Joseph the tax collector is credited with engineering the monopolistic unity of Pharaonic Egypt (Gen. 47:13–26), as the census-taking David is credited with founding the Jerusalem kingship for Israel.

If we cannot offer a full raison d'être for the very generous measure of personality accorded Joseph and David, we still may paradoxically explain their independence (i.e., as operators) as a function of their mediating different kinds of history. But why do personalities loom large in the authors' reconstruction of the given historical transitions? Is this efflorescence of "character" explained as the function of a changing history that changes people, as it were, into themselves, while using their lives to advance a destiny across the critical generations? Why might these personalities, at the place that tribal saga is replaced by political history, have a perceivable unity of psychological life, that is, a psychological life that seems to exist independently of the ideological and epochal life of patriarchs, priests, judges, prophets, and kings otherwise characterizing the biblical norm?

One of our answers has been that the autonomy of the two princely characters is merely the foreshadowing of the sufficiency or sovereignty of their given princely houses. Personality itself would figure in the equation because historical changes are spoken through persons, and because each of these founder-figures finds his personality in the form of a personal authority in the historical juncture, as opposed to his finding a legacy in the historical continuum. Joseph comes into his own on his own, i.e., in Egypt, not because he is the son of Rachel, but because he is a man of demonstrated ability in foreign eyes and in a foreign court. David similarly comes into his own, first against Goliath and then among the Philistines, not because he is armed or sponsored by the king, but because he is himself a man of demonstrated ability and personal resourcefulness on the field of battle. Even if both characters attribute their ability to their sponsorship by God, each exhibits a presence of mind indissociable from exceptional self-command. One notes that those characters in the narrative who stand up to the princely personages of Joseph and David also seem to find *their* voice, even as they take over responsibility for what is happening as a result of the authoritative personage they are bearding—Reuben or Judah in the case of a severe Joseph-in-disguise, Abigail or Mephibosheth in the case of a potentially vindictive David.

However, by the same rule, the "historical juncture" opens not only to make the princely character's life story visible in conjunction with that of other individuals, but also to limn the competing "life story" or history of the other major house. For not only is each princely character the founder of his line, he is also to be "found" in the presence of the other line that his own eminence tends to obscure. Thus Joseph is not made present to us without the acknowledgment of the presence of "Judah" and its future, while the Judaic David is not made present to us without acknowledgment of the presence of Rachel's children

"Benjamin" and "Joseph." For Saul, Shimei, and Jeroboam are all descended from Rachel, while David is Leahite.

"Judah," the youngest son of Leah, is repeatedly present in the story of the older son of Rachel: in Judah's motion to sell Joseph rather than kill him; in his getting (through Tamar) the twins that create the critical third generation from the twin Jacob; in his being named and employed as the go-between and spokesman between Joseph and his family; in his personal assumption of the Cain-like consequences of failure as his brother's keeper (the ostracizing curse); in his inheritance—from Jacob —of the patriarchally transmitted blessing of Abraham; and in that blessing's fulfillment in the exceptional numerosity of Judah's tribe in the reckoning recorded at Numbers 26 (v. 22:"seventy-six thousand five hundred men"). It is of some importance to check this blessing against its prehistory in the story, for it does not itself mention offspring. Nonetheless, it contains the blessing of victory over enemies that coordinates the kinsmen's blessing on Rebekah (Gen. 24:60) with God's promise to Abraham (Gen. 22:17), and both of these earlier utterances pair victory with fertility. But the blessing also shows how Joseph is shadowed by "Judah," for Jacob's promise to Judah, that "your father's sons will bow down to you," repeats while it replaces the promise made to Joseph by his dreams (cf. Gen. 49:8, with Joseph's dreams at 37:7, 9): in effect it is a promise to David.

In the establishment of the Davidic throne and the deposal of the Benjamite Saul, "Joseph" is likewise conversely present: in the dissent of Shimei ("the first of all the House of Joseph"), and in the activation of Shimei's dissent by the Ephraimite Jeroboam, when he leads the Northern secession and establishes the Northern sanctuaries. For Jeroboam acts as a second Moses, reacting to Solomon and then Rheoboam as a second Pharaoh: Solomon had given Jeroboam "charge over all the forced labor of the House of Joseph" (1 Kings 11:28), and like Moses fleeing Pharaoh, this future leader finds refuge abroad (in Egypt), until the head of state (Solomon) dies, when the rebellious fugitive returns to lead the departure of "Israel" out of the imperial jurisdiction. Thus each princely character's story has its counterweight in the other, because the promotion of each one is shadowed by the ultimately independent future of the other house.

As the characters that are dramatized, Joseph and David are also endowed by the narrative with a style that allows them to take a double part. Joseph adopts the guise of foreign authority to eavesdrop on his brothers' consciences; David feigns or affects madness to escape Philistine suspicion. The princely characters have the freedom to make these departures from their identity in order to conserve their existence. They are characters with the capacity for compassion and self-observation;

they are shown compromising with others without compromising themselves. David's versions of the self- dramatizing question, "Who am I?"
have a double significance, for they are echoed by the question "Who
is David?" These are not so much the questions of a character like
Shakespeare's Richard II, that is, a narcissistic ego contemplating its
own demise, as the questions pertaining to the destiny of a founder-
figure: e.g., "Who am I, Lord Yahweh, and what is my House, that
you have led me as far as this?" (2 Sam. 7:18b). The question asks who
David is politically, what significant power or position he will enjoy.
What serious interest can another party—Saul, the Philistines, Nabal,
Shimei, Ittai—take in him or his party? (Cf. 1 Sam. 21:10, "Is not
this David the king of the land?"; 1 Sam. 25:9, "Who is David? Who
is the son of Jesse?"; and 1 Kings 12:16, "What portion have we in
David?/We have no inheritance in the son of Jesse.") But the "I" question
asks who David is to himself: Who is he personally, what can he signify
or be to David, How seriously should David be taking himself, as a
self? (Cf. David to Saul at 1 Sam. 24:14:"After whom has the king
of Israel come out? After whom do you pursue? After a dead dog!
After a flea!" and 1 Sam. 18:19, "Who am I, and who are my kinsfolk,
my father's family in Israel, that I should be son-in-law to the king?")

Where did David's power to refer to himself—whether as a somebody
or as a nobody—come from? What enables this self-objectifying mode
of reference? Is there not perhaps a significant parallel in Joseph's and
his brothers' ability to see how they might look before God and before
each other (Gen. 37:29; 39:9; 42:18, 21–22, 28)?

Self-referential questions belong particularly to the Davidic narrative.
Their rhetoric is heard, for example, in the self-humiliation of
Meribaal, "son of Jonathan son of Saul": "What is your servant, that
you should show favor to a dead dog like me?" (2 Sam. 9:6, 8). Although
to opposite effect, Jonathan's son speaks with an idiom like that of the
Saulide loyalist Abner, who is furiously asserting his claim to Ishbaal's
(Ishbosheth's) tolerance for his high-handedness: "Am I a dog's head?"
(2 Sam. 3:8). Within the narrative of the kingship, this rhetoric of self-
abnegation originates with Saul himself, at his calling by the prophet
Samuel: "Am I not a Benjamite," Saul asks, "of the smallest of the tribes
of Israel?" (1 Sam. 9:21). Gideon protests divine appointment similarly
(at Judg. 6:15), and the reluctant Saul is also found among several reluctant and self-objectifying biblical prophets; but Saul himself never seems
to say such things with much cognizance of what it is he might be saying.
Saul, in the episode at Gilgal (1 Sam. 13)—perhaps not a little like the
temporizing Jacob in the episode of the rape of Dinah at Shechem (Gen.
34)—has been seen through by others, but he is a temporizer who does
not readily see through himself.[29] Again it seems to be no accident that

the most problematic identities in the canon of biblical character, namely the first "Israel" (Jacob), and the first Israelite "king" (Saul), introduce the two "princely" characters, the ones with the greatest measure of self-possession in relation both to a self and to a story to be possessed.

Apparently the question being asked about the individual person (Who am I?) cannot be asked without the question about the royal or sovereign party (Who is David?). The individual person cannot be understood as self-sovereign until the kingship has provided him with the royal metaphor for personal sovereignty. As popular phrases like "a man's house is his castle" and "every man a king" show, the king alone originally enjoys the rights with which society eventually comes to credit all its individual members. The Psalms are a case in point: they speak with the accents of the conscious ego, yet they are assigned to the utterance of the king. Originally, the kingship did the individual's living for the individual and enjoyed the individual's rights or entitlements representatively. David's question thus partly refers to his substantiality as a party, as a faction, as an "estate." David, in the current idiom, does not need to "get a life," but perhaps a character like David's victim Paltiel does: the tearful husband of Michal only has Michal, as Uriah only had Bathsheba.

Thus the new autonomy of the new kingship in David anticipates and prerepresents the autonomy of the individual per se. But the feeling that David represents the kingship of the common man still does not mean that he represents the individual potentially divorceable from all his connections. On the contrary.

We are now in a better position to restate the relation between Joseph and David. King David is the "sovereign" side of the self-sovereign individual, the one who is responsible for his own actions, and who cannot really wish them off on Uriah, or Joab, or the rich man in Nathan's parable. The princely Joseph is the "self" side, the character who can see his life as it will look to God, and so as a kind of work of art. The story of Joseph was probably first introduced into the tradition of the saving history during the time of David, and thus near the time when the history of David itself was being written: when the expansionary ideal of the monarchy was also enlarging the domain of the individual Israelite citizen while diminishing the importance of the tribe—and therefore enlarging the individual's chances both for distinction (at court) and for obscurity (one could become a foreigner in one's own land, particularly as a servant or hireling—indeed, one could sell oneself as a slave). Thus Joseph is employed in the service of foreign masters, and David serves under the Benjamite Saul and the Philistine Achish.

Taken together, the stories of David and Joseph might suggest to us the subject appropriating sovereignty and rights for himself from the exclusive party of the sovereign, while at the same time the stories could also show a sovereignty that is made correspondingly more subjective, with the loss of tribal cohesion: Joseph is the master of a world within himself at the expense of relations to kin. The same individuality is also made more objective, by means of the new master-slave relation —with the result that the inner life of character can become that much more the object of fictional and critical investigation. The stoical slave's empire over himself is brought into existence by the impositions of an imperial despot who throws him into prison.

These stories create complete individuals, with depths to cry out of that are uniquely their own, but they must nonetheless be understood as exceptions that are not really allowed to break the Ptolemaic rules of biblical characterization, for their context is ineradicably the biblical text of the national history. Joseph's reconstitution of his father's house in Egypt and David's projection of the building of the house of God in Jerusalem by his son both attest to the design that the biblical character has upon the greater design of God and history. For biblical characters there is always such a futuristic factor that tends to qualify a personalized teleology or closed circle of personal recognition and recapitulation, so distinctively a part of the novelistic and biographical storytelling attaching to purely literary characters. But the bones of Joseph are long since buried in the Northern Kingdom, and all that remains is his story; the throne of David, likewise, has been dismantled, and all that remains of the Messiah ben David are the messianic psalms from which scholarship has belatedly tried to reconstruct the coronation liturgy.

The house of Israel in the north was the kingdom of Israel, but also the house of Joseph; in the south, the kingship in Judah was otherwise the house of David: God promises Solomon that Israel shall never lack for a man to occupy the throne of David. But if the Lord giveth and taketh away personal identity, he also giveth and taketh away political and institutional identity. Thus even the "collective" explanation of our two characters' autonomy subjects them to contingency: the contingency of the international history that gives either the house of Joseph or the house of David only an episodic purchase upon its existence in historical time. The northern kingdom and the Davidic throne are only conserved archivally, through the keeping of the record, and not through any genetic or social keeping of Joseph by his brothers, nor any civic or national keeping of Zion and its hymnists by David's God. These considerations of a mortality writ large bring the princely characterization back within the norm of "other-determination" observed by the narrative of the Hebrew Bible as a whole.

As we have said, the Psalmist's relation to God was not destined to be understood conventionally, as the relation of the divinity to the royal ruler as the god's adopted son. On the contrary, the adopted son of the divinity in the Bible is originally Israel, a corporate individual that can represent the rights of a people, rather than the privilege of a prince. Thus the biblical revolution against a conventional form of divine favor—the preferring of the ruling house alone—is coordinated with the events of the Exodus and the death of Pharaoh's firstborn son, for the preferring of the ruling house alone is virtually the political form of primogeniture, and the Bible regularly speaks of the taking away of all such inherited expectations and privileges. As good democrats we might see such expectations and privileges being divinely conferred on a people as a whole; but in the Old Testament this conferral could hardly mean the giving of rights to an individual who had no people, for if one had no people one could not be given anything worth having. What self could there be for him, if he were not the son of his people?

The mother typically names the child in the Bible, and in all the Bible's vast onomasticon of personal names, she seems to have most often named him Zechariah or Zachariah. This is a name suggesting the Hebrew word for a male, *zachar*: but "zachar" no less suggests the root *zkr*, "to remember." Consider, for example, the story of Ruth the Moabitess. Genetically, Ruth was ultimately Nahorite: yet her people think they are the sons of Moab, "our father," so her parentage was Moabite. Legally or adoptively, as a wife, she is Judaic. Dynastically, as a mother, she will become proto-Davidic. Her son Obed connects her Judaic husband Boaz's father, Salmon, with David's son Solomon: one of Solomon's two pillars will accordingly be named Boaz. Ruth seems to have become a mother mainly in order to provide a grandchild or godchild for her husband's kinswoman, Naomi. And Ruth would not have it any other way. For hers is one of the so-called "orphan" books: the text vaguely attaches itself to the time of the Judges, and yet it is not found in the canon of the "Former Prophets," but in the "Writings." From Ruth's point of view, she exists to be conscripted or reclaimed by all her other identifications, which are all that she would call her own; she does not seek to call anything of herself her own. Her design is not to have her will or her way in our sense of securing self-fulfillment; hers is rather a design upon a place within the larger design.

"Oh that Ishmael might live before thee," Abraham cries out (Gen. 17:18), protesting what seems to be God's regular sacrifice of this Patriarch's firstborn. Moses tells God to blot him out of his book, unless Israel is included in it (Exod. 32:32)—they are the people he has "borne" (Deut 1:9); but God will not in fact blot Israel out of His book (2 Kings 14:27), for Israel has found grace in His sight (Exod. 33:16f). Thus

Ruth the Moabite is seeking to recover what the nameless daughters of Lot originally lost for her: that is, a place in the national registry. By the beginning of the Gospel of Matthew she has got it, through her son Obed, between Salmon and Solomon, which also means between Rahab the harlot and Bathsheba the adulteress.

The first of the three installments of the genealogy that begins Matthew's Gospel starts from Abraham and ends on David the King. The third installment ends on a latter-day Joseph, dreamer of dreams and son of Jacob. Joseph's name also turns up, at significant intervals, no less than three times in the analogous genealogy in Luke, which is a kind of calendrically conceived periodic table for the prediction of Jesus over eleven genealogical "weeks" reckoned from God to Joseph the carpenter.[30] The seventh week from God is headed by another Joseph, whose week issues in another Jesus, and the seventh week before Jesus is headed by David, whose week issues in this earlier yet post-Davidic Joseph. The list is contrived to show that Jesus is truly "son of David," being the adopted son of the latter-day "House of Joseph." The attempt of the original Joseph to direct his father's blessings on his sons, and that of the original David to direct the royal succession, show that "Joseph" and "David" again observe the biblical rule: one expects one's name to be preserved in Israel through one's offspring. And as our examples from the New Testament imply, their names no less than Ruth's want to be remembered in any final fixing of the text.

UNDERSTANDING THE BREAD: DISRUPTION AND AGGREGATION, SECRECY AND REVELATION IN MARK'S GOSPEL

John Drury

The study of the New Testament Gospels as literature has emerged out of one of the most spectacular failures in the history of criticism: the long drawn-out collapse of the quest of the historical Jesus. Albert Schweitzer was its obituarist. In the last chapter of his splendid book by that title, he described, with pathos, the hopes of a century and more of dedicated critics that Jesus, released from the bands which fastened him to "the stony rocks of ecclesiastical doctrine," would walk "straight into our time as a teacher and saviour." But their own historical methods turned against them, like the sorcerer's apprentice, by not stopping where, or when, they hoped. Nor, correspondingly, would Jesus. "He does not stay. He passes by our time and returns to his own."[1] They appealed to history, and to history they have gone.

The movement of gospel criticism in our own generation has shown that Schweitzer was right about the way things were going. Although the historical quest has been sustained, and sustained by the same good-ish intentions, our understanding of first-century Christianity has increased at the expense of our certainties about Jesus. Form critics examined the separate units of the gospels in terms of the needs and achievements of the primitive Christian communities. Then redaction critics examined whole gospels in terms of the mentalities of their authors: internally known by the shapes and themes of their literary art, externally by relation to similar contemporary texts in Greek, Latin, and Hebrew.

But what has been failure to Christian proprietorial hopes has been achievement in the refining and enriching of historical method. What started as the attempt to recover one all-important man, reclaiming what he actually said and did by cleaning away and discarding what his successors made of it—hoping to gaze on the actual face of Jesus as Schlie-mann had (too credulously) gazed on the gold mask at Mycene which he took to be the face of Agamemnon, and using techniques of excava-tion as crude as his—this attempt has ended up as the current recovery of a whole world in its intricate symbolic structure and in the process of change. (The aim of today's gospel scholars must be the sort of cul-tural reconstruction so brilliantly achieved for Holland's golden age by Simon Schama's *The Embarrassment of Riches*.)

So metaphors of retreat and loss are not adequate. There has been huge gain in scope and resources. When gospel scholars have admitted that their texts are historical fictions or fictionalized histories—at any rate cultural constructions—they can sit at table with literary critics who know more than they about the whole business of literary representation as an art, with historians who know more about the societies which shaped the gospels. The Christian critics went looking for their man. But they have found a whole past world in all its social, religious, and literary vivacity. And they have been rewarded in the present by the refreshing company of Jewish scholars, literary critics seasoned in Proust and Joyce, anthropologists, structuralists, and historians of antiq-uity. It has not turned out as they hoped. But it has not turned out at all badly—even from the religious point of view, if intelligent convivi-ality among human beings is a greater religious good than proprietorial pride in the recovery of pristine title-deeds, or if the intelligent charity evoked by the study of religions not our own is a greater religious good than crusading.

The Riddle

Necessity is the natural mother of critical invention. The critic is most needed and most welcome when the reader is flummoxed. And this is the likely mental state of any reader of Mark's gospel who gets to 8:14–21.

> Now the disciples had forgotten to take bread, neither had they in the ship with them but one loaf. And [Jesus] charged them, saying, Take heed, beware of the leaven of the Pharisees, and of the leaven of Herod. And they reasoned among themselves, saying, It is because we have no bread. And when Jesus knew it, he saith unto them, Why reason ye, because ye have no bread? perceive ye not yet, neither un-derstand? have ye your heart yet hardened? Having eyes, see ye not? and having ears, hear ye not? and do ye not remember? When I brake the five loaves among the five thousand, how many baskets full of

fragments took ye up? They say unto him, Twelve. And when the
seven among four thousand, how many baskets full of fragments took
ye up? And they said, Seven. And he said unto them, How is it that
ye do not understand?

But you don't, and the commentaries fail you. Half way through the
book, you are presented with a pointed resumé of what you have recently read. And you are at a loss. Two things may happen. First, you
may bash on regardless. It is a technique of reading which sometimes
works and you will be in numerous company. It is what most modern
readers of Mark have done, including the learned. And it is what Mark's
disciples do—characters with whom the reader may well identify. After
all, it is realistic enough, since in real life we leave behind us trails of
unsolved and evaded problems and survive. Or, second, you may stop
until you have worked it out, realistically judging that this is one of
those times in reading, as in life, when the disciplines of the *vita
contemplativa* must be given space if the *vita activa* of carrying on is to
carry on in good form. This is what I decided to do in my contribution
to the Alter/Kermode *Literary Guide to the Bible*.[2] I now mean to give
a much fuller exposition of the solution to Jesus's riddle which I
sketched there. It was clear that the critic owed the reader some sort
of a solution then and there. Since then it has become clear that riddle
and solution are far more intricately and deeply tied into Mark's gospel,
far more crucial to its evangelistic strategy, than I had thought—and
also far more vitally and polemically connected with the life of early
Christian societies at the critical point of the status of gentiles within
them. As a result the proportion of repetition in this paper is small.

The riddle itself points imperiously back into the text, and makes
us thankful that at least this is a text which we can go back to and
look things up in, that we are not just at the mercy of the time-bound
and unstoppable oral storyteller. The greater fullness which I intend
now is primarily textual. Not only will we have to scrutinize Mark's text
at large, if selectively concentrating on chapters 6 through 8. We will
need to consider the texts on which it draws, the sacred scriptures of
Judaism. For Mark, along with the other early Christian writers, spoiled
the Jews as the Jews had once spoiled the Egyptians. In the course of
their exodus from the old religion, seen by the more radical among
them as a sort of captivity, the Christians stole the jewellery of the Torah
for their own uses and adornments. The aim of my study is, in fact,
to trace a part of the course of that Christian exodus, bursting the
bounds of sacred tradition and going through deadly baptismal waters
to become a new society sustained by a new food. As with all transitions,
it mixes continuities with discontinuities. But in Mark's book it is all

concentrated in Jesus and dramatized by his story. It is a major reason for the vitality of early Christianity that it did this, packing all the complexities of religion into the simplicity of a single biography.

The Christians represented that biography by bread before they put it into their biographical texts. The society which eventually produced Mark's gospel was a society which met to eat bread. It understood that bread and eating in narrative wise. Its story was Jesus's story, assimilated as their own. "Grub first, then ethics," said Brecht. "Grub first, then gospel text" would also apply. Jesus as the new Passover bread was the nourishing focus of this new religion in its transition phase between being a Jewish sect and being an independent, universal religion with scriptures of its own. We will understand that bread if we do as they did and trace its story.

When Robert Lowth set himself to the critique of Hebrew poetry in the middle of the eighteenth century, he warned:

> if the reader be accustomed to habits of life totally different from those of the author, and be conversant only with different objects; in that case many descriptions and sentiments, which were clearly illustrated and magnificently expressed by the one, will appear to the other mean and obscure, harsh and unnatural; and this will be the case more or less, in proportion as they differ, or are more remote from each other in time, situation, customs sacred or profane, in fine, in all the forms of public and private life.[3]

This will not be easy, and as some encouragement for the ardors ahead we may use what the twentieth-century art historian Edgar Wind said about recovering the secrets of pagan mysteries in the art of the Renaissance, because it is so apt to the riddle in Mark 8, a lucid modern voice to put against its antique obscurity.

> The process of recapturing the substance of past conversations is necessarily more complicated than the conversations themselves. A historian tracing the echo of our own debates might justly infer from the common use of such words as microbe or molecule that scientific discovery had moulded our imagination; but he would be much mistaken if he assumed that a proper use of these words would always be attended by a complete technical mastery of the underlying theory. Yet, supposing the meaning of the words were lost, and a historian were trying to recover it, surely he would have to recognize that the key to the colloquial usage is in the scientific, and that his only chance of recapturing the first is to acquaint himself with the second. The same rule applies to an iconographer trying to reconstruct the lost argument of a Renaissance painting. He must learn more about Renaissance arguments than the painter needed to know; and this is not,

as has been claimed, a self-contradiction, but the plain outcome of the undeniable fact that we no longer enjoy the advantages of Renaissance conversation. We must make up for it through reading and inference. Iconography is always, as Focillon observed with regret, *un detour*, an unavoidable round-about approach to art. Its reward . . . is that it may help to remove the veil of obscurity which not only distance in time (although in itself sufficient for that purpose) but a deliberate obliqueness in the use of metaphor has spread over some of the greatest Renaissance paintings. They were designed for initiates; hence they require an initiation.[4]

We certainly do as we match up to Mark, a deliberate dancer with veils of obscurity whose artistic purpose is to make readers initiates.

Decoding

Most obviously, the riddle refers to the two miraculous meals of bread and fish which have just happened in Mark's book and is about the numbers of fish, and more emphatically about the numbers of loaves and baskets of leftover fragments. The numbers are crucial.

At 6:35–44, Jesus looked up to heaven and broke five loaves and two fish. His disciples distributed them among five thousand people who ate and were satisfied. Then they took up twelve great industrial-sized baskets, *kophinoi*, full of fragments.

At 8:1–10, Jesus took seven loaves, gave thanks, and let the disciples distribute them to four thousand people. This time they took up seven ordinary domestic baskets, *spuridai*, of fragments.

I have put these numbers in a table on the fourth page of the accompanying chart. The contemplation of that table is not immediately enlightening. But Jesus and Mark together do not seem to think that that is any excuse. What disciples and readers have witnessed ought to enlighten them, give them a key to the conundrum. We need to retrace our steps—being more leisurely and spacious about it than our shame and panic press us to be, as always when we have lost, say, the car key.

What have we been told about bread and eating so far—that is, up to 6:34? Some odd and sketchy things, but that could be part of their point. The first of them was John the Baptist's raw diet of locusts and wild honey: apt nourishment for the prophet who summoned Judaism back to nature from culture (1:6). (The last, oddest, and most revolting, was John's own severed head served on a plate at Herod's feast [6:28]. In between we read about people not eating, eating in irregular ways, or going about the preliminaries of eating. There were two of these preliminaries. At 1:16–20 two fishermen cast nets into the sea, and two mended their nets in their boat. All four became disciples, and so were taken into the story as narrative seed of the church-to-be. In chapter 4 there are parables of sowing and the harvest of the church-to-be. So we have witnessed the first stages of preparing fish and bread to eat.) At 2:15–27 there was much irregularity and untowardness about eating. Jesus sat at table with publicans and sinners. His disciples failed to fast when John the Baptist's did, and Jesus vindicated them by appeal to the special time of his own coming as bridegroom to the feast. His disciples plucked ears of corn on the sabbath, and Jesus vindicated them by an appeal to David in scripture. At 3:20 the crowd "could not even eat." Likewise at 6:31 "they had no leisure even to eat." And the disciples sent out to exorcize at 6:8 were told by Jesus to take "no bread." Up to and including Mark 6:31, not eating or eating irregularly seems to be the norm. (The only unambiguously positive and straightforward instances were Peter's wife's mother at 1:31 serving, presumably with food, Jesus and the four fishermen-disciples, and Jesus's command to Jairus's household to give the daughter "something to eat." Both of these were laconically noted and made unusual, more wonderful than straightforward, by their association with women just recovered from sickness or death. Positive and ordinary eating is for those on the other side of collapse. In a society to which eating customs were as important as that of Jews and gentiles in the first century, this must matter.)

So these incidents combine to destabilize and postpone ordinary eating, right through to the threshold of the first of the miraculous meals. One of them is particularly important, the plucking of grain on the sabbath at 2:23–27. We should give it more time. It is both irregular and preparatory for bread. We sense its importance if we notice that the reference which Jesus makes there to Jewish scripture, the story of David and the showbread in 1 Samuel 21, implies numbers that come up again in the two miraculous meals and Jesus's riddle about them. (See the table on p. 107.) The regulations for the showbread are in Leviticus 24. It consisted of twelve loaves, set before the Lord every sabbath on behalf of the people and as a little model of the twelve-tribe nation, in two rows of six. The story in 1 Samuel 21 (see p. 104) tells how David unceremoniously took five of these twelve loaves to satisfy the hunger of himself and his campaigning companions. So seven were left after the royal sacrilege.

We are now in business, possessing three of the four numbers used by Mark in the meals and the riddle. They have scriptural holiness and come from a scriptural passage which Mark indicated with unusual emphasis. They are: 12, 5, and 7. Something holy, or sacrilegious, or both,

UNDERSTANDING THE BREAD

I.

MARK

1:1 *John's raw food*
1:16 *Fishermen (church-to-be)*
1:31 *Simon's mother in law serves*
2:15 *Jesus eats with sinners*
2:18 *Jesus's disciples don't fast*

2:23 Showbread

²³One sabbath he was going through the grainfields; and as they made their way his disciples began to pluck heads of grain. ²⁴And the Pharisees said to him, "Look, why are they doing what is not lawful on the sabbath?" ²⁵And he said to them, "Have you never read what David did, when he was in need and was hungry, he and those who were with him: ²⁶how he entered the house of God, when Abi'athar was high priest, and ate the bread of the Presence, which is not lawful for any but the priests to eat, and also gave it to those who were with him?" ²⁷And he said to them, "The sabbath was made for man, not man for the sabbath;²⁸ so the Son of man is lord even of the sabbath."

3:20 *"they could not even eat"*
4 *Seed parables (church-to-be)*
5:43 *"give her to eat" (Jairus's daughter)*
6:8 *"no bread" (disciples sent out)*
6:14 *John's head on a dish*
6:31 *"no leisure even to eat"*

Leviticus 24:5

⁵"And you shall take fine flour, and bake twelve cakes of it; two tenths of an ephah shall be in each cake. ⁶And you shall set them in two rows, six in a row, upon the table of pure gold. ⁷And you shall put pure frankincense with each row, that it may go with the bread as a memorial portion to be offered by fire to the Lord. ⁸Every sabbath day Aaron shall set it in order before the Lord continually on behalf of the people of Israel as a covenant for ever. ⁹And it shall be for Aaron and his sons, and they shall eat it in a holy place, since it is for him a most holy portion out of the offerings by fire to the Lord, a perpetual due."

1 Samuel 21:1

21 Then came David to Nob to Ahim'elech the priest; and Ahim'elech came to meet David trembling, and said to him, "Why are you alone, and no one with you?" ²And David said to Ahim'elech the priest, "The king has charged me with a matter, and said to me, 'Let no one know anything of the matter about which I send you, and with which I have charged you.' I have made an appointment with the young men for such and such a place. ³Now then, what have you at hand? Give me five loaves of bread, or whatever is here." ⁴And the priest answered David, "I have no common bread at hand, but there is holy bread; if only the young men have kept themselves from women." ⁵And David answered the priest, "Of a truth women have been kept from us as always when I go on an expedition; the vessels of the young men are holy, even when it is a common journey; how much more today will their vessels be holy?" ⁶So the priest gave him the holy bread; for there was no bread there but the bread of the Presence, which is removed from before the Lord, to be replaced by hot bread on the day it is taken away.

see 12:35 etc, below

Numbers 27:15

¹⁵Moses said to the Lord, ¹⁶"Let the Lord, the God of the spirits of all flesh, appoint a man over the congregation, ¹⁷who shall go out before them and come in before them, who shall lead them out and bring them in; that the congregation of the Lord may not be as sheep which have no shepherd." ¹⁸And the Lord said to Moses, "Take Joshua the son of Nun, a man in whom is the spirit, and lay your hand upon him."

2 Kings 4:42

⁴²A man came from Ba'al-shal'ishah, bringing the man of God bread of the first fruits, twenty loaves of barley, and fresh ears of grain in his sack. And Eli'sha said, "Give to the men, that they may eat." ⁴³But his servant said, "How am I to set this before a hundred men?" So he repeated, "Give them to the men, that they may eat, for thus says the Lord, 'They shall eat and have some left.'" ⁴⁴So he set it before them. And they ate, and had some left, according to the word of the Lord.

6:32 First Miraculous Meal

³²And they went away in the boat to a lonely place by themselves. ³³Now many saw them going, and knew them, and they ran there on foot from all the towns, and got there ahead of them. ³⁴As he went ashore he saw a great throng, and he had compassion on them, because they were like sheep without a shepherd; and he began to teach them many things. ³⁵And when it grew late, his disciples came to him and said, "This is a lonely place, and the hour is now late; ³⁶send them away, to go into the country and villages round about and buy themselves something to eat." ³⁷But he answered them, "You give them something to eat." And they said to him, "Shall we go and buy two hundred denarii worth of bread, and give it to them to eat?" ³⁸And he said to them, "How many loaves have you? Go and see." And when they had found out, they said, "Five, and two fish." ³⁹Then he commanded them all to sit down by companies upon the green grass. ⁴⁰So they sat down in groups, by hundreds and by fifties. ⁴¹And taking the five loaves and the two fish he looked up to heaven, and blessed, and broke the loaves, and gave them to the disciples to set before the people; and he divided the two fish among them all. ⁴²And they all ate and were satisfied. ⁴³And they took up twelve baskets full of broken pieces and of the fish. ⁴⁴And those who ate the loaves were five thousand men.

6:45 *"they did not understand about the loaves."*

7   *Jesus defends dirty eating;*
        appeals to defecation
        "all foods clean"

(Understanding the Bread—*continued*)

II.

MARK

7:24 The Dogs Eat the Crumbs

24And from there he arose and went away to the region of Tyre and Sidon. And he entered a house, and would not have any one know it; yet he could not be hid. 25But immediately a woman, whose little daughter was possessed by an unclean spirit, heard of him, and came and fell down at his feet. 26Now the woman was a Greek, a Syrophoeni'cian by birth. And she begged him to cast the demon out of her daughter. 27And he said to her, "Let the children first be fed, for it is not right to take the children's bread and throw it to the dogs." 28But she answered him, "Yes Lord; yet even the dogs under the table eat the children's crumbs." 29And he said to her, "For this saying you may go your way; the demon has left your daughter." 30And she went home, and found the child lying in bed, and the demon gone.

7:31 *Deaf stammerer cured*

8:1 Second Miraculous Meal

8 In those days, when again a great crowd had gathered, and they had nothing to eat, he called his disciples to him, and said to them, 2"I have compassion on the crowd, because they have been with me now three days, and have nothing to eat; 3and if I send them away hungry to their homes, they will faint on the way." 4And his disciples answered him, "How can one feed these men with bread here in the desert?" 5And he asked them, "How many loaves have you?" They said, "Seven." 6And he commanded the crowd to sit down on the ground; and he took the seven loaves, and having given thanks he broke them and gave them to his disciples to set before the people; and they set them before the crowd. 7And they had a few small fish; and having blessed them, he commanded that these also should be set before them. 8And they ate, and were satisfied; and they took up the broken pieces left over, seven baskets full. 9And there were about four thousand people. 10And he sent them away; and immediately he got into the boat with his disciples, and went to the district of Dalmanu'tha.

8:11 *No sign for Pharisees*

8:14 First Riddle—Bread

14Now they had forgotten to bring bread; and they had only one loaf with them in the boat. 15And he cautioned them, saying, "Take heed, beware of the leaven of the Pharisees and the leaven of Herod." 16And they discussed it with one another, saying, "We have no bread." 17And being aware of it, Jesus said to them, "Why do you discuss the fact that you have no bread? Do you not yet perceive or understand? Are your hearts hardened? 18Having eyes do you not see, and having ears do you not hear? And do you not remember? 19When I broke the five loaves for the five thousand, how many baskets full of broken pieces did you take up?" They said to him, "Twelve." 20And the seven for the four thousand, how many baskets full of broken pieces did you take up?" And they said to him, "Seven." 21And he said to them, "Do you not yet understand?"

8:45 Son of Man came to serve (cf. 1:31)

Galatians 2:11

[11]But when Peter came to Antioch I opposed him to his face, because he stood condemned. [12]For before certain men came from James, he ate with the Gentiles; but when they came he drew back and separated himself, fearing the circumcision party. [13]And with him the rest of the Jews acted insincerely, so that even Barnabas was carried away by their insincerity. [14]But when I saw that they were not straightforward about the truth of the gospel, I said to Peter before them all, "If you, though a Jew, live like a Gentile and not like a Jew, how can you compel the Gentiles to live like Jews?" [15]We ourselves, who are Jews by birth and not Gentile sinners, [16]yet who know that a man is not justified by works of the law but through faith in Jesus Christ, even we have believed in Christ Jesus, in order to be justified by faith in Christ, and not by works of the law, because by works of the law shall no one be justified.

1 Corinthians 10:16

[16]The bread which we break, is it not a participation in the body of Christ? [17]Because there is one bread, we who are many are one body, for we all partake of the one bread.

Leviticus 24	12 showbreads					
1 Samuel 21	12 showbreads	5 taken	(7 left)			
Mark 6:35–44		5 taken	(7 left)	12 *kophinoi* of bits	5000 fed	5 fed
Mark 8:1–10		7 taken		7 *spuridai* of bits	4000 fed	4000 fed

(Understanding the Bread—*continued*)

III.

MARK

12:35 Second Riddle—David and His Son

[35]And as Jesus taught in the temple, he said, "How can the scribes say that the Christ is the son of David? [36]David himself, inspired by the Holy Spirit, declared,

'The Lord said to my Lord,
 Sit at my right hand,
till I put thy enemies under thy feet.'

[37]David himself calls him Lord; so how is he his son?" And the great throng heard him gladly.

14:3 *Jesus anointed for burial at table*

14:22 Passover Meal

[22]And as they were eating, he took bread, and blessed, and broke it, and gave it to them, and said, "Take; this is my body." [23]And he took a cup, and when he had given thanks he gave it to them, and they all drank of it. [24]And he said to them, "This is my blood of the covenant, which is poured out for many. [25]Truly, I say to you, I shall not drink again of the fruit of the vine until that day when I drink it new in the kingdom of God."

see 2:23 etc., above

1 Corinthians 10:16

[16]The cup of blessing which we bless, is it not a participation in the blood of Christ? The bread which we break, is it not a participation in the body of Christ? [17]Because there is one bread, we who are many are one body, for we all partake of the one bread.

1 Corinthians 5:17

[6]Your boasting is not good. Do you not know that a little leaven leavens the whole lump? [7]Cleanse out the old leaven that you may be a new lump, as you really are unleavened. For Christ, our paschal lamb, has been sacrificed. [8]Let us, therefore, celebrate the festival, not with the old leaven, the leaven of malice and evil, but with the unleavened bread of sincerity and truth.

is going on. Closer attention to Mark's first miraculous meal, in chapter 6, will disclose the something holy. Subsequently, in chapters 7 and 8, we will get on to the sacrilege.

Mark begins his account of the first miraculous meal, in chapter 6, by saying that it was motivated by Jesus's pity for the crowd who were "as sheep without a shepherd." David was a shepherd. Moses was a shepherd. So was Jesus: not only the Jesus of the Christians but the Jesus of Jewish scripture translated into Greek by the legendary seventy: Joshua the son of Nun who was Jesus of Nazareth's namesake. At Numbers 27:17 Moses worried about his succession. When he is dead who will continue his shepherding work "that the congregation may not be as sheep which have no shepherd"? God answered, "Take Jesus the son of Nun." He will be the next shepherd of Israel.

So Mark 6:34–44 is the feeding of the congregation of Israel by Jesus the Son, not of Nun, but of the much more august David. The congregation of thousands in the desert sits in companies of hundreds and fifties (Mark 6:40)—as did Israel under Moses in the desert according to Deut. 1:15. The types are coming in thick and fast, but according to Mark's cornfield story, David is the key. (Look again at the table on p. 107.) David took five of the twelve showbreads, leaving seven. Like father, like son: Jesus takes five loaves too. But he feeds five thousand people with them rather than five. And he leaves, not only the seven remaining loaves, but twelve very big baskets of leftover fragments. Jesus the son is mightier than David the father. He is mightier than Moses who was at a loss, as Jesus's disciples were, how to feed the people: "Where am I going to get meat to give to all this people?" "Shall all the fish of the sea be gathered together for them, to suffice them?" (Numbers 11:13, 22). Two fish were enough for Jesus, recalling to the reader the fishermen called two by two in chapter 1—Peter and the other apostles to the Jews. Jesus, greater than David or Moses, is also greater than Elisha who gave Mark the structure which he augmented and enhanced with typological excess:

> A man came from Baal-shal-ishah, bringing the man of God bread of the first fruits, twenty loaves of barley and fresh ears of grain in his sack. And Elisha said, "Give to the men, that they may eat." But his servant said to him, "How am I to set this before a hundred men?" So he repeated, "Give them to the men, that they may eat, for thus says the Lord 'They shall eat and have some left.'" So he set it before them. And they ate, and had some left, according to the word of the Lord. (2 Kings 4:42–44)

So much for the first miraculous meal. But not really or conclusively. Disciples of Roland Barthes know that narrative incident as full of "indi-

ces" as this must have functional energy to drive the rest of the story
along. A reader—a scripture-learned first-century Christian reader now,
rather than a postmodern one—who is being as doggedly attentive to
the numbers as he should be will have noticed that of the twelve showbread loaves, seven are still there: not taken by David nor, yet, by his
extraordinary son. So he too will suspect that the narrative energy of
this first meal is not exhausted, that there is more to come. And the
readers, or hearers, in Mark's first-century church would have noticed
the markedly Jewish character of this meal, and expected more: knowing that Jesus and his bread were the nourishment of gentile Christians
too. He, or she, would have been waiting for something to correspond
to the gentile element in Christian commensality and conviviality. We
ought to hold on to these presentiments while we read on.

After the meal, Jesus and his disciples cross the lake to Jewish territory
and Bethsaida. On the way Jesus calms a storm, astounding his disciples
who "did not understand about the loaves, but their hearts were hardened." Then comes half a chapter of teaching, the *leitmotiv* of which
is sacrilege, the desecration of Jewish purity tradition by an attack on
sacred food hygiene. Jesus says that his disciples are right to eat with
dirty hands, because all this tradition is but a cover for spiritual alienation, giving the Corban casuistry as an example of its dishonesty. This
is Jesus's negative justification of his messy associates. Mark adds that
the Jews were obsessive washers: not only of their own persons, but
also, absurdly, "baptizing" pots and pans, whereas the Christians bap-
tized people. Mark's Christians apparently made it a point of honor
to eat out of dirty dishes as well as with dirty hands. It showed how
they were different. Jesus's next demystifying *pronunciamento* gives them
positive justification. The body itself sees to cleanliness. It has a digestive
system. It defecates. "Thus," interposes Mark, "he declared all foods
clean." People should worry, not about the natural stuff they put into
themselves, which their insides will sort out, but about the unnatural
or metaphysical muck which they spew from their hearts: envy, murder,
adultery, deceit, and the rest. These really do defile. This is profanation
with a vengeance, bringing the walls of ritualized purity tumbling down
to disclose the real source of our troubles with one another, the real
dirt. Coming so soon after the care for Israel in the miraculous meal,
this is untoward and shocking. It is done in the name of a religion of
inward goodness with no time for outward boundaries.

But the pendulum swings back. In the next incident Jesus, having
attacked Jewish custom on Jewish soil, meets a gentile woman in gentile
territory and plays the stuffy defender of Jewish privilege and priority
—another surprise. When she asks him to exorcize her possessed daughter he replies with a metaphor which keeps the food-theme going. "Let
the children first be fed, for it is not right to take the children's bread

and throw it to the dogs." This is strange as well as surprising. For the children *have* "first" been fed: five thousand of them, recently and miraculously. Jesus knows this as well as the reader does. He knows too that there was a lot left over: twelve baskets full. Precisely. He knows it all well enough. For when the woman rejoins "Yes, Lord; but even the dogs under the table eat the children's crumbs" he concedes completely and her daughter is exorcized and at rest. It was precisely the right rejoinder—as usual in folk tales like this which consume all that they lay out, with peasant thrift. There was an excess from the miraculous feeding of Israel. She takes it. The twelve baskets of crumbs are now accounted for.

Jesus moves down to Decapolis. There he cures a deaf stammerer by physical exertions that are well up to his exacting standards of disregard for decency and daintiness. He pokes his fingers into his ears. He spits. He touches his tongue, "looking up to heaven" as he did when he broke the five loaves and using the magic word *ephphatha*, "be opened." Clear speech and hearing result. Restored sight will come later. Now comes the second miraculous meal.

Like the first, it is in a desert. But the eaters are different. Instead of the flock of 6:34 they are just a large crowd, *polus ochlos*—heterogeneous too, since some of them are "from far away." When they sit, it is not in the previous ancient order of hundreds and fifties. They just flop to the ground where they are at his command. The fish they get are not two *ichthuai* but an unspecified number of *ichthudia*, which means little fish or few fish. The diminutive recalls the little dogs, *kunaria*, invoked by the Syrophoenician woman. If it was right to relate the two fish in chapter 6 to the pairs of apostles to the Jews, then these are Paul and Barnabas and their associates who went to the gentiles. Hence Paul called himself "the least of the apostles" (1 Cor. 15:9). Now for the numbers. The Syrophoenician woman has commandeered the leftovers from the first meal already. So expectation is concentrated on the seven loaves that remain of the showbread. They are eaten now, blessed by Jesus and distributed by his disciples to the motley and informal crowd. Seven baskets full of crumbs are taken up. In line with the tendency to diminution here, which we noticed with the fish and can see again in the number of eaters which is a thousand less than before, this is less than the previous twelve baskets. But it has the symmetry of fulfillment (seven loaves, seven baskets) and achieves it with the number seven, which has signified completion since the week the world was made. For all its informality and its lesser numbers, this second meal is fulfillment and completion. It images the universality of the gospel for all humanity, for the lesser gentiles as well as the privileged Jews. The sacrilegious teaching in chapter 7 prepared for it.

But we must go on a bit further. After this second meal the Pharisees seek a sign from heaven. They are blind to these signs on earth. Jesus leaves them. But his disciples are no better. The riddle, which we have at last and laboriously made some sense of, is opaque to them. They do not yet understand. The fulfillment eludes them. The story goes on. A blind man gets his sight back and sees clearly, but they are intellectually blind. And then, suddenly, one of them does, for a moment, see. "Thou art the Christ" says Peter at 8:29. Three verses later he is in the dark again, rebuking Jesus for asserting that the Christ's way will go through rejection and death. Then comes the great iconic epiphany of the transfiguration at 9:2–8.

It is essential that we read on, at least this far. Only so do we get at the full and ultimate answer to the riddle. It is not so much a question of what should be understood as of who should be understood. The solution to the riddle is Jesus himself. He is what all these numbers, all that typology, are about for Mark. The first words he wrote, as title and key for everything that was to follow, were "The gospel of Jesus Christ, the Son of God." Then he set himself to his biographical writing. So it is only when we have read it all that we will understand. If the truth is a man, then we can only get it when he has lived through everything that his life had to be, and is dead. Then we will understand. Meanwhile, in life as in reading, we blunder on because, as creatures of time, we have to. Things happen, like those meals. We make something of them at the time, or little, or nothing. In the future there may be moments of understanding that throw revelatory and corrective light on what we half saw, or got wrong, at the time. Mark has things in common with Proust, because he too is realistic about human understanding and time. So it is at the moment of Jesus's death that the gentile centurion can give the real answer, "Truly this man was the Son of God" (15:39). Only then has Mark's authorial and textual title at 1:1 become human property. What Mark wrote at the head of his book, what God said at Jesus's baptism and transfiguration can then be said by a human being. It is a breakthrough. And what is broken through is the boundary between God and humanity, between sacred and profane: as the sky's firmament was split at the baptism, so now the temple veil splits apart at the death.

That is still way ahead. But there are moments of illumination in the interim. I will mention two that connect with the bread riddle.

We have uncovered the Davidic typology in the first meal. Jesus was David's son—and more. This was the key to the bread riddle. At 12:35, nearing the end of his road, Jesus is teaching in the temple at Jerusalem and puts a second riddle:

> "How can the scribes say that Christ is the Son of David? For David himself said by the Holy Ghost, The Lord said to my Lord, Sit thou

on my right hand, till I make thine enemies thy footstool. David therefore himself calleth him Lord; and whence is he then his son?" And
the common people heard him gladly.

Notice those last words. What the scribes got wrong when they read
Psalm 110 ("The Lord said to my Lord") the common people hear gladly.
"Common people" is the King James translation of *polus ochlos*, which
is what the people at the second miraculous feeding were called. They
understand, their intelligence led, as Simone Weil said the intelligence
must be, by joy. For Jesus is more than David's son. He is the anointed
Messiah for all and sundry, regardless of nationality. Here at 12:35,
readers who are still unsure about the exact meaning of the David typology in the first feeding, resting as it did upon Jesus's previous appeal
to David and the showbread, are given a further chance to make up
their minds.

The second moment is the Passover supper in the upper room at
12:22–25. This is of the utmost importance. It is the climax of all the
preceding meals, and it fastens the identification of Jesus with the Christians' common bread which was so central to them. Their religion got
its force from its concentration on this single life and death. But when
it had become a matter of history, though vitally sacred history, it needed
an objective correlative in the center of their (later) lives. They needed
more than mere memory. They need presence: memory with present
power. Before they had gospel books like Mark's, the single bread, the
one loaf, gave them that. Here in the upper room, Jesus makes that
crucial identification, taking the loaf, which he has blessed and broken,
and giving it to them—precise repetitions of his actions at the miraculous meals, and so meant to recall them. But this time there is no distri-
bution by the disciples to a crowd. It is just for them. And this time
he makes the crucial identification which constitutes the Christian society: "Take; this is my body." His actions with the loaf send our minds
back to the feedings. Its singleness, its being just one (in Greek there
are no separate words for bread and loaf; *artos* does for both)—this
oneness sends our minds back to the mysterious phrase in the narrative
run up to the bread riddle in chapter 8. It began with "Now they had
forgotten to take bread, neither had they in the ship with them but
one loaf." We can take the ship of disciples as Mark's image of the church
in transition. It contained this one loaf. But Mark was ambiguous about
it. He said that it was there just after he had said that they had forgotten
to take bread. The disciples, two verses later, denied that it was there
by saying "We have no bread." Jesus began the speech in which he put
the riddle with "Why reason ye that [*hoti*] ye have no bread?" He is
not agreeing with them. He is fiercely adversarial. So the ultimate aim
of the riddle is to hector them into understanding the one loaf, which

is himself—not himself in isolation; rather, himself as their nourishment. We realize this only now, at the Passover supper in chapter 14. That is part of that proto-Proustian handling of time and understanding which we have noticed in the gospel. Now that we do realize it, all that typology in the two feeding narratives which hinted that Jesus's identity was what they, in line with the stated intention of the whole book, were about—all that is confirmed with material definition in the one loaf. It was ambiguous and elusive at the time of chapter 8, the time of transition in the ship. But now it is utterly clear. "This [loaf] is my body" —the shared singleness of the new society. Only now have we really solved the riddle. And with the understanding of the gospel's center which we get from it we can read the passion narrative which follows as salvation. For what Jesus did with the bread to make it their food —taking and breaking—will be done to his body to make it the source of salvation.

Taking Stock of Mark

Enough reading. If we read because we are exhausted by the battering excess of actual living, there are times when, as readers, we are tired out by the battering excess in a book. Then we turn to the contemplative generalities of criticism for a while. Exhaustion is an important factor or dysfactor in reading which our professional pride may make us shy to acknowledge. Mark is a particularly exhausting read because he combines very tight and spare symbolic articulation with what Wind called "deliberate obliqueness." He has a love of burying things to make us dig them up, of putting lamps under bedsteads before getting them to the lampstand (4:21). The reason for this in literary history is that he combines, in his writing, the apocalyptic world-view with folk tale. Both flourished in his milieu. Apocalyptic literature is trying reading because it is deliberately obscure. It puts us in the dark, and there shows us weird dreams and visions which we cannot understand until an interpreter unlocks them. We are alternately baffled and illuminated, which is not much of a holiday from life itself. Folk tale is trying because its sparse compactness, its utter lack of loose and merely picturesque detail, makes very exacting demands on our attention. Of all folk tale's wanderings, transgressions, riddles, and returns, we cannot afford to miss a single thing. So although the folk tales collected by the Grimm brothers are short, we cannot read more than two or three of them on the trot, and do best to concentrate on one alone.

In more modern and elevated terms, Mark compares to Dostoevsky. He has the same passion, the same love of transgressions of order that fosters those *Skandal* scenes in which energy and error, blundering and insight, impel the trespassings which tear the veil from the truth. In historical terms, Mark was an apocalyptist writing folk tale: articulating an elaborately interconnected series of folk tales into an apocalyptically revelatory gospel for initiates. It makes an energetic and demanding hybrid. But he is not an entirely hostile writer. In his grim way, he gives his readers rests and chances. For all its aggressive interrogation, that bread riddle was meant to help. It was a time for readers to let their minds play with types and numbers so they could get their bearings and understand what was going on. A book is held together by its persistent deployment of a few central themes and persons, reflecting on one another as they go through time and space. Readers have to understand them.

The bread riddle was Mark's attempt to get his readers to use their own wits and resources to get a grip of those themes and persons. He wrote for first-century Christians, for initiates, and with "deliberate obliqueness." In the late twentieth century we have the extra trouble of what Wind called the "veil of obscurity" made by "distance in time." We have had, as he warned, to recover in a roundabout way things that were part of first-century Christian conversation. If time-consuming, this was not impossible, because fortunately the Jewish scriptures, which were the great resource of first-century Christian conversation, have survived. We needed to raise our knowledge of them up to something like that of those Christians: people of sprightly intelligence who, very unlike us indeed, had few, if any, other books to confuse or dissipate their intellectual energies. Having done that, we found that, in the matter of the themes and persons that make up a book, Mark was not ultimately complex. In the last analysis he had, as he told us in his first verse, only one theme and person: Jesus. And it was because he was so blatant and downright about that at the start that he could then whip and sway the narrative (which he had so firmly pegged down at the beginning) through so many subsequent loops, obscurities, and regressions. The phase of the narrative on which we concentrated ran from chapters 6 through 9 and was continually preoccupied with bread —more so than any other long phase in Mark's narrative. But that was not adding a new theme. In the end we got to know that the bread was single and it was Jesus.

Who was Jesus? At the beginning of our stretch of Mark, at 6:14–16, Herod wondered. For some said that he was John the Baptist resurrected, some that he was Elijah, others that he was one of the ancient prophets. Herod took the first option, which was as wrong as the others. He was John resurrected. The story of John's gruesome end followed. At the end of our stretch, at 8:27, Jesus asks his disciples who people say he is and gets precisely the same list: John resurrected, Elijah, or one of the old prophets. "But who do you say that I am?" he asks.

Peter replies with something not on the list at all: "You are the Christ." There follows teaching on the way to life through death and the epiphany on the mountain: the iconic tableau which reveals practically all (there is the death still to come). With these two episodes of identification framing it—the first negative and the second positive—we can be in no doubt that all the stuff about bread in between was about Jesus.

Taking Stock of Markan Christianity

We have now got materials that enable us to reconstruct Mark's primitive Christian society and enjoy its conversation. It was table talk, because Jesus was their single and common loaf of bread. And it was scripture talk, because all the scriptures were fulfilled in Jesus. Jesus was the content of both bread and scripture. So their conversation was particularly animated and resourceful when the two coincided and the scriptures spoke of bread. Mark's Christians were a mixture of Jews and gentiles—probably more gentiles—who had Jesus in their own present, and assimilated him into themselves, by eating bread and interpreting scriptures. This was the social life which Mark wrote into his book. I will end by dwelling on it, or in it, a little.

That there were gentiles in Mark's church was due to his predecessor, Paul, who had fought for it like a tiger. There were different kinds of community in the preorthodox Christianity which produced the New Testament books. Mark's community was radically Pauline, which Matthew's community was not. There is a record of one of Paul's fights for mixed but single community in his letter to the Galatians. "When Peter came to Antioch I withstood him to his face, because he stood condemned. For before certain men came from James, he ate with the gentiles; but when they came, he drew back and separated himself, fearing the circumcision party. And with him the rest of the Jews acted insincerely" (2:11–13). If other people had doubts about Jews and gentiles sharing together in the common Christian food, Paul had none. He was ready for the riskiest confrontation because to lose this was to lose all. He was a Kennedy equal to his Cuba. He was just as intolerant of divided table fellowship in his church in Corinth as he was with the Galatians. "The bread which we break, is it not a participation in the body of Christ? Because there is one loaf, we who are many are one body, for we all partake of the one loaf" (1 Corinthians 10:16–17). The "many" of Mark's gentile crowd, Mark's all-important "one loaf" which is Jesus's sacrificed and shared body—there they are. When they get into Mark's gospel thirty years later they are the trophies or insignia of Paul's hard fight for gentile Christianity, taken up for a last push against conservatively Jewish Christianity. In the conversation of Pauline communities like Mark's, something like "one loaf for the many" may have been a slogan and rallying cry to pit against any lingering pockets of Petrine resistance and separate tables.

It is particularly striking that Paul was so ardent and unyielding about the bread. He had difficulty in being remotely positive about material matters, most notoriously marriage and sex. He gives himself away at 1 Cor. 6:13 with "Meats for the belly, and the belly for meats: but God shall destroy both it and them." His headlong concentration on Christ crucified—"nothing but Jesus Christ and him crucified" (1 Cor. 2:2) —had bankrupted the world. It had swept aside all religious boundaries, making one man as good as another—and in his more heady rhetorical moments, one woman as good as a man. It had come perilously near to sweeping away terrestrial affairs altogether as lacking any strong bearing on religion. Paul wanted to die and be "with the Lord"—and only hung around on earth for other people's benefit. He had felt a power, and had unleashed it on others, which was very like that felt by listeners to that masterpiece of death and love, Wagner's *Tristan und Isolde*, with its bankrupting of the world of social differences like marriage for the sake of fulfillment in an undifferentiated and unbounded elsewhere. If he stood so intransigently on guard over that very material thing, the one common loaf for the many, it could only be because it was the only socially constructive symbol and actuality of that lethal power. The loaf showed forth the death of Christ (1 Cor. 11:26), which broke the bounds of old holiness and made, through the profanation, a new and wider holiness where there had been profanity before. And that, in fact, is exactly what he thought the loaf was, and why he told the Corinthians to eat it with self-critical reverence and social charity beyond party spirit, lest they profane the Lord's body and there be nothing sacred in the world at all. Wagner, having blown the world away in *Tristan*, returned to it to write two operas centered on Christian sacraments: *Meistersinger*, which is set on St. John the Baptist's day and climaxes in the quintet that baptises Walther's new song, and *Parsifal*, which is about the Eucharist. St. Paul, to whom the world had died with the death of Christ, was a stickler for both those rituals. They were essential as the only significant markers in an otherwise symbolically devastated world.

There were also the scriptures. For Christians with no scriptures of their own they were as sacred and authoritative as any text could be. But precisely what that meant we can see by contrasting them with the more orthodox rabbis. From Jamnia on the rabbis went about collecting rabbinic exegetical sayings and anecdotes, pinning them to the appropriate point in the sacred text, as the votive offerings of their wisdom and piety to their one remaining altar. A quick look at the gospels suggests that the Christian writers did the reverse, pinning bits of scripture to the altar of their one Lord and rabbi's life and death—Jesus's. But this does not do justice to the power of the old scriptures over them.

For that, we need to look at the typology which was so major and energetic a part of their handling of the scriptures. As Anthony Collins observed in 1724, "Perfect novelty is a great and just exception to a Religious Institution; whereof Religious Sects of all kinds have been so sensible, that they have ever endeavoured to give themselves, in some manner or other, the greatest antiquity they well could; and generally the utmost antiquity."[5] Typology, which Collins subsumed under allegory, is one of those manners, a pipeline by which a new religion draws on the banked capital of sacred tradition. Even a Christian as happy with the shock of the new as Mark or Paul used it liberally. In particular, Mark used it to understand the bread, in two major instances. One was his David-typology of Jesus, justifying Jesus's profanation of the sabbath in the cornfield by David's profanation of the showbread—and then exploiting it in arithmetical detail. Another was the Passover typology in Jesus's last supper with his disciples. Mark, following Paul, gave it a new, Christian *haggadah* by way of the extraordinary profanation of the Passover cup being filled with Jesus's blood for his disciples to drink. This a part of the Christian takeover of Passover by the death of their crucified Messiah. As Paul said, "Christ our passover is sacrificed for us" (1 Cor. 5:7). It was not much less of an abomination in Jewish food law for being symbolic. Since the beginning of food laws with Noah, blood had been banned, and in Passover ritual the lamb's blood was reserved for God and splashed on doorposts or temple altar. Blood was very holy; defiling and divine. Christians made it, very precisely, common. But if it had not been holy, too, and if they had not known it, their sacrilege would have been symbolically vacuous.

Typology faces both ways, its Janus face looking toward holy and profane, past tradition and present vitality. If it only copies past tradition it is not vital. To be vital it needs to break bounds and get into the profane. To make the profane wonderful and holy it needs to look back and pay pious tribute to the past by means of some sort of continuity with it. Typology is a mode of creativity in religion as in literature. James Joyce drew, from his Jesuit education, holy Christian types and tropes which he applied to the profane details of Dublin life. He was creative, revelatory, sanctifying even, by way of committing sacrileges. By transgressing the bounds of holiness, as drawn by orthodox Christianity, he achieved what he called "epiphany"; the sudden "revelation of the whatness of a thing," the moment in which "the soul of the commonest object . . . seems to us radiant." According to Richard Ellmann, Joyce felt that the artist

> was charged with such revelations, and must look for them not among gods but among men, in casual, unostentatious, even unpleasant moments. He might find a sudden spiritual manifestation either "in the vulgarity of speech or of gesture, or in memorable phrase of the mind itself." Sometimes the epiphanies are "eucharistic," another term arrogantly borrowed by Joyce from Christianity and invested with secular meanings. These are moments of fullness or of passion.[6]

To the officials and adherents of formalized religion their sacrilege is blasphemous. To the secular reader they may convey an odd sense of holiness, including the constitutive shiver and edginess by which Rudolf Otto identified the holy. The Jews in exodus spoiled the Egyptians, the Christians in exodus spoiled the Jews, and now the modern and postmodern writers in exodus are spoiling the Christians. When Albertine gave Proust's narrator her lingual kiss it reminded him of the host put on the tongue at mass, putting the reader right on the very dodgy boundary between sexual devotion and excitement, and religious devotion and excitement.

How are such transgressions justified? By formal, traditional religion they cannot be. They are condemned. But most of us do not belong to that or, if we do, make up our own minds about its sexual and literary prescriptions. Perhaps that is why we enjoy Mark so much: his bias against officialdom, his enthusiasms for transgression and vulgar gestures, his tales of individual response. We must decide on grounds of quality. Such decisions take a good deal of time in which a transgression becomes memory. Then we can tell if the memory is "eucharistic," evoking gratitude for its power to deflate the inflated, to soothe exacerbations and insults rather than just inflicting them, to feed rather than to poison. Such judgments are partly aesthetic. Is the transgression not just done, but well done? Is it merely sensational, or does it combine, like Walther's song or Joyce's *Ulysses* or Proust's *Remembrance*, a residual but obstinately tenacious reverence for the old canonical/scriptural masters, with bold new adventure into where literature has not been before? If so, then it has a quality that is also moral and is not merely insulting. By its regard for the unregarded, its inclusion of the outcast, its veneration of the profane, it has exercised the virtue of charity and increased, for its readers, the area in which intelligent charity can be exercised.

LITERARY EXEGESIS OF BIBLICAL NARRATIVE: BETWEEN POETICS AND HERMENEUTICS

Adele Berlin

Literary exegesis, as I will term various ways of reading the Bible that call upon methods used by literary critics, has many faces and employs many techniques. Because the field is young, growing rapidly, and still rather undisciplined, its rules and procedures have yet to be spelled out. The situation in literary studies of the Bible is somewhat like that portrayed in the Book of Judges: each person does what seems right in his or her eyes. Yet from out of this diverse array some lines can begin to be drawn, some common modes of operation discerned. One such mode of operation is the discovery of verbal and/or thematic similarities in two distant narratives, often, as it happens, from Genesis and the Deuteronomic history. These similarities then become the basis of a comparison of the narratives, which leads, in turn, to the interpretation of one in light of the other. I would like to focus attention on this practice because it is increasingly widespread and appealing, and because I think it is misunderstood. To anticipate my argument, I think that we have here an interpretive strategy—a hermeneutic procedure—and not, as its practitioners think, a compositional device. I will not attempt to judge the validity of this procedure as an interpretive tool. My concern is merely to point out how its use has obscured the distinction between the strategies that the Bible uses in composing its narratives and the strategies that the reader uses to interpret them. To put it more succinctly, hermeneutics has been mistaken for poetics.

A number of studies of the Book of Samuel have noted certain resemblances between the stories of Michal and Rachel.[1] The most obvious, though the most enigmatic, is the reference to *teraphim* (household idols) —in both instances used by the woman to effect a deception. And by this deception the woman promotes the interests of her husband and undermines those of her father.

On the larger structural plane, both stories, at least according to the Masoretic text, involve situations in which a younger sister is married to the hero, after more than usual machinations on the part of a devious father who has less than cordial feelings toward his prospective son-in-law. In both cases the younger sister is the father's second choice as bride: Michal is an alternative to Merab and Rachel is a supplement to Leah. This younger sister motif, whereby these biblical Cinderellas end up married to a future patriarch and a future king, both of whom are younger brothers, forms a nice complement to the younger brother motif that marks heroes.

In both stories the word "love" (*'hb*) is rather prominent (Gen. 29: 18, 20, 30; 1 Sam. 18:20, 28). Love was not, as far as we know, a crucial factor in the arrangement of marriages, yet it figures in the motivation for both of these. Note also the reversal in direction: the man loves the woman in the Rachel story but the woman loves the man in the Michal story.

Related to love and marriage is the matter of progeny. The motif of the barren mother is common in special birth stories, and Rachel is an example. In addition, barrenness is often the plight of the favored wife—Rachel again exemplifies this (Gen. 29:31), as does Hannah (1 Sam. 1:5). But the barrenness in special birth stories is, of course, temporary. Michal's barrenness is permanent. Moreover, she is not a favored wife. She loves but is not loved. In the case of Michal, the literary conventions of love and barrenness have been reversed.

I want to look more closely at the way various authors express their perceptions of the relationship between these stories, but first let me take an opposite position. Just as I made the most convincing case that I could for the similarities, I will now argue that the perception of these similarities is exaggerated.

First of all, in highlighting the parallels I have ignored or subordinated the many divergent parts of these stories.[2] Even some of the parallels may be distorted by the comparison. Take the mention of "love." Although this is, indeed, a point of contact between the two stories, the mention of "love" has a raison d'être, and a different one, in each story taken separately. Michal's love for David echoes that of Jonathan and the people (1 Sam. 18:16), and shows the growing support for David among Saul's own family. It is an important element in the shift from Saul to David which occupies the narrative. Jacob's love for Rachel is a prelude to his love for her children (Gen. 37:4; 44:20), and perhaps an echo of Isaac's love for Esau and Rebekah's for Jacob (Gen. 25:28) in a family where favoritism and the jealousy it provokes are a major force in the dynamics of the narrative.

As for the *teraphim*, their occurrence in both stories may be coincidental. They certainly do not signify the same thing in both stories and may not represent a common motif. Perhaps they were simply the natural objects to use in each situation.

If we look outside of the Masoretic text to the Septuagint, we find that among the many verses lacking in the Greek of 1 Samuel 17–18 are 18:17–19, the Merab episode. Thus in the Septuagint version there is no younger sister motif; there is only one marriage arranged and that is with Michal.

Despite the objections I have raised, I think that a convincing case can be made for the parallels between the two stories, at least to those sympathetic to a literary approach. The reasons for this are informative in understanding how a literary approach works and what its assumptions are. Differences between the Masoretic text and the Septuagint are not taken into account because each text is analyzed in its own right. Each text is a different story, not the same story in earlier or later, or better or worse form. The Masoretic and the Septuagint stories could be compared, with good results, but this comparison would be no different than comparing a biblical story with, say, a Babylonian one.[3] As for coincidental similarities that may have other explanations, like the mention of "love" and "*teraphim*," that is no deterrent, for in these literary approaches there are no coincidences. Every similarity is potentially meaningful. This point is crucial, for it shows something about the hermeneutic system at work here, about which more will be said later. For now, though, let us grant that there are resemblances between the two stories. The next questions are: how did they get there and what do they mean? Answers to these questions can be found in the comments of several critics.

Robert Alter says of Michal's placing of the *teraphim* in the bed:

> This is obviously an allusion to Rachel, who, in fleeing with Jacob
> . . . steals Laban's *teraphim*. . . . Perhaps the allusion is meant to fore-
> shadow a fatality shared by Michal with Rachel, who becomes the ob-
> ject of Jacob's unwitting curse because of the theft (Gen. 31:32); what
> is certain is that the allusion reinforces our sense of Michal as a woman
> who has renounced allegiance to her father in her devotion to her
> husband.[4]

Peter D. Miscall, usually an advocate of indeterminacy, has no doubt that Alter's interpretation of the allusion is correct; Miscall sees "no reason to qualify the statement [i.e., Alter's] with a 'perhaps.'"[5]

J. P. Fokkelman, not surprisingly, has the most well-developed set of connections, which he says "provides a foundation for a homology of Laban: Jacob: Rachel = Saul: David: Michal." He adds that "The parallel is extensive enough to be interpreted as an invitation to the reader to stay awhile and look at the similarity in the fate of the patriarch par excellence and the king of Israel par excellence."[6]

These three citations refer specifically to the stories of Michal and Rachel, but there are a host of other commentaries, by these scholars and their colleagues, in which one pericope is compared with another in a similar fashion. Often the comparison involves a narrative from Genesis and one from Samuel. The discourse in which the comparison is couched may vary, as may the literary orientation of the critic, but these differences are superficial. Basically they are all comparing one narrative with another and using the comparison to further the interpretive process. A few examples:

Yair Zakovitch has called attention to mirror-image stories—instances in which one story reflects another, often with some type of reversal.[7] Zakovitch views this as a technique of characterization, for a character in one story may come into sharper focus when compared with a character in a structurally or thematically similar story. He compares, among others, the episode of David and Bathsheba with the story of Judah and Tamar. Although he does not cite the stories of Michal and Rachel, they would seem to fit this category. Like Alter, Zakovitch sees allusions made by a later writer to an earlier story to be part of narrative poetics.

The most far-reaching use of comparisons is that which Moshe Garsiel presents in his study of 1 Samuel. He notes all kinds of parallels and analogies within the Books of Samuel and between Samuel and other parts of the Bible. For instance, he sees similarities between the Joseph and David stories (as do Alter, Miscall, and Nohrnberg).[8] Again, Garsiel attributes these parallels to the author's intentional imitation of, or allusion to, earlier stories.

A rather different move is that of Joel Rosenberg, who speaks in terms of "allegory" rather than "allusion" or "analogy." He notes the "compelling affinities that exist between Genesis and I/II Samuel," but, in reverse of the previously cited scholars, views Genesis as a "companion work to II Samuel, a 'midrash,' if you will, upon the Davidic history."[9]

These are just a few of many similar literary analyses. Whether they call it allusion, homology, parallelism, narrative analogy, or allegory, they are all identifying what they perceive to be compositional techniques. The difference in terminology by which this is expressed says more about the critic's preference in literary theory than about biblical narrative.

Is this really a compositional technique? Is it the work of an author or editor? I think it is something in the mind of the reader, not the writer.[10] By saying this I am not advocating a reader-response approach, nor am I, like the New Critics, afraid of the intentional fallacy. There are certainly interbiblical allusions and parallels, but the ones I have been citing are not they. It strikes me that to compare the Michal and Rachel stories in the manner described above is rather like making a *gezerah šawah*, a type of analogy used in rabbinic exegesis. In other words, this is an exercise in hermeneutics. The comparison of characters, plot structures, specific terms, and the like, is a principle of hermeneutics in the new literary exegesis.

The proof is that the point of the comparison is to derive added meaning from the story. The comparison in and of itself is of little interest; so what if one story resembles another?—this is not a Proppian analysis of the formal structure of narratives. The payoff comes if the comparison has an exegetical gain. A sign of the newness of this hermeneutic principle is that the exegetical gain is not always very large. But the exegetes are reaching for it, even if they must qualify it with a "perhaps," or only indicate, as Fokkelman does, where to look without actually finding it. Ironically, the better we get at finding meaning in these comparisons—the more compelling our interpretations become—the less conscious we will be that we are engaged in hermeneutics. It is when the interpretation is less than compelling that we begin to realize what is happening. Occasionally even a great literary *darshan* like Robert Alter fails to convince, and then we see more clearly the weak points in his exegetical edifice. We will examine one such case in detail, but before doing so, let us focus on the most common criterion for identifying comparable narratives: verbal correspondence. The occurrence of the same words or phrases in two different stories often triggers a comparison between them. Sometimes just one word in common is sufficient to launch the comparison.

Now this, of course, is close to what the Midrash often does. It finds meaningful connections between pericopes which share the same words or phrases. But there is one major difference: the connections are *exegetical, not compositional*. The Midrash uses the connections to derive meaning, not to make a statement about narrative poetics. One brief example: commenting on the word *'admoni*, "reddish," in connection with Esau in Gen. 25:25, *Genesis Rabbah* 63, 8 says: "R. Abba bar Kahana said: as if he were a spiller of blood. And when Samuel saw David [who was] *'admoni*, as it is written [in 1 Sam. 16:12]: 'And he sent and brought him, and he was *'admoni*,' he became alarmed and said, 'Will he, too, be a spiller of blood like Esau!?'" On the strength of the use of the same word in reference to Esau and David, the Midrash draws a conclusion about their shared characteristics. (It then hastens to qualify this with an explanation of their differences.) And, since Esau lived before Samuel, it assumes that Samuel knew of the midrashic interpretation of *'admoni* as applied to Esau. But it does not suggest, as the modern literary commentaries might, that the story of Esau influenced the story of David—that the author of the David story intentionally employed the word *'admoni* in order to create an echo of the Esau story.

Now look what Alter has done with the same type of verbal correspondence. Noting that both the Gideon story (Judges 8) and the Joseph story (Genesis 37) interchange the terms "Midianites" and "Ishmaelites," he says:

> Whatever the reasons for the working of both Ishmaelites and Midianites into the older [i.e., the Joseph] story, I would suggest that the ancient audience was familiar with the conspicuous switch in designation in Genesis 37, and that a similar switch here, in conjunction with the peculiar prominence of the Midianite-Ishmaelite camels . . . , may have been used as a marker of allusion. The recollection, however teasingly oblique, would set up a background of tension to the narrated events: a flickering memory of the moment of fraternal betrayal as the Israelites entreat Gideon to be their king. Joseph himself is a figure who climbs from slavery to royal status but is ultimately the king's high functionary and will found no dynasty.[11]

Was the author of the Gideon story really alluding to the Joseph story? Can we say so based on the use of one term? Alter is careful to protect himself with "may have been" even as before he did with "perhaps." But his intent is clear. He cites but dismisses a more obvious reason for the use of the double terminology, that "Ishmaelites" is a later gloss.[12] Alter does not hazard to guess why the two terms occur in Genesis 37, but he suggests that the author of Judges 8, having found them in Genesis, used them in his own story as a subtle allusion. It seems more reasonable to me that the two terms were included in Judges 8 for the same reason that they were included in Genesis 37, whatever the reason may have been. The reason for the inclusion is immaterial; the fact is, the same terms are present in the two stories. That being the case, *we can use their presence, if we so wish, for our own exegetical purposes.* But the presence of the terms, in and of itself, says nothing about the relative chronology of the pericopes. It does not even suggest that there *is* a chronological relationship. To think otherwise is to confuse hermeneutics with poetics. Alter can have his midrash without calling it an allusion. By referring to the second story as an allusion to the first, Alter, the arch-opponent of historical criticism, is, irony of ironies, using the supposedly synchronic literary approach to learn diachronic lessons about the relative dating of the texts.

I offer another example, one even more tenuous than Alter's because it is based on a lack of understanding of an element in the story. David Damrosch makes the following connections between 1 Sam. 18:25–27 and Genesis 34:

> The truly bizarre detail that enters into Saul's second effort at seducing David through the offer of a daughter is the nature of the proof he requests that David has killed the hundred Philistines: a hundred fore-skins. . . . What are we to make of this strange evidentiary proceeding?
>
> Most directly, Saul's stratagem recalls the tactic employed by the sons of Jacob in Genesis 34. . . . Here too the request for circumcisions as pre-condition for marriage is a trap. . . . The parallel is clear, and there may even be an echo of Hamor's reaction to the brothers' proposal when David receives Saul's offer: their reactions of pleasure at the proposals are described in similar terms (*wayyitevu divreyhem be'eyney Hamor*, Gen. 34:18; *wayyishar haddavar be'eyney Dawid*, 1 Sam. 18:26).[13]

What can one say about Damrosch's "clear" parallel? Firstly, Saul's request for the foreskins is neither "bizarre" nor "strange." He wants proof that David has killed Philistines and there is no better proof than body-parts.[14] Why foreskins instead of, say, ears or hands? Because he wants proof that *Philistines* have been killed. The Philistines, as the Bible often makes a point of noting, stood out among the population of Ca-naan in that, unlike Israelites, other Semites, and Egyptians, they were uncircumcised. The best evidence of a dead Philistine is his foreskin.

Having said that, I think that the parallel is much diminished. All that is left is that the Hivites, like the Philistines, were uncircumcised and that this somehow offended the Israelites. That both stories contain requests "for circumcision as a pre-condition for marriage" is, to say the least, stretching the plots a bit. As for the verbal correspondence, it is based on the occurrence of "words in the eyes of," a common phrase occurring innumerable times in narratives (cf., e.g., Gen. 21:1; Gen. 41:37; 2 Sam. 17:4).

Damrosch's is, admittedly, a poor example, but his methodology is the same as that used to produce more satisfying interpretations. Even in the better interpretations, the identification of "allusions" or "echoes" does not prove anything about the literary history of Genesis and the Deuteronomic history. If anything, it merely corresponds to the order in which we now have the material (i.e., Genesis before Samuel) or to the critic's assumptions about the textual history of the Bible. The use of literary analysis for the reconstruction of compositional history is, as Damrosch[15] has recognized, a hermeneutic circle: dating is based on textual analysis and textual analysis is based on presumed dating. Damrosch is one of the few literary critics with a sophisticated understanding of source and redaction criticism and a sympathetic attitude toward it.[16] He realizes, as more literary critics are coming to admit, that one cannot understand a text if one is ignorant of its context and history. He chides Alter[17] for harmonizing away the gaps, doublets, and contradictions in biblical narrative. Yet his own historical reconstruction neatly harmonizes the current disagreements among historical critics.

> If the materials of Genesis 12–36 were reworked by an exilic Yahwistic author . . . then one may well see Deuteronomistic influence in the presentation of the themes of memory and exile. It is perfectly possible, on the other hand, that the unified Yahwistic corpus antedates the Deuteronomistic history; in this event, the lines of influence on these themes would presumably run the other way.[18]

This either/or situation is harmonized under the rubric of "reciprocal influence, with an early Yahwistic story influencing the History of David's Rise and then in turn being revised in light of the later Succession Narrative."[19] Perhaps Damrosch's reconstruction of literary history is correct. It is certainly not impossible and has some things to recommend it. But how did he arrive at it? On what is his textual analysis, on which the reconstruction is built, based? Edward L. Greenstein, in a review of Damrosch's book, isolates three strategies—narrative analogy, doubling of episodes, use of type scenes—which Damrosch identifies as compositional techniques. Greenstein suggests that these strategies "may also be viewed as a general approach to *reading*: making meaning through the internal comparison of relations among characters, motifs, and narrative sequences."[20] In other words, despite Damrosch's disagreements with Alter's approach (parts of the book are a polemic against Alter), when it comes to the interpretation of the text, he ends up doing much the same thing.

There are two points that this discussion aims to make. (1) We must be cautious in using literary analysis for purposes of dating texts. It may be possible to do so—indeed, there is often little else to go on —but the criteria must be carefully worked out. I don't know if it is possible to break out of the circularity of most of the present arguments, but at least we should be aware of it. This is especially important now, as there are encouraging signs that literary criticism and historical criticism may be coming together in new and fruitful ways.[21] (2) We should not mistake hermeneutic principles for compositional techniques. Hermeneutics is not poetics. To be sure, there is a close relationship between them;[22] but they are not one and the same. I would not deny that parts of the Bible echo other parts, that there is inner-biblical exegesis, that internal allusions exist—but the comparisons that I have cited in this paper are of a different order. They are comparisons generated by the reader. The discovery of similar words and/or themes in different pericopes is, in one sense, no different from the discovery of other types of correspondence like, say, the numerical correspondence in *gematria*. If it seems preposterous to base an interpretation on the latter, and quite reasonable to base it on the former, it only means that tastes in hermeneutic principles have changed.[23] Some of that change is reflected in the popularity of this form of literary exegesis.

If, then, verbal correspondence does not point to a compositional technique, does not prove the existence of an allusion, how can we identify allusions? This is a subject that requires more discussion, but I think that we can qualify it by saying that verbal correspondence *may* indicate an allusion but does not necessarily do so. To confirm an allusion we would generally need more than the correspondence of a single term or usage, and, more important, we would want some independent evidence of the borrowing of one story's words by another.[24] In the end, it may remain a subjective judgment, but it is worth thinking through the criteria more carefully than has been done thus far, both in the interest of developing sound exegetical principles and in the interest of untangling the literary history of the Bible.

THE RIGHT CHORALE: FROM THE POETICS TO THE HERMENEUTICS OF THE HEBREW BIBLE

Bernard M. Levinson

In his brilliant *The Poetics of Biblical Narrative*,[1] Meir Sternberg argues that the Bible of the ancient Israelites is fundamentally modern in the interpretive demands it places upon its readers. As such he clearly repossesses the Hebrew Bible for the contemporary intellectual. Like Auerbach before him, Sternberg works from the perspective of the entire scope of Western literature to demonstrate the rich complexity of biblical narrative.[2] Moreover, he does not rest content in providing a simple descriptive aesthetics of narrative structures and authorial techniques. Instead, Sternberg derives cultural theory from his narratological analysis. On the basis of his poetics, Sternberg provides an account of the nature and significance of the Israelite revelation. That revelation, according to Sternberg, is epistemological in character and has as its literary reflex the genesis of a new narrative technique: free indirect discourse. Mediating thereby between the method of poetics and the theoretical formulation of the content of revelation is Sternberg's thesis concerning the central contribution of Israelite to world literature: the omniscient narrator whose privileged knowledge reflects the divine omniscience of the Creator.

With extreme self-consciousness, Sternberg brings to the fore the issues of the methodology and theory of biblical studies. He begins his book with the following questions: "What goals does the biblical narrator set himself? What is it that he wants to communicate in this or that story, cycle, book? What kind of text is the Bible, and what roles does it perform in context?" (p. 1). These questions, with their focus on the communicative intent of the Hebrew Bible, lay the conceptual and methodological foundations for his overall interpretive project. Sternberg attempts to provide a prescriptive model for how the study—not just the literary study— of biblical narrative should be carried out. Indeed, the intention of his methodological shift from the paradigm of genetics to that of poetics, from *genesis* to *poesis* (p. 68), is to permit a coherent and comprehensive exposition of the text and its significance. Precisely that concern with theory—significance, meaning, coherence—is frequently absent in conventional biblical scholarship, whose nearly exclusive concern is with method.[3] Sternberg's commitment to both is an immense contribution to the field and accounts for his astute if often sharply polemical demonstrations of the inadequacies of prior research.

Given the questions Sternberg sets for himself, it is both appropriate and necessary to ask whether he succeeds in answering them. To the extent that he aims at providing a prescriptive model for the study of the Bible altogether, the query may be broadened to a more important issue: is the conceptualization of the Bible in terms of a narrative poetics both methodologically and theoretically adequate? A second look at the questions that open the book reveals one of the key strategies in Sternberg's approach. Sternberg shifts all but imperceptibly from referring in the first question to "the biblical narrator" to, in the third question, "the Bible" as a whole. Two issues emerge immediately. The first is Sternberg's deliberate focus on the narrator as the agent of the biblical text's communication. The second and more striking issue is the implicit equation of the work of the narrator, which clearly can at most refer to the narrative texts of the Bible, with the text of "the Bible" as a whole, and, on the basis of that assimilation of the one to the other, then to generate comprehensive theoretical claims concerning Israelite literature.

Can indeed the narrative texts of the Bible adequately be comprehended as the work of a "narrator"? Can, further, the Bible be comprehended primarily in terms of its narrative to the exclusion of its other literary genres, in particular its law? Finally, perhaps most importantly, does Sternberg's characterization of revelation in terms of an epistemological breakthrough accurately represent the nature of the Israelite revelation?

To raise these questions in this way is, of course, to suggest their answer and the issues I will address in this article. First, I shall attempt to demonstrate that the use of a synchronic method, a *poetics* of narrative, cannot provide a comprehensive reading of crucial biblical narrative texts. To the contrary, the conventional diachronic (historical-critical) method not only is essential but also points to just those textual aspects of the Bible that the newer literary critics should find most engaging. By means of a study of the biblical Flood-narrative I shall attempt to illustrate the contributions of a methodology informed by source-criticism to the newer literary approach to biblical narrative.

Second, I will argue that Sternberg's characterization of the nature of the Israelite revelation as epistemological in fact is a necessary consequence of his literary methodology. Its restriction of methodological legitimacy to a synchronic poetics of *narrative* in effect creates a canon within the canon— those parts of the Hebrew Bible which are not narrative, not susceptible to reading in terms of poetics, are de facto excluded. For the purpose of establishing literary and cultural theory, this narrative canon can indeed be construed only in terms of epistemology, its literary features involving such issues as point of view, ambiguity, gapping, and repetition. The consequence of Sternberg's effective exclusion of the biblical legal corpora from his poetics is the omission from his account of the Israelite revelation of that which is truly distinctive: the formulation of ethics and law in covenantal terms, the attribution of law to Sinai.

Third, and finally, I will contend that not only must the legal corpora of the Bible be made central to a theoretical conception of revelation, they must also be made central to the *literary* study of the Bible: no less than the narrative texts, the legal texts of the Bible reflect its unique textuality and point to techniques of authorship that should be of most interest to literary theorists.

The broad conspectus of Sternberg's book and its concern for both methodological and theoretical comprehensiveness impose a responsibility upon his readers. To take seriously his larger claims requires a willingness to confront a broad range of important exegetical, methodological, and indeed theological and philosophical issues, each of which could be the subject of its own article or monograph. Within the scope of a single article, therefore, to address the range of issues that Sternberg raises, I will focus my analysis on the overall orientation toward the biblical text that he proposes. I will attempt to provide a critique of Sternberg's double dichotomies of method (synchronic versus diachronic) and content (narrative versus law). As a more adequate orientation to the Hebrew Bible, I will propose a notion not of poetics but of hermeneutics: a method informed by both synchronic and diachronic analysis of the text and a theory of revelation derived equally from narrative and law.

The Problem of Method: Synchrony and Diachrony

Sternberg's methodology, his substitution of poetics for genetics, involves a double critique: of conventional critical scholarship (literary criticism in the established sense of source criticism) for being exclusively concerned with establishing the historical context out of which the Bible emerges, and of the new literary approach, for so removing the Bible from that context that the innovative force of its narrative strategies is lost. Recognizing that biblical study "is the intersection of the humanities par excellence" (p. 21), Sternberg attempts to avoid the double reduction of the text either to its origins or to a decontextualized, merely self-referential closed system and urges instead a historical reading of Israelite narrative conventions in the light of their comparative literary history (pp. 7–22). There is no doubt that he indeed illuminates the literary techniques and conventions of a broad range of ancient Near Eastern literature (pp. 81–89, 101–7, 127, 232) and elucidates the harmonistic exegesis embedded in the Samaritan Pentateuch and the Septuagint (pp. 371–74). In each case, his recourse to comparative literary history highlights the distinctiveness of biblical narrative by showing the generic conventions that Israelite writers transform or how the versions often soften interpretive difficulties posed by the Hebrew.

Despite this studied investigation of literary history, however, Sternberg's actual analysis of the biblical text is consistently and exclusively synchronic. He makes his sole focus the narrator as the reflex of the author; the text is construed as a compositional unity, the product of the artistic control of its author. This approach permits Sternberg to analyze the narrative rules underlying the text's composition. As such, although he is concerned with history to a far greater extent than many other practitioners of the newer literary approach to the Bible, his explication of the text is synchronic rather than diachronic: his expositions never refer to an editor or redactor or view the text as deriving from multiple hands, as a unity redactional rather than compositional in origin. Sternberg's expositional model thus rejects Higher Criticism, which rather analyzes the text in diachronic terms as the product of a compositional history involving a succession of editors or redactors.

Although Sternberg invokes modern literary theory—the terminology of *poetics*—to formulate his synchronic method, in fact his respect for the integrity of the text and the intentionality of its details derives much of its inspiration from the great tradition of ancient rabbinic exegesis. In a sense Sternberg does not simply reject but moves chronologically behind the methodology of historical-critical biblical scholarship in order to obtain new principles of interpretation. He implicitly employs rabbinic conceptions of the text's coherence and the purposiveness of its details to restore to biblical studies a concern with meaning— with what and how the text communicates—often absent in critical scholarship. Indeed, he begins his book by invoking the "ancient rabbis" whose "interpretive genius" and deftness with biblical language he praises, while noting his "variance from their premises" (p. xiv). Rabbinic exegesis thus provides Sternberg with an important methodological counterpoint to the primarily analytical or dissecting force of conventional diachronic criticism.

At least in its origins, however, the diachronic method no less than the synchronic was concerned with the question of meaning. Even if diachronic method as currently practiced is not true to its origins, that method is still essential to the proper understanding of Israelite literary creativity. Therefore, in order to understand the consequences of Sternberg's recourse to a synchronic model of textual exposition that is at least partially grounded in precritical assumptions, it is essential to analyze the intellectual origins of the historical-critical method as a response to traditional rabbinic exegesis.

Although there are a few significant exceptions, the point of departure for all rabbinic interpretation of the Pentateuch is the assertion, "There is neither early nor late in the Torah."[4] Rabbinic exegesis therefore is fundamentally synchronic in its orientation and method. The postbiblical attribution of the whole of the Pentateuch to Moses means that rabbinic exegesis is constrained to deny the very literary history that brings the Pentateuch into being. The attribution of Mosaic authorship, the presumption of the text's original coherence and revelatory origins, militates against a type of literary analysis that can recognize accretion, contradiction, revision, or redundancy in the text of the Pentateuch. Such textual phenomena are in effect explained away in synchronic terms by rabbinic midrashic hermeneutics, which understands them to have a didactic purpose, as referring to separate narrative or legal cases. A transformation of the just-quoted rabbinic assertion, shifting from chronological to textual terminology, results in the following formulation: "There is neither redundancy nor contradiction in the Torah."

Herein lies the divergence of ancient and medieval rabbinic exegesis from the Enlightenment hermeneutics that give birth to the modern historical-critical method. Already in 1670, Spinoza drew on scattered hints in medieval rabbinic commentaries to provide a reading of the Hebrew Bible which candidly asserts its profusion of inner contradictions as well as the post-Mosaic origins of the Pentateuch. For this reason, Spinoza's biblical analysis in the first fifteen chapters of the *Theologico-Political Tractatus*[5] is correctly understood to be crucial for the later, more systematic elaboration of the historical-critical method.[6] Nonetheless Spinoza's concerns in this portion of the *Tractatus* were not to void the text of significance and authority.[7] That such is the prevalent understanding of Spinoza, however, accounts for the unease about his work that endures among scholars of Judaica. In turn, in their nearly exclusive focus on Spinoza's philological and historical arguments, historians of the critical method misconstrue the intent of the earlier chapters concerned with biblical criticism by taking them out of the context of the work as a whole and by essentially ignoring chapters 16–20, those chapters in which Spinoza provides the theory for a prototypically modern democratic state founded upon the rights of free thought and expression.

The latter chapters, whose concern is freedom, share a common conceptual structure with the earlier chapters, whose concern is hermeneutics. Spinoza argues in chapters 1–15 that neither philosophy nor theology[8] should be subordinate to the other, that neither the reader nor the biblical text should be subordinate to the other, that neither the individual nor the state should be subordinate to the other. He attempts to grant each autonomy, respect, and freedom in relation to the other. Spinoza's concern is to permit the reader to deal with the biblical text on its own terms and thereby to emancipate the Bible from two forms of alien hermeneutics: first, the reduction of theology to philosophical truth (the requirement by Maimonides that the Bible conform to the laws of identity and noncontradiction that derive from Greek philosophy) and second, the reduction of philosophy to theological truth (the requirement by Judah Ibn Alfakhar that the reader unquestioningly subordinate his or her critical intelligence to the authority of the biblical text).[9] Spinoza argues that the contradictions that cannot but engage the Bible's attentive reader must not be explained away through allegorical exegesis (Maimonides) nor be used to contradict reason itself (Alfakhar). Nor do they render the text itself false (unprofitable) at the level of meaningfulness. The need to establish and legitimate an autonomous biblical hermeneutics has as its counterpart the need to legitimate the individual's right of free expression with respect to the state, which Spinoza defends in chapters 16–20. Although the individual participates in a political contract, Spinoza acutely argues, the intent of such participation is to permit, not suppress, "free reason and judgement" (p. 258). The sovereignty of the state does not preclude the autonomy of the individual. "No one can ever so utterly transfer to another his power and, consequently, his rights, as to cease to be a man: nor can there ever be a power so sovereign that it can carry out every possible wish" (p. 215). Spinoza's hermeneutics, whereby the truth of the Bible is not contradicted by its manifest contradictions and redundancies, thus has as its corollary his philosophical claim that the "true aim of government is liberty" (p. 259): that the democratic state must tolerate contradiction comprehended as dissent (p. 263).

What modern biblical criticism has taken from Spinoza is exclusively the historical-critical method without his equal concern for the "truth" (p. 101) of the biblical text and for the interrelation of biblical hermeneutics and intellectual history or ethics. Most specialists over the past century have concerned themselves primarily with philology, text criticism, history, and the reconstruction of the allegedly earliest and original version of the text. The result, an analytically dissecting method often lacking an accompanying concern for synthesis or textual significance, all but bastardizes the very Spinoza claimed as "father." Despite its real contributions to the understanding of the history of Israelite literature, historical criticism has intellectually impoverished itself in its separation from the larger tradition of which it was once part.

The contemporary application to the Hebrew Bible of a new form of the synchronic method by the Bible as Literature movement must be understood in this context as an attempt to restore meaning—a nonreductive scholarship—to the biblical text. The meaningfulness and integrity of the Bible are reconceptualized, however, in artistic rather than explicitly religious terms. This same context of a primarily analytical and at times desiccating biblical scholarship helps account for why non-"specialists" in Bible (Auerbach, Barfield, Burke, Fromm, Voegelin, Frye, Schneidau, and Alter, among others)[10] have made such important contributions over the past half-century. Their independence from the philological conventions of the discipline allows them not only to deal synthetically and conceptually with the Bible but also, in some of these cases, to generate a theory of literature or an approach to intellectual history informed by the Hebrew Bible.

For these reasons, many contemporary practitioners of a literary approach to the Bible disdain the historical-critical method, rejecting it as altogether invalid. Although Sternberg grants the method its legitimacy, he effectively restricts its role to *ancilla*, interpretation's handmaiden assisting the "inquiry into the historical processes of composition" of the text but barred from crossing the rigid line imposed by Sternberg's poetics "between source and discourse" (p. 22). Sternberg's distinction establishes an implicit hierarchy: diachrony elucidates the *genesis* but not the *poesis* of a biblical text. As I have attempted to suggest with my account of the origins of the historical-critical method in Spinoza, diachronic analysis can be part of an interpretive framework that overcomes the dichotomy of "source" and "discourse" and, no less than a synchronic method, points to important issues of theory and textual significance. Indeed, Spinoza's explicit rejection of the medieval convention of hierarchy—his assertion at the beginning of chapter 15 that neither philosophy nor theology should be "subordinate" (*ancilla*) to the other—provides a model for a proper hermeneutics of the Hebrew Bible.

I contend, and will attempt to demonstrate, that the two methods, synchronic and diachronic, cannot be bifurcated in their application, the former concerned with "the structure of the product," the latter, with genetic "reconstruction of the [compositional] process" (p. 22). To the contrary, adequate comprehension of the structure and significance of the biblical text must be informed by both. Viewing the text diachronically in many instances reveals the dynamics of the formation of Israelite literature and the particular literary creativity of biblical authors and editors. Sternberg's restriction of diachronic analysis to genetic reconstruction risks "detextualizing" the Bible by obscuring precisely those elements of biblical literature that should be of most interest to contemporary literary theorists.

Perhaps more than any other single literary feature of the Bible, the issue of repetition forces the question of methodology. So important is the issue of how a literary method construes narrative repetition that Sternberg devotes his longest chapter to it. Sternberg frames the chapter as a sharp critique of three exegetes, two medieval rabbinic (Ibn Ezra and Radak [R. David Kimḥi]) and one modern (Cassuto). His demonstration of the medievals' and Cassuto's common reduction of narrative repetitions to meaningless rule is effective: the medievals reduce repetition to mere rule either of language or of biblical storytelling,[11] while Cassuto reduces the repetitions to "the tradition of Canaanite epic to which the Bible supposedly belongs" (pp. 370–71).[12]

Sternberg argues that the counter to such a reductive analysis of repetition is the model of poetics: to assume the purposiveness and intentionality of the repetitions. "The text has devised a redundancy on some level with an eye to a definite effect; that is, in order to impel the reader to transfer it to another level (pattern, context, framework) where it will duly fall into place" (p. 369). Sternberg's presupposition that the text is everywhere purposive implicitly reformulates as an important heuristic principle of poetics (p. 75) the similar notions of textual coherence and absence of redundancy that ancient rabbinic exegetes characteristically assumed for dogmatic reasons. Rabbinic synchronic exegesis therefore does double duty for Sternberg: just as it provides him with a vantage point for a critique of the reductively analytic method of modern Higher Criticism, as noted above, so here it silently underlies his cogent critique of the two medieval exegetes and Cassuto for their common explanation of the text in terms of rules which do not bespeak intentionality.

Although in this chapter Sternberg does not discuss it in these terms, repetition is equally one of the primary sources of evidence that historical critics employ in their attempt to analyze and isolate the separate documentary sources from which, they maintain, the Pentateuch derives. Given the importance of repetition both to poetics and to historical criticism, the close study of a text in which repetitions are central provides a valuable opportunity to demonstrate that both synchronic and diachronic analysis are essential to the literary study of the Bible. As such, I would like to provide an analysis of the biblical Flood story (Genesis 6–9) as an example of a narrative text which clearly demonstrates that a diachronic method is essential to revealing the striking textuality of the Hebrew Bible.

I will begin by recalling the narrative background of the Flood story. Discovering to his chagrin that the humanity he has made devotes itself only to evil, God repents—this is one of the most extraordinary lines in the Bible—that he has made humans (Gen. 6:6) and sets out to destroy all life. "Yahweh said, 'I will blot out [*'emḥeh*] from the earth the men whom I have created—from men to cattle to creeping things to birds of the sky; for I regret that I made them'" (Gen. 6:7; cf. 7:23).[13] The divine intent signaled by the verb is to transform the earth into a *tabula rasa*, to wipe the slate clean.[14] The telling sequence of the life-forms listed ominously concretizes the verbal action. God cites in chiastic order (A B C : C' B' A') his series of creative acts of days five ("birds of the sky," Gen. 1:20) and six ("cattle and creeping things" as a pair, Gen. 1:24,[15] and "men," Gen. 1:26). The as yet unspecified form of destruction is thereby planned to be a precise and thorough reversal of the creation of life.

There the story would abruptly end—not only leaving the scholar without a Bible to discuss but more seriously leaving the reader embarrassed by a Yahweh who, however omnipotent, patently lacks divine omniscience—but for the omniscient narrator's qualification, "But Noah found favor with Yahweh" (Gen. 6:8). Noah will become the basis for an experiment in divine eugenics: by means of Noah, Yahweh hopes to create a new human stock from an obedient root, the wicked rest of humanity extirpated. God thus commands Noah to build an ark, informing him:

> (17) "For my part, I am about to bring the Flood—waters upon the earth—to destroy all flesh under the sky in which there is breath of life: everything on earth shall perish. (18) But I will establish My covenant with you, and you shall enter the ark, with your sons, your wife, and your sons' wives. (19) And of all that lives, of all flesh, you shall take two of each into the ark to keep alive with you; they shall be male and female. (20) From birds of every kind, cattle of every kind, every kind of creeping thing on earth, two of each shall come to you to stay alive. . . ." (22) Noah did so; just as God commanded him, so he did. (Gen. 6:17–22)

God's command that Noah collect two of every species of animal to be taken onto the ark, so that not only human but also animal life will survive the Flood, is followed immediately by the narrator's noting Noah's prompt obedience. The narrator uses a compliance formula: "just as God commanded him, so he did." Noah having thus perfectly executed the command to collect the animals, it should cause the close reader some consternation to find Noah once again commanded to collect animals, as if he had not already done so, although this time according to a different numerical criterion:

(1) Then Yahweh said to Noah, "Go into the ark, with all your household, for you alone have I found righteous before Me in this generation. (2) Of every clean animal you shall take seven pairs, males and
their mates, and of every animal which is not clean, two, a male and its
mate; (3) of the birds of the sky also, seven pairs, male and female, to
keep seed alive upon all the earth. (4) For in seven days' time I will
make it rain upon the earth, forty days and forty nights, and I will
blot out from the earth all existence that I created." (5) And Noah
did just as Yahweh commanded him. (Gen. 7:1–5)

Although this text follows immediately upon the preceding one, it
cannot logically be read as chronologically consequent upon it without
immense hermeneutical contortions. The first compliance formula renders the subsequent divine command otiose and the second compliance
formula inexplicable. Not only is the second passage redundant in light
of the first, it is also inconsistent with it in the system of categorizing
and enumerating the creatures to be saved and in its conception of the
origin and duration of the waters which are to destroy life.

In the first passage life is to be preserved, "of all flesh . . . two of
each" (6:19), without exception. In contrast, in the second passage, animals and birds are categorized as either clean or unclean (7:2; problematically anticipating the dietary laws which are not revealed to Israel
until Leviticus 11 and Deuteronomy 14). Of the clean animals, seven
pair are to be preserved; of the unclean, but a single pair. Even the
terms employed in each case to denote the two genders of a sexual
pair are altogether discrepant. The full extent of the inconsistency is
regularly obscured by English translations which use a single word,
"male," for two different Hebrew words: in the former passage, "male
and female" [*zākār ûnĕqēbāh*] (6:19); in the latter, "a male and its mate"
[*'îš wĕ'ištô*] (7:2, bis).[16]

There is a further fundamental inconsistency between the two passages in the conception of the nature and origin of the waters which
are to destroy life. In the former passage (Gen. 6:17), the water is "the
Flood, waters upon the earth": in other words, an inundation whose
duration is not here specified but which lasts, it emerges, a year and
ten days (cf. 7:11a and 8:13–14).[17] The waters of the Flood are not
nature's ordinary water: the phrasing of 7:11b makes it clear that they
are rather the primordial waters above the vault of the firmament and
below the fundament of the earth.[18] God's plan is to restore the earth
to watery chaos, in effect to pull the plug and submerge the earth, reversing his second great act of creation, the separation of the waters
(Gen. 1:6–8). The Flood is effectively a mythological reversal of creation.[19] By contrast, in the second passage quoted, the waters are de-

scribed more straightforwardly as rain which will begin in seven days and last for forty (7:4).

But for special pleading, the unavoidable conclusion is that there are *two* Flood stories, or more precisely, a flood and a downpour story, commingled, just as there are two problematically contiguous sequences of command and execution. The relation between the two accounts cannot be rendered in narrative terms: Noah does not move from the first to the second. Rather there are clearly two mutually exclusive accounts, each of which preserves independent traditions concerning the origins of the water which destroys life (primordial waters versus rain), the duration of the water (one year versus forty days), and the categorization (recognizing or not recognizing cultic status as pure and impure) and enumeration of the creaturely life to be saved (two of each species or rather seven pair of the clean, one pair of unclean). Further it is not only by means of these substantive or topical criteria that the competing discrepant traditions can be distinguished; each is marked by its own characteristic syntax and lexicon.

Herein lies the justification for the diachronic analysis of the Bible according to the standard historical-critical method. The two contiguous passages cannot construe in terms of a narrative poetics that derives the text from the artistic genius of the *narrator*. The interpreter's methodology, to comprehend the text, must consequently shift from a synchronic poetics to a method informed by diachrony, an analysis of the text as the work of a *redactor* who has conjoined originally separate literary documents.[20]

Although therefore valuable for its diachronic perspective on the text, by itself standard historical-critical scholarship would not suffice for a comprehensive textual exegesis. Instead, it would be much more concerned to isolate the separate literary or traditional strata to which narrative or legal passages belong, determine their distinctive features, and attempt to date them relative to one another. In fact, older commentaries frequently separate their expositions of the Flood story according to the J-source and the P-source without providing a coherent interpretation of the text as it stands.[21]

What has not been adequately studied, either by conventional historical-critical scholarship or by the newer, synchronic approaches, is the impact upon the mind of ancient Israelite scribes of such mutually exclusive traditions, each of which is authoritative. There has been growing attention to the clear evidence within the biblical text that ancient Israelite authors were not only transmitters of texts but also interpreters of them and that significant elements of the Bible clearly derive from sophisticated exegetical activity on the part of ancient Israelite authors. This attention to so-called "inner-biblical exegesis" is one of the most important recent developments within biblical scholarship within the past two decades.[22] What evidence is there in the narrative for the editors' awareness of the fearful asymmetry of the accounts concerning Noah?

Immediately after the last passage quoted, the editor announces the Flood's onset:

> (6) Noah was six hundred years old when the Flood came, waters upon the earth. (7) Noah, with his sons, his wife, and his sons' wives, went into the ark because of the waters of the Flood. (8) Of the clean animals, of the animals that are not clean, of the birds, and of everything that creeps on the ground, (9) two of each, male and female, came to Noah into the ark, as God had commanded Noah. (10) And on the seventh day the waters of the Flood came upon the earth. (Gen. 7:6–10)

Noah, having already been credited for complying with each of the two previous inconsistent divine commands regarding the animals, is now for the third time credited for obedience as he presumably watches the animals enter the ark apparently of their own volition. However the force of this third compliance formula, the note that the animals entered the ark "as God had commanded Noah," is absolutely unclear: the final creaturely cargo of the ark complies properly with neither prior divine command. In this new formulation the categorization of the animals as clean or unclean, which refers back to 7:2 (the second passage quoted), is rendered contextually problematic since only two of each, not seven pair of clean and one pair of unclean as originally commanded, are here to be preserved. Even on its own terms, of course, this passage cannot logically be construed. If "two of each" are to be preserved, irrespective of their cultic purity, why make the clean/unclean distinction at all? As lacking any clear referential force and thereby rendered contextually meaningless, the clean/unclean distinction is therefore rather a lexical tag by means of which the writer of the verse attempts to preserve the categorization of the creatures found in the second source while harmonizing it with the number scheme of the first source, in which a single pair of each creature is to be preserved by Noah (6:19–20).[23]

To recapture the literary and intellectual dynamics responsible for this text, the attentive reader must adopt *hermeneutics* as a theory of reading. Although ostensibly a consecutive *narrative*, the passage cannot be read on its own terms without its forcefully breaking down the reader's expectation of the text's coherence. Far from deriving from a narrator whose goals are to produce an artistic text, whose accomplishments are discerned by means of *poetics*, the verses derive from a redactor confronted by a hermeneutical crisis: clearly contradictory traditions concerning the flood, each of which is equally authoritative. The Israelite conception of the authority of the canon required the preservation of each of these traditions: the canon is conservative in its hermeneutics (see Deut. 4:2; 13:1 [12:32 in English versions]). The editor therefore retains the two texts in sequence. Confronted thereby by their clear inconsistency, he attempts in a third, new text, to provide an exegetical harmonization of their differences that serves only to underscore them. He purchases a nominal lexical consistency at the cost of revealing his diachronic editorial hand. In his anxious attempt to preserve each source, he subverts both: the compliance formula signals the breach of both previous divine imperatives. Consistent with neither, the now exegetical text is in fact a new literary creation whose origins have no direct ground in tradition (revelation); the text derives from exegesis. The canon is radical in its hermeneutics: the very requirement for conservation requires its breach.

There are other texts in the Bible, particularly in the legal corpora, in which biblical editors highlight the very discrepancies they are concerned to reconcile. Such harmonizations cannot be read but as profoundly exegetical artifice whereby the Bible calls attention to its own textuality; thus they form *aporia* whereby the Bible deconstructs itself. On the one hand, at the stage of the formation of the Pentateuch, this and other equally inconsistent texts were retained and redacted together. On the other hand, this very explicitly contradictory (inconsistent) canon imposed upon the editor the burden of exegesis. As Sarna, Sanders, Childs, Fishbane, and others have so powerfully demonstrated, exegesis is not what happens only *after* the biblical text is complete. Rather exegesis is part of the very literary—hermeneutical— dynamic that produces the text. The text itself is a product of what it engenders; its modern readers respond in kind to, and thereby sustain, the interpretive activity that gave it birth.

I have tried to demonstrate in this section the contributions that diachronic analysis can offer to the interpretation of the biblical text, together with the literary and hermeneutical issues it raises. Although Sternberg's formulation of *poetics* stresses (literary) history as providing an essential context for the interpretation of biblical narrative in a way that many practitioners of the Bible as Literature movement do not (p. 70), he shares with them the effective restriction of expositional legitimacy to synchronic textual analysis. That methodological dualism, whereby diachronic source-critical analysis is retained merely as ancillary, illuminating only the background of the text, cannot, I think, be sustained in light of the issues I have pointed to here. As such, the new literary method which invalidates the old, privileging synchrony to the exclusion of diachrony, flattens, obscures, or lacks the means of explicating some of the most exciting features of the biblical text, and

much of ancient Israelite literary creativity. Further, the exclusive derivation of the text from a single author (narrator), even if only heurist-
ically maintained, risks returning a modernizing scholarship to the
precritical midrashic method of the early rabbis who, for dogmatic reasons, were constrained to avoid the intimations of literary history within
the Pentateuch.

Common to the synchronic methodology of both ancient rabbinic exegesis and Sternberg's poetics is a notion of the text's coherence, its unitary derivation from a single author. Contradictions and redundancies
are conceptualized as everywhere legally or didactically (rabbinic) or
artistically (Sternberg) purposive and intentional. In contrast, the analysis here draws on Spinoza to allow the contradictions and redundancies
to stand. Such *aporia*, made central to hermeneutics by Spinoza, alone
allow the recovery of the literary history of the Bible and its implications
for interpretation.

The Nature of the Israelite Revelation

Sternberg's book alternates between a consideration of the proper methodology for narrative exposition and the thesis that biblical narrative
can be comprehended only in light of the ideology that it both narrates
and reflects. Sternberg is concerned with providing not merely a descriptive aesthetics of narrative but, more profoundly, a theory concerning the cultural and intellectual context of Israelite literature.

Sternberg argues that the unique form of omniscience that distinguishes biblical narrative from other ancient forms of apparent narra-
torical omniscience, Homeric and Near Eastern, is unprecedented in literary history. He properly does not countenance any notion of a natural
or inevitable evolution of this prose form either from Israel's cultural
neighbors or within Israelite literary history itself. Instead, "the Bible's
poetics appears to have sprung full-blown" (p. 232). Sternberg argues
evocatively for a profound cultural breakthrough, a revolutionary
transformation of experience and cognition unique to ancient Israel,[24]
as alone accounting for the unique attributes of biblical narrative.
Although the factuality of such a radical break with the past cannot
be doubted, he contends, its actual historical dynamics lie beyond the
realm of analysis or reconstruction and are marked rather as miraculous:

> Within the same mode of narration—the omniscient—the Bible's
> reality model and its compositional status are poles apart from the
> Homeric or Near Eastern. It all goes back to an epistemological revo-

lution, which shifted the center of gravity from existence to knowledge. The shift . . . manifests itself all along the biblical line: doctrine, value, interest, plotting, narration, reading process. (pp. 88–89)

Working independently, the Bible and Homer created a remarkable art of sequence, with the possible difference that the Bible broke with time-honored conventions of narrative in the process and the certain difference that its artistic revolution correlated with an ideological revolution. How this triple miracle happened in Israel, God only knows; but there can be no doubt that it did happen. (pp. 231–32)

Although he never uses the word directly, it seems clear that Sternberg is here providing an account of the Israelite revelation. In its drive to account for the distinctiveness of Israelite literature, Sternberg's poetics of narrative becomes, at least in part, a secular narrative theology: the text points to the omniscience of the Creator.

Sternberg formulates the distinctiveness of Israelite literary culture in terms of monotheism's "epistemological revolution"—the assonance with revelation is evocative—that rejects the pagan concern with "existence" to emphasize instead "knowledge." He argues that both "Homer and Oriental [Near Eastern] paganism" conceptualize the difference between the divine world and the human world in terms of "existence": the gods are immortal, humans are mortal. In contrast, Israel's revelation reformulates that divine/human distinction in terms of knowledge: "God is omniscient, man limited, and the boundary impassable" (p. 46). The epistemological revolution confers informational privilege: the revelatory conceptualization of God in terms of omniscience has as its literary reflex the omnisciently privileged narrator, unrestricted by empirical human knowledge (p. 87). The literary device which that omnisciently conceived narrator permits, free indirect discourse (pp. 52–53), is equally a textual reflex of the Israelite conception of unrestricted divine knowledge. As God sees into the human heart, so does the narrator reveal interiority.

Is it indeed the case that a revolution in epistemology is central to the Israelite experience of God such that the Bible's narrative "serves the purpose of staging and glorifying an omniscient God" (p. 89)? I believe that Sternberg misstates the case in characterizing revelation in terms of epistemology.

Earlier I pointed out Sternberg's conceptual slide in the book's opening sentences from biblical narrative to the Bible as a whole. To be sure, Sternberg himself points out his exclusive focus on narrative, noting in his preface, "I reserve for separate treatment issues like the Bible's generic variety" (p. xi). In effect, however, he restricts that variety, as far as a possible incorporation into a poetics is concerned, to the genres that are most obviously "literary": on the next page he presents as a brief sample of "generic variety" the "meaningful opposition between prose narrative and poetry or parable" (p. xii). Consistent both with this note concerning the artistically interesting biblical genres and with the shift from narrative specificity to the more comprehensive question, "What kind of text is *the Bible* . . . ?", is a striking generic omission. The legal corpora of the Bible play a minimal role in both Sternberg's conception of the genres to which a literary method may be applied and his conception of revelation.[25]

Despite the truly extraordinary intellectual scope of his book, key biblical texts are absent. Not found among his expositions are any examinations of Sinai, biblical law, the covenant and its commandments, the Mosaic reformulation of the law on the plains of Moab, or the texts that refer to them.[26] Nor, to be fair, should Sternberg in a book concerned with *narrative* be expected to refer to them (although the omniscient narrator figures importantly in them too)—were it not for the book's own aim and claim: from the standpoint of a narrative poetics to address the question, "What kind of text is the *Bible* . . . ?", and to provide thereby an account of Israelite literary and cultural distinctiveness.

The issue is not simply one of being comprehensive as regards the generic variety of the Bible. The question is rather one of the biblical text's own priorities. At the descriptive level it is accurate to note the ideology implied by "the segments of law interspersed (say) throughout the story of Exodus" (p. 41). Conceptually speaking, however, it is rather the law which contains the narratives. In the Decalogue's first commandment, the entire antecedent narrative of the Exodus is reduced to but a relative clause in God's introductory self-identification: "I Yahweh am your God *who brought you out of the land of Egypt, the house of bondage*: You shall have no other gods besides me" (Exod. 20:2–3). The narrative of liberation provides the basis for the nation's obligation to God and, thus, the justification for the nation's first priority: fidelity to the covenant. The text presents revelation as primarily the revelation of cultic, ethical, and civil law; indeed all biblical law is consistently presented as revelatory in origin. The primary concerns animating biblical authors relate therefore to problems of action and obedience rather than of knowledge. These concerns constitute a constant motif in the narrative corpus. From the garden story of Genesis on, the major focus is the interplay of obedience and disobedience, whether individual, patriarchal and matriarchal, tribal, royal, priestly, or national. This motif of obedience is strikingly absent in Sternberg's own précis of the Bible (p. 48).

Indeed, Sternberg's brief reference to the narrative of the Fall (Genesis 3) provides striking confirmation of my argument that he privileges epistemology at the expense of law (morality). As proof of "how the Bible's new departures in poetics and epistemology make the most of each other," Sternberg astutely shows that, of the two trees in the center of that garden, only "the Tree of Knowledge . . . has no trace in pagan mythology" (p. 89). Sternberg's emphasis on epistemology, however, causes him to truncate his reference to the biblical text which, whenever it uses the qualititative attribute, speaks of "the tree of knowledge *of good and evil*" (Gen. 2:9, 17). Sternberg's telling omission of the attributive genitive, absent also in his other references to the tree (pp. 12, 89, 104, 278), restricts to terms of absolute knowledge, or epistemology, a tree whose fruit rather provides knowledge of moral discernment.[27]

The narrative corpus, which Sternberg makes his sole focus, by itself necessitates his conception of revelation as epistemological. Given his exclusion of ethical and legal texts from the corpus of texts on which he grounds his theory, what real content can the Bible have, other than what emerges from the analysis of a decentered narrative: "gaps, ambiguities, redundancy, exposition, temporal ordering, omniscient viewpoint, reading process, patterns of analogy, alternative forms of reference, indirect characterization and rhetoric" (p. xii). All these have as their theoretical reflex the question of the narrator's control, which then points to his knowledge, which raises the question of epistemology, which in turn becomes the cultural foundation for the literary strategies. The argument is circular: the corpus of texts admitted into the literary canon itself controls the literary and cultural generalizations that can be made from them. In effect, Sternberg restricts primary expositional legitimacy to the narrative texts of the Bible: he creates an ungrounded canon within the canon in which only the narrative texts are salutary for interpretation.

So central is law to the hermeneutics of the Hebrew Bible that Rashi (R. Solomon ben Isaac, 1040–1105 C.E.) begins his commentary on the Bible's first verse by forcefully raising the question of the justification for narrative altogether: "R. Isaac said, 'The Torah should have begun with, "This month shall mark for you [the beginning of the months]" [Exod. 12: 1], for that was the first commandment that Israel was commanded. What is the reason, then, for beginning with the [narrative of] creation?'"[28] Transforming R. Isaac's provocative question into the terms of genre theory, it may be rendered, "Why is there narrative rather than law?" In other words, why does the Bible not simply begin immediately with the heart of God's revelation to Israel, the law, which, although textually later, is conceptually prior?

Sternberg's larger point, that the Bible is fundamentally modern in its literary structure and in the interpretive demands it places upon its readers (pp. 53, 409, 436–37), would in fact be corroborated with reference to the legal corpora. Sternberg astutely refuses to equate chronological antiquity with conceptual primitivism and recognizes that the structure of the biblical text constitutes thought, even if not discursively or philosophically formulated (pp. 46, 89). In a superb comparative study of cuneiform and biblical law, J. J. Finkelstein cogently argues that the Bible is the very source of the (modern) idea of the person— that biblical law is modern in implicitly providing a coherent formulation of the person as unquantifiable in finite terms, as morally infinite in value. In contradistinction, Finkelstein argues, the cuneiform legal corpora remain conceptually as well as chronologically ancient. Their system of penalties does not register a consistent distinction between offenses against the person and against property: in other words, that the two constitute separate ethical categories, infinite person and finite chattel, is not fully articulated. Finkelstein attempts to confirm his hypothesis in each case with reference to the conception of the human in other literary genres.[29]

Sternberg's dichotomy in *method*, synchrony versus diachrony, involves a parallel dichotomy in *content*: narrative versus law. In each case, Sternberg restricts his interpretive attention to the former to the effective exclusion of the latter. The narrative focus of Sternberg's poetics, which does not refer to the implications of the legal corpora for the conceptualization of revelation, points to the interrelation between a canon and the theory of textual significance, or hermeneutics, derived from it. Sternberg's narrative canon, in which the law plays no meaningful theoretical (literary, artistic) role, which effectively silences Sinai and law-giving, comes closer to imposing a Pauline law–gospel dichotomy in its conception of what is salutary than to providing a coherent reading of the Hebrew Bible. If biblical law indeed constitutes a stumbling block to a literary approach, the law is nonetheless essential to a theory of revelation and of the communicative aims of Israelite authors. That the study of biblical law is also essential specifically to the *literary* study of the Bible, I shall now attempt to demonstrate.

The Literary Implications of Biblical Law

The legal corpora of the Bible are not only central to an exposition of the Bible's revelatory content, they are also central to a proper conception of the Bible as literature. If the convention of anonymity characterizes the narrative texts of the Bible, as Sternberg rightly stresses, what characterizes the legal texts is the convention of voice, the divine or prophetic attribution of law. Each convention—voice and anonymity—

equally constitutes a claim for textual authority, strikingly in each case by disclaiming explicit human authorship. Sternberg uses the anonymous narrator's omniscience, echoing that of God, as evidence for the place of absolute knowledge in the text's ideology. The claim to absolute authority differently asserted in the legal corpora by means of divine or prophetic voicing provides an independent means for the recovery of the conception of authority in ancient Israel. This latter conception in turn may be compared to that which Sternberg posits for the narrative texts.

The issues already pointed to in the discussion of the Flood story emerge even more sharply in the study of the hermeneutics of biblical law. The redactional preservation of discrepant yet equally authoritative texts leads to editorial attempts at their harmonization, which in turn introduces additional inconsistencies that further break down the text's (literal) authority. Central to what the Bible communicates, in other words, through the *aporia* which emerge by means of a method informed by diachrony, is the Bible's own textuality: both the interpretive issues out of which it emerges and those which it mandates its readers to confront. The legal corpora demand a shift from poetics to hermeneutics as a theory of biblical reading.

There is an initial impediment, of course. The legal corpora have been essentially excluded from the literary study of the Bible because they are conventionally read as legislative texts rather than as *literary* ones. As practical texts, they are perceived to lack both the freedom from direct external reference and particular aesthetic features that distinguish literature from other forms of writing. There are, however, several reasons why the legal corpora should in fact be understood in literary terms.[30] Although both biblical and ancient Near Eastern legal corpora seem like judicial texts to the modern reader (and the cuneiform legal texts were so understood when first discovered less than a century ago), recent scholarship has demonstrated that in fact they were never implemented as law, nor were they intended to have a direct application to society. Among the many thousands of court dockets in existence from southern Mesopotamia, there is no record, for example, of Hammurabi's Code (1792–50 B.C.E.) ever being cited in an actual judicial proceeding, despite its continually being recopied as part of the scribal curriculum for over a millennium.[31] Not only is there little external evidence for the judicial citation or implementation of the legal corpora, but even on internal grounds they lack "laws" critical to the organization of any society. In the case of the Pentateuch, for example, there are no laws to regulate either normal marriage or inheritance.[32] Rather than constituting "legal codes," therefore, the legal collections of the ancient Near East, and the biblical corpora influenced by them, represent theoretical reflections on ethical issues, considerations of the proper thing to do in a certain case, such reflections the product of a scribal intelligentsia and primarily circulated within scribal schools.[33] As the intellectual products of an ongoing literary and exegetical tradition, the texts are much closer to literature than conventionally assumed.[34]

There are two further important correctives to the view that the legal corpora are not literary. First, the legal corpora, everywhere attributed to an authoritative speaker known from the narrative frame, can be analyzed—no less than the narratives—in terms of voice or persona, point of view, gapping, repetition, structure, and so on. As such they contain many of the stylistic features characteristic of literary texts.[35] Second, the contributions of literary theory to the study of contemporary legal texts is increasingly being recognized as important.[36] Indeed, one recent study suggests parallel paradigm shifts in new approaches to biblical studies and the Critical Legal Studies movement so far as the conception of the text is concerned.[37] The benefits of conceptualizing the legal corpora in literary terms, of enriching the literary study of the Bible through recourse to biblical law, can best be demonstrated by turning to an examination of the literary issues they raise.

I have already noted that one of the features that distinguishes the biblical concept of revelation is that it is a legal revelation. The attribution of the ultimate authorship of a corpus of law to God and its designation as his personal will are unique in the ancient Near East to the Hebrew Bible. By way of contrast, the convention of the great second millennium B.C.E. cuneiform texts, like Hammurabi's Code, is a royal speaker: Hammurabi is both the textual speaker of the laws and, in terms of the text's explicit assertions, their author.[38] In this context of the literary history of the genre, the Israelite attribution of law to God, whatever the precise historical experiences it reflects, represents the attempt to assert the absolute authority of the law. It most likely also represents an attempt to validate Israelite values in the face of the more established high cultures of Mesopotamia and Egypt, whose literary canons —the very word "canon" is ultimately Sumerian in origin[39]—were already ancient when Israel emerged as a historical state.[40] Few cultures have been more aware than ancient Israel of their "belated" position in intellectual history and of the authority of prior texts.

This convention of the attribution of all law to God, either directly or through Moses, his prophetic intermediary, leads in turn to a series of fascinating hermeneutical issues. The very convention of authoritatively voiced law, combined with notions of canonicity, led to the preservation in ancient Israel of multiple and originally independent legal corpora, much as separate legal collections are to be found in cuneiform literature. Beginning during the Exile, however, confronted with a threat to their national existence, Judaean scribal editors began to collect these originally separate legal collections and combine them together with narratives. The text they eventually created, the Pentateuch, thereby embeds in its narrative three separate collections of laws: the Covenant Code (Exod. 21:1–23:19), the Holiness Code (Leviticus 17–26), and the laws of Deuteronomy (chapters 12–26).

The hermeneutical implications of this redactional feat are enormous and, indeed, the very achievement points to political compromise between different social groups in Israel as well as to a sophisticated body of accompanying oral interpretation.[41] On the one hand, because each of these three legal collections originates either from a separate period of Israelite history or from a separate social stratum of ancient Israelite society, they are frequently inconsistent with one another in their content or requirements, if not actually contradicting or even polemically reformulating one another. On the other hand, each of the three mutually inconsistent legal corpora is made simultaneously and equally authoritative: each is attributed to divine revelation.[42] The corpus of law thereby ascribed to revelation becomes contradictory, incomprehensible without interpretation. The interpretive resolution of such contradictory laws is possible in either of two basic modes: either synchronic rabbinic exegesis or diachronic historical-critical scholarship. What is particularly striking in this connection is not only that the attempt to resolve (synchronically) the contradictory legislation of the Pentateuch has its origins within the Bible itself, but that the *exegesis* of authoritative Scripture within Scripture should itself acquire authoritative status as Scripture. Even more striking is that such harmonistic exegesis should assert itself as conforming to the original stipulations involved, thereby presenting *exegetical law* as the original signification of the law. For example, the postexilic Chronicler, in 2 Chron. 35:13, asserts as "according to the law" his legal harmonization of the contradictory Passover laws of Exod. 12:9 and Deut. 16:7—although it conforms to neither![43] The parallel with the narrative harmonization in the Flood story, where the redactor's "just as God had commanded Noah" (Gen. 7:9) signals conformity more exegetically wished for than evident, should be obvious.

Literary history here—human authorship and revision of law, the obvious need for new laws to develop in response to ongoing social and economic change—is everywhere ostensibly denied by means of the attribution of law to God or Moses. Yet precisely the thoroughness of such attributions parts the veil of redactional illusion. The very repeated denial of literary history succeeds in affirming it. The achievement of the biblical editors is that they retain the *aporia* which reveal their hand even as that hand is dissembled or camouflaged. The hermeneutical implication of this retention of *aporia* is that the very assertion of textual

authority itself is made inseparable from its interpretation and ultimately, for the reader who thinks in historical terms, its deconstruction.
The divine attribution of the laws points finally to the divine voice of
human exegesis.

A clear example of the Bible's deconstructing itself in this way is found
in the book of Leviticus, which concludes with a colophon, standard
in Near Eastern ritual texts, that functions as a catch-line to summarize
the book's contents:

> These are the commandments that Yahweh gave Moses for the
> Israelite people on Mount Sinai. (Lev. 27:34)

The catch-line marks the foregoing legal and ritual material as deriving from God's revelation to Israel upon Sinai. Such an attribution is
fine, except that it is preceded by one nearly identical, although somewhat more detailed, at the conclusion of the immediately preceding
chapter:

> These are the laws, rules, and directions that Yahweh established,
> through Moses on Mount Sinai, between Himself and the Israelite
> people. (Lev. 26:46)

This colophon clearly marks a *terminus ad quem* for the priestly prescriptions of Leviticus whose authority is asserted through their attribution to Sinai. The identical claim at the end of the following chapter
clearly constitutes an embarrassment of colophonic riches and points
to the book's last chapter, concerned with vows, as a literary appendix
to Leviticus. The attempt to authorize it as equal in authority with the
preceding material by means of the authority claim of the colophon,
calls that claim, in its contextual redundancy, into question. The very
assertion of the authority of the text precludes credulity; the text, which
doth protest too much, betrays its own textuality and compels its interpretation.

Perhaps the greatest trope of textual authority, of profound hermeneutical significance, is the Book of Deuteronomy, the work of seventh-
century B.C.E. scribal intellectuals concerned to effect a series of important transformations of Israelite religion, paramount among which was
the restriction of sacrifice to a single, central site: the Jerusalem Temple.[44] In doing so they had to controvert an ancient altar law, ascribed
to Yahweh at Sinai and which immediately follows the Decalogue, that
tolerates precisely the opposite: sacrifice is acceptable "in any place"
(Exod. 20:24 [20:21 in some printings]). Moreover, as the necessary consequence of restricting all legitimate sacrifice to the Jerusalem sanctuary,
they had to make a second fundamental innovation in Israelite cultic

life. Previously all slaughter of domestic animals was a ritual act not distinguished from sacrifice in that it had to be carried out at an altar (cf. Exod. 20:24a and Lev. 17:3–7). For the Deuteronomists to permit nonresidents of Jerusalem to eat meat in the context of the restriction of sacrifice to Jerusalem, it was also necessary to legitimate *secular* slaughter as distinct from cultic *sacrifice*. The reforming authors of Deuteronomy had therefore to overcome a hermeneutical problem created by ancient Israel's emerging literary canon. They had to sanction a pair of cultic innovations, centralization of sacrifice and permission for secular slaughter, that contradicted authoritative "Scripture."

Their fascinating technique for justifying these innovations in Israelite literary and legal history shows the sophistication of the intellectual and exegetical culture of ancient Israel. First the authors of Deuteronomy altogether disclaim their own authorship and instead take refuge in the device of pseudepigraphy. They employ the authoritative voice of Moses as textual speaker, although Moses would have lived fully half a millennium before. Second, they cite and reformulate the very Exodus lemma they must overcome, repeatedly recontextualizing it in such a way as to make it command both of their cultic innovations (see Deut. 12:13–14).[45]

Through this technique of citation and transformation, the authors of Deuteronomy paradoxically borrow from the authority of the Exodus lemma in order to authorize their subversion of its original meaning. In so doing, and in their recourse to the pseudepigraphic voice of Moses, the authors of Deuteronomy disclaim their own authorship and deny literary history. They cloak their fundamental transformation of Israelite religious history, that is to say, of the formative canon, as nothing new, as but a Mosaic report of what God required at Sinai: "as I commanded you" (Deut. 12:21). As a result of their studied transformation of literary history, the Deuteronomists become the authors of the very authoritative traditions upon which they ground their innovations. They "author- ize" their own revisionist originality. Remarkably, precisely their denial of their own voice enables them all the more profoundly to assert their authority to revise an authoritative text attributed to revelation! In their gesture of exegetical deference and nonoriginality, they radically assert their freedom to revise the received cultural canon. The explicit denial of an innovation in literary history enables its implicit, and true, creation.

The dialectical hermeneutics of Deuteronomy raises the question of the self-understanding of the text's authors. Do the authors of Deuteronomy believe their transforming exegesis of the altar law is what Exod. 20:24 intended; or is the exegetical recourse to the lemma a merely formal way of maintaining the authority of the text? This hermeneutical

issue is not only characteristic of many similar problems concerning the
legitimation of innovation within the legal literature of the Hebrew
Bible. The same issue is in fact central to much subsequent Jewish literary and intellectual history, as Gershom Scholem brilliantly demonstrates for the postbiblical period.[46] He points to a long postbiblical trajectory in which literary *history* is in fact camouflaged in two ways.
Explicit authorship is denied through recourse to pseudepigraphy, the
attribution of the text to authoritative figures from the past,[47] while
innovation is denied through the text's self-presentation as a mere exegetical exposition of what was latent in the original revelation.[48] Does
the rabbinic claim concerning the Sinaitic origin of the Oral Law represent what early scholars actually thought, for example, or was it an attempt to legitimate *halakhic* innovation in the face of cultural safeguards
precisely against such innovation? Similarly, do the kabbalists believe
the tenets of the *Zohar* to be Sinaitic in origin, their teachings Tannaitic?
Or is the *Zohar*'s Tannaitic voice a subterfuge by Moses de León (c. 1240–
1305 c.e.) to sanction innovation by conferring upon it the mantle of
instant antiquity?[49] It is clear that the origins of this trajectory in intellectual history, both the technique of pseudepigraphy and the stance of
exegetical passivity, lie in ancient Israel, as Michael Fishbane demonstrates.[50]

That the revelatory authority of the legal texts is a redactional trope
forces a reconsideration of Sternberg's claim that the absolute authority
of the omniscient narrator reflects the absolute authority of the omniscient God. Sternberg sharply bifurcates divine and human knowledge
and makes that claim of epistemological difference central to his reconstruction of the ideology of ancient Israel. "God is omniscient, man limited, and the boundary impassable" (p. 46). This barrier that Sternberg
establishes between finite human knowledge and infinite divine knowledge is no less rigid in its formulation than his methodological formulation of "the line between source and discourse" (p. 22), which, so far
as the explication of textual meaning is concerned, confines diachronic
method to genetic *ancilla* and restricts expositional legitimacy to a synchronic poetics. In each case the structure is that of hierarchy and of
dualistic opposition. Given his conceptual structure of an absolute, divine omniscience distinct from—independent of—merely finite human
knowledge, how then does Sternberg conceptualize the merely human
text, with its *aporia*, as the source for the revelation of divine omniscience? Is not authoritative omniscience—the claim of epistemological
completion, whether narratorial or divine—itself a trope, itself finally
to be repossessed as a textual strategy, as an interpretive assertion?
Sternberg's dichotomy between divine and human must itself be inter-
pretively overcome.[51]

Authority itself is an interpretive trope, whether it be asserted through anonymity or through voicing, through narrative or through law. The use of a synchronic method, poetics as a systematization of narrative rules, tends to underemphasize the extent to which the text's own claims of authority reflect an ongoing process of redactional reformulation. Sternberg's recourse to a notion of a narrator whose authority is unimpeachable works unintentionally to reify—to detextualize—the concepts both of the narrator and of God, to shift attention away from the role of editors in the formation of biblical literature. These issues strongly emerge through the study of the legal corpora and the use of a method informed by diachrony. The Hebrew Bible therefore requires hermeneutics as a theory of reading to overcome not only Sternberg's double bifurcations of method (synchronic versus diachronic) and content (narrative versus law), but also of authority (divine versus human): to recognize their necessary interrelation and the centrality of interpretation to all.

Arguably one of the most important dynamics within ancient Israel is the simultaneous creation of literary history and the obscuring of it, authorship and its obfuscation. This double movement can be comprehended only in terms of the dialectic of hermeneutics, not in terms of a bifurcating poetics. The exclusive privileging of the divine or prophetic voice in the legal corpora paradoxically lends greater dignity to the human voice as that voice pseudepigraphically asserts its right to supplement and reformulate authoritative texts, as that human voice ascribes its compositions to revelation. The creation of literary history through the attempt to obscure innovation, the paradoxical privileging of the human voice by means of the trope of the divine or prophetic speaker, the retention of multiple, competing, and inconsistent texts, each ascribed with equal authority to revelation and therefore together unintelligible without interpretation: all these issues cut to the heart of what is most creative about ancient Israelite literature. They also clearly overlap with contemporary literary theory's concern with the history of authorship,[52] with the impact of a literary canon upon subsequent creation (including the anxiety of influence),[53] and with deconstruction. To have access to what is most compelling about ancient Israelite literary creativity requires a hermeneutics grounded jointly in synchronic and diachronic method and in the Bible's legal corpora no less than in its narrative.[54]

> This is the thesis scrivened in delight,
> The reverberating psalm, the right chorale.
> Wallace Stevens, "Esthétique du Mal," XV

THE INTEGRITY OF
BIBLICAL PLURALISM

James A. Sanders

The current decline of literature and the attendant rise of literary theory in English graduate programs was anticipated by the curricula of theological seminaries, which have long emphasized scholarly-critical methodologies over the biblical text itself. The future pastor, rabbi, or priest has been expected to know the latest theories in the history of the formation of the various literary units of the Bible, but so far as the academically reputable seminary is concerned, Bible content is left almost entirely to the student.

Such a curriculum may have worked well up to the liberal period, the first half of this century (though I wonder even about that); however, it has produced a generation of ministers reasonably adept at reciting basic histories of the formation of the Bible but ignorant for the most part of the Bible itself. The common seminary curriculum in Bible presupposes that Bible content was learned at home, or in synagogue or church. Such curricula were designed to be built on a student's basic knowledge of Bible content but are currently continued despite the patent lack of it. And I suspect that part of the reason for increasing specialization in guilds of biblical scholars is that many of those who now teach Bible in seminary are largely ignorant of Bible content beyond their areas of specialization. I often tell students that we must stop attributing our ignorance of Scripture to the New Testament writers.

What knowledge there is of Bible content among lay folk usually comes by a route other than sitting and reading the text. Jacob Petuchowski, distinguished professor of rabbinics at the Hebrew Union College, once remarked that an orthodox Jew knows the Bible by the folio in the Talmud on which it is cited. Similarly a Protestant usually knows the Bible by the hymn in which it is paraphrased or perhaps a Gospel tractate in which a verse is cited totally out of context. And these are the very people who go to seminary or take courses in Bible in college. Bible taught as literature in college has become perhaps the best entry point for basic knowledge of Bible content. The supposition

that Bible is learned at home or in the place of worship is largely a
false one, and yet seminaries continue to make this assumption in making their curricula.

Most students today come to seminary without having read the Bible.
Those rare arriving students already familiar with the text have been
taught to believe in its harmoniousness and to suppress their inevitable
questions about discord. It is for these rare students that current seminary curricula are designed—and with the specific purpose of "defunda-
mentalizing" them. These students learn what form-historical critics
have to teach them, and often what they learn is what European-trained
scholars think certain biblical texts originally meant, or what the original
speakers, writers, and sources really said; and often these constitute
a canon within the canon consonant with scholars' needs and presuppositions. Not only do most seminary students not know what the Bible
itself says, they also do not know why the formation or source-critical
theories were devised; that is, they know neither the content nor the
discrepancies, anomalies, and contradictions which an honest reading
of the Bible exhibits and that so-called higher criticism is supposed to
explain.

George Steiner's lament of current general ignorance of the Bible,
in his review of the Alter-Kermode *Literary Guide to the Bible*, could have
been sadder than it was. He wrote, "The lapse of the scriptural from
the everyday in the commerce of ideas and proposals, of warning and
of promise in our body politic in the West entails a veritable breakdown
of solidarity, of concord within dissent. . . . As a result . . . the Bible
is today an active presence not in the everyday but in historical and
theological scholarship, in comparative anthropology, and, most recently, in the study of semantics and of literature."[1] But it is not even
very active in theological scholarship since the triumph of so-called Biblical Higher Criticism, as Hans Frei and David Kelsey have noted.[2]

There is simply no substitute for reading the Bible itself, preferably
in Hebrew and Greek but at least in a responsible, formal-equivalence
translation such as the New Revised Standard Version. A firm knowledge of Bible content, thereafter conjoined with the best of what the
form-historical method has discerned of how to account for the anomalies, discrepancies, and contradictions that abound in biblical texts, provides the best possible standpoint from which to deal with the Bible's
pluralism. The student is then in a position to perceive how the pluralism that exists in the early Jewish literature of the Persian, Hellenistic,
and Roman periods emerged forthrightly and "honestly" out of the
pluralism of the First Testament itself.

The invidious substitution of biblical criticism for biblical content, or
even biblical thinking, brought Brevard Childs of Yale in 1964 to decry

the current state of affairs and to launch by 1970 his mode of studying and reading Scripture in canonical context.[3] The main point of this mode of reading Scripture is that of respecting the final form of the Masoretic text of the First Testament as the context in which to read its parts, instead of reading layers of the text discerned by the form-historical deconstructionist exercise and then attributing authority only to the earliest levels—those that might possibly have derived from the so-called original authors.[4]

Early believing communities, according to the available manuscript evidence and according to early postbiblical literature, appear not to have been as concerned as we about such origins. There appears to have been a denomination in early Judaism for which the Psalter was not yet closed, but like the Third Section, the Writings or *Ketuvim* of the *Tanak*, was still open-ended.[5] We had already learned, largely due to the discovery of the Scrolls, that Judaism was quite pluralistic in the Persian and Hellenistic periods, and if there was a stabilized Psalter for parts of Judaism it could have been open-ended for others. It would be difficult, furthermore, for anyone to deny that these non-Masoretic psalms functioned authoritatively or canonically for the faithful at Qumran.

This clearly raises the issue of a dual understanding of the word "canon." Canon implies both *norma normata*, its internal and external shape—the questions of inclusion and order—and *norma normans*, its function in a believing community. Function helps us to answer an important question about shape: since the entrance into the land of Canaan was such an integral part of the early recitals of the Torah story, Israel's epic history, in prophetic books, psalms, and histories, why was Joshua not included in the Torah, which is also called the Pentateuch? The Torah could just as well have included Joshua, the story of the fulfillment of the promises to Abraham and Sarah, and encompassed what is called the Hexateuch.

A viable answer lies in the fact that a primary function of the recitation of the Torah was to keep the identity of the faithful ever fresh in their minds no matter where they lived.[6] When, according to biblical tradition, Ezra the scribe brought the Torah in its final edited form from Babylonia to Jerusalem in c. 445 B.C.E. (Nehemiah 8), the many Jewish communities outside Palestine, especially the very large community in Babylonia (whence the official Talmud would eventually come), required assurance that they could retain their religious identity outside of Palestine/Israel. The hope for return to the land would henceforth be forever an integral aspect of the promises to Abraham and Sarah in the first place, while the primitive story of its original fulfillment in Joshua would become the first book in the prophetic corpus. The focus was both on the shape of the Torah, which would eventually be recited in full in annual or triennial cycles, and on its function in Jewish believing communities. The story of the entrance into the land was joined with the Early Prophets as the beginning of the venture in Israel rather than as the climax of the Abraham-Sarah story and its promises.[7]

Canon in the sense of *norma normans*, or function, focuses on the interrelationship of a canon's stability and its adaptability, as well as on the hermeneutics which would render the stable adaptable in the ongoing lives of believing communities in ever changing circumstances. While differing denominations might have canons that differ in content and order of books, from Protestant to Orthodox, from Jewish to Christian, they all have found ways to seek their Bible's relevancy to their ever changing lives. The hermeneutics by which they do so is the mid-term between adaptability and stability. Canon in this sense is best understood as a paradigm of the monotheizing process compiled over a period of fifteen hundred years, from the Bronze Age to the Roman, and compressed into a disparate but single body of literature.[8]

Text and Canon

These and similar observations have led to a near revolution in the technical exercise of "text criticism," which tries to determine the best text of the Bible from the hundreds of ancient and medieval manuscripts available today. From the beginning of the eighteenth century until recently, text criticism mostly was understood to have as its task the establishment of "the original text" of a specific portion of Scripture. Text criticism therefore was servant to and part of historical criticism. One decided by critical theory what a given biblical author probably ought to have written or said, and then one cast about among the available texts and early versions to try to reconstruct the text in the light of the theory advanced. The goal was to come as close as possible to what the ancient individual contributor actually said or wrote. A number of English translations done in the middle of this century, such as the New English Bible and the Jerusalem Bible, exhibit that desired goal; they are full of scholarly emendations and conjectures about how texts might originally have read, whether there is existing manuscript evidence for such readings or not. Such a procedure in effect decanonized the text because it bypassed the actual manuscripts inherited from ancient communities of faith, instead attempting to reach back of them to so-called original speeches and compositions.

To counter this procedure, the United Bible Societies Project in Stuttgart and the Hebrew University Bible Project in Jerusalem undertook to rewrite the history of the transmission of the text.[9] The former project, launched in 1969, intended for the First Testament what it had done for the Second, which has produced *The Greek New Testament* and ancillary literature. The latter project has produced five volumes of preliminary report, and Dominique Barthélemy has so far written and published two volumes of the projected six volumes of the final report.[10] The reasons each of the six invited scholars joined the project varied, but for the most part it was because it had become clear that text criticism as it was currently practiced was deeply flawed. The apparatuses in the four editions of *Biblia Hebraica* reinforce the hermeneutic of suspicion toward the Masoretes that began with Luther in the sixteenth century.[11]

The importance of the relation of studies in canon to studies in texts became increasingly clear. The availability of a plethora of biblical manuscripts through the discovery of the Dead Sea Scrolls indicated quite clearly that before there had been stabilization of the text into a proto-Masoretic form, by the end of the first century of the common era, there had been a lengthy period of textual fluidity reaching back through the earliest manuscripts available. The practice of rendering the texts adaptable and relevant to the needs of believing communities was evident in the copying and translating done for those communities. The process of stabilization of the Hebrew texts became rather intense in the period beginning in the middle of the first century B.C.E. and culminating in the proto-Masoretic biblical manuscripts discovered in the caves other than at Qumran, principally at Murraba'at and Masada.

The so-called hermeneutic rules or techniques of Hillel, Ishmael, and finally the official thirty-two rules associated with Jehudah ha-Nassi, were devised and came about to bring controls on the totally natural and ongoing efforts in the believing communities to render the increasingly stable text as adaptable as it had been in the earlier oral period and then in the period of textual fluidity. One aspect of the stabilization process was a decisive move in Judaism toward verbal inspiration of Scripture away from earlier, more shamanistic views.[12] The move to a view of literal inspiration soon followed, which led to the practice of *gematria* and other such interpretations, and to the ultimate Masoretic concern with ever more accurate modes of scribal copying of texts as witnessed by the introduction of scribal *masorot* in the lateral, top, and bottom margins and as end-notes, and by the counting of words and even letters, recorded in end-notes for later scribes to utilize.

The more one works on facsimiles and microfilms of ancient manuscripts the more one sees misconceptions and perpetuation of errors in critical apparatuses and in commentaries. After the narrative (hi) story related in the Torah and Early Prophets (Genesis to 2 Kings) the order of books is only relatively stable until printing was invented. Printing provided as great a stimulus to stabilizing the order of books after Kings as had the invention of the codex centuries earlier. The order

of the Five Scrolls in the *Ketuvim* varies considerably in the various manuscripts, with no apparent pattern evident. Ruth often is the first book
in the *Ketuvim*. With the advent of printing, early editions of the Jewish
Bible placed the five in the calendar order of the four feasts and one
fast at which each was read (the Song of Songs at Passover, Ruth at
Weeks, Lamentations on the Ninth of Ab, Qohelet at Tabernacles, and
Esther at Purim); but apparently no medieval manuscript so ordered
them. A simple example of the perpetuation of a late custom is that
of *Biblia Hebraica—Kittel* (3rd edition) and *Biblia Hebraica—Stuttgartensia*
continuing to place Chronicles at the end of the *Ketuvim*, whereas the
great Tiberian manuscripts including Aleppensis and Leningradensis
(the latter being the single text used in *Biblia Hebraica*, and the former
the single text used by the Hebrew University Bible Project) both place
Chronicles first in the *Ketuvim*. Israel Yeivin recently affirmed, "The
order of the Books in the Torah and the Former Prophets has been
established from earliest times; however, the order of the books in the
Latter Prophets and the Writings is not fixed."[13]

One cannot entirely trust any of the apparatuses in BHK[1-3] or BHS,
a major reason for the establishment of the Ancient Biblical Manuscript
Center in Claremont. Scholarship has too long been captive of the conceptions of earlier scholars as well as their errors. Printed critical editions of any manuscript of necessity reflect the interests, concerns, and
biases of competence of their editors as well as the scholarly *Zeitgeist*
of the time of the editor.[14]

Canon as Paradigm

Studies in text criticism thus led to the conviction that the results of
earlier studies in the history of canon formation were also flawed. A
new look was required at how canonization actually took place. It became clear that those earlier studies had been largely based on extraca-
nonical references in Sirach, 2 Maccabees, Josephus, the Second Testament, and the Talmud.[15] Careful study of the actual manuscripts
bequeathed to us by ancient believing communities gives a different picture from that which the earlier focus on extrabiblical lists and supposedly authoritative councils had yielded. This led to the question of what
a canon really is.

Whereas the Koran may be characterized as a human record of a
revelation from God, the Jewish and Christian Bibles may be viewed
as human responses to divine revelations. When one uses the word
"canon" one must specify to which denomination or community of faith
it refers even within Judaism and Christianity; within both there is now
and was in antiquity more than one canon in the sense of limited lists

of sacred books considered canonical. The literature considered canonical by the Jewish denomination at Qumran was apparently open-ended. The library there reflects the prestabilization period quite well, both in terms of some individual books, such as the Psalter, and in terms of the high respect shown there for what we call apocryphal books. Some scholars think that the Torah or Temple Scroll from Qumran Cave 11 was deemed to be as authoritative as the Pentateuch itself.[16] The Church of the Latter Day Saints is perhaps the latest Christian denomination to claim the canon to be open-ended, and Jacob Neusner (and not a few orthodox Jews) uses the word "canon" to refer to the rabbinic corpus of literature. If one looks for clues in actual extant manuscripts for the closure of the Christian canon one may be somewhat disappointed: there are only three uncials and fifty-six minuscules which contain the whole of the Catholic-Protestant New Testament; and while there are 2,328 manuscripts of the Gospels there are only 287 of the Book of Revelation.[17]

Jewish and Christian Bibles may best be understood as paradigms of the struggles of Israel, early Judaism, and early Christianity to pursue the integrity of reality, or the Oneness of God. The popular concept of canon as a closed box of ancient jewels, which somehow continue to be valuable and negotiable, needs reexamination. Since canons have varied so much through the ages, even within orthodox Judaism and Christianity, one needs to take seriously not only the shape (*norma normata*) of canon, but also the function (*norma normans*) of what is considered canonical.

Intertextuality

Consideration of the function of the canonical begins with appreciation of biblical intertextuality from the earliest discernible strata to the last editorial hands. Important to sound exegesis of any biblical passage is discerning the function of recognizable traditions. The key word is function, and in order to be able to perceive how the tradent wanted his or her appeal to the tradition to work, one has to try to discern the ancient hermeneutics by which the tradent understood that tradition and how he or she marshaled it to the point of the new composition. There is hardly a passage in the Bible outside reports of court or temple (civil or cultic, even wisdom) records which does not build upon older traditions, and invariably they are fluid in reference and citation (except for Mic. 3:12 in Jer. 26:18, which is almost verbatim). The fluidity of citation which marks most of the First Testament functioning in the Second is standard within the First and common in early Jewish literature. That which was commonly viewed as authoritative from the past was first and foremost relevant and adaptable; its relative stability of phrasing was important largely for the recognition of its authority.

The stability and the adaptability of authoritative and eventually of canonical traditions must be seen as complementary. Paraphrase of the canonical or older word in the composition of a new word can only go so far, or the authority of community recognition of the older word is lost. This was undoubtedly a factor in the move toward stabilization in the first century B.C.E. While biblical exegetes are not prepared to say with some literary critics that every time a text is reread it is rewritten, some of us nonetheless recognize that every time a text or tradition is cited it is resignified to some extent. This recognition is quite important in understanding the canonical nature of biblical literature. And each time one observes the resignification of the older word in the newer, one must try to discern the ancient tradents' hermeneutics; in the Bible that entails discerning their view of reality, that is, their view of God.[18]

There are many passages in the Bible where the Torah story is referred to, whether in the histories, the prophets, the psalmists, or the Second Testament. The tradents' views of God, or reality, determined how they applied the text or tradition. This is especially evident in working on the phenomenon of true and false prophecy in either testament; for in those instances where ancient contemporaries disagreed on the significance, or resignification, of a common text or tradition, it was hermeneutics that divided them.[19] Neither personal character, nor good or bad theology, is a criterion for discerning true and false prophets; the hermeneutic they exhibit, in applying authoritative texts and traditions to the situations they face, makes the crucial difference. The very sorts of interpretations opposed by the so-called true prophets in the pre-exilic period are presented in Isaiah 40–55 and other exilic prophets as prophetic truth. The hermeneutics evident in the pre-exilic prophets could, however, include declamations of judgment not only against Israel but also against foreign nations.

Studies in biblical intertextuality led to the view that three factors, which may be thought to form a triangle, have to be considered together to understand the function of the canonical in the new situation: the written text or oral tradition called on, the sociopolitical situation to which the adaptation is made, and the hermeneutics by which the older word functions in the new. Other factors are multivalency and pluralism. Multivalency, because the nature of canonical literature is that it passed the tests of value and cogency over a number of generations, and in a number of communities, before it finally was considered sacred. Everything that made it into a canon had first to pass through and function

in the lives of believing communities, specifically the liturgical and in-
structional programs of believing communities. Nothing made it in by
a side door, not even if attributed to an ancient, highly regarded name.
It has been observed that much of biblical literature is pseudepigraphic,
and that is true.[20] But so is much of nonbiblical or noncanonical literature. Attributing a piece of literature to a famous ancient name would
not have been sufficient to establish it with the people of a believing
community if the composition itself did not interest them or meet their
needs.

Equally important is recognizing the Bible's pluralism. It has been
argued that pluralism is too modern a term to apply to the Bible.[21]
Nevertheless, the Bible, whether Jewish or Christian, is a collection of
literature deriving from five different cultural eras from the Bronze
Age to the Roman. It bears in it the cultural traits of the west Semitic
and Hamitic worlds, the Persian, the Hellenic, and the Hellenistic. It
is expressed in the idioms and mores of those cultures and of many
locales.

Four points about its pluralism need to be made: (a) the Bible has
its own internal self-corrective apparatus; (b) no theological or social
construct based on the Bible long endures without a prophetic challenge
to it from within the Bible itself; (c) no one community of faith or mode
of theology can encompass the whole canon any more than one theology
can encompass the concept of God: some communities need to say
"debts" in the Lord's Prayer so others can say "transgressions"; some
need to stress that Christ's sacrifice was "once for all" so that others
can celebrate Christ's perpetual sacrifice in the mass; and (d) if the Bible
as canon is viewed not as a box of jewels but as a paradigm of ancient
struggles to monotheize, then its limited pluralism may provide a sufficient model or paradigm for modern efforts to pursue the integrity
of reality in a seemingly more pluralistic world.

The fact is that the Bible contains multiple voices, and not only in
passages clearly recording differences between disagreeing colleagues
(so-called true and false prophets), but between the priestly and the
prophetic, between Wisdom and tradition, between the orthodox and
the questioning voices of prophets such as Jeremiah in his confessions,
between Job and his friends who represented aspects of orthodoxy, between Qohelet and the Torah, between Jonah and Nahum (both of
whom addressed God's concern for Nineveh), among varied voices
within a book like Isaiah, between Paul and James, and even among
the Gospels with their varying views of what God was doing in Christ.
And these are only a few of the intrabiblical dialogues one might mention. One needs also to recognize the measure of pluralism in the doublets and triplets in the Bible, the same thing told in quite different

ways, making different even contradicting points. We should celebrate the fact that the Second Testament includes four quite different Gospels and all the riches of their differences.

It is in large measure because of this kind of limited pluralism that the Bible has spawned some six hundred denominations. The Bible has steadily through the centuries given rise to dissenting voices about what it says on crucial matters. Challenges to the orthodoxy of one view come in their turn to be challenged by others.

Honesty demands recognition of the Bible's internal dialogues. It is healthy to listen in on them and learn just how impossible it is to limit God or reality to any one set of propositions. To insist that the Bible is harmonious or even homogeneous has led to diabolical abuses. If someone challenges a dogma or view based on portions of the Bible, the response is often that "the Bible" supports or teaches the view espoused, meaning thereby that the Bible is totally consistent on the point; and often those making the claim simply refuse honestly to admit biblical pluralism out of fear of loss of the kind of authority they think the Bible gives them. What results is that the dogmatist has both God and the Bible reduced to a certain schema in support of what he or she believes independently to be true. If a countervailing view from the Bible is submitted, the biblicist then resorts to the ploy that the contradictory passage is not yet fully understood. Fundamentalism of this sort becomes almost purely a political ideology.

Canonical Hermeneutics

In our understanding of canon as paradigm, the ancient hermeneutics which lie unrecorded in almost every page of the Bible may be as canonical as the ancient texts themselves.[22] Not only are such intra-biblical hermeneutics discernible where clearly recognized older traditions and texts are resignified in a later text, they are also discernible in three other ways: in the adaptation of non-Israelite traditions or international wisdom into biblical literature; in the determination of a text's eligibility to progress toward canonical status; and in what can only be called the monotheizing process.

When duplicate literary materials are available from other ancient Near Eastern cultures one has a control factor for discerning how such international wisdom was adapted to biblical use. There was apparently a four-fold process: it was depolytheized, Yahwized, monotheized, and Israelitized.[23] Not all the steps were fully carried out, fortunately, so that we often get a glimpse of the process at work.

Mention of gods other than those who could be resignified as Yahweh, or at least as one God, was eradicated. Where suggestions of a number of gods remained they were relegated to membership in a heavenly council. The heavenly council, the biblical accommodation to pantheon and to the human tendency to polytheism, but actually the best guarantee against it, was probably made up of gods Israel came in contact with in her long journey and history from the earliest days. Such gods were retired, as it were, put on a pension and consigned to duty in the heavenly council under the aegis of the One God who alone had power and authority (see, e.g., Pss. 82 and 89, 1 Kings 22, Isa. 40:1 –11, and Job 1). They could serve either as ministering angels, or in the heavenly army, or in the heavenly choir (see, e.g., Ps. 148).

Those Albrecht Alt called tutelary deities, such as the Shield of Abraham, the Fear of Isaac, and the Mighty One of Jacob, would simply give their names over to the One God as epithets. The rabbinic tradition that God has seventy names derived from the monotheizing process. *El Elyon*, or God Most High, was probably the high god of ancient Jebus, or Canaanite Jerusalem. *El Shaddai* would perhaps have been a mountain god. The One God took over the attributes and functions of the gods and goddesses of other peoples. Yahweh thus has male and female attributes as well as the functions of the otherwise heavenly, earthly, and chthonian deities, the last accounting for what has been called the dark side of Yahweh.

It is clear from the discovery of many female goddess figurines, as well as from some inscriptions, that popular theology in ancient Israel was about as polytheistic as elsewhere. The canonical process filtered out what in itself did not have a monotheizing thrust or could not itself be monotheized in one way or another. If one takes seriously all the laws against polytheism and all the prophetic declamations against it, one must allow for an actual history of polytheism in popular and even official thought (see, e.g., Jer. 44 and Ezek. 16).

The next step was to call Yahweh, or at least God, what other peoples called by another name or by other names. Stories familiar in international wisdom became Yahwistic stories, whether creation stories, flood stories, lists of ancient worthies, stories of child sacrifice, tales of royal courts and their courtiers, dramas about foreign *magoi*, etc.[24] It is interesting to note the texts where the word God seemed sufficient without invoking the name Yahweh; but it is also interesting to note the texts where foreigners call upon Yahweh, as in the case of Balaam (Num. 22–24). The exilic Isaiah was satisfied to say that Cyrus of Persia did not know Yahweh even while Yahweh was acting in and through Cyrus (Isa. 45:4).

The third step is the most interesting, the monotheizing. It would not be sufficient simply to reduce many gods to the status of pawns in heaven or collapse them into one; nor would it have been sufficient to superimpose Yahweh's name over names of other gods. Where the monotheizing step is most impressive is in those instances where Yahweh takes over the work of destroying deities, as in Exod. 4:24–26, and indeed in the killing of Egypt's firstborn in the Exodus as well as the Egyptian army at the Red Sea. In the latter cases one might simply take it that Yahweh was a highly partisan denomi*natio*nal deity who fought as Holy Warrior for his own chosen people, but that Yahwistic function is anticipated and adumbrated in the Exodus 4 passage where Yahweh threatens to kill Moses himself.

Though some source critics claim that these three short verses could easily be excised without disturbing the rest of Exodus 4, in fact they render the "saving" work of Yahweh, in the Passover and at the sea, theologically acceptable and not simply a polytheizing story of national superiority. Exod. 4:21–26 reads as follows:

> 21 And Yahweh said to Moses, "In your proceeding to return to Egypt, note carefully all the miracles which I have placed in your power, and execute them in Pharaoh's presence; but I will encourage his own thinking so that he not let my people go. 22 And you shall say to Pharaoh, 'thus says Yahweh, "Israel is my son, my first born. 23 And I said to you, 'let my people go that they may serve me, but you refused to let them go; hence I am going to kill your son, your first born.'"'" 24 Then on the way, at a lodging, Yahweh encountered him and sought to kill him. 25 But Zipporah took a flint, cut off her son's foreskin, touched his [Moses'] genitals [with it] and said, "You are thus a bridegroom of blood to me." 26 Then he left him alone. Whereupon she recited, "A bridegroom of blood for circumcisions."

Just as interesting is how the text insists that Yahweh hardened the heart, or better, encouraged the thinking of Pharaoh, when considering the demands of the community organizer who was himself already guilty of murder and had been a fugitive from justice.[25] Pharaoh is impressed over and over again by Moses's demonstrations but each time remembers his duty as Pharaoh and his responsibility to the Egyptian economy. He would finally back off each time from letting Moses pull the rug of cheap labor out from under his economy. What were they? Ingrates? After all, Egypt had supplied food to them when they had had droughts in Palestine. The text allows us to do the monotheizing ourselves because the text itself moves in that direction. The Torah story is about God's emancipation proclamation, not Pharaoh's. And ultimately it will be God's Torah and not Israel's alone. Why? Because the Exodus as canon can and, I think, should be read as a paradigm of God's signifying one of the many slave rebellions in the late Bronze Age as the Exodus, and not as one denomination's box of jewels which others come and steal.

The prophets later will agree with the so-called false prophets that

God was indeed Holy Warrior, but in the massive power flows in the ancient Near Eastern Iron Age, God would be at the head of the Assyrian or the Babylonian armies attacking Israel and invading Jerusalem. Isaiah will present perhaps the hardest thinking of all when he says that God actually commanded him in his early ministry to preach comfort to the people so that their hearts would be fat, their ears heavy, and their eyes closed (Isa. 6:9–10).

The first three Commandments of the ten are against polytheism (the fragmentation of truth or reality), against idolatry (worshipping creation instead of the Creator), and against taking the name of God in vain (co-opting the One God of all for a particular group, party, or point of view). They are perhaps the greatest challenge to the workings of the human psyche that it has ever confronted. The human mind just does not want to monotheize; it is repelled by aspects of it. But the Bible as canon does so. Not in all its parts equally well, but the thrust is there. And I am prepared to say that nothing that ends up in the Jewish or Christian canons can escape a rereading by a monotheizing hermeneutic. This is not to say that it was the intention of all the original authors. Clearly not. The question is whether one cannot take the monotheizing thrust of the Bible as a whole, that is as a canon, and go back and read the parts in the light of the whole. Unfortunately, those who claim to find their identity in these texts, including current believing communities, while commanded to do so rarely have ever done so.

The fourth step of Israelitizing was not always followed. Indeed the Flood story is a fine example of the failure to adapt this international story all the way. Instead of the ark's landing on Mt. Zion, as one might think it should, it lands on Ararat. The story remained universal even as Yahweh was being universalized.

These four steps are extrapolated from close study of many instances of borrowing from others, or simply claiming what was common wisdom of the ancient Near East and the later Hellenistic cultures. Graphically they might be seen as forming an arc. The move to depolytheize a non-Israelite or common bit of wisdom, law, proverb, or story might be seen as a thrust from the particular culture whence it came toward the universal; the move to monotheize constituted the further thrust toward affirming the integrity of reality beyond the fragmentation of truth inherent in polytheism; the moves to Yahwize and finally to Israelitize, while still affirming the monotheizing thrust, nonetheless should be seen as paradigmatic of reapplying the universal to the particular, in this case, the Abraham-Sarah story.

The Bible's hermeneutic bent toward the universal in its monotheizing thrust is thus matched by a countervailing incarnational thrust. The

Bible, when viewed as God's story, presents a series of divine pastoral calls, in judgment and in grace—on God's first parishioners in Eden's bower, on Abraham and Sarah in Haran, on Pharaoh to release Sarah from his harem, on Jacob at the Jabbok, on Joseph in the pit, on the slaves in the huts and hovels of Egypt, on Moses on the mountain and in the desert, on David behind the flock, and finally, perhaps, on and in a baby Jew threatened by Herod's jealous sword. Without the particular the universal would be lost, and vice versa: without the Yahwizing the monotheizing would have no particular base in the human experiment; and without the monotheizing the Yahwizing would remain tribalistic.

The source-critical view that the two principal appelatives for God, *'elohim* and *yaweh*, derive from two distinct written or even oral sources in Israelite antiquity, while quite possibly historically true, must finally be absorbed into the Bible's canonical pluralism which alone can exhibit its overarching integrity. This hermeneutic clue pervades the Bible. For example, the two accounts of Creation, in Genesis 1 and in Genesis 2, even though they may indeed come from quite different ancient cultic sources in Israel, make by the sheer fact of their successiveness a uniquely poignant statement that could not be made otherwise, either by one of the chapters alone or by a homogeneous blend of both: God is at once awesome, transcendent, and majestic, *and* pastoral, immanent, and self-giving. Nor should the two be harmonized; for it is in the *plerosis* and the *kenosis* they suggest that the integrity of reality is indicated even though it can never be fully contained by doctrine.

The title of the present volume is derived from Deut. 30:12 through a story recorded in the Talmud in which the phrase is cited as affirmation that once God had given Torah to Moses and Israel it took on a life of its own. Lodged neither in Platonic ideal nor Aristotelian form, Torah lives instead among those of the divinely circumcised heart (Deut. 30:6); it is in their mouth and in their heart to do it (30:14). Israel had been exhorted to circumcise their own hearts (Deut. 10:16; cf. Jer. 4:4); but they could not do it by themselves, so God in the adversity of exile and deprivation has done it for them, performing through adversity a kind of divine operation, an open-heart surgery (Jer. 30:12 –17, 31:31–34; cf. Hos. 6:1–3, Ezek. 36:26–27, Isa. 51:7). The operation has rendered Israel as a whole, corporately, similar to the prophets earlier in whose mouths God had placed the divine Word or words (Jer. 1:9, 15:16, 20:9; Ezek. 2:8–3:3) that needed to be said in their situations and in their times. That Word, or Torah, though stable enough, is not statically to be found in a heavenly treasure, but is ever alive and adaptable to new situations, as and when they arise.

Paul's understanding of Deut. 30:12–13 lies along the same trajectory

but in celebration of the incarnation of Torah in Christ (Rom. 10:6–
10).[26] Rabbi Joshua appeals to the ongoing exegetical process of Torah
in Israel; Paul bases his christology on the nearness of the Word of
God ("in your mouth and in your heart"), Jesus Christ as experienced
in the Christian community. Both christologies, Paul's and Joshua's, have
wrested the whole concept of Torah, hence canon, from those who
would lock God into particular boxes, and have placed it securely in
dynamically conceived processes responsive to ever changing needs.

The Canonical Process

What became canonical was not only that which was multivalent and
pluralistic enough, but also that which had the rugged power for life
that would see Israel and Judah through their death throes and into
the resurrection called Judaism, God's first New Israel (Ezek. 37). That
power claimed that God was One, not only the God of life but also
of death (Deut. 32:39; 1 Sam. 2:6), not only the God of risings and
successes but also the God of defeats and fallings (1 Sam. 27–28; Luke
1:52–53). The climax of the story of the two promises to Abraham and
Sarah in Genesis is reached in 1 Kings 10, which tells of a famous sovereign of a foreign land, the Queen of Sheba, coming to Jerusalem to
be an international witness to the fulfillment of the promises of progeny
and a place to live.[27] But beginning with the next chapter, 1 Kings 11,
it is all downhill until both Israel and Judah are destroyed. In the Jewish
canon, Kings is followed not by Chronicles but by the Latter Prophets
to explain the defeat and to affirm that God could restore the fallen
and could resurrect the dead, even turn an Assyrian siege-stone into
a precious cornerstone of a sure foundation (Isa. 28:16).

Such is the monotheizing process which became the Bible's own basic
canonical hermeneutic. And it is so not because some final great redactor waved an editorial wand over all the disparate but compressed literature called Bible.[28] It is so because what got picked up and read again
and again, and was recommended to the children and to other communities nearby, and continued to give value and to give life, was what made
it into the canon. Morton Smith seems satisfied to say that the reason
the Bible was finally monotheistic (a term I prefer not to use) was that
the "Yahweh-only political party" won out in the fifth and later centuries
B.C.E.[29] Perhaps. But we have to ask a further question: why did that
party win out, if party it was? The word "canon" is often used in a
largely political sense; even so such users occasionally recognize the factors contributing to canonization of emulation, by artists of earlier art-

ists, and of timing, but rarely recognize, except implicitly, the factor of readers themselves.[30]

What deep-seated need of ancient Jewish and Christian communities did the monotheizing remembrances and recitals meet? They needed to know there was integrity to reality, both ontological and ethical, that good and bad, winning and losing, light and darkness could be seen as parts of a whole. Human experience of reality is its ambiguities, as Reinhold Niebuhr was wont to say, and as the Bible in its limited pluralism realistically portrays. But what the Bible also very realistically witnesses to in the splendor and the squalor, the risings and the fallings of life, is the human need for belief in the integrity of reality, the very Oneness of God. In this canonical view, God thus becomes vulnerable to the human scene of protagonists and antagonists, pros and cons, by granting divine fellowship and even sharing human suffering.

Christians would add to the paradigm that that fellowship and vulnerability took an ultimate shape in another defeat and fall, the crucifixion of the Christ, and in another rising, the resurrection through and beyond death. One does not need to affirm Christ's resurrection as historical event to assert the canonical paradigm which affirms that God is the God of death as well as of life. If the Second Testament is read by a monotheizing hermeneutic, then the Jews and Romans portrayed in it would be read as humans in another not uncommon but deeply moving and poignant paradigm of acceptance and rejection, of protagonists and antagonists, and not as the ancestors of current Jews and gentiles. And Christ would be read as the deity's Christ and not as the Christians' Christ. In such a rereading Pharisees might mirror Presbyterians or Catholics, and Romans might mirror Americans in yet another monotheizing rereading of the Second Testament text. Just as the Torah in a monotheizing reading is God's Torah and God's emancipation proclamation for humanity, so the Christ is God's Christ. To fail to monotheize these two great canonical events is to tribalize them and engage in what R. G. Collingwood called human corruption of consciousness which is human sinfulness.

To go back and read all the parts in the light of the whole would revolutionize reading of the text. Such a rereading would for most people amount to a rewriting of the text but without changing a single word preserved on leather, parchment, and papyrus. It could revive Judaism as Judaism and not only as Zionism, and it could revive Christianity apart from its deepest sin of all, the tendency to make Christ an idol of a new though mixed tribe.

GENESIS 22:
THE SACRIFICE OF SARAH

Phyllis Trible

This essay plays with tradition and innovation. It interprets Genesis 22 in context, as it appears and as it subverts appearances.[1]

A Prologue for Orientation

Traditionally, two topics identify the story: the sacrifice or binding (Akedah) of Isaac and the testing or trial of Abraham. The first focuses on the son as object and potential victim of a divine command; the second on the father as subject and potential perpetrator of the command. These topics provide the common ground upon which author and reader stand.[2] We proceed, then, from familiar terrain. But our subtitle indicates a movement into unknown territory: "The Sacrifice of Sarah" yields surprise, elicits puzzlement, and builds suspense. Innovation separates reader from author because it indicates that the latter knows what the former does not. Near the end we regain parity, only to face another challenge.

A rhetorical critical method and a feminist hermeneutic shape the study.[3] Though insightful analyses of Genesis 22 are already available,[4] a nonpatriarchal perspective requires a thorough rereading. At first method prevails, but in the end hermeneutics. This skewed interplay orients the reader while subtly disorienting the text.

Introduction

With the narrator as interpreter, continuation and surprise begin the story, "And it came to pass after these events that God, indeed God, tested Abraham" (22:1).[5] The little phrase, "after these events," collects a tortuous saga of multiple dimensions. Long ago and far away, a preface of genealogy and geography initiates the action. Terah, descendant of Shem, takes his son Abram, his barren daughter-in-law Sarai, and his

170

grandson Lot from Ur of the Chaldeans to Haran (11:10–32). There Terah dies, and the narrative proper commences. Swiftly the story moves: the call of Abram, his journey with Lot and Sarai to the promised land, a sojourn in Egypt, struggles to secure the land, the rejection of Ishmael, the destruction of Sodom and Gomorrah with its aftermath, the debacle in Gerar, and throughout it all the haunting specter of no heir. But at long last God keeps promise. Sarah conceives and bears Isaac, the child Laughter. Then life resumes with the expulsion of Hagar and Ishmael, his near death in the wilderness, and a dispute over wells in Beersheba. Barrenness, deception, warfare, surrogacy, manipulation, destruction, incest, jealousy, envy, rivalry, and malice (12:1–19:34)—all press upon a single line, fraught with the burden of continuity. "And it came to pass after these events. . . ."[6]

Surprise joins that burden. "God, indeed God, tested Abraham." Though such a procedure is implicit throughout the preceding stories, only here does the verb *test (nissāh)* appear.[7] The explicit use startles the reader. It portends a crisis beyond the usual tumult. How many times does Abraham have to be tested? Enough is enough is enough. After delays and obstacles Isaac, the child of promise, has come. Let the story now end happily, providing readers and characters respite from struggle and suspense. But vocabulary and syntax prevent such a respite. The divine generic *Elohim* occurs with the definite article *hā*, suggesting "the God, the very God." Reversing the usual order of a Hebrew sentence, this subject precedes its verb. The narrator makes clear that an extraordinary divine act is taking place. "God, indeed God, tested Abraham."

As the narrator's interpretation of what follows, the verb *test* evokes ambiguous responses. What kind of God tests human beings?[8] The kind who remains faithful even when Abraham fails? If so, the reader need not fear the outcome of this episode. Why, then, have the test at all? Does it imply that this time God might punish failure? Or have the advent of Isaac and the expulsion of Ishmael brought a new dynamic to the story, an unprecedented crisis of faith? Whatever, by using the verb *test*, the narrator poses a problem rather than providing an explanation. The ambiguity of surprise joins the burden of continuation. "And it came to pass after these events that God, indeed God, tested Abraham."

God's Command

In this exquisitely wrought narrative, the introduction leads to three sections (22:1b–2; 22:3–10; 22:11–18) plus the conclusion (22:19). The first section is divine command, where the narrator recedes, giving only verbal indication of dialogue. God calls (*'mr*) Abraham to attention by speaking his name: "Abraham." Matching the divine utterance comes the human response: "And Abraham said (*'mr*), "*Hinnēnî*." This is no simple reply, but a strong word of immediacy, even obedience. Older translations use the interjection, "Behold, I."[9] If we reject that archaism, let us retain its power. "Here now am I," at your service, giving full and total attention. Simply, even naively proclaimed, this obedient stance precedes a command of terror. It is carefully constructed, with the particle *nā'* joining the imperative "take" (*lqḥ*) to suggest consequence: "Take, so I require of you." The grammatical combination indicates that God knows well what is coming. Soon Abraham also will know because the object of the verb is not a simple word but heavy-laden language. It moves from the generic term of kinship, "your son," through the exclusivity of relationship, "your only one," through the intimacy of bonding, "whom you love," to climax in the name that fulfills promise, the name of laughter and joy, the name *yishāq* (Isaac). Language accumulates attachments: "your son, your only one, whom you love, Isaac." Thus far every divine word (imperative, particle, and objects) shows the magnitude of the test. Yet the horror awaits disclosure.

After the divine imperative *take* comes a second command, *go*. Familiar language harks back to the call of Abram in Genesis 12:1. There in a two-word formula, *lēk-lᵉkā*, God orders Abraham, "Go you." The prepositional phrases that follow move from generic identification of land through particular designation of clan to intimate specification of family, thereby isolating Abram. (He is not, however, cut off from Sarai and Lot.) "Go you from your country, and from your clan, and from your father's house to a land that I will show you." Abram receives no security for the present, only promise for the future. "I will make of you a great nation." The divine assurance vies with the narrated preface that "Sarai is barren; she has no child" (11:30). Threatened by barrenness, the verb *go* constitutes a radical act. Trials and troubles ensue, but the outcome is fruitful, as subsequent episodes relate. Now, after all these events, the same words *lēk-lᵉkā* occur again. "Go you," this time "to the land of Moriah." As it was in the beginning, so now in the end, "Go you."

At the beginning, this command, though scary, held promise and hope; at the end, how different is the implication. Yet the reader and Abraham do not immediately know the difference. Allusions to Genesis 12 may mislead. Only with the third imperative and its cognate object does the shock come: "Offer him there as a burnt offering upon one of the mountains which I shall tell you." The "him" is "your son, your only one, whom you love, Isaac." In other words, sacrifice the one to whom you are attached; "offer him upon one of the mountains of which I shall tell you." The non-specificity of the location matches the non-specificity in the call "to a land that I shall show you." But the meanings of the two occasions, the call and the test, decisively oppose each other. The promise of the beginning, "I shall make of you a great nation," and its potential fulfillment through Isaac unravel in the test. As Abraham once broke with the past, so now he must destroy the future.[10] Genesis 22:1b–2 intends and portends the unwriting of Genesis 12:1 –3. If the imperative of the call be radical, how ominous is the imperative of the test. It awaits the response of Abraham, to be given in the second section of the story.

Abraham's Response

In the call episode Abram's answer is succinct and unequivocal. "So Abram went as Yhwh had told him" (12:9a RSV). In the sacrifice story his response is lengthy and hesitant. It alternates between narrated and direct discourse to vary the perspective of text and reader (22:3–10). Four units constitute this section of mounting suspense as murder draws near (22:3, 4–6, 7–8, 9–10).

1. Obedience Begins

Within the opening unit (22:3), the divine imperatives of section one, *take* and *go*, reappear as indicatives. "Take your son" becomes "Abraham took . . . his son." "Go yourself to the land of Moriah" becomes "Abraham went to the place of which the-God had told him." So far obedience prevails; its fulfillment depends upon the third verb, *offer* or *sacrifice*. No indicative match for that verb appears here, but a link occurs through the noun *'olāh*, burnt offering. The connection suggests yet does not confirm perfect obedience. Besides responding to vocabulary in section one, verse three is an artfully arranged sentence that harbingers the destiny of Isaac:

> So-rose-early Abraham in-the-morning
> > and-saddled his-ass
> > > and-took two-of his-young-men with-him
> > > > and <u>Isaac his-son</u>
> > > and-cut wood-for a-burnt-offering
> > > and-arose
> > and-went to-the-place which God, indeed God, said-to-him. (22:3).[11]

At the beginning three indicative verbs describe Abraham's meticulous activity: rose, saddled, and took. An appropriate object or adverbial phrase attends each verb, though significantly the last of these verbs, *took*, has two objects: "two of his young men with him" and "Isaac his son." Content and structure indicate that stress comes at the end: "Isaac his son." These words stand apart for emphasis. The remainder of the sentence underscores the point. Like the beginning, three indicative verbs describe Abraham's preparation: cut, arose, and went. In the center, framed by six verbs that signal terrible obedience (rose, saddled, took; cut, arose, went), is the phrase "Isaac his son." The father's activity surrounds his son not to protect him in life but to prepare him for death.

2. Obedience Continues

Unit two (22:4–6) begins by advancing the story three days but still falls short of the destination. "On the third day Abraham lifted up his eyes and saw the place from a distance" (22:4). References to sight, especially the verb *see* (*r'h*), are proleptic, anticipating a major motif. For the time being, however, the story turns to other vocabulary. It also switches to dialogue. Abraham speaks (*'mr*) to his young men (*na'ar*). "Stay-yourselves here with-the-ass" (22:5a). They are not to witness the deed. He continues, "I and-the-young man (*na'ar*), we-will-go over-there, and-we-will-worship, and-we-will-return to-you" (22:5b). The speech achieves ambivalent effects. Separation and union contend; detachment and attachment compete. Opposing the category young men (you) is the set Abraham and Isaac (we). Yet use of the term *na'ar* (young man) connects the two groups. Abraham identifies his companion by the same word that the narrator has employed to cite the attendants. "I and the young man," he says, not "I and my son" or "I and Isaac." Otherness undercuts oneness; detachment vies with attachment. Establishing distance, *na'ar* avoids the pain of paternal bonding. "Your son, your only son, whom you love, Isaac" in the language of God has become in the speech of Abraham "the young man," like the other "young men."

Father and son are united, however, in three first person plural verbs that follow one upon the other: "we will go, and we will worship, and we will return to you." If the young men, the attendants, are suspicious, the last verb reassures them that the end will restore the beginning. Abraham makes no distinction between the subjects of the three verbs. Separation will return to union. While allaying suspicion, his speech also promotes deception. Abraham may misrepresent what will happen in order to accomplish it. Or perhaps he misunderstands what is at stake.

Or perhaps he knows what the reader does not. In any event, his first words confound characters and readers.

These words yield to the narrator whose structure, syntax, and vocabulary sound familiar rhythms:

> And-<u>took</u> Abraham the-wood-of the-burnt-offering
> and-laid [it] upon-<u>Isaac his-son</u>
> and-<u>took</u> in-his-hand the-fire and-the-knife. (22:6abc)[12]

Three verbs provide the action. The first and last are identical, "took" (*lqḥ*). They allude to the divine command, "take" (22:2), and the response "he took . . . his son Isaac" (22:3). This time the objects, wood of the burnt offering and fire and knife, surround "Isaac his son." Ironies abound. Isaac carries the wood that will ignite him. Yet unkindled it is not dangerous material, unlike the fire and the knife that Abraham takes in his own hand.[13] The father embraces his son with potential destruction even as he protects him from immediate danger. Syntactically and thematically this sentence echoes verse three to trap Isaac. A narrated conclusion pairs unequals as it unites father and son: "So-they-went, the-two-of-them, together" (22:6d). The report plays on the theme of union and separation. "I and the young man, we will go," Abraham said earlier in a speech that established both distance (detachment) and inseparability (attachment). That ambivalence hovers subtly in the juxtaposition of "two" and "together." "Two" designates separate entities while "together" merges them. "So they went, the two of them, together." Silence speaks.

3. Isaac Interrupts

The poignant conclusion of unit two also advances the story. "They went." But Isaac interrupts, initiating unit three (22:7–8). Structurally, the narrator shows this break in Abraham's obedient journey by repeating the entire conclusion of unit three at the end of unit four (22:8b) so that the narrative later resumes by returning to the place before interruption. Thus, the sentence, "So-they-went, the-two-of-them, together," forms an inclusio around the words of Isaac and Abraham. It holds together these two, son and father.

Relational language within heightens the unfolding terror. "And-said (*'mr*) Isaac to-Abraham his-father. And-he-said: 'My-father!'" (*'ābî*). Once God addressed the patriarch by name (22:1); now Isaac employs a term of intimate possession. Replying as he did to God with a strong word of immediacy, *hinnēnî*, Abraham adds the possessive vocative, "my-son" (*bᵉnî*). Again, the language suggests full attention, bound this time to a precious relationship. "Here now am I" [here for you], my son." Isaac's next words play on that particle of attention and immediacy. "Look (*hinnēh*)," he speaks, "the fire and the wood, but where is the lamb for a burnt offering?" Two ingredients he specifies, fire and wood. The absence of another, lamb, he questions. Never does he acknowledge the knife, the instrument that will be raised to murder him.

Abraham's reply pits touching evasiveness against terrifying subtlety: "And-said ('*mr*) Abraham, 'God will-see-for-himself the-lamb for-a-burnt-offering, my-son'" (22:8). The Hebrew sentence, like the English, begins with God and ends with son, the two poles in Abraham's life. These boundaries conflict rather than harmonize. And indeed they must. Divine and human do not balance. God is the subject of action, power, and authority. This recognition may mean either good or bad news. To say that God will see to the lamb evades the choice, at least for a time. If the narrator has Abraham seeing (*r'h*) the place from afar off, Abraham has God seeing (*r'h*) to the sacrificial lamb before the place is reached. So God dominates the reply in this sentence where syntactic order reverses with subject preceding verb: "God, indeed God, will see to it. . . ."[14]

At the opposite end comes "my-son." Besides rounding off the sentence, this vocative reverberates with the companion address, "my-father." Thus the first word spoken in this entire unit (my- father) finds resonance in the last (my-son). The bonding of parent and child encircles their conversation. Nevertheless, the meaning of "my-son" remains indeterminate. Its juxtaposition to '*olāh*, burnt-offering, allows the horrendous reading of apposition. "God will see to the lamb for a burnt-offering," namely, "my-son." The language functions on two levels. "My-son" is both speech to and speech about, direct address and direct reference. What it gives in poignancy, it retracts in cruelty. With this word, dialogue ceases. The refrain that concludes the unit locks in the tenderness and the terror. Both father and son are trapped; they are snares for sacrifice. "So they went, the two together." Silence shouts.

4. Obedience Climaxes

In unit four (22:9–10) the journey continues, with the narrator repeating vocabulary, changing nuances, and achieving destination. The opening sentence belongs to a pattern woven through the units. At the end of unit one, Abraham "went (*hlk*) to-the-place which the-God had-told him" (22:3). At the end of unit two (22:6) the singular verb becomes plural, "they-went (*hlk*), the two of them together," while the clause of destination is dropped. The end of unit three repeats "they-went (*hlk*), the two of them together." Now at the beginning of unit four, the verb *came* (*b'*) in the plural, rather than *went*, signals completion of the journey, along with repetition of the theological destination. "And-they-came to-the-place which the-God had-told him" (22:9).

Immediately separation occurs. Syntax and content tell the tale. Abraham alone is subject of six verbs, with Isaac appearing as object after each group of three. He receives center-stress and end-stress:

> And-<u>built</u> there Abraham the-altar,
>> and-<u>arranged</u> the-wood,
>>> and-<u>bound</u> <u>Isaac his-son</u>.
> and-<u>laid</u> him on-the-altar, from-upon the-wood.
>> And-<u>put-forth</u> Abraham his-hand
>> and-<u>took</u> the-knife to-slay <u>his-son</u> (22:9b–10)

Irony, poignancy, and suspense abound. The reader remembers Isaac's innocent question "Where is the lamb?" and Abraham's ambiguous reply (22:7–8). Now the narrator equates burnt offering and son, an equation that Abraham's words previously suggested. Isaac the questioner is the answer burnt offering. He is the lamb for sacrifice. Further, the knife that he omitted in his list of sacrificial equipment reappears. When Abraham first "took [it] in his hand," along with the fire, he protected Isaac from the dangerous weapon (22:6). Now, by contrast, Abraham put forth "his hand" and "took the knife to slay his son."[15] Protection yields to destruction. The moment, not just the hour, is at hand. And yet the fire is missing. Does the omission thwart the ritual? Or is the fire next time? An attentive reader permits the ambiguity. But no ambiguity characterizes the action of Abraham. In obedience to the divine command, he stands poised to plunge the knife. His response is complete; the suspense, insurmountable. Thus ends the second section of the story.

God's Resolution

With variations, the third section corresponds to the first and the second. It comes, however, as a doublet, for a single resolution cannot embrace both characters evenly. Parallel units (22:11–14 and 22:15–19) contain a three-fold pattern: the narrated appearance of deity, a speech to Abraham, and the narrated response.[16] These two units do not introduce God speaking (*'mr*) directly to Abraham, as in section one, but rather the messenger of Yhwh calling (*qr'*) to him from heaven. If the difference connotes distance, it also bespeaks transcendence. From beyond, deity interprets the text. The responses of Abraham indicate that he understands.

1. Yhwh Provides

The first unit (22:11–14) begins just as Abraham is poised, knife in hand, to slay his son. The messenger of Yhwh diverts his attention by uttering his name (22:11a).[17] This time the verb *say* (*'mr*) comes from heaven. Further, it leads not to a single vocative, as in the beginning of the story, but to a repeated one. The emphasis reinforces the diversion, to compel a response, the familiar reply of obedience:

> And-he-said, "Abraham, Abraham"!
> And-he-said, "*Hinnenî*" (Behold,-here-am-I). (22:11b)

Abraham has not swerved in all the story; steadfastly he has remained faithful. Parallel commands now relieve the dreadful suspense. The first negates verbatim the narrated action in the climax of section two. "And Abraham put-forth (*slḥ*) his-hand" (22:10a) becomes "Do-not-put-forth (*slḥ*) your-hand. . ." (22:12a). At this point the vocabulary reverts to the word *na'ar*, young man, that Abraham earlier used for the child (22:5). The reversion hints at a shift in perspective yet to be realized. "Do-not-put-forth your-hand to-the-young-man." In contrast to this specificity, the second negative generalizes, thereby ensuring the total safety of Isaac. "Do-not-do to-him anything." No harm shall befall the young man. These two prohibitions remove terror and relieve suspense. Yet the meaning remains obscure, awaiting a special word.

A deictic clause announces that word. "For (*kî*) now I-know that (*kî*). . . ." The formula signals climax, consequence, and conclusion.[18] "For now I know that a fearer of God are you because you have not withheld your son, your only one, from me" (22:12b). Fearer of God! To fear God is to worship God. The term "fearer of God" embodies awe, terror, and devotion in the presence of *mysterium tremendum*.[19] And the worship of God abolishes all idolatries, specifically now the idolatry of the son. "You have not withheld your son, your only one, from me." This interpersonal language takes the reader back to the beginning of the story, to the words, "your son, your only one, whom you love, Isaac." The repetition underscores the issue to clarify the test. Abraham had formed an attachment to his son. Attachment threatened the obedience, the worship, the fear of God. Thus the test offers Abraham an opportunity for healing, an opportunity to free both himself and his son.[20]

To attach one's self to another is to negate love through entrapment. In surrounding Isaac, Abraham binds himself and his son. To attach is to know the anxiety of separation. In clinging to Isaac, Abraham incurs the risk of losing him—and Isaac suspects it. To attach is to practice idolatry. In adoring Isaac, Abraham turns from God. The test, then, is an opportunity for understanding and healing. To relinquish attachment is to discover freedom. To give up human anxiety is to receive divine assurance. To disavow idolatry is to find God. "Do not lay your hand on the young man or do anything to him, for now I know that you fear God because you have not withheld your son, your only one, from me."

The divine vocabulary of "young man" and "your son" discloses in retrospect a subtle truth hidden in Abraham's speech to his young men. At that time, he distanced himself from Isaac while affirming their unity. "Then Abraham said to his young men, 'Stay here with the ass. I and the young man, we will go yonder and we will worship and we will return again to you'" (22:5). The term "young man" undercut the bonding in the pronoun "we"; in turn, the pronoun "we" undercut the aloofness in the designation "young man." By neutralizing each other, these identifications allowed, though they did not compel, movement beyond attachment-detachment to nonattachment. Thus Abraham's words held potent meaning. Realization of that meaning comes now as the divine messenger juxtaposes the two ways of identifying Isaac: "young man" (detachment) and "your son, your only one" (attachment). Separating these two identifications is the crucial affirmation, "for now I know that a fearer of God are you." Structure and content together break the dangerous dialectic; it is transcended in the worship of God:

> Do not lay your hand on the young man or do anything to him,
>   for now I know that you fear God
> because you have not withheld your son, your only one, from me.
> (22:12)

The inseparability of what is said and how it is said yields the meaning. Fear of God severs the link between detachment and attachment to save both Abraham and Isaac.

Fear of God also brings vision. "Abraham lifted up his eyes and saw (*r'h*). . . ." Whereas earlier these words introduced "the place from afar" (22:4), this time Abraham sees differently: not afar off but, at hand, behind him an animal. Freed of attachment, he beholds an answer to Isaac's question, "Where is the lamb for a burnt offering?" (22:7d).

> And-lifted-up Abraham his-eyes and-saw.
> Lo-behold (*hinnēh*), a-ram behind-him
>   was-entangled in-a-thicket by-his-horns. (22:13a)

Right vision inspires proper action. Three indicative verbs now answer the divine imperatives spoken to Abraham at the beginning of the story. "Take, go, and sacrifice" (22:2) become "Abraham went, took, and sacrificed." Between these grammatical pairings, however, Abraham's world has changed. Contrasting objects, *ram* and *son*, establish the dissonance:

> and-went Abraham
>> and-took the-ram
>> and-sacrificed-it for-a-burnt-offering
>>> instead-of his-son, (22:13b)

Strikingly unlike the syntactic patterns of previous sentences,[21] the son stands here outside the action of the father. Further, this sentence eliminates the ambiguity of apposition that once linked "burnt offering" and "my son" in Abraham's speech (22:8). By location and meaning, the preposition *taḥat*, "instead of," separates the two nouns.

As substitute for Isaac (and for the lamb), the ram vindicates Abraham's prediction that "God will see to" the sacrifice (22:8). The ram symbolizes the succesful completion of the test.[22] Accordingly, an appropriate etiology concludes this unit of section three.

> So Abraham called the name of that place
>> "The Lord will see"
> As it is said to this day,
>> "On the mount of the Lord it will be seen." (22:14)

What is seen is that God provides. To be a God-fearer is to have this vision.

2. God Blesses

But the story cannot and does not end here. While the substitution of a ram for Isaac brings comfort and closure, it also reopens the issue that the test was designed to resolve. Is the sparing of Isaac license for Abraham to reattach himself to his son? If Abraham has demonstrated willingness to relinquish attachment, is he now allowed to keep it? In assuring the reader that Isaac is safe, this first of two resolutions allows misunderstanding. It invites betrayal and folly. Precisely to prevent such an interpretation, the story provides a second resolution in tandem with the first (22:15–19).[23]

The clue for parallel units is the little word *she'nith*, "second time." "The messenger of the Lord called to Abraham a second time from heaven." An oath empowers the divine speech: "By myself I have sworn, utterance of the Lord." Two motivational clauses frame four promises:[24]

<u>Motivation</u>
Now (*kî*) because (*ya'an*) you have done this thing
and-not withheld your-son, your-only-one
<u>Promises</u>
1. Therefore (*kî*) surely I-will-<u>bless</u>-you
2. and-surely I-will-multiply <u>your-descendants</u>
   as-the-stars-of the-heavens
   and-as-the-sand that (is) on-the-seashore.
3. And-will-possess your-descendants the gate-of their-enemies,
4. and will-<u>bless</u>-themselves by-<u>your-descendants</u> all the
   nations-of the-earth.
<u>Motivation</u>
Because (*'eqēb 'asēr*) you-have-obeyed my-voice. (22:16b–18)

In the opening motivation (22:16b), the introductory particles *kî ya'an*[25] point back to the deictic words "for now (*kî 'atah*) I know that" (22:12). And the content of this clause also recalls earlier divine speeches. The assertion "you have done this thing" alludes reversely to the prohibition "Do not do to him anything" (22:12). The recognition "you have not withheld your son, your only one" contains a direct quotation (22:2). Verification of these emphases comes in the concluding line, "because you have obeyed my voice" (22:18b). Framing promises of blessing, these motivational clauses underscore not just Abraham's willingness but indeed his relinquishment of idolatry. No longer is he attached to Isaac. He has not withheld his son; he has obeyed the divine voice.

Conclusion

By structure, use of particles, and repetition, the narrator has relentlessly secured meaning. Abraham fears God, worships God, obeys God. Alone Abraham returns from the place of sacrifice. It can be no other way. If the story is to fulfill its meaning, Isaac cannot, must not, and does not appear.[26] Abraham, man of faith, has learned the lesson of nonattachment. Before the crisis he asserted that "we will return" (*šûb*, 22:5). But now the narrator perceptively returns to the verb in the singular: "So Abraham returned. . ." (*šûb*, 22:19). To go yonder and worship (cf. 22:5) returns one to social discourse healed of interpersonal idolatry. A narrated report concluding this unit likewise ends the entire story:

So-returned Abraham to-his-young-men
   and-they-arose
   and-they-went together to-Beersheba
And-lived Abraham in-Beersheba. (22:19)

So much has been at stake that the story requires two conclusions. They give parallel messages: All is well with Isaac; God provides (22: 11–14). All is well with Abraham; God blesses (22:15–19).

The Sacrifice of Sarah

Our rhetorical-critical reading demonstrates the ways structure, vocabulary, and content embody meanings. What a piece of work is Genesis 22! And yet, hardly do I complete the first two verses before a great uneasiness descends. So attached to patriarchy is this magnificent story that I wonder if it can ever be what it purports to be, namely a narrative of nonattachment.[27]

With all-consuming power, the patriarchal bonding of father and son threatens to destroy not only Abraham and Isaac but also another— Sarah. Why is she not in this story? Where is she? What does it all mean for her? Over centuries, many commentators have answered such questions by composing stories outside the text to fill gaps within it.[28] Another approach wrestles from within, using scripture to interpret scripture. Adopting this procedure, I should like to show how the biblical depiction of Sarah works to expose the patriarchy of Genesis 22, how that exposure alters the meaning of the story, and how the resultant interpretation challenges faith. A feminist hermeneutic takes over the rhetorical analysis to yield a different reading.

In the genealogical preface to the so-called Abrahamic narratives, Sarai receives special attention. A recital of descendants originating with Shem lists, in each case, a single male heir followed by reference to "other sons and daughters" (11:10–25). The pattern ceases with the introduction of Terah, "father of Abram, Nahor, and Haran" (11:26). Of the three sons named, only Haran, who dies early, is identified by a male descendant, his son Lot. All three, however, are associated with women:

> And Abram and Nahor took wives.
>   The name of Abram's wife was <u>Sarai</u>,
>   and the name of Nahor's wife, <u>Milcah</u>,
>   the daughter of Haran the father of
>   <u>Milcah</u> and Iscah.
>   Now <u>Sarai</u> was barren; she had no child. (11:29–30)

Here male genealogy relinquishes structure and content to herald a story that names characters.

Contrast emerges between Sarai and Milcah, whose names appear in alternating sequence. The contrast moves between the silence and voice of the text. Nothing is said of Sarai's lineage, but Milcah is "the daughter of Haran"; she also has a sister. On the other hand, nothing is said about Milcah's fertility (cf. 22:20–23), but "Sarai was barren; she had no child." These ominous words haunt the narrative to come. They bring Sarai to center stage while Milcah recedes, as does her husband Nahor. The three remaining men, Terah, Abram, and Lot, go forth with the lone woman Sarai, the one who has neither pedigree nor fertility, neither past nor future.

> Terah took Abram his son and Lot the son of Haran, his grandson,
> and Sarai his daughter-in-law, his son Abram's wife,
> and they went forth together from the Chaldeans . . . to Haran. . . .
> (11:31)

Unique and barren, Sarai threatens the demise of genealogy. The death of her father-in-law Terah in Haran reduces the generations to two. The generational preface stops (11:32), and the call of Abram begins (12:1–3).

In his journey from Haran to the promised land, Abram takes Sarai his wife as well as Lot his brother's son (12:5). Upon their arrival, Yhwh assures Abram descendants but does not take account of Sarai's condition. When famine sends the group to Egypt, the tension builds. Speaking for the first time, Abram addresses Sarai (12:11–13). With flattery he manipulates her to justify deception and protect himself. He disowns the beautiful Sarai as wife, calls her his sister, and allows Pharaoh to use her, thereby ensuring his own survival, even his prosperity. For her sake Pharaoh dealt well with Abram (12:16) but also for her sake Yhwh afflicted (*ngʿ*) Pharaoh (12:17). Sarai remains the pivot in the story. At the end, Pharaoh reprimands Abram and holds him accountable for the use of his wife (12:18–20). Pharaoh respects another man's property. Throughout it all, Sarai has neither voice nor choice. Though she is central in the episode, patriarchy marginalizes this manhandled woman.

Object of special attention, Sarai eventually speaks, seeking to fulfill herself within cultural strictures. Her words concern fertility and status; they also reveal her as a voice of realism, decisiveness, and command:

> And Sarai said to Abram,
> "Because Yhwh has prevented me
> from bearing children,
> go to my maid.
> Perhaps I shall be built up from her." (16:2a)

Thus this barren woman proposes a plan whereby she may obtain children through her Egyptian maid Hagar (15:1–6). As property of Sarai,

Hagar is female enslaved, used, and demeaned. Abram once gave Sarai
to Pharaoh; Sarai now gives Hagar to Abram. This time, however, no
deity intervenes; the arrangement is legal and proper.

But no happy solution results (16:4–6). Inevitably the women clash.
The pregnant maid sees the lowering of hierarchical barriers, and the
barren mistress resents loss of status. Reasserting power, Sarai afflicts
(*'nh*) Hagar, who then flees to the wilderness. The blessed and exalted
woman has become malicious and tyrannical. Her authority reaches into
the wilderness. Finding Hagar by a spring of water, the messenger of
Yhwh orders her not only to return to her mistress but also to "suffer
affliction (*'nh*) under her hand." The cruelty of Sarai continues, this
time with heavenly sanction. Who will deliver Sarai from such dis-ease?
Who will make possible healing reconciliation? Not Abraham, not her
son, not the narrator, and not even God. To the contrary, the story coun-
tenances the division between the women.

As the narrative proceeds, God makes clear that only Sarai, no other
woman, can bear the child of promise. She is destined for great things:

> And God said to Abraham:
>   "As for Sarai your wife,
>   Call not her name Sarai
>   for Sarah (is) her name.
> I will bless her
>   and also will give from her to you a son.
> I will bless her
>   and she will become nations;
>   royal people from her will be." (17:15–16)

Sarah's apotheosis is complete. If Hagar is woman in the gutter, Sarah
is woman on the pedestal. Their positions illustrate well the strictures
of patriarchy.

The exaltation of Sarah continues as Abraham responds to the divine
words. Falling on his face and laughing,[29] he utteres two speeches. The
first, inward dialogue, poses through rhetorical questions an impossible
situation:

> Abraham . . . said in his heart
>   "Shall a son be borne to one
>   who is a hundred years old?
>   Shall Sarah, the daughter of ninety years old,
>   bear?" (17:17)

These words of Abraham specifically name Sarah. His second response,
outward dialogue, pleads for the legitimacy of Ishmael, but it does not
name Hagar:

And Abraham said to the God,
  "If only Ishmael might live in your presence!" (17:18)

Abraham's responses bring yet again divine sanction for Sarah as the sole designated mother of the chosen heir. A single speech makes three declarations (A, B, C, below). It begins by citing Sarah and Isaac (A). Conversely, it closes with Isaac and Sarah (C). Hers, then, is the first and last proper name. Between the two declarations occurs a promise of blessing for Ishmael, without reference to Hagar (B). Although central in the structure, the promise becomes peripheral to the story line. In other words, the beginning stress upon Sarah and Isaac and the ending stress upon Isaac and Sarah confine Ishmael. The extremities of the divine speech show in particular the special, exalted role of Sarah as mother.

	God said,
(A)	"No, but Sarah^a your wife will bear for you a son,
	and you will call his name Isaac.^{b}
	I will establish my covenant with him
	as an everlasting covenant
	for his descendants after him.
(B)	As for Ishmael, I have heard you.
	Surely I will bless him
	and I will make him fruitful
	and I will increase him more and more.
	Twelve princes he will bear
	and I will make him a great nation.
(C)	But my covenant I will establish with Isaac$^{b'}$
	whom Sarah$^{a'}$ will bear to you by this time next year."
	(17:19–21)

Yet another story ensures the status and destiny of Sarah (18:1–16). Disguised as three men, Yhwh visits Abraham by the oaks of Mamre. After receiving the hospitality of rest and food, the guests inquire about Sarah (18:9). Told that she is in the tent, the visitor (now singular) promises to return in the spring "when surely a son will be to Sarah your wife" (18:10). At this point the narrator intervenes to focus on Sarah. Four times her name appears in a report about her location and activity, her old age and infertility, and her immediate response to the promise.

Now-Sarah was listening at the entrance of the tent
  behind him.

Abraham and-Sarah (were) old, advanced in the days;
  it was past to be to-Sarah (in the) manner of women.

So-laughed <u>Sarah</u> within herself. . . . (18:10b–12a)

Only after this narrated intervention does Sarah's direct response to the divine promise come:

> After being worn out, (is there) to me pleasure—
> and my lord, (who) is old? (18:12b)

Yhwh replies, however, not to Sarah but to Abraham. Questions of reprimand precede a reiteration of the promise, with the name Sarah occurring at the beginning and end.

> Why (is) this, <u>Sarah</u> laughed saying
> "Now shall I indeed bear when I am old?"
> Is anything too difficult for Yhwh?
> At the appointed time I will return to you in the spring
> and to <u>Sarah</u> (will be) a son. (18:13–14)

Sarah's laughter "within herself" (18:12) has been heard,[30] but out of fear she denies (*kḥs*) that it ever happened. "Not I-laughed." This time the divine reply comes directly to her. "No, for you-did-laugh." For the first and only time the deity speaks to Sarah. Yet not even this curt rebuke diminishes her exalted and unique status.

Elect among women, only Sarah can bear the legitimate male heir. And so, at long last, it comes to pass. "Yhwh visited Sarah . . . and did to Sarah as Yhwh had promised" (21:1). She bears a son to Abraham in his old age. Abraham names him Laughter (*Yishaq*) but Sarah interprets its meaning:

> Laughter God has made <u>for-me</u> (*lî*).
> All who hear will laugh <u>for-me</u> (*lî*). (21:6)

If Laughter (Isaac) is special to Abraham, how much more to Sarah! She claims the child for herself, "for-me." After all, he is her, not Abraham's, one and only son.

Ishmael, the other male child in the family, is thus a threat. So jealousy continues to breed rivalry between the two women: Sarah, wife of Abraham, and Hagar, wife of Abraham; Sarah, woman on the pedestal, and Hagar, woman in the gutter; Sarah, mother of Isaac, and Hagar, mother of Ishmael. Potential equality between sons counters actual inequality between their mothers. Power belongs to Sarah; powerlessness to Hagar. Sarah asserts authority against the other woman, as she did once before, and now against her child. Speaking to Abraham, she orders:

Cast out this slave woman and her son,
for the son of this slave woman
  will not inherit with my son,
            with Isaac. (21:10)

Language of contrast achieves several effects. First, the single phrase "her son" and the double phrase "with my son, with Isaac" show the lack of equality between the sons. Second, the name Isaac accords him dignity and power in contrast to the namelessness, and hence powerlessness, of both the slave woman and her son. Third, the combination "my son Isaac" bespeaks possessiveness, indeed attachment. It foreshadows language that in Genesis 22 applies to Abraham, rather than to Sarah. Yet in chapter 21 Abraham has no exclusive relationship with Isaac. He uses no speech of intimacy for either son. But the narrator and the deity attach him to Ishmael and to Hagar:

The matter was very distressing
  in the eyes of Abraham
  on account of his son.
But God said to Abraham,
  "Do not be distressed in your eyes
    on account of the lad
    and on account of your slave woman." (21:11–12a)

Possessive language, "his son," links Abraham and Ishmael, a paternal-filial connection that endures until Abraham's death (25:9).

Through direct and narrated discourse Genesis 21:1–11 delineates a decisive parental difference between Sarah and Abraham. Sarah speaks directly, using the vocabulary "my son Isaac." Her exclusive speech owns her one and only son. On the other hand, Abraham speaks not at all; he claims no father-son relationships. They appear only in the distancing of narration. The storyteller makes the claim for Abraham regarding both sons, "his son Isaac" (21:4,5) and "his son" Ishmael (21:11). Accordingly, unlike the bond between Sarah and Isaac, no unique tie exists here between Abraham and Isaac. Other texts support the observation. Before Genesis 22:7 Abraham never utters or implies the possessive "my son" for Isaac, though he does imply the epithet for Ishmael (17:18). Such witnesses, most especially chapter 21, dispute the father-son pairing of Genesis 22 to compel a closer look at Sarah's relationship to Isaac.

With single, unqualified attachment to "my son," Sarah prevails once more over against Abraham because God supports her.

Everything that Sarah says to you, heed her voice;
for in Isaac will be named to you descendants. (21:12)

Sarah, the chosen vessel of the legitimate heir, remains secure on the pedestal that patriarchy has built for her. To keep her there protects her from a test, but in doing so it exacerbates her tyranny, deprives her of freedom, and renders impossible reconciliation with Hagar.

If the phrase "my son Isaac" in 21:10 foreshadows the language of chapter 22, while reversing the parental figures, other associations similarly challenge the content.[31] In the wilderness with his mother Hagar, Ishmael comes close to death; a messenger of God intervenes to save him. On the mountain with his father Abraham, Isaac comes close to death; a messenger of God intervenes to save him. Thus are joined the two sons and the divine representatives. The presence of Hagar the mother and Abraham the father, however, skews the pairing. Chapter 21 shows that the proper match in parents are the mothers, Hagar and Sarah. This pairing argues correspondingly for the appearance of Sarah, not Abraham, in Genesis 22. As Hagar faced the imminent death of Ishmael, so Sarah ought to have faced the imminent death of Isaac. Explicit parallels between chapters 21 and 22 sustain the logic of the argument, and yet a bias for father-son bonding has defied the connection.

Another observation demonstrates the inappropriateness of Abraham as the parental figure for Genesis 22. Nowhere else in the entire narrative sequence does he appear as a man of attachment.[32] To the contrary. When Yhwh calls him, Abram obediently leaves his country, his clan, and his father's house to journey to an unknown land (12:1–4). Immediately after that commendable relinquishment comes an unflattering one: Abram passes his wife Sarai off as his sister (12:10–20). Later he even repeats this act of extraordinary detachment (20:1–18). In reference to the land, Abraham shows no possessiveness but instead allows Lot to choose (13:2–12). After warring with kings from the East and recovering all the goods and people captured, Abraham gives the king of Salem a tenth of everything, besides refusing to take anything not his own (14:1–24). Similar behavior appears in his less generous treatment of Hagar. On two occasions he gives power over her to Sarai and God (16:1–6 and 21:1–14). Hints of his involvement with Ishmael (17:18; 21:11) are negated when he sends the child away, along with Hagar. In another episode he gives gifts to Abimelech as they settle a dispute over wells (21:22–34). Be the incident an occasion for weal or woe, nowhere prior to Genesis 22 does Abraham emerge as a man of attachment. That is not his problem. How ill-fitted he is, then, for a narrative of testing and sacrifice.

Attachment is Sarah's problem. Nevertheless, Genesis 22 drops Sarah to insert Abraham. The switch defies the internal logic of the larger story. In view of the unique status of Sarah and her exclusive relationship to Isaac, she, not Abraham, ought to have been tested. The dynamic of the entire saga, from its genealogical preface on, requires that Sarah be featured in the climactic scene, that she learn the meaning of obedience to God, that she find liberation from possessiveness, that she free Isaac from maternal ties,[33] and that she emerge a solitary individual, nonattached, the model of faithfulness. In making Abraham the object of the divine test, the story violates its own rhythm and movement. Moreover, it fails to offer Sarah redemption and thereby perpetuates the conflict between her and Hagar. As long as Sarah is attached to Isaac (both child and symbol), so long Sarah afflicts Hagar.[34]

The text, however, permits the banished Hagar to forge for herself a future that God and Sarah have diminished. She chooses an Egyptian wife for her son and so guarantees the identity of her descendants (21: 21; cf. 25:12–18). If it yield but small mercy, her act is nonetheless a sign of healing for this abused woman. By contrast, the biblical story allows no opportunity, however small, for Sarah to be healed. It attributes to her no action or word that might temper her affliction. Instead, it leaves her a jealous and selfish woman.

Patriarchy has denied Sarah her story, the opportunity for freedom and blessing. It has excluded her and glorified Abraham. And it has not stopped with these things. After securing the safety of Isaac, it has no more need for Sarah; so it moves to eliminate her. The process begins obliquely, yet with the telling phrase, "and it came to pass after these events" (22:20). As this phrase introduced the story of testing and sacrifice (22:1), so it returns to make a transition that continues the larger narrative.

Once again, continuation holds surprise. The narrative begets a genealogy (22:20–24). Its subject reverts to the family of Nahor, thereby recalling the genealogical preface to the entire saga (11:27–32). An unidentified speaker addresses only Abraham, who has just returned from the mount of sacrifice. Unlike the preface, this passage says nothing explicit about Sarah. Silence begins her removal. The words commence, "Behold Milcah also (*gam*) has borne children to your brother Nahor" (RSV). The particle "also" contrasts the two wives.[35] Though Sarah has borne only the singular child Isaac, Milcah has birthed eight sons. Bethuel, the last of them, holds special meaning because "Bethuel became the father of Rebekah" (22:23). Reference to this daughter forecasts a future for Isaac. The concluding item in the genealogy likewise implies contrast between women: "Moreover, his concubine, whose name was Reumah, bore Tebah, Gaham, Tahash, and Maacah" (22:24, RSV). Though Hagar, second wife of Abraham, bore the one son Ishmael, Nahor's concubine Reumah bore four sons. Yet the small family of Abraham and Sarah, excluding Hagar, and not the large family of Nahor

and Milcah, including Reumah, carry the promise. The two families
join later when the one and only child Isaac finds a wife in the daughter
Rebekah (24:1–67).

If at the beginning of this entire saga barren Sarai threatened the
demise of genealogy (11:30), at the end genealogy portends the demise
of Sarah. Immediately after the report of 22:20–24, patriarchy dismisses
Sarah. It has no further need of her, and so it writes a lean obituary
(cf. 25:7–8).

> Sarah lived a hundred and twenty-seven years;
>   these were the years of the life of Sarah.
> And Sarah died at Kiriath-arba (that is, Hebron)
>   in the land of Canaan. . . . (23:1–2a, RSV)

The place of Sarah's death suggests another facet of her story. After
the test, Abraham returns to dwell in Beersheba. But Sarah dies in Hebron. Thus the text reads as though husband and wife were never re-
united in life. Indeed, "Abraham *went* to mourn for Sarah and to weep
for her" (23:2b).

Sarah died alone. Then Abraham went to her. But immediately the
story turns from Sarah to a long section in which Abraham bargains
with the Hittites for burial ground (23:3–18). Only after some sixteen
verses does Sarah re-enter the narrative. "After this, Abraham buried
Sarah his wife in the cave of the field of Mach-pelah east of Mamre
(that is, Hebron) in the land of Canaan" (23:19). Where she died, there
was she buried. If early on patriarchy casts out the woman in the
gutter (Hagar), the time comes when it also dismisses the woman on
the pedestal (Sarah). Moreover, it allots Sarah no dying words. It leaves
the reader to remember as her last words only the harsh imperative,
"Cast out this slave woman with her son; for the son of this slave woman
shall not be heir with my son Isaac" (21:10). This utterance haunts
Sarah's portrait, crying out for release from possessiveness and attachment. And though the story for healing is at hand, it remains captive
to a patriarchal agenda.

From exclusion to elimination, denial to death, the attachment of Genesis 22 to patriarchy has given us not the sacrifice of Isaac (for that
we are grateful) but the sacrifice of Sarah (for that we mourn). By her
absence from the narrative and her subsequent death, Sarah has been
sacrificed by patriarchy to patriarchy. Thus this magnificent story of
nonattachment stands in mortal danger of betraying itself. It fears not
God but holds fast to an idol. If the story is to be redeemed, then the
reader must restore Sarah to her rightful place. Such a hermeneutical
move, wed to rhetorical analysis, would explode the entrenched bias

to fulfill the internal logic of the story. And it would do even more: it would free divine revelation from patriarchy. Yet even there the matter does not end.

An Epilogue for Disorientation

We have presented two interpretations of Genesis 22. They share the theme of attachment, detachment, and nonattachment. They diverge in appropriating this theme to Isaac's parents. The patriarchal interpretation, given in the text, elects Abraham and so makes paternal bonding the idolatrous problem. The feminist interpretation, inspired by the text, chooses Sarah and so makes maternal bonding the idolatrous problem. An author's intentionality and a reader's response have thus yielded competing views. Although the two readings might coexist, however uneasily, becoming attached to either or both of them would violate this narrative of nonattachment.

To be faithful to the story no interpretation can become an idol. And so the essay concludes with a disorienting homily. After we perceive the sacrifice of Sarah and move to free the narrative from attachment to patriarchy, after and only after all these things, will we hear God testing us: "Take your interpretation of this story, your only interpretation, the one which you love, and sacrifice it on the mount of hermeneutics." If we withhold not our cherished reading from God, then we too will come down from the mountain nonattached. In such an event, we and the story will merge. Interpretation will become appropriation. Testing and attachment will disappear, and the worship of God will be all in all.

THE HISTORIES OF DAVID: BIBLICAL SCHOLARSHIP AND BIBLICAL STORIES

Regina M. Schwartz

The so-called Deuteronomistic history, the narratives spanning the Book of Judges through 2 Kings, is explicitly engaged in constructing Israel's history, but this history is informed by presuppositions that are rarely explored in biblical scholarship. Instead and ironically, biblical scholarship is itself preoccupied with history, not the same history that the Bible is anxious to have remembered, but a history to which the Bible offers clues: the political and religious history of the ancient Near East. This essay is an effort to make distinctions between those projects, that is, to make distinctions between the writing of history in the Bible and the writing of history in biblical scholarship, especially because they are so often and, I will argue, so dangerously blurred.

Biblical Scholarship

"Traditional history," as Michel Foucault characterizes it, "retracing the past as a patient and continuous development," aptly describes the major pursuit in biblical studies for the past two centuries; specifically, the project that has dominated modern biblical scholarship is the historical reconstruction of the biblical text.[1] This project is marked by its quest for origins—the origin of a given passage, the origin of a cultic practice, the original setting of the text—and by a deep commitment to charting development, whether the formation of the text, the development of the ancient Israelite religion, or the development of political organizations in ancient Israel. Much biblical scholarship has been devoted to ascertaining sources (even though the Bible has obscured its sources) and many of the historical reconstructions of ancient Israel have been markedly teleological (even though the Hebrew Bible depicts a history that resists fulfillment or completion). A brief survey of the major posi-

192

tions held by biblical scholars in this century shows how consistent their presuppositions are despite their different conclusions regarding the nature and extent of the two layers of redacted material in the biblical text and how those two layers came together.[2] All of these positions are attempts to explain the development of the biblical text—a project that has its own history. Throughout the nineteenth century, biblical scholarship always saw itself as part of the larger Germanic historiographic tradition in which it flourished. Robert Oden asserts that this is not just a question of influence; "rather, the broader historiographic tradition shared the same methods, the same goals, the same prejudices, and the same world of understanding as biblical scholarship."[3]

What were these assumptions?—that history charts development, that its focus should be the development of the nation, the German nation in particular, and that the nation should be understood as an individual entity with its own unfolding spirit, its own internal laws of development. Philosophic idealism joined to the project of national revival in the Wars of Liberation gave nineteenth-century German historicism this special cast in which the nation's quest for power was an ethical imperative. As one historian characterizes the thinking of Leopold von Ranke: "It must be the uppermost task of the state . . . to achieve the highest measure of independence and strength among the competing powers of the world, so that the state will be able to fully develop its innate tendencies."[4]

One of the key figures in German historicism was Johann Gustav Droysen (1808–94). Throughout his writings, the idea of a "divine order," of "God's rule of the world" recurs, along with the insistence that a divine plan is working itself out in Prussia in particular. Droysen worked on his *History of Prussian Politics* for decades, leaving it unfinished at his death; he tried to argue, implausibly enough, that ever since the fifteenth century, Prussian rulers (conscious of Prussia's German mission) followed a consistent plan of action, a plan still unfolding in Germany.[5] An emphasis on teleological development insistently marks his thought: "The moral world, ceaselessly moved by *many ends*, and finally, . . . by the *supreme end*, is in a state of restless development and of internal elevation and growth, . . . With every advancing step in this *development* and *growth*, the historical understanding becomes wider and deeper" (my emphasis).[6]

Droysen's philosophy of history is indebted to that of Wilhem von Humboldt, who in his famous essay "On the Task of the Historian" sounds at first surprisingly at odds with the prevailing notions of coherence and continuity. "What is apparent," he writes, "is scattered, disconnected, isolated," but then he explains that it is the historian's task to take what is "apparent" and show something else: the coherence that heretofore had been hidden. Historiography is that process in which he "takes the scattered pieces he has gathered into himself and work[s] them into a whole." Events are "only in part accessible to the senses. The rest has to be felt (*empfunden*), inferred (*geschlossen*), or divined (*errathen*)."[7] Leopold von Ranke also begins by talking about isolated events, but his interest soon turns to the notion of a cohesive, hidden order informing the seeming chaos. "Although [history] pursues the succession of events as sharply and accurately as possible, and attempts to give each of them its proper color and form . . . , still history goes beyond this labor and moves on to an investigation of origins, seeking to break through to the deepest and most secret motives of historical life." For Ranke, Humboldt, and Droysen, historiography unveils an inner logic to the randomness of events. That logic is the course of national development.

For ancient Israel, the Book of Samuel was among its founding fictions.[8] It set the terms by which the institution of monarchy was to be understood and by which the nation of Israel was defining itself; it was the kind of narrative engaged in the formation of identity—not just of David or Saul but of the nation. Nationalism was the paramount concern in that other set of founding fictions—and I use the term fiction here advisedly—the founding fictions of German historicism. History was called upon to narrate the ideals of the German nation, its various "progresses," moral, military, political, religious. Because the story of ancient Israel was written by historians who were also thinking about, or even writing the story of Germany, it is no wonder that the two stories were often confused. All that development so faithfully outlined in the growth of the German nation was all too easily found in the growth of ancient Israel.

We can see this brand of historicism at work in one of the most prominent biblical scholars of the late nineteenth century, Julius Wellhausen, when he writes in the introduction to his *Prolegomena to the History of Ancient Israel*: "It is necessary to trace the succession of the three elements [the Jehovist, the Deuteronomic, and the Priestly] in detail, and at once to test and to fix each by reference to an independent standard, namely, the inner development of the history of Israel." With this commitment to charting such "inner development," he cannot help but find it. The metaphors he uses to discuss the literary composition of Judges, Samuel, and Kings are revealing:

> we are not presented with tradition purely in its original condition; already it is overgrown with later accretions. Alongside of an older narrative a new one has sprung up, formerly independent, and intelligible in itself, though in many instances of course adapting itself to

the former. More frequently the new forces have not caused the old root to send forth a new stock, or even so much as a complete branch; they have only nourished parasitic growths; the earlier narrative has become clothed with minor and dependent additions. To vary the metaphor, the whole area of tradition has finally been uniformly covered with an alluvial deposit by which the configuration of the surface has been determined.[9]

He shifts from the metaphor of a plant with a new branch, to a plant that has only parasitic growths; next, it is overgrown with accretions; then, he dresses it (the plant wears "minor and dependent" clothes), and then he drops the plant altogether to opt for geologic history: now the biblical text is composed of layers of alluvial deposits, and presumably scholars can take out their spades and dig right through it. Whether as the growth of an organism or the accretion of geologic deposits, this is the picture of history that he quickly applies not only to the development of the text, but to its plot, that is, to the biblical narrative's own sense of history. Deftly, almost without our noticing, the story of Germany has become the story of Israel. According to Wellhausen, the history spanning Deuteronomy to 2 Kings offers "a connected view of large periods of time, a continuous survey of the connection and succession of race after race, the detailed particulars of the occurrences being disregarded; the historical factors with which the religious pragmatism here has to do are so uniform that the individual periods in reality need only to be filled up with the numbers of the years."[10] Needless to say, such thinking is in marked contrast to Nietzsche's historical sense of disruption and discontinuity described in his *Untimely Meditations*, where he reacts against the "consuming fever of history" from which he believes his age suffers, and where he critiques the kind of history that seeks to reduce the diversity of time "into a totality fully closed upon itself . . . a history whose perspective on all that precedes it implies the end of time, a completed development."[11]

When we read contemporary secondary literature about David with this notion of German historicism in mind, we can detect signs of it virtually everywhere. Its presuppositions not only inform many scholars' accounts of the development of the text, but also inform their accounts of the history of ancient Israel. Their story tells of the accretion of David's power, alluvial deposit by alluvial deposit. Finding this presupposition of development in one too many places, I began to be suspicious. If biblical scholars reconstructed the *text* that way because the whole discipline of textual studies (including philology) was hopelessly permeated by the assumptions of German historicism, so be it. But find that development in the story of David—a story marked by discontinuity, duplications, and ideological conflicts? How were biblical scholars going to reconcile their need to find continuity and development with this messy text? They did it by chopping up the text into different documents, first into big pieces, then into smaller ones; they took the amorphous, heterogeneous story we have been given and separated it into strands, each governed by the criterion of development and continuity.

Here is one of the many source theories: a historian or historical school wrote a strand that bridges Judges to Kings according to a coherent principle, that Israel's fate was determined by its responses to the law in Deuteronomy. The narrator "considered the whole of past history in relation to this law, concluded that the prescriptions of the law should have been observed at all times (2 Kings 22:13,17), and thus reached an unfavorable judgment on the history of Israel, seeing it as a period of going astray from God for which it was punished."[12] That part was written in exile, from the point of view of a hope for an Israel that failed. However, amid all of the narratives describing the disobedience and failures of Israel, there was also a recognizable drive to idealize David. The contradiction between the pessimism of the Deuteronomistic historian and the optimism about David is resolved by separating the documents. To be coherent, one document must believe one thing— say, that Israel is continually going astray from the law and Israel must be punished for her sins—and the other document believe something else—say, that David is the ideal of kingship and kingship is ideal for Israel. There simply cannot be contradiction, for narrators are consistent, histories are consistent, and they must have consistent ideologies.

To a surprising degree (surprising, because most of us assume that these decisions about sources were based only on linguistic data), the criterion of a consistent sympathy or ideology or plot continuity, whether pro- or anti-monarchical, pro- or anti-Saul, pro- or anti- whomever or whatever the scholar chooses to focus on, has been *determining* in separating strands of narrative and ascribing authorship. Sources have even been named for the character the author ostensibly sympathizes with —the Saul source, the Samuel source—and when two basic sources did not resolve all the contradictions, more narrative strands had to be isolated to account for them. When these were not named for a character, they were named for some continuous thread in the plot; hence, we have the "ark narrative," or "the rise of David narrative." Note how blithely Kyle McCarter, the scholar who wrote the impressively scholarly Anchor Bible commentaries on 1 and 2 Samuel, can take for granted in his introduction that *his* demand for coherence is also felt by his readers: "Numerous internal thematic tensions, duplications, and contradictions stand in the way of a straightforward reading of the story." What does he mean by a "straightforward" reading of the story? Does reading

forward and reading straight mean reading straight for the goal, reading teleologically, reading for development? Or is he defining "straightforward reading" in his sentence tautologically to mean the kind of reading we do when there are no "thematic tensions, no duplications or
contradictions"—"straightforward reading" as simple reading? Surely
contemporary theory has taught us that there is no such reading, that
there are no such texts, and that the nature of language is to be fraught
with tensions. Furthermore, our vanguard historians—who are quick
to admit that they are not recording events but constructing them by
their very selection and organization—see randomness, contradictions,
and tensions of all kinds as the very processes of history, where successive events have nothing particularly forward or straight (let alone
straightforward) about them. But McCarter tells us that because "the
narratives about Samuel, Saul, and David that make up our book have
a heterogeneous appearance even to the untrained eye" and because
its "thematic tensions, duplications, and contradictions stand in the way
of a straightforward reading of the story," he and many other biblical
scholars must set out on a determined course to offer us that straightforward reading, even if the cost might be smoothing out its puzzling ideological tensions, eliminating its teasing duplications, and ironing out its
provocative contradictions. The Bible gets rewritten into a group of coherent stories, and the difficult one we have in our Bibles is either neglected, or worse still, it is "solved."

Biblical Stories

Writing on Nietzsche's *Genealogy of Morals*, Foucault distinguishes "effective history" from traditional history. If traditional history is devoted
to searching out sources, establishing continuity, finding resemblances,
and charting development, with some goal ever in sight, "effective history," in contrast, is devoted to charting ruptures and discontinuities,
to disrupting the fiction of the unity of the subject, and to breaking
the commitment to seek origins and ends.

> History becomes "effective" to the degree that it introduces disconti-
> nuity into our very being—as it divides our emotions, dramatizes our
> instincts, multiplies our body and sets it against itself. "Effective" his-
> tory deprives the self of the reassuring stability of life and nature,
> and it will not permit itself to be transported by a voiceless obstinacy
> toward a millennial ending. It will uproot its traditional foundations
> and relentlessly disrupt its pretended continuity. This is because
> knowledge is not made for understanding; it is made for cutting.[13]

In complicated and contradictory ways, the Hebrew Bible depicts history as a series of ruptures in which various identities are cut and recut,
formed, broken, and reformed, rather than as a continuous process
in which a stable entity called Israel develops. In a narrative like Genesis
15, where Abraham is told to cut three birds in half for a mysterious
covenant ceremony in which fire passes between the pieces while the
promise of a future nation is made to the patriarch, does cutting signify
constituting identity or destroying it? Or both? Animals are not the only
entities severed here; Abraham's descendants are to be separated from
their home, "sojourners in a land not theirs" as part of the process of
creating a new home, and yet Yhwh will threaten to cut off Israel's
inheritance. Israel is already "cut off" in that it is separated from the
other nations; that separation is defining, and it means that not Israel
but its enemies have been "cut off" before it (2 Sam. 7:9). Other forms
of rupture characterize this history; in Israel's story, "cutting" is joined
by an emphasis on tearing away and breaking, and what is broken is
not always Israel's enemies, nor, for that matter, is it always Israel. Defeating the Philistines, David rejoices that Yhwh has "broken through"
his enemies, comparing this bursting or breaking to the breaking of
waters (2 Sam. 5:20). The comparison of defeating enemies to breaking
waters can be read as an allusion to the defeat of Egypt and the separation of waters at the Exodus; Israel is formed by such breaking. But
in another kind of internal rending (1 Sam. 15:27–28), the kingdom
is torn away from Saul, a metaphor that is theatricalized in the story
of Saul tearing Samuel's cloak in a desperate attempt to hold on to the
priest's, and hence divine, favor. Later, the kingdom is torn away from
Solomon as it was torn from Saul (1 Kings 11:11-13), but in this instance,
we are told that, for the sake of David, it is not all torn away. But if
"for David's sake" means not cutting off here, elsewhere David is told
that the sword will never be far from his house (2 Sam. 12:10). I rapidly
enumerate some of the ruptures in the story of Israel—ruptures that
the language of cutting so overtly signals—because they run counter
to the strong drive we have seen in biblical scholarship to read that
story as a development.

One version of "development" that has been ascertained frequently
in the Books of Samuel is the rise of David, and with it, the corollary
demise of Saul; supposedly, Saul's paranoia, ineffectuality, and estrangement from Yhwh develop, and David's political astuteness, military
success, and favor from Yhwh develop. But the depiction of Saul is more
difficult than a progressive demise, and David is not always on the rise.
In the very passage asserting that David's power is made secure by God
—the oracle of Nathan that David will have a permanent House, a secure dynasty—there is a curiously contradictory exchange. David has

been enjoying a brief period of peace; he has successfully taken over the house of Saul; he has been made king of both the south and the north and is at rest from his battles; and he would like to build a house for God in the city of David. The response comes from the Almighty: "*You* want to build *me* a house?" (the pronouns are emphatic). David is reminded that he is not God's patron; God is *his* patron. But then, after Yhwh corrects David on this score, clearly *limiting* the sphere of his influence, he proceeds to *expand* his power. It sounds as though David's ambition is simultaneously rebuked and rewarded. Yhwh says, "Are you going to build me a house for me to live in: I haven't lived in a house from the day I brought up the Israelites until this very day! Instead I've gone about in a tent wherever I happened to go throughout Israel. Did I ever speak with one of the staff-bearers of Israel whom I appointed to shepherd my people Israel and say, 'Why haven't you built me a house of cedar?'" Yhwh continues, "I took you from the sheep pasture to be prince over my people Israel. I was with you wherever you went, clearing all your enemies from your path. And I shall make you a name like the names of the nobility in the land. I shall fix a place for my people Israel and plant it, so that it will remain where it is and never again be disturbed." In this passage, God clearly suggests that the idea of a house, of permanence, of stability, is abhorrent, and yet he offers David a house as though it were desirable indeed; as the passage reads, the promise of a House is not an unequivocally welcome one. We readers could probably wrench our imaginations into some resolution of this conflict—certainly many scholars have separated the account into independent strands so that there is no conflict left—but the price would be the elimination of one of the key conflicts in the Bible: the tension between, on the one hand, a nostalgia for an Israel that is not fixed and not "like the nations," nostalgia for a period of wandering dispossessed, for associating tent-dwelling with godliness and moral rectitude, and, on the other hand, a longing for stability, for landed property, for a standing army, a dynastic leadership, in short, for becoming a nation among the nations.

Four chapters later, someone other than Yhwh will also refuse the offer from David to take up residence in a house. Called back from the front to cover up the king's adultery, Bathsheba's husband, Uriah the Hittite, will remind the king of Israel that "the ark, and Israel, and Judah, abide in booths; and my lord Joab, and the servants of my lord, are camping on the face of the field; and I, shall I go into my house to eat and to drink, and to lie with my wife? As you live, and as your soul lives, I will not do this thing" (2 Sam. 11:11). The passage casts a shadow back upon the earlier promise of a stable House. Everyone else has rallied to the field to meet a national threat—only David dwells in a house—and it is while he stays in that house that he commits adultery and orders murder, thereby undoing that promise of stability to his House. Henceforth, the nation is rent with civil strife, and Nathan prophesies that the sword will never be far from David's House. It seems that a House is a bad idea after all; but then, what about the promise of permanence to David's House? It is possible that conflicts and ruptures like these are frequent because this text is not simply about the people, the nation, or its king *amassing* power, but is instead everywhere ambivalent about power. Even as the story of Israel depicts its efforts to become "like the nations," it depicts that very project as pernicious, for Israel depends for its identity on its distinctiveness, on being drawn "from the nations."

The institution of monarchy itself is presented from wildly divergent points of view, often broadly drawn. How can the narrative depict the "development of the monarchy" when it is unsettled about what monarchy is, what the nation is, and what it means for this entity called a nation to be ruled by this entity called a king? Rather than presupposing settled answers, these stories are intently interested in exploring such questions of definition. Is a king one who will enslave the people and seize their property, as Samuel warns them in his stirring testimonial against the abuses of kingship? If so, why does the same Samuel who delivers this scathing critique against monarchy anoint not one king but two?

> "He will take your sons and assign them to his chariot and cavalry, and they will run before his chariot. He will appoint for himself captains of thousands and captains of hundreds from them. They will do his plowing, harvesting, and grape-gathering and make his weapons and the equipment of his chariotry. Your daughters he will take as perfumers and cooks and bakers. Your best fields and vineyards and olive groves he will take and give to his servants. Your seed crops and vine crops he will tithe to make gifts to his officers and servants. Your best slaves, maidservants, and cattle, and your asses he will take and use for his own work; and your flocks too he will tithe. You yourselves will become his slaves. Then you will *cry out* because of the King you have chosen for yourselves." (1 Sam. 8:11–18, my emphasis)

The Israelites had "cried out" in Egypt, groaning under slavery to Pharaoh, and the Promised Land was intended as the hope of deliverance from such unbridled tyranny, not as a reenactment of their enslavement. But, at the height of Israel's peace and prosperity, when the proverbial milk and honey were flowing, King Solomon married—could it be?—a daughter of Pharaoh? Shortly after his adultery, David himself had set a captured population to work as slaves, brickmaking, to be precise, as the Israelites had done in Egypt. Is this why Israel's liberator, Moses, is an Egyptian, to suggest that Israel is not simply delivered from Egypt, but fundamentally, delivered to Egypt? How could Israel become like Egypt when from its inception it is the antithesis? These questions are not repressed in the "Deuteronomistic history"; rather, they are its subject, and they simply will not fit neatly into a scheme of Israel's development.

On yet another level, the story has trouble keeping its agenda straight. If we thought it was preoccupied with the serious business of political and military history, the rise (or whatever that is) of monarchy (whatever it is), the narrative is interrupted by disturbing sex scenes like the story of David taking Bathsheba when from his roof he spots her bathing, or of Amnon, overcome with passion, raping his half-sister. Do the struggles for Israel's definition have anything to do with these sexual scenes? The way in which these scenes are carefully interwoven with political events would indicate that they must. The Bathsheba affair is surrounded by the war with the Ammonites; their insult to David's emissaries (emasculating them) and their alliance with the Syrians against Israel are positioned at the beginning, and the siege of Rabbah follows. Immediately after the Israelite victory over the Ammonites, the narrative turns to the rape of Tamar, which is followed by Absalom's murder of his elder brother (and the heir to the throne) and ultimately the story of civil war. Simply put, Israel is threatened from without and from within and in the very midst is an act of adultery and rape. What, if any, development could we ascertain in this random welter of isolated, confused events? Do these rapes cause the political anarchy, or vice versa? Mieke Bal has made it clear that the Book of Judges, which is so explicitly about war and political intrigue, is also about sexual violence; she even labels that sexual violence a kind of countercoherence.[14] These are not separate spheres, public and private, that merely affect one another—such a reading would say that the private acts of David have public consequences, that David is torn between private desires and public duties, that David's private affections get in the way of his public role.[15] The quest for such causality is misguided because politics *are* sexual, and sexuality is political. The text itself claims their synonymity in the scene that delivers the divine judgment on David's illicit affair: "Thus says the Lord, 'Behold, I will raise up evil against you out of your own house; and I will take your wives before your eyes, and give them to your neighbor, and he shall lie with your wives in the sight of this sun. For you did it in secret; but I will do this thing before all Israel, and before the sun'" (2 Sam. 12:11–12). What David might have imagined as a private affair in fact implicates the entire nation: Absalom will sleep with David's concubines in a declaration of civil war.

There is no question that owning the sexual rights to a woman (or stealing her, as the case may be) confers power. As this is overtly the case for marriage to the king's daughter or sexual intercourse with the king's concubines, it is no less the case in other sexual exchanges. Levi-Strauss taught us that the exchanges of women establish power relations between men; hence, David's dominance over other men is signaled by both military and sexual conquests.[16] When he is a fugitive from King Saul, garnering the support of the masses (the so-called rise of David), he turns for provisions to a man he had previously protected with his guerilla band. The man refuses to recognize the power of David and his obligation to him: "Who is David? Who is the son of Jesse? There are many servants nowadays who are breaking away from their masters. Shall I take my bread and my water and my meat that I have killed for my shearers, and give it to men who come from I do not know where?" In an unsubtle commentary on his poor judgment, the man is named Nabal or Fool. David decides to destroy Nabal and his household. But then, this test of David's power and of his right to the throne takes an interesting turn; the way the story unfolds, David does not kill Nabal (Nabal conveniently drops dead just hearing of David's threat to him), instead, David takes Nabal's wife. The power gain is presumably equivalent. The Fool's wife, Abigail, is no fool, and her way of acknowledging David's power is to collude in her own exchange, engaging in a seduction that is purely political—or should I say, politics is her seduction? "And when the Lord has done to my lord according to all the good that he has spoken concerning you, and has appointed you prince over Israel . . . and when the Lord has dealt well with my lord, then remember your handmaid" (1 Sam. 25:30–31). David remembers right away.

Sexual and political power are so completely fused again in the story of Saul's concubine that it is not quite right to claim that one is a metaphor for the other; they are not distinct enough to stand in for one another. Upon the death of Saul, his general, Abner, sleeps with one of the deceased king's concubines, Rizpah. When the king's son learns of it he is incensed; the act is clearly a sign of pretension to the throne, for the competition over who will succeed Saul—his son or his general—is fought out over sexual ownership of the concubine. The king's general does not like competition from the king's son: "Am I a dog's head? Here I am full of goodwill toward the House of Saul your father, and you find fault with me about a woman!" (2 Sam. 6:8). That "a woman" could be the subject of such irony in the passage only shows her grave importance for conferring power. Abner is sufficiently incensed over the contest about "the woman" to vow to betray Saul's son by joining the enemy David in a treaty. Needless to say, his betrayal is cast in the same terms—traffic in women—for the condition David sets to enter into any agreement with Abner ups the ante: David will take, not one of Saul's concubines, but Saul's *daughter*, Michal, thereby crushing all hopes for succession for both Abner and Saul's son. But then, the story pauses to portray a poignant scene of the emotional cost of taking Michal away from her husband: "Paltiel son of Laish went with her, weeping behind her, as far as Bahurim where Abner told him to turn back, and he did so." There is silence on the cost to Michal. Has the biblical narrator suddenly gone soft on us and decided to depict the moving devotion of a man for a woman? Are women more than property in political exchanges after all? Or is this an effort to remind us that David's political alliance to Michal is at another man's expense, a man whose name is not Fool, a man who is not an enemy, a man who is a neighbor of the king (Paltiel's home is Gallim, a Benjamite town north of Jerusalem [1 Sam. 25:44, Isa. 10:30]); and is this seizing of Michal a kind of prelude to David's taking Bathsheba from yet another man, also a loyal servant of the king and no fool?

Unlike Mieke Bal, I have not argued for the synonymity of sex and politics to establish another order, a countercoherence, but to clear away a specious distinction to get to the deeper ruptures in this narrative. It will turn out that David's seizures of other men's women—Abigail, Michal, and Bathsheba—are not all alike by any means, for they are not simply acts of garnering power from men who are in his way. Taken together, the three episodes of David's difficulty with such sexual exchanges demonstrate his difficulty as king, and perhaps they even demonstrate the difficulty of kingship for Israel. Abigail seems to offer the paradigm of how it "should" be done, how David should acquire power, for when he takes Abigail, he manages to keep his hands unbloodied: "my lord shall have no cause of grief, or pangs of conscience, for having shed blood without cause or for my lord taking vengeance himself" (1 Sam. 25:31).[17] The story even unfolds improbably, with Nabal dying of fright, to keep David from actually taking the woman from his neighbor. There is another normative sign: he has the requisite children by Abigail. But when David takes Michal, it is from another man—Paltiel weeps—and later when Michal treats David with contempt for his sexual display before the ark of God, she is condemned to childlessness, condemned to be the "widow of a living man" like the concubines who were taken by his son. David has not taken Saul's daughter with such clean hands, he has not succeeded in establishing an alliance with the House of Saul, and there will be no heir to the House of Saul and the House of David.

When David takes Bathsheba, he does not need her; he is at the height of his power, king of all he surveys, including Bathsheba. She is still the property of another man; in fact, two other men have rights to her before David, as the careful inclusion of her near-patronymic "daughter of Eliam" reminds us. Her husband is a loyal servant of the king, and moreover, a loyal servant of God, fighting his holy war while David lolls about at home during "the time when kings go to war." Hence, taking Bathsheba contrasts with the way he garnered power as a fugitive. In fact, the roles have reversed: now, David is the Fool. The king is greedy as Nabal had been, and he denies his neighbor what is rightfully his, as Nabal had denied David provisions and hospitality. Nathan's parable of the ewe-lamb drives home the point that this adultery is a violation of a property right: Bathsheba is compared to an animal, a favored animal, to be sure, one that is like a daughter (alluding to the Hebrew wordplay on Bathsheba's name), and the only one the poor man has; the polluting of his woman is analogous to the slaughter of his animal. As Levi-Strauss observed, "the exchange of brides is merely the conclusion to an uninterrupted process of reciprocal gifts [from, say, wine to animals to women], which effects the transition from hostility to alliance, from anxiety to confidence, and from fear to friendship. As the regulated exchange of women is designed to establish cooperative relations between men, so the rules governing those exchanges —taboos on adultery and rape, determinations of brideprices and bride labor—are designed to maintain and protect that cooperation."[18] Like the incest taboo which enforces an exchange and alliance with an outside group, the adultery taboo protects the peaceful alliances. But when women are stolen rather than peaceably exchanged—as Michal sort of is and Bathsheba certainly is—all of the relational directions reverse, toward fear, anxiety, and hostility. The Bathsheba story shows that the consequence of stealing another's wife is the murder of a loyal servant. Upon such an infraction of the social order, only chaos can follow: "you have killed with the sword so the sword will never be far from your House." And the death of a child born of such infraction is overdetermined. The biblical division of the universe into pure and impure makes Tony Tanner's understanding of adultery as adulteration apt. "Adulteration implies pollution, contamination, a 'base admixture,' a wrong combination. . . . If society depends for its existence on certain rules governing what may be combined and what should be kept separate, then adultery, by bringing the wrong things together in the wrong places (or the wrong people in the wrong beds), offers an attack on those rules, revealing them to be arbitrary rather than absolute."[19]

The meaning of *nabal* will deepen, for David's act of adultery with Bathsheba should be seen not only in the light of the exchanges that characterize his other marriages, but in light of the much larger issue of adultery that pervades the biblical text. Israel is continually whoring after other Gods, as the Bible pointedly puts it; the faithfulness or faithlessness of the people toward their God is always cast in sexual terms: "I am a jealous God, you will have none but me." It is a narrative obsessed with the possibility and actuality of betrayal, with "going astray" as the term for both faithlessness and sexual transgression. Idolatry is repeatedly figured as sexual infidelity: "So shameless was her [Israel's] whoring that at last she polluted the country; she committed adultery with lumps of stone and pieces of wood" (Jer. 3:9). It is in that context that the king of Israel goes astray. Even within the Bathsheba story itself, desire for God and human desire are homologized, for David's adultery is set in stark relief—not, as we would expect, to the fidelity of Bathsheba's husband to her, but to Uriah's faithfulness to God. Under the injunctions of holy war, to sleep with his own wife would be to be faithless to God; it is that fidelity that Uriah maintains despite his abstinence at war, despite the obvious attractiveness of his wife, despite his drunkenness, and it is that fidelity to God that he finally dies for. Meanwhile, David, so very careful about idolatry, has "gone astray" from God after all. While Abigail had successfully forestalled David's violence against *her* husband, he is driven to kill Bathsheba's husband, and Abigail's warning haunts the plot: "when Yahweh appoints you prince over Israel, this must not be an obstacle or stumbling block to my lord, that blood was shed in vain and that my lord gained victory by his own hand."

It is no accident that adultery leads to murder, that adultery is the crime that is explicitly exposed, rather than any of David's many other politicial machinations and assassinations in the House of Saul that are only hinted at. For in this act, David violates a whole series of commandments: "You shall not kill; you shall not commit adultery; you shall not steal; you shall not bear false witness against your neighbor." And just before these injunctions regulating social order are the commandments about the exclusivity of desire for God. "You shall have no gods except me." A relation between the final five commands and the earlier ones that specify loyalty and gratitude and exclusivity of love toward God is thereby established. The logic could be paraphrased: "you shall love only me, you shall not love your neighbor's God" and that means that "you shall not covet your neighbor's god, you shall not covet your neighbor's wife." We should not be surprised to note that in Yhwh's response to David's adultery with Bathsheba, it is not at all clear whom David betrayed, her husband or God, for the infidelities are inseparable: "A sword will never be lacking in your house, because you treated *me* with contempt and took the wife of Uriah the Hittite to be your own wife." The analogy needs further refinement, for it is cast in specific terms: as Israel is to God, so woman is to man. You shall have no god except me; you shall have no man except me. Fidelity to God is not like fidelity to a woman; this is a culture that has institutionalized polygamy, not polyandry. Just as Israel's identity is contingent on God, so a woman's identity in the Bible is contingent upon a man. Women are created for man, as Genesis 2 makes vivid, and they exist only in relation to man (whether husband, brother, father, sons), as the story of Ruth reinforces. Hence, to violate her is to violate him: Uriah is killed, Paltiel weeps, Absalom becomes murderous, and the women themselves—Bathsheba, Michal, and Tamar—are not subjects who are entitled to a response.

Both sexual fidelity and divine fidelity are preoccupations of a narrative that tends to construct identity as someone or some people *set apart*, with boundaries that could be mapped, ownership that could be titled. But if, as I have been arguing, the parameters of Israel's identity are at issue—which God is allowed and which is not, which woman is allowed and which is not—then the identity of the nation and the people is not already mapped, but in the process of being anxiously drawn and redrawn, and we must address the prior question: *is* this people set apart? or is its hankering to "go astray" an effort to cross boundaries, or at least to blur them by being God's and someone else's too? Which people are outside and which are inside the boundaries of the community of Israel? To seek clearly circumscribed definitions in this text is to be frustrated at every turn. What is a king, a priest, a military leader, and what is the difference? That question is the story of Samuel and Saul. What is an assassin, what is a politician, and what is the difference? That is the story of David. And what is a family? Is Jonathan David's brother? Is Absalom Amnon's brother? What is a wife? If she is someone who belongs to someone else, what is she when the belonging is switched?

The narrative's effort to construct Israel's past is no less than an effort to construct Israel, but it is not a construction in the sense of building a building, nor is it a national spirit unfolding, an institution growing, or an organic personality flowering. Instead, Israel is an inconsistent, fractured, complex, and multiple concept: a people who believe in their God and who do not, who are bound by a law that they refuse to obey, who have no land but the promise of one, who have a land only to lose it. And even these formulations are misleadingly stable, for each presupposes "a people" when defining them is very much a part of the task of the "history." One way the story defines the people is as those who claim a united history, and they are only a people so long as they remember (or adopt) that shared history; and yet they are forever forgetting, needing to be reminded. Another way is that they are a people who have entered into a covenant with their God—a covenant that stipulates they must not go astray—and yet they are continually doing just that. Whatever Israel is, even provisionally, it is always threatened with being "cut off," disinherited by Yhwh, even with being not-Israel. For once disinherited, Israel will not be on its own, struggling for independent survival; once disinherited, Israel will cease to be. The deal struck in Exodus, "I will be your God if you will be my people," could be rephrased as "You will be *a* people, if and only if, I, and only I, am your God." That means that when Israel "goes astray" it risks losing not just prosperity, but its identity—not only because whoring after Baal and Asherah means losing some version of cultural distinctiveness, nor because Israelites risk becoming indistinguishable from other Mesopotamians, but because these are the terms of the contract: Israel will be destroyed by its enemies if she is unfaithful, will be rewarded as a nation if she is faithful. She is constituted by the exclusivity of her object choice. "You shall have no gods except me." If the people forget their history or go astray from their God, they will "be no more." Adultery, rape, the people going astray: these violations are not just violations of commandments, they are violations of various identity-constructs, and they become tests of definition in a text that is anxious about whom this story is about, and whose story it is anyway.

All of this anxiety about identity, political and sexual definition, has been succinctly summarized in that one biblical word: *nabal*. It means not only fool, but also outcast, as in David's lament for Abner when he asks why he should have died as an outcast, a *nabal*. It refers to someone who has severed himself from society through a moral transgression, someone who has forfeited his place in society by violating taboos that define the social order. As a verb, it means to violate, and it is used especially to indicate sexual violations: the rape of Tamar, the rape of Dinah, the rape in Judges 19, adultery in Jeremiah 23; but it is also used to indicate uttering false words and thereby disrupting the order of language. Its Akkadian stem was used to indicate breaking away (as a stone) or tearing away, and that Akkadian sense of rupture is still attached to the Hebrew word used for an adulterer and rapist in ancient Israel where sexual violation signals breaking away, rupturing the norm. A variant of *nabal* means corpse, and in ancient Israel, a corpse represents another rupture, this time not only from the social order, but from the order of life itself. Death represented the strongest degree of uncleanness, an "irreparable separation from God's life-giving power and from the centre of life, the cult."[20] But the outcast is not so very far from the corpse, for as bearers of evil, those cast out of society had not only no home, but "no name" (Job 30:8). The book of Job offers a Lear-like description of their pitiful undoing:

> They used to gnaw the roots of desert plants,
> and brambles from abandoned ruins;

and plucked mallow, and brushwood leaves,
making their meals off roots of broom.
Outlawed from the society of men,
who, as against thieves, raised hue and cry against them,
they made their dwellings on ravines' steep sides,
in caves or clefts in the rock.
You could hear them wailing from the bushes,
as they huddled together in the thistles.
Their children are as worthless as they were,
Nameless people, outcasts of society.

Job 30:3–8

Who is a *nabal* and who is not, what makes one cast out and another not, is of course another way of asking who is an Israelite and who is not, what is Israel and what is not, for the outcasts define Israel's borders.

The Derridian insight that the margin is the center becomes, in this case, a perception not only that the Israelite is defined by the outcast, but that the Israelite defends himself with such ferocity against the outcast out of fear of the outcast, the violator, within him, even out of attraction to that violator. *Nebalim* is used for Israel's enemies, the "other," but it is also used for the Benjamites when they make themselves the enemies of Israel's other tribes, and it is eventually applied to all of Israel herself (Deut. 32:6). When Amnon rapes Tamar, she protests that he should not act like a *nabal*. Her objection, "This is not a thing men do in Israel," condenses all of the allusions the term has to moral, sexual, and national identity. In fact, rape is a thing men do in Israel and the law has provided for it: if the woman belongs to no one else, then he need only marry her, as Tamar reminds her assailant (Deut. 22:28–29). But Tamar is his half-sister, and incest is not a thing men do in Israel. Like adultery, incest confuses the carefully drawn kinship boundaries, the narrow space permissible between exogamy and incest. His rape makes Amnon virtually a non-Israeli, like all the *nebalim*, a nonentity. This may be a thing men do in other nations, but this is not a thing men do in Israel; in Israel there is no place for Amnon. Following his sexual violation, he will die (fulfilling that other sense of nabal, corpse), and even his death is engulfed in an ever widening circle of violence, moving from his brother (Absalom murders him and is murdered) to the entire family (the civil war, the usurpation of Adonijah, the assassinations of the kings of Judah, and eventually the forced exile of the population). This kind of violence attends each instance in the Bible where *nabal* signals a sexual violation. In Genesis, the rape of

Dinah leads to war with Israel; in Judges, the rape of the concubine gives way to war with Israel; and in both cases, these are wars of definition, establishing borders—who is Israel and who is not.

Significantly, the term *nabal* occurs especially frequently in the David narratives. David's adultery is followed by Amnon's rape, but it is immediately preceded by a story of *nebalim*. David had sent his men to the Ammonites to reaffirm their covenant with the new king, but the Ammonites distrust these emissaries and humiliate them, shaving off half of their beards and cutting off their tunics to the buttocks; that is, they are symbolically raped and castrated (note the Akkadian sense of tearing, even where the word is not used but its meaning is enacted), and David understands them to be outcasts now, telling them not to return to Israel until their beards have grown back. It is a story of a violation that issues in liminality; Israel's definition has been challenged, and she will have to fight the enemy to define herself against him. Israel's effort to affirm a covenant, to establish its borders peaceably and proceed with that settled identity issued instead in a struggle in which its borders were defied and had to be redrawn: a struggle of definition.

Finally, to return to that prominent story about *nabal* in the David narratives, the story of David's dealings with Abigail's husband: "Nabal is his name and nabal is his behavior." Nabal has violated the covenant agreement by which David protects him and in turn has earned protection; he becomes first an outcast from the order, then a corpse, allegorizing the meanings of his name. In all this, David is made the foil for Nabal; unlike the Fool, David is wise, knows the rules and follows them, knows wise words when he hears them, knows, that is, not to shed blood so that he may inherit the kingdom. But in the parallel scene with Bathsheba, where David marries another wife of another man who dies, David is not contrasted to Nabal. David becomes the *nabal*. While it is not made an explicit appellation in this scene, the term is most consistently used for an adulterer, and we saw that it is explicit in the next scene where Amnon rapes Tamar in an echo of David's forcible taking of Bathsheba. Retrospectively, what Tamar says of Amnon becomes an indictment of David: "this is not a thing men do in Israel." And like all the other scenes where *nabal* is used to signal sexual violation, David is engulfed in violence. This is not a thing men do in Israel, but David *is* Israel. At his height, when the House of David is synonymous with the nation, David behaves like an outcast. How can the House of David both define Israel and be cast out of Israel? Where is the nation when the King is in exile? What happens to the promise of a House that will be stable forever when its recipient is a *nabal*, like the nameless, homeless ones?

Foucault asserts that

> the world we know is not this ultimately simple configuration where events are reduced to accentuate their essential traits, their final meaning, or their initial and final value. On the contrary, it is a profusion of entangled events. . . . We want historians to confirm our belief that the present rests upon profound intentions and immutable necessities. But the true historical sense confirms our existence among countless lost events, without a landmark or a point of reference.[21]

I have argued that despite the Bible's effort to make sense of the profusion of events, in this case in the narratives of the Books of Samuel, the historiography offered by the Bible largely confirms the sense of confusion. The history of biblical interpretation has been engaged in the effort to discover "profound intentions and immutable necessities," and it has ferreted out any efforts the Bible has made to create such order and called them dominant. But perhaps it is time that we begin to listen to other voices in the text, the voices of biblical historians who depict history as we know it and as we live it. When we read the very discontinuities, duplications, and contradictions that biblical scholars want to smooth out, perhaps we could take note of them, not at all surprised at the instability in these stories: how could it be otherwise, when there is no stable ground from which to tell this story? We may even like ancient Israel's founding fiction better, not despite, but for all the cracks in its foundation.

ESTHER PASSES: CHIASM, LEX TALIO, AND MONEY IN THE BOOK OF ESTHER

William T. McBride

Ezra's production of a second Torah after the original was destroyed by Babylonian fire hints at the unresolvable question of biblical authorship in general, and necessarily casts doubt on the distinction between biblical text and tradition; at the same time it "authorizes" a continuation of Pharisaic-rabbinic hermeneutics willing to "obscure the boundaries between composition and interpretation" and attentive to hidden subtleties.[1] As Joyce Baldwin tells us of Esther: "No other book of the Old Testament has come down to us in so many variant forms."[2] So, in the spirit of high-serious play, throughout the course of this essay on Esther I deliberately smooth over textual distinctions of origin and canon, referring to apocryphal stories, Greek and Semitic additions, various rabbinic commentaries and translations, as well as to the authorized versions of the Book. My methodology, therefore, is "midrashic" in the sense that current scholars of literary criticism and midrash give the term, where "text" and "critical text" production are not absolutely distinct. When I speak of the "Book of Esther," I intend what Geoffrey Hartman has called a "continuum of intertextual supplements" or "text milieu."[3] Like the tyrant Xerxes, I homologize the rhetorical, legal, and fiduciary, while at the same time I emphasize difference and dissymmetry as a result of such operations. For the purpose of reading the overdetermined crossing and double-crossing nature of this sublime chiastic work that is the Book of Esther, as well as the chrematistic, postal, and imperial legacy associated with the lineage Cyrus, Darius, Xerxes, I prefer to call the Persian King Xerxes with its fortuitous double x's rather than Ahasuerus, and therefore follow Carey Moore's *Anchor Bible* translation on this point.[4] Unless otherwise noted, citations are from the Authorized King James Version.

I

Chiasm, the Hebrew poetic form par excellence, derives its name from the Greek letter X or "chi" and signifies a rhetorical and thematic figure similar to inverted parallelism, whereby words, clauses, phrases, characters and plot elements are exchanged in a mirror-like inversion. The Alter/Kermode *Literary Guide to the Bible* defines chiasm as a "formal patterning of any literary or rhetorical unit that preserves symmetry while reversing the order of the terms, to produce the sequence ABBA." Sternberg finds the effect of chiasm to be "closure" and rounded-off parallels.[5] Indeed an overwhelming majority of philosophers and rhetoricians who analyze chiasm, as well as most Esther commentators, read the trope's effect as symmetrical, as a figure of closure.[6] The Book of Esther indeed tempts its readers to find a certain symmetry, balance, and cancellation without residue, particularly in its recapitulation of events in 9:1, where, according to the *Anchor Bible*, it is declared that in place of the pogrom, the "opposite happened"—Purim. Virtually all exegetes of Esther concerned with the book's chiastic results speak of "completeness," "integration," "perfect harmony," "closure," rounded-off parallels, "exact opposites," "true reversals," and "fully resolved situations."[7] Like Haman who wishes to eradicate Jewish difference, readers of Esther tend to purge the book of its chiastic difference.

There are, however, some notable exceptions to this predisposition to symmetry. Yehuda Radday has diagramed what he terms the "perfect chiasm" as the sequence ABC–D–C'B'A'.[8] A number of critics have each in their way pointed out that this middle member, "D"—this dividing element, center, plane, axis—although valueless and substanceless with regard to the exchange, acts nonetheless as the "general space" of that transaction's possibility; that is to say, it acts as its "ground."[9] They go on to stress a *"strategic dissymmetry"* as the result of the chiastic transaction.[10]

James Kugel argues convincingly—although his subject is biblical parallelism in general rather than chiasm specifically—to correct the tenacious analysis of parallelism spawned by Robert Lowth and his followers, addressing its "disastrous effect on subsequent criticism. Because of it, synonymity was often imposed where it did not exist . . . , and the real nature of biblical parallelism" was lost "in the enthusiasm following the discovery of the pairs." Kugel writes that the "ear" of the Bible's original audience "was attuned to hearing 'A is so, and *what's more*, B is so.'" The excess of this "what's more" marks the "expectations the ancient Hebrew listener, or reader, brought to every text."[11] And it was the "rabbinic genius" of midrash to seek out such differentiation "central to that whole search for nonapparent significance that is midrash." For the rabbis, the "ways of wisdom consisted of looking deeply into things for their slight differences, their tiny nuances, allusions, hidden connections."[12] As for those readers of Esther sensitive to Kugel's "what's more," David J. A. Clines compares Haman's and Mordecai's decrees and discovers they "neither directly contradict nor cancel one another out," and makes a point of saying such "divergences are often significant"; Carey Moore mentions that "the provisions of Mordecai's letter . . . must duplicate, *if not exceed*, the harsh terms of Haman's letter in order to nullify" it.[13] More on this excess in terms of monetary, strategic, and memorial interest will follow. As a visionary metaphor of chiasm, we might substitute prismatic refraction for mirror-like reflection, and thus avoid the habitual smoothing over of the logical antinomies that radiate from chiasm.

II

In the Book of Esther, King Xerxes inhabits the characterological "center" of the book's chiasm, acting as a kind of Postmaster General *in absentia*, presiding over the mechanical sorting and shifting of subjects and scrolls, mediating between Haman and Mordecai, Vashti and Esther. He mediates, however, without neutralizing. As Derrida puts it in "The Double Session": "What takes place is only . . . the place, the spacing, which is nothing." "The word 'between' has no full meaning of its own." That is to say, it "forms a syntactical plug [*cheville syntaxique*]," what "philosophers from the Middle Ages to Husserl's *Logical Investigations* have called an incomplete signification."[14] As I hope to show soon, with Xerxes's constant deferral of decision making he performs like Derrida's *cheville syntaxique* or syntactical "kingpin," little more than a protected place-holder or "figure" head.[15] Not only is the chiastic central element characterized by a certain absence, but the trajectory of its surrounding members is dissymmetrical.

Esther does not merely inhibit Vashti's throne; she transforms that previously passive office into a vehicle for legislative action by issuing edicts and by *breaking* the racial barrier with her "inter"-marriage.[16] Likewise, Mordecai does not simply replace Haman, matching his extreme personal favor with the king, but gains the acceptance of and promised wealth and peace for "all his seed" (10:3). The field is hardly left intact. The formerly repressed (Semitic) elements now erupt and graft onto the previously privileged (Persian) ones, thereby exceeding those original values and creating new ones—for example, gentile Jews, that is, the increase in followers of Judaism from the pool of Xerxes's

subjects due to the chiastic countermanding of Haman's edict for a pogrom (8:17). This excess of favor, obtained by Mordecai's and Esther's
thrift and restraint, indicates, not only the effect of the chiasm to go
beyond its mirror function, but the Book of Esther's overdetermined
dialectic (which is not one) of excess and restraint, concealment and
discovery, expedience and delay, injury and compensation.

Compensation as punishment in the Book of Esther invariably entails
the principle of lex talionis—i.e., the chiastic measure for measure, eye
for eye—the ancient Hebrew law stated most explicitly in Exod. 21:
24, Deut. 19:21, and Lev. 24:20. Vashti will not appear when bidden
and is ordered to disappear (1:19); Haman provides a gallows (Heb.,
tree) fifty cubits high for Mordecai, and is hung (crucified)[17] on it instead
(7:10), along with his ten sons (9:10, 25). As the rabbis would have it:
"he is boiled in his own pot," and citing Ps. 7:15, "is fallen into the
ditch which he made."[18] Those who were prepared to act on Haman's
decree to destroy all Jews are themselves destroyed. The Targum Sheni
notes: "All this happened that thou [reader] mayest know that God
never fails to punish with measure for measure."[19] Werner Dommershausen remarks on the suitability of the chiastic word order to express
retaliation, and, indeed, both the chiasm and talio share similar
exchangist attributes.[20] In his chapter "Lex Talionis" in *Studies in Biblical
Law*, David Daube meditates on the law's "central" preposition: "in place
of."[21] It is this substitutive, tropic character of lex talionis which also
operates in the chiasm: Esther *in place of* Vashti on the throne, Haman
crucified *in place of* Mordecai, and so forth. As most scholars see a symmetrical exchange as the result of the chiasm, so too, many see a balance
restored as a result of the exaction of the talio.[22]

What is so symmetrical, however, about being awarded your attacker's
inert eye "in place of" your previously sound, now gouged one?[23] Deut.
19:19 seems to allow retaliation even on those who merely contemplate
evil, but where is the "balance" in murdering seventy-five thousand foes
(Esther 9:16) who had only *prepared* to assault you? The law of taliation
was established, according to Daube, to prevent measureless retribution,
and the "ruthless kind of retaliation" the ancient gentiles exacted
(Daube, 105), which George Knight says was not "'tit for tat,'" but, in
an allusion to Matt. 18:21, rather up to "seventy times seven."[24]

With the introduction of a money economy and, hence, money thinking, a further "advance" was made possible by moving away from the
literalness of "eye for eye" to the fungibility (exchangeability in money)
of man already inherent in the law (Daube, 108). This gives a new twist
to Daube's talionic phrase "paying back an enemy in his own coin"
(Daube, 144).[25] Rather than a specious, "mere" cancellation, however,
something is left over in a chiastic exchange. In fiduciary terms such

an excess or remainder is to be understood as a gain of interest. *Black's Law Dictionary* defines "interest" as the "compensation" for the "use or forbearance or detention of money," and I would add for the detention of information and of people as well.[26] It is the book's characteristic deferring, delaying action—this "detention"—that occasions its exchanges and their residua.[27] The exchangist ideology of the chrematist (coin-making) King Xerxes and of his empire permeates the actions and chiastic transactions that come to pass in the Book of Esther. Each of the king's gestures and edicts is calculated to unify his kingdom and strengthen his realm's economy of people as well as his economy of coins.[28] Although Herodotus and others celebrate Xerxes's postal system for its efficiency—like the bureaucratic machine of which it is a part —detour, deflection, and delay are at its root.[29] Xerxes deflects responsibility for banishing Vashti by deferring to Memucan (1:15–16), distances himself from culpability for the pogrom by turning over the signet ring and its authority to Haman (3:10–11), and detours Haman's poisonous letter by rechanneling his royal authority to Esther and Mordecai (8: 2). By obscuring the source of these decisions, Xerxes neatly launders his role, allowing him to claim what has been recently termed "deniability," the first rule of covert operations.[30]

Another significant delay in the book is the extraordinary eleven-month deferral of the pogrom, which may cost the Jews even greater anxiety than a swift death. As Deut. 28:66 puts it: "And thy life shall hang in doubt before thee; and thou shalt fear day and night, and shalt have none assurance of thy life." But the delay certainly affords the time for Esther and Mordecai (employing their own deferral tactics) to reverse the death sentence. While the cruel, and responsibility-deflecting, cast of the die decides the Jews' fate by means of an "atrocious lottery," in fact, these "arithmetics of fate" work in their favor from the outset by granting them ample time to escape.[31] It is fitting that the festival, Purim, be named after the typically heartless device *pur* which, this time, allowed time for escape, and enabled the Jews, in the spirit of the talio, to turn "mourning into dancing."[32]

Esther's delay in making her request of Xerxes to save the Jews serves to predispose the king toward granting it; his anticipation builds (he cannot sleep the night of the first banquet), as his jealousy of Haman grows. The Targum Sheni has Esther think: "I shall excite the jealousy of Ahhashverosh against Haman, for the king will say:'What must be the reason that of all my governors Esther invited none but Haman to the banquet?'" (Targum, 152) Haman's head swells as he awaits Esther's cleverly delayed banquet, since the invitation to "make haste" (5:5) to the first banquet left no time to ponder it. This delay, what Clines calls a "retardation of the main plot" from chapters five through seven, allows Haman time to indulge in self-aggrandizing boasts of riches and of his promotion "above the princes and servants of the king" (5:1), and to overindulge in a fifty-cubit-high "gallows" meant for Mordecai.[33] When, at the second banquet, Esther performs the double unmasking of her identity as Jew and Haman's as Jew-killer and queen-defiler, she cashes in, is paid in full, and with interest. She realizes the extreme of Xerxes's favor, obtaining not merely "half the kingdom" offered in 5:3 and again in 7:2, but Haman's death, the full "house of Haman" (8:1), and, along with Mordecai, the king's signet ring (8:2) —not the promised half, but the entire kingdom. The Purim postal practice of sending and receiving "portions" commemorates this excessive favor.

The book's most *interest*-bearing deferral is the delay of Mordecai's reward for saving Xerxes's life. The initial denial occurs at that jarring gap between chapters two and three, where the entering of Mordecai's efforts into the Catalogue of the King's Benefactors[34] is followed instantly by the unprecedented promotion of Haman (3:1). The reader is momentarily perplexed. For example, Sandra Berg says the first verses of chapter three "unexpectedly report the promotion of Haman, not Mordecai."[35] The reader is then forced to make a metonymic link by contiguity between Haman and Mordecai which positions Haman in a debtor's (not to say a chiastic) relation to Mordecai. Haman somehow wrongs Mordecai; he literally "steals his promotion," which serves to escalate the enmity between the two. If the book ever lays bare its artifice, it does so here with this inversion at the gap between chapters two and three.[36]

Near the end of an extraordinary six-month "potlatch," inebriated from wine, the power of rule, and the camaraderie of his stag-party cronies, Xerxes decides to flaunt his wealth further by demanding the presence of his wife, Queen Vashti, wearing *only* her crown. The Megilla, Targum Sheni, and Midrash Rabbah, along with other ancient commentaries, insist on Vashti's nakedness.[37] Herodotus depicts a similar husbandly excess by the Lydian King Candaules who displays his naked queen to his servant Gyges, thereby necessitating regicide and a transfer of the crown.[38] After hearing Xerxes's request, Vashti answers in the Targum Sheni: "Ever since I was born no man has seen my body except thou alone, and if I now appear before thee and before the hundred and twenty-seven crowned kings, the end will be, they will slay thee and marry me" (Targum, 121).[39] Both Xerxes and Candaules transgress this law and bring about courtly crises: Gyges sees the queen's nakedness and must kill Candaules in order to restore order; Vashti refuses to be a party to such transgression and is divorced and deposed ostensibly to restore order.

On the strength of the decision to punish Vashti's refusal as precedent, Xerxes publishes an edict throughout his land that wives should obey their husbands. The letters are authorized by the king and validated by the impression of his signet ring. In keeping with imperial procedures, the tyrant attempts to abolish disparity and resistance among his subjects by circulating this piece of legal tender, ensuring that each husband's household is a microcosm of the king's unquestioned dominion. This totalizing, homogenizing effect is characteristic of both a money economy and of tyranny, whereby things are reducible to their representation in money. Percy Neville Ure highlights the arguments of Busolt and Radet for a connection between the origin of coinage and tyranny, pointing out the Lydians of 700–600 B.C.E as the producers of the first metal coins resulting from their middleman role in industry and commerce between the Greeks and the Far East.[40] Citing the *Persepolis Treasury Tablets*, Carey Moore relates how Xerxes improves upon his father's new money economy by for the first time paying off the Persepolis builders in monetary units rather than paying in kind.[41] Seth Benardete in *Herodotean Inquiries*, writes:

> The trust in art is the tyrannical replacement for the trust in the customary. The tyrant tries to wipe out the memory of the old things with innovations [minting coins], but he puts them on a different basis, his own fame. He tries to replace the embodied customs with a name, which, attached to artifacts [coins], might survive him; and he sometimes succeeds.[42]

Xerxes also has an imperial need for a homogenized, raceless domain, or at least for a tolerance of all races, in order for the empire to expand, and hence prosper.[43] Haman, Xerxes's chief of police, attempts his own version of tyrannic homogenization by means of a Jewish pogrom that will eliminate the scattered, diverse people who refuse to "keep . . . the king's laws: therefore it is not for the king's profit to suffer them" (3:8), and hopes to insure his plan with a baksheesh of ten thousand talents of silver. By citing the threat of Jewish heterogeneity to Xerxes's unified empire, Haman strikes at the heart of that empire's power base and is hence accorded a free hand to work the genocide. But is it not rather Haman and his pogrom which pose the threat to Xerxes's unity, not Mordecai and his religious allegiance? Remember that chapter three, verse fifteen reports how "the city Shushan was perplexed" by the deadly plan. The financially astute Esther will successfully suggest that should Haman intend to sell her people as slaves, thereby increasing the king's coffers, she would assent, but an outright destruction of so many subjects (the queen included) would only deplete the royal treasury, since the annihilation of so many Jews, she implies, would mean doing away with a substantial population of taxpayers. In other words, it does not profit the king *not* to suffer them.

Esther's survival in Xerxes's court is due, in part, to her restraint and, in part, to her presentation of an assimilated, i.e., homogeneous, countenance to all she meets. Since Esther's ethnicity is unknown, Xerxes grants a "remission of taxes to the provinces" (RSV, 2:18). The Targum Sheni has the king ask her: "Pray tell me, who are thy people, and what is thy family?" Upon Esther's answer that she is an orphan, the king "universally remitted the taxes, and gave presents to the provinces, because he thought and said to himself, I will do good to all the nations and governments, among whom is certainly the people of Esther" (Targum, 128). This tendency to universalize is manifest in the generalizing decrees of Xerxes: here by making Esther the daughter of all races and religions, and earlier when he legislatively restricts all wives based upon Vashti's singular action. Haman makes a similar synecdochical move when, instead of seeking the death of Mordecai alone, he attempts to annihilate all Jews. These examples of what Kenneth Burke calls synecdoche's "relationship of convertibility, between the two terms," i.e., part *for* whole and vice versa, point up, once again, the profoundly exchangist nature of Xerxes's empire and of the chiastic Book of Esther.[44] To Mordecai, Esther is the loyal daughter/wife/Jewess.[45] To Hegai, Haman, and Xerxes she is the prudent virgin/gentile. The *Encyclopedia Judaica* cites *Megillah 13A* in order to note that "everyone took her to be one of his own people,"[46] resembling the recognizable wine each satrap is served, which comes from his own province,[47] and resembling each royal decree which is written in that province's own familiar script. Esther mimes the homogenized and homogenizing status of Xerxes, who claims, in his letter reversing the pogrom (whose text we find in the Targum Sheni): "I am the same from one end of the land to the other" (Targum, 165). Esther, like Xerxes, also acts as the sorting, shifting, chiastic "middleman." As "queenpin," she carries Mordecai's assassination plot discovery to Xerxes, plays Haman and Xerxes off one another with her ruse of two banquets—a superb double-cross—and in the apocryphal Semitic *Vorlage* "Mordecai's Dream" and the "Interpretation of Mordecai's Dream," Esther represents the mediating stream turned torrent between the two dragons, Haman and Mordecai.[48] R. Phinehas forges his interesting reading of the line from Esther 9:3, "Because the fear of Mordecai was fallen upon them," this way: Just as "the king's coinage was current throughout the land," so "Mordecai's coinage was current. What was the coinage of Mordecai? It had Mordecai on one side and Esther on the other" (*Midrash Rabbah*, 121). Now, given that by 9:3 Mordecai has emerged from behind the scenes, where he worked as a spy for Xerxes and as a broker for Esther, to the front lines of the battle to reverse Haman's pogrom plans in the name of the reluctant king, I see the coinage of Mordecai rather as a two-headed, incuse coin whose obverse side features Mordecai in sackcloth and ashes with the legend "Blessed be Mordecai" stamped under the figure, and whose reverse side represents Xerxes's crowned head sunk in intaglio carrying the legend "Cursed be Haman," with Esther providing the unacknowledged alloy at its center.[49] Were Esther figured numismatically, she would be like the realm's talents of pure silver: all things to all people. We read in 2:15: "Esther obtained favour in the sight of all them that looked upon her." Rabbi Judah says: "She was like a statue which a thousand persons look upon and all equally admire" (*Midrash Rabbah*, 77).

According to the Megilla's reading, Mordecai shares Esther's assimilability by virtue of his polyglottal prowess in that, as a Sanhedrin, he is conversant in over seventy languages (*Encyclopedia Judaica*, 6:908). He is, therefore, additionally valuable to the king, and will exceed the space marked out by his predecessor, Haman. Perhaps it is Mordecai's linguistic ability which serves him early in the book by enabling him to overhear the treasonous contrivance which Bigthan and Teresh believed they had indecipherably cast in a foreign tongue. Xerxes establishes legal homogenization by issuing his edicts "to each province in its own script, and to each people in its own language" (1:22, *Anchor Bible*). It is worth noting again in passing that this particular edict serves to smooth over any wifely insubordination.

So Esther, like an infinitely exchangeable coin, first passes from her natural parents (who had passed away) to her adoptive father/husband /cousin Mordecai. She then passes herself off as a gentile and a virgin, gaining passage to Xerxes's house of virginal candidates for queen in this other lottery, the beauty pageant. By passing up Hegai's offer of unlimited indulgence, and prudently displaying her unsurpassed beauty, Esther gains favor as the most valuable of virginal candidates.[50] Each candidate, like a sum of ill-gotten money, is deposited for twelve months where she is laundered, homogenized, i.e., purified: "six months with oil of myrrh and six months with sweet odours for the purifying of women" (2:12). Each night Xerxes exercises his *jus primae noctis*, and every morning another spent virgin passes over to Shaashgaz's counting house of concubines. Prudent Esther does not make this deflationary passage; instead she is crowned Xerxes's queen, completing the book's first manifest reversal/crossing. Vashti had refused to show herself to the King's drunken fellows and was punished with divorce and disinheritance; Esther holds in reserve her true racial/religious, familial, and hymenal status, and is rewarded with the crown. Vashti passes up her chance to remain queen; Esther passes for a virginal gentile and usurps Vashti's royal crown, throne, and bed. Esther also exchanges her master /husband/guardian, passing from Mordecai to Xerxes. She counterfeits, however, her allegiance to Xerxes, while remaining faithful to Mordecai's commandment not to reveal her people or kindred.[51]

By keeping her ethnic origin hidden, by depositing it secretly away, Esther increases in potential value. Esther, the adept speculator (ably assisted by Mordecai, the broker) cashes in her familial stock by revealing her secret identity at precisely its maturing moment. She not only goes unpunished for her duplicity, her cryptic heterogeneity, but realizes the double dividend of Haman's descent/Mordecai's ascent and the rescue of her otherwise doomed people. Esther will later appeal to her potentially counterfeit-detecting sovereign for validation: "If it please the King, and if I have found favor in his sight, . . . and I be pleasing in his eyes" (8:5), i.e., if you test me and find me to be genuine coin of the realm, then reverse counterfeit Haman's decree. Such phrases are more than mere idiomatic expressions or typical Old Testament polite locutions; as Clines asserts, the phrase "To 'please' is the oil in the wheels of the Persian bureacracy."[52] (These phrases are also chiastically constructed—see note 51.) Mordecai, not surprisingly, is himself described in fiduciary terms. According to the *Anchor Bible*, Mordecai was "great in the King's house . . . for this man Mordecai waxed greater and greater"; like an interest-earning sum, he "was growing and was great" (9:4, *Anchor Bible*).[53]

At a number of moments in the book, Mordecai proves himself the knowledgeable speculator by manipulating the kingdom's economy of information. He advises Esther to conceal her race/religion until the appropriate moment for disclosure; he learns of the assassination plot and deposits it with the king through Esther to his (eventual) great advantage; and he effectively floats his Jewish identity to some of Xerxes's men who tell Haman but not Xerxes, which in part prompts Haman to the excess of unilaterally demanding a pogrom. In a future chiastic reversal (4:15–17), Esther will exchange roles with Mordecai and become initiator and manipulator. Esther instructs Mordecai to do her bidding by carrying to their people the message to fast, perhaps taking a cue from Mordecai's initial "sackcloth and ashes" response to news of the pogrom—a fitting contrast to Haman's excess.

When Mordecai refuses to bow to Haman, following the Jews' allegiance to only one God,[54] he chiastically replicates Vashti's earlier refusal to bow to imperial whim; Mordecai eventually is raised up to take Haman's place, while Vashti's refusal culminates in her dismissal. Haman follows Xerxes's order to serve Mordecai during the latter's triumphant parading, yet ultimately is punished; Mordecai disobeys Xerxes's order of obeisance to Haman and is ultimately rewarded. Esther twice risks sovereign displeasure by appearing in front of the king unbidden and is rewarded; Vashti risks displeasure by not appearing and is punished. Haman hazards ten thousand talents of silver to see his plan through; Esther wagers her life twice ("If I perish, I perish," 4: 15) by approaching the king unbidden in order to assert her queenly role as counsel. Haman formulates his chiastic relation to Mordecai in Targum Sheni this way: "Thy sackcloth and ashes have won the victory over the ten thousand talents of silver" (Targum, 157).

Esther gains the king's friendly ear by passing her hand passionately over the top of his golden scepter.[55] With her stroking supplication, Esther raises her sovereign's excessive interest and is hyperbolically promised half the kingdom should she desire it.[56] Esther's restraint, proven earlier by her passing on Hegai's offer of unlimited indulgence, accounts for her passing up this extravagant offer as well. Other than in this scene, Esther proves to be a sobering influence on her king, not prompting such excessive demands and actions as had Vashti and as will Haman when the king thinks he discovers his right-hand man "making a pass" at his queen. The rabbis have Xerxes and his subjects drinking from the *pakta*, "a kind of large loving-cup used by the Persians," which is also an Aramaic word meaning "to excess" (*Midrash Rabbah*, 41, n. 4). And Sandra Berg finds a paronomastic connection "between Vashti and the 'drinking' which highlights the king's banquet [1:8]—a link which subsequent events clearly establish."[57] Vashti's link to drinking-to-excess nicely contrasts with Esther's sobering presence. Esther's restraint is echoed later by the victorious Jews who slaughter tens of thousands of their enemies, but wisely pass on Xerxes's allowance to plunder.[58] While the Book of Esther teaches temperance, it also authorizes excess by establishing a festival wherein, according to the Mishnah, "celebrating Purim Jews were to drink wine until they were unable to distinguish between" the chiastic elements "Blessed be Mordecai" and "Cursed be Haman."[59]

III

Visibility and invisibility are the mechanisms by which Xerxes obtains and maintains power.[60] His subjects remain visible to him at all times by the employment of spies like Mordecai who is witness to the assassination plottings of Bigthan and Teresh. Xerxes's law of forbidding uninvited entry to the king's house ensures both the visibility of each of his people and his own invisibility. What goes on behind those walls? Like all tyrants, Xerxes's hold on his realm depends on the people's belief in the unseen. Such fealty enables the monarch to pay the builders of his Persepolis in monetary units that *stand for* the absent amount of silver or whatever other standard the money bears. In this way, the tyrannical bureaucrat wields his scriptorial power through coinage.

Xerxes's entire bureaucratic kingdom hinges on his issuing coins and edicts, printed by his scribes, validated by his signet ring, and distributed by his efficient postal system. This efficiency is tested when the king pits writing against writing. In his attempt to reverse the Haman-authorized decree to destroy all Jews, he authorizes Esther's and Mordecai's countermanding decree to destroy all enemies of the Jews. When Bigthan and Teresh are crucified, how fitting that it is not the actual execution that warrants Xerxes's presence, but the writing of its details into the official book of chronicles.[61] It is also by reading the chronicles late one sleepless night that Xerxes discovers, with the aid of double-entry bookkeeping, a lacuna, that gap between chapters two and three: Mordecai was never rewarded for his spying. Just as our kingpin Xerxes occupies the characterological center of the chiastic cluster Vashti-Esther /Haman-Mordecai, this sleepless evening's event arguably maintains the book's narratological center, occurring as it does in chapter six, verse one of the book's ten chapters. This determination of the book's center is Yehuda Radday's reading. Radday echoes the consensus that "biblical authors and/or editors placed the main idea, the thesis, or turning point of each literary unit, at its center." As he asserts, a work's chiastic structure is more than an "artistic device," rather it is "a key to meaning."[62]

While few would dispute that Xerxes's consultation of his ledger inaugurating Mordecai's ascent is *a* turning point in the Book of Esther, Radday betrays uneasiness at the event's "apparent lack of profundity," and unconvincingly cites the rabbis for "ample theological justification for the central position of the king's sleeplessness."[63] A rather more profound center of the book, one that presents a chiastic crossing in the middle of the more general chiasm that is the Book of Esther, occurs at 5:9 (arguably as central as Radday's 6:1), which stages Haman and Mordecai *crossing* paths at the king's gate. The last time we see Mordecai before this momentous meeting with Haman is at the end of chapter four, where he has chiastically changed places with Esther: following her lead now, doing "all that Esther had commanded him," he "went his way," literally "he *crossed*" (*wayyaᶜăbōr*) (*Anchor Bible*, 51). This first face-to-face meeting, with Mordecai refusing either to tremble in Haman's presence or to bow to his *de facto* kingly authority,[64] prompts Haman's excessive call for pogrom, the mainspring of the drama. Haman's initial restraint in deferring an immediate confrontation with Mordecai also allows time for his anger and head to swell; when he cashes in this retributive note in return for the pogrom, he is in excess.

The doubling nature and middle position of 5:9, the manner in which it represents the rise of one and the fall of another element in the chiasm by means of its own internal chiastic crossing, serves well as the central, though—because prism-like in its doubling—insubtantial, pivot of the entire book. Radday's 6:1 and 5:9 form an uncannily double center that is no center at all—that is, one with an X through it.

A final question of *interest*, posed earlier but deferred, remains: Why are so many enemies of the Jews killed in the Book of Esther? It is possibly due to the author's excessive, hyperbolic style, although that hardly answers the question. Perhaps the slaughtered tens of thousands is a talionic response devised to match Haman's ten thousand talents of silver. More likely the author's desire to legalize a festival not mentioned in the Torah leads to such a *memorable* slaughter. Chapter nine, verse twenty-eight reads: "And that these days should be remembered and kept throughout every generation, every family, every province, and every city; and that these days of Purim should not fail [Heb. *pass*] from among the Jews, nor the memorial of them perish from their seed." What is "left over" then from the chiastic exchange of pogrom for Purim is its memory.

NOTES

Introduction

1. Of the recent literary theorists who have noted the contemporary applicability of this scene, long a favorite among Talmud scholars, Daniel Boyarin has drawn out its fullest implications, in *Intertextuality and the Reading of Midrash* (Bloomington and Indianapolis: Indiana University Press, 1990), pp. 33–37.

2. Babylonian Talmud, Tractate *Baba Metzia*, 59 a,b. We rely on the Vilna edition of the Talmud (1880–86) and on the Hebrew translation by Adin Steinsaltz (Jerusalem: Israel Institute for Talmudic Publications, 1983).

3. We can justify the figure of oven as text by applying talmudic hermeneutics. The passage on the oven of Akhnai, associating coherence with impurity, evokes another famous talmudic passage that identifies textual canonicity with impurity: "R. Judah said in the name of Samuel, '[The scroll of] Esther does not make the hands unclean'" (Babylonian Talmud, *Megillah*, 7a). The sages decreed that the coherent body of Holy Writ renders unclean the hands of those who touch it. If the Book of Esther does not make one's hands unclean, it is excluded from the canon, fragmented, and therefore clean—like the oven of Akhnai according to R. Eliezer. In Tractate *Yadayim*, the rabbis declare that love motivated their decree: to protect Scripture from being used to no purpose, or to prevent it from being stored in the Temple together with the priestly tithe on produce, which would attract scroll-gnawing mice. One could of course read this decree profanely, as advisory: interpretive boldness, such as R. Joshua's, requires that one be willing to get one's hands dirty. Violation attends creation.

4. The twelfth-century French scholar known as the Rabad implies the analogy by appropriating the Talmud's verb "encompassed" in describing the plastering of the oven. His commentary appears in the sixteenth-century compilation *Shittah Mekubbetzet* of Bezalel Ashkenazi.

5. Maimonides, Preface to the *Mishneh Torah*.

6. Maimonides, *Mishneh Torah*, Yesodai HaTorah 9, 1.

7. For midrashic prooftexts, see Isaak Heinemann, *Darchei HaAggadah* (Jerusalem: Magnus, 1970), pp. 11, 201.

8. Jerusalem Talmud, Tractate *Pe'ah*, 17, a.

9. See Jerusalem Talmud, Tractate *Kelim*, Chap. 5, Mishnah 8.

10. Solomon Molcho, *Sefer ha-Mefo'ar* (1529); cited by Steinsaltz, *Baba Metzia*, p. 248.

11. To complicate matters further, and to throw into relief R. Akiba's ostracizing rather than his consoling of R. Eliezer, a modern rabbinic sage reads the talmudic scene as a political allegory based on Isa. 31:9 ("the Lord, whose

fire is in Zion, and his furnace in Jerusalem"). The oven in dispute is Jerusalem; the question is whether the trials of persecution are fragmentary and transient or durable and a sign of imminent messianic redemption; and the real opponents are R. Akiba the revolutionary and R. Eliezer the quietist. In this powerfully sustained reading, every detail, from the carob to the heavenly echo, is explained by a prooftext and related to a specific historical episode in the Bar Kochba rebellion. See *The Writings of Rabbi Joseph Elijah Henkin* (Hebrew), vol. 2 (New York: Ezrat Torah, 1989), pp. 211–14.

12. Even so, at the end Abraham's psyche is inaccessible. Sternberg's analogy between divine and narrative omniscience may suggest that the *machpelah* episode progresses from cave-in-a-corner to field and then to land, to dramatize not only Abraham's victimization by the Hittites but also his dawning recognition, emphasized by narrative repetition, that God's promise of nationhood is slowly being fulfilled. Sternberg asks of Abraham, hitherto "the known quantity" in the reader's relation to the otherwise seemingly objective narrative: "Does he see the numerology ["the link between four hundred shekels and four hundred years, the Fourth Generation and the City of Four"] as a contradiction or as a confirmation of the Covenant? Or does he oscillate . . . between fear and hope?"; and answers, "We simply cannot tell."

13. See *The Poetics of Biblical Narrative* (Bloomington: Indiana University Press, 1985).

14. Gabriel Josipovici, *The Book of God* (New Haven: Yale University Press, 1988), p. 301.

15. We can see the same split in recent interpretation of medieval literature, earlier critics finding parataxis primitive, later critics finding it sophisticated, and not exclusively a feature of oral culture. See especially Fred C. Robinson, *Beowulf and the Appositive Style* (Knoxville: University of Tennessee Press, 1985).

16. Cited in the discussion following her presentation at the Georgetown conference.

17. See James L. Kugel, *The Idea of Biblical Poetry* (New Haven: Yale University Press, 1981).

18. Hans-Georg Gadamer, *Truth and Method*, 2nd ed., trans. Garrett Barden and John Cumming (1975; New York: Crossroad, 1982), p. 273.

19. Frank Kermode, *The Genesis of Secrecy* (Cambridge: Harvard University Press, 1979), p. 145.

20. For additional remarks on the nature of this interpretive tension, see Joseph C. Sitterson, Jr., "Will to Power in Biblical Interpretation," in *Mappings of the Biblical Terrain: The Bible as Text*, ed. Vincent L. Tollers and John Maier (Lewisburg, Pa.: Bucknell University Press, 1990), pp. 45–53.

21. *The Literary Guide to the Bible*, ed. Robert Alter and Frank Kermode (Cambridge: Harvard University Press, 1987), p. 6.

Biblical Imperatives and Literary Play

1. Gabriel Josipovici, *The Book of God: A Response to the Bible* (New Haven: Yale University Press, 1988), p. 300.

2. Harry Levin, *The Gates of Horn* (New York: Oxford University Press, 1963). Gary Saul Morson, in his recent study of *War and Peace* (*Hidden in Plain View* [Stanford: Stanford University Press, 1987]), makes a related point—that Tolstoy's aim was nothing less than the radical subversion through fiction of both

historiography and novelistic narrative in the interests of what he conceived as the truth.

3. The relevant volumes are Robert Alter, *The Art of Biblical Narrative* (New York: Basic Books, 1981); Meir Sternberg, *The Poetics of Biblical Narrative* (Bloomington: Indiana University Press, 1985); Northrop Frye, *The Great Code: The Bible and Literature* (New York and London: Harcourt Brace Jovanovich, 1982); David Damrosch, *The Narrative Covenant* (San Francisco: Harper & Row, 1987).

4. Harold Fisch, *Poetry With a Purpose* (Bloomington and Indianapolis: Indiana University Press, 1988).

5. Fisch, p. 78.

6. Fisch, p. 149; Herbert N. Schneidau, *Sacred Discontent: The Bible and Western Tradition* (Baton Rouge: Louisiana State University Press, 1976).

7. Fisch, p. 77.

8. Stanley Fish, *Self-Consuming Artifacts: The Experience of Seventeenth-Century Literature* (Berkeley, Los Angeles, London: University of California Press, 1972).

9. Eric Auerbach, "Odysseus' Scar," in *Mimesis: The Representation of Reality in Western Literature*, trans. Willard Trask (Princeton: Princeton University Press, 1953), pp. 2–23.

10. Fisch, p. 12.

11. See Alter, *The Art of Biblical Narrative*; George Savran, *Telling and Retelling: Quotation in Biblical Narrative* (Bloomington and Indianapolis: Indiana University Press, 1988); Sternberg, *The Poetics of Biblical Narrative.*

12. Alter, *The Pleasures of Reading in an Ideological Age* (New York: Simon and Schuster, 1989), p. 81.

13. Leo Lowenthal, "Sociology of Literature in Retrospect," in *An Unmastered Past* (Berkeley and Los Angeles: University of California Press, 1987), p. 171.

Double Cave, Double Talk

1. For the underlying theory of inset-frame relations peculiar to mediated discourse, see especially my "Proteus in Quotation-Land: Mimesis and the Forms of Reported Discourse," *Poetics Today* 3 (1982):107–56, and "Point of View and the Indirections of Direct Speech," *Language and Style* 15 (1982):67–117. Some further aspects of the theory have been developed with special reference to the Bible. Thus, on reported speech, *The Poetics of Biblical Narrative: Ideological Literature and the Drama of Reading* (Bloomington: Indiana University Press, 1985), pp. 365–440; on reported thought, "Between the Truth and All the Truth: The Rendering of Inner Life in Biblical Narrative," *Hasifrut* 29 (1979):110–46, and "Language, World and Perspective in Biblical Art: Free Indirect Discourse and Modes of Covert Inside View," *Hasifrut* 32 (1983):88–131; on the middle ground between speech and thought, directly relevant to the present essay, "The World from the Addressee's Viewpoint: Reception as Representation, Dialogue as Monologue, *Style* 20 (1986):295–318.

2. Double, at least, because it combines formal negation by grammar ("no" or, applied to the verb, "not") and semantic negation by lexis (built into "deny" = not give), with the negative intensifier *ish . . . lo* (not *a single man*) thrown in.

3. In biblical context, the novelty in the treatment of these prepositions is poetic rather than linguistic, attaching to the contrastive linkage and rhetoric

of their senses, not to the individual senses themselves. On the contrary, the respective senses occur elsewhere even in the sociopolitical framework of citizen rights. Thus *with* as a pointer to inequality: "If thy brother falls into poverty . . . thou shalt support him, as an alien and a resident he shall live with thee" (Lev. 25:35), or, by way of analogy from human to divine scale, "The land shall not be sold in perpetuity, for mine is the land, for you are aliens and residents with me (25:23). Conversely, *amidst* as an indicator or recommendation of equality: "These six cities shall be for refuge for the people of Israel and for the alien and the resident amidst them" (Num. 35:15), or "You shall allot [the land] as an inheritance for yourselves and for the aliens who dwell amidst you and have begotten children amidst you: they shall be to you as native-born sons of Israel (Ezek. 47:22; see also Exod. 12:48–49, where the change from *with* to *amidst* marks the alien's progress to full enfranchisement). So the poetics exploits and sharpens a fine distinction available in the language system—just as, by allusion to the equalizing spirit of the above quotes and many related normative commands, it implicitly opposes the Canaanite to the Israelite social system.

4. Nor is the link between the two occasions fortuitous, I would further suggest, because Abra(ha)m was likewise sojourning in Hebron at the time (13: 18, 14:13). Moreover, the witnesses to his grand gesture included a trio of Hebronite "allies"—Mamre, Eshkol, Aner—all, significantly again, "Emorite" rather than Hittite (ibid., and 14:23). Again, if he dwelt then "by the oaks [or, terebinths] of Mamre, which are at Hebron" (13:18, 14:13, 18:1), now he has not only returned to the area but even buys a resting-place, trees and all, "east of Mamre (that is, Hebron)": things have come full circle. And that the tales originate in such disparate sources—on all genetic accounts—only heightens the sense of their poetic composition. This fine continuity across (temporal, textual, situational, normative, genetic) discontinuity also bears on the wider problem of our tale's role and integration within the Abraham cycle as a whole, on which more later.

5. On the operations of hearing in discourse and reported discourse, with special reference to the Bible, see my "The World from the Addressee's Viewpoint.

6. A victim to his antisemitism, Hermann Gunkel casts Abraham (and with him "Jewry" at large) in a Uriah Heep role, whereby he assumes humility and deference so as to impose his will on the gentiles that he secretly despises (*Genesis* [Göttingen: Vandenhoeck & Ruprecht, 1910], p. 275). If anything, as Benno Jacob counters, the exact opposite is true here (*Genesis* [Berlin: Shocken, 1934], pp. 506–7); and indeed grows even more so the deeper we penetrate the layers of motive concealed-and-revealed in verbal behavior throughout this chapter. At the same time, the Bible neither makes nor invites any sweeping generalization one way *or* the other, and as a matter of principle at that, as I argued elsewhere in regard to its avoidance of "typal" character. (See also notes 3 above and 16 below.)

7. The relation between internal and external interpreter, dramatized rather than monopolized by opaque dialogue and not always so harmonious as here, is a theme that runs through my *Poetics of Biblical Narrative* as part of the general issue of point of view.

8. As the Double Cave, Machpelah (from the root *kpl*, "fold" or "double") embodies a wonderful figure of duplexity/duplicity—a miniature in space of the narrative's overall dynamics. The two*fold* (or should we say, *double*-barreled?) root meaning of "Machpelah" is itself appropriately evocative; so is, to glance

at an old dispute, its twofold reference: to a cave made up of an inner and an outer chamber (one within the other, like the inset within the frame of our dialogue), and to one consisting of an upper and a lower level (two-storied, like the narrative surface in relation to the depth). This structural miniature ramifies still further, actually, as do other sides of the cave question, from the linguistic to the topographical, which have exercised critics since the rabbis. (See *Eruvin* 53a, the ancient translations, the medieval and modern commentaries.) More recently, Herbert Marks has explored the resonance of Double Cave, and its implications beyond our tale, in a yet unpublished study of poetic etymology.

9. This ugly word, or its converse "buy," never surfaces during the negotiations but only later: first in nominal form (*lemiknah*, "as a possession," v. 18), when the chapter comes to detail Abraham's purchase in contractual language, and then in the bluntest verbal form (*kanah*, "bought") appropriate to distant retrospect on the transaction (25:9–10, 49:13). These later appearances emphasize by contrast the word's suppression in the dialogue. But in A. E. Speiser's rendering, "sell" does appear as early as vv. 4 and 9 (*Genesis* [Garden City, N.Y.: Doubleday, 1964], p. 168). Considering the translator's fine scholarship, the gulf between sociohistorical and (socio)poetic competence leaps to the eye.

10. Rashbam (echoed by Speiser, *Genesis*, p. 170) glosses "amidst you" as "before your eyes," and though he omits to say why, one may supply a reason in keeping with my own argument: Abraham would thereby cleverly switch the bearing of the word from the sociopolitical to the dialogic situation, and with it the role of the Hittites from neighborly company (unintended by them, unwanted by himself) to collective witness. A nice touch, except that the story both opposes "amidst" to "with" in a systematic way, as status terms, and also reserves the witnessing role for the properly sense-oriented legalisms "before the eyes" and "in the ears" (vv. 11,13,16,18).

11. Or, as Moshe Greenberg has suggested to me, with performative force: "I (hereby) give." This performative reading comes to much the same thing as the past—except that it does not quite explain the removal of possessive particles from the object—and the two may well join forces to secure the giving.

12. For example, "No" to the intercession (as Abravanel takes it), or to the offer of money (Rashi), or to the modesty of the site requested (*or Hahayyim*)? As so often with gaps, in or out of dialogue, the various interpretive attempts to narrow down the range of reference are a measure of its actual width and openness. They also bring out how the Bible, instead of aiming or settling for some univocal closure, yokes together assorted, even incompatible-looking possibilities, this time with a view to ironic opposition between levels of discourse.

13. In a much-cited article, Manfred R. Lehmann proposes a very different line of motivation by reference to the Hittite Code, which stipulates that the services due to the king from a landowner pass to a buyer only if he acquires the entire holding. This supposedly reveals the question at issue: Abraham asks for the cave and Ephron insists on the field, because each would avoid the feudal duties attached to the property. ("Abraham's Purchase of Machpelah and Hittite Law," *BASOR* 129 [1953]:15–18.) One need not be a stickler for evidence to wonder at the currency gained by a hypothesis so obviously out of touch with both the narrative's detail and drift, with its textual and contextual realities alike. (It is even doubtful whether the chapter's "Hittites" are at all the Hittites known to history, legal history included.) More recently, however, a number of scholars have not only attacked this Hittite connection (plus motivation) on its own ground but also shifted the frame of reference to neo-Babylonian dialogic sale documents, with interesting points of comparison. See especially Gene

M. Tucker, "The Legal Background of Genesis 23," *Journal of Biblical Literature* 85 (1966):77–84, and Herbert Petschow, "Die Neubabylonische Zwiegesprächsurkunde und Genesis 23," *Journal of Cuneiform Studies* 19 (1965):103–20.

14. This mock embarrassment is even advertised in the syntactic disorder of Abraham's opening—literally, "If thou, pray hear me," shifting in mid-sentence from conditional to optative form—with its suggestion of a false start, a polite stammer. (In terms of classical rhetoric, one may see here a figure of anacoluthon, as many have in fact done: thus the Gesenius-Kautzsch grammar, 110e, or John Skinner in *Genesis* [New York: Charles Scribner, 1925], p. 337).

15. Contrast Abraham's advance belittling ("a morsel of bread") of the feast he puts (literally, "gives") before his guests (18:2–8).

16. This accords with the master principle of "foolproof composition" (*Poetics of Biblical Narrative*, pp. 48ff.) whereby the Bible supplies, among other aids to understanding, progressive or retrospective enlightenment of matters implied earlier in the text, if only to be on the safe side and to carry the maximum audience with it. In our tale, given the multiple web of indirections, the narrator's and the dialogists', the ongoing clarification effected by this better-later-than-never policy would variously benefit different (to an extent, all) types of readers: from those with some lingering doubt, through those vacillating among hypotheses, to, above all, those innocent (or noble or hurried) souls who have been completely taken in by the bland surface and might otherwise remain so. To mention one extreme instance on record, even an interpreter like Kalisch, who for thirteen verses persists in taking the Hittites as genuinely moved, respectful, and altruistic, cannot help changing tack in face of the four hundred shekels: the silver thrust upon him, Ephron is "unable to withstand the temptation" of taking, indeed making easy money (*Genesis* [London: Longman, 1858], p. 456). To be sure, nothing in communication, biblical or otherwise, is proof against ingrained prejudice, such as Gunkel's antisemitism (n.6 above): excluding him from the implied circle of readers in the first place, it neutralizes the effects of textual dynamics on sense-making and attitude- formation, along with much else. He ends as he began, a biased counter-reader, and of a particularly misleading and unrewarding kind, too. Misleading, since he operates in the name of objective historicism, among all approaches. Also unrewarding, because he does not so much oppose the text's value system (by, say, judging *its* inferred judgments, counterbalancing its theses, laying bare its persuasive strategies) as superimpose his own on it to the point of inversion and confusion. Gunkel's accordingly illustrates a mode of (counter) reading that is neither constructive nor reconstructive nor even, if only because of its security, deconstructive— all somehow open in principle to the foolproof composition—but just projective. And as with bias against, so with bias for; as with racism, so with far less explosive issues, down to questions of realism or manners or usage.

17. See note 13.

18. Appropriately, the reference here is not to Samuel (2 24:24) but to the later version in Chronicles (1 21:25), with which the Midrash shares the transparent desire to raise the cost from fifty silver to six hundred gold shekels: the larger the payment, the stronger the right of possession as well as the payer's merit.

19. All the more remarkable, therefore, that Acts confuses or perhaps conflates the two acquisitions in retelling how Jacob's body was "carried back to Shechem and laid in the tomb that Abraham had bought for a sum of silver from the sons of Hamor in Shechem" (7:15–16). But then the Shechem site

did become the resting place for *Joseph's* bones (Josh. 24:32)—a further link between the two accounts of patriarchal land-buying, which on the one hand radicalizes their difference in scale within Genesis itself and on the other may have occasioned their mix-up by the New Testament speaker, Peter.

20. His personally as well as his offspring's: note the recurrence of "give to *thee*" on all three covenantal occasions quoted above. At the same time, once our horizon widens into covenantal magnitude, the increasingly pointed reference to his Hittite opponents as "the people of the land" assumes a wider thematic bearing to include the Canaanites in general.

21. Thus Franz Delitzsch, *Genesis* (Leipzig: Dörfflin & Frank, 1853), p. 413, approvingly quoted by Gerhard von Rad, *Genesis*, trans. John H. Marks (London: SCM Press, 1970), p. 241. Two millennia before, Josephus's version of biblical history implies much the same judgment in its contrastive *re*proportioning of the Binding and the Purchase stories. They are of about equal length in the original telling—nineteen and twenty verses respectively—but his retelling elaborates upon the one, while reducing the other to the barest summary, with no trace of dialogue left. (*Jewish Antiquities*, 1.13.222–36 vs. 14.237). In genetic terms, again, Gunkel holds that the Machpelah affair originally circulated not as a full-fledged "saga" but as a mere "notice"—comparable to the one-verse record of Jacob's land acquisition at Shechem—which the Priestly writer then "spun out into circumstantial narrative" (*Genesis*, p. 262). Such conjecture about the source would have little interest, except that its underlying sense of proportion and coherence meets, and in effect vindicates, Josephus's practice of discourse: as if, by an instinctive and corrective reverse movement, his retelling cut the tale down to its proper, ante-Priestly, notice-length size. A suggestive convergence of (low) opinion, this, considering the disparities in expression and approach as well as time among the parties, all likewise at one in their regard for the masterpiece and cornerstone that goes immediately before.

Princely Characters

1. Robert Alter. *The Art of Biblical Narrative* (New York: Basic Books, 1981), pp. 137–40, 157–76 (Joseph), pp. 78–81, 114–29, 147–53 (David); Meir Sternberg, *The Poetics of Biblical Narrative: Ideological Literature and the Drama of Reading* (Bloomington and Indianapolis; Indiana University Press, 1985), as cited below. The present essay combines my remarks on biblical characterization from two reviews of these books—mainly unpublished—which were written shortly after the books' respective publications.

2. The phrase is the translated title of the book by Erich Kahler, *The Inward Turn of Narrative*, trans. Richard and Clara Winston (Princeton: Princeton University Press, 1973). Two essays that suggest the fictional side of Alter's and Sternberg's themes are "Recognition and Deception" and "Secrecy and Narrative Sequence," chapters 4 and 6 in Frank Kermode, *Essays on Fiction: 1971–82* (London: Routledge & Kegan Paul, 1983), pp. 92–113, 133–55.

3. Sternberg, *Poetics*, p. 519, n. 3, is very wry on this theme in the scholarly literature. Sternberg's account (originally with Menakhem Perry) shows how the exchanges that pass among parties to the story successively convict David of adultery, intention to perpetrate fraud, conspiracy to murder, complicity in unnecessary military risk and the resulting loss of life, falsification of battlefield intelligence, and obstruction of justice (*Poetics*, pp. 196–214).

4. Cf. Alter, "Narration and Knowledge," in *Art*, pp. 155–77. The "epistemological overtones" are discussed by Sternberg, *Poetics*, pp. 84–99, 230–35, and esp. for David, pp. 190–93, and pregnantly hinted at for Joseph by Alter, *Art*, pp. 157–59. Both Alter and Sternberg would rule out a modern novelist's epistemological skepticism in the Bible's scheme of things; yet our doubts about what Uriah knows about David's relations with Uriah's wife, and about what Abraham's ambassador to Nahor-land can know about Rebekah's family, do tend to put certainty, verifiability, and the whole truth ultimately out of human reach (it will go with Uriah to the grave, as Sternberg remarks). In the case of the ambassador—who does not finally get Rebekah's genealogy right, despite three earlier accounts of it—the text in effect undermines its own authority, for reasons having to do with both the trustworthiness or "keeping" of the tradition, and with the "novelty" of the generation-crossing Rebekah herself. (See also Sternberg, *Poetics*, pp. 181–85, on Robert Polzin's dubieties in his *Moses and the Deuteronomist* [New York: Seabury Press, 1980].)

5. The tale of *Joseph and Asenath* (c. 100 B.C.E.-200 C.E.), as ed. C. Burchard, in James H. Charlesworth, gen. ed., *The Old Testament Pseudepigrapha*, Vol. 2 (Garden City, N.Y.: Doubleday, 1985), pp. 143ff., is early evidence of the novelistic impulse in question. Fielding's *Joseph Andrews* senses that the biblical recognition-scenes may be assimilated to those of New Comedic form and to the restorations and reunions of the de′nouement in Greek prose romance. The possibility for both of these comic plots (or, in R. S. Crane's terms, "synthetic" plots), namely plots turning on the replacement of impermissible attachments by permissible ones, is biblically planted in the original story: for the vindicated Joseph is married to the *daughter* of a Potiphar at Gen. 41:45, as opposed to a *wife*: Joseph is now lying with the right—or permissible—Potipheran.

The Davidic history becomes the stuff of tragic novels in Hardy's *Mayor of Casterbridge* (Henchard/Farfrae = Saul/David) and Faulkner's *Absalom, Absalom*. Puzo's *The Godfather* casts Vito Corleone's "Sonny" as Absalom. (Puzo's next novel was called *Fools Die*, echoing David's question about the fate of Abner.) Biblical critics have perhaps already guessed something of the extended correspondence. Alter, in *Art*, p. 102, implies that Abner and Amasa are victims of gangland-style rub-outs (Joab being the "toughest of ancient Near Eastern mafiosi"), and I have also lately heard of biblical scholars referring to David's final instructions to Solomon as "the godfather scene." Puzo's contemporizing of the building of Solomon's temple-house as the Corleone family's eventual move from illegal New York rackets into legitimate gambling casinos in Las Vegas seems to me quite as witty as any of the analogous topical correspondences worked into Dryden's *Absalom and Achitophel*.

6. Hermann Gunkel, *The Legends of Genesis: The Biblical Saga and History*, trans. W. H. Carruth (1901), (New York: Schocken Books, 1964), pp. 60–67. Cf. also Erich Auerbach, *Mimesis*, trans. Willard R. Trask (Princeton: Princeton University Press, 1953), pp. 11–12, on the "unexpressed" (roughly Alter's "reticence") in biblical characterization.

7. "Givenness" is Sternberg's fine and economic term, *Poetics*, p. 327.

8. Sternberg discusses the clues to the "internals" in *Poetics*, pp. 342–48.

9. Ammon and Moab are recognized as Lot-ites at Deut. 2:9, 19, but the story of their generation is designed to give them no clue to this "Nahorite" identity. Lot in conceiving his children is drunk, and the names they are given are ambiguously eponymous, and anonymous (i.e., the names are references to their being fathered by a nameless generic father). I have explained the story in relation to sexual indistinction in Sodom, in "The Keeping of Nahor," in

The Book and the Text: The Bible and Literary Theory, ed. Regina M. Schwartz (Oxford: Basil Blackwell, 1990), pp. 161–87. Cf. the following from a longer version of the Nahor essay:

> The "saving history" is always accompanied with the saving *of* history: this will be a history saved out of earlier occasions for its obliteration, and transmitted across the fissionary dispersion and differentiation that separates one people from another people. Thanks to Noah, the post-diluvian Shemite knows his precursor in the ante-diluvian Sethite. Thanks to Terah and Abraham, the extra-territorial Nahorite (who was a Mesopotamian Shemite) knows his precursor in the territorial Nahorite. And thanks to the Egyptianized Israelites who conserved the remains of Joseph, the Mosaic Israelites know their precursors in the Patriarchs, who included that wandering Aramaean who wandered into Egypt. Thus the Exodus-installment of the saving history begins in Egypt, upon the datum of the Pharaoh who *knew not Joseph*; and it re-begins upon God's declaration to Moses that He is to be *remembered* as the God of Abraham, Isaac, and Jacob.

10. See Gen. 24:58—"And they called Rebekah, and said unto her, Wilt thou go with this man? And she said, I will go"—with Gen. 27:6ff: "And Rebekah spake unto Jacob her son, saying, Behold, I heard thy father speak unto Esau thy brother, saying, Bring me venison, and make me a savoury meat, that I may eat, and bless thee before the Lord before my death. Now therefore, my son, obey my voice according to that which I command thee." *Before the Lord* is Rebekah's own ideologically significant addition (to her otherwise close citation of Isaac's words at Gen. 27:4). For the contrast between Abraham and Jacob in the "ethnic" transmission of genetic and cultural thickness and thinness, see Nohrnberg, "Keeping of Nahor," *passim*, in *Book*, ed. Schwartz.

11. See Nohrnberg, "Moses," in *Images of God and Man: The Old Testament Short Story in Literary Focus*, ed. Burke O. Long (Sheffield: Almond Press, 1981), pp. 37–40, for this Joseph-Moses interface.

12. Nohrnberg, "Keeping of Nahor," *passim*, in *Book*, ed. Schwartz.

13. So Sternberg, *Poetics*, pp. 298f. The proof of Sternberg's hypothesis is missing. It is that the Ishmaelite traders who bought Joseph for silver, *and then sold him*, carry much the same goods as the brothers' caravan takes to Egypt to buy more grain (cf. Gen. 37:25 with 43:11–12); the brothers are thus taking Benjamin down to Egypt, as the Ishmaelites took Joseph: conceivably as part of what they have to sell. Alter, *Art*, pp. 138–40, considers why the brothers might open (or be made to open) their sacks twice, once before each other, and again before their father; the mystery of iniquity and God's knowledge of it is here, but Sternberg makes clear what exactly the inquity is, and why the brothers' pretense to be opening the sacks for the first time in front of their father might be pardonable if desperate strategy on their part. Perhaps both authors are also saying what I wish to say about the brothers' motivations in this case: despite their worst suspicions, *they don't want to know*: this appears to be the case with Jacob himself, when he seizes upon the explanation of a wild beast for Joseph's bloody coat. Such a reluctance to know the worst helps explain why, in the first instance, the brothers go no further after opening the first sack, rather than finding out then and there if the rest of the sacks will

also turn out to be endowed with unexplained money. The narrator has found a way to show us the characters' will-to-ignorance playing itself out.

14. Alter points out, *Art*, p. 164, that the brothers' alleged spying on "the nakedness of the land" might otherwise be the biblically taboo viewing of the nakedness of kin: a taboo that is violated when Joseph is stripped of his coat. My original reviewer's reaction was: "Alter finds Joseph's accusation a non-sequitur in its place, but *abreaction* might be a more telling interpretation. For Joseph, we learn delayedly, has been eavesdropping on his brothers' speech in their own language. He has been spying on their nakedness before each other, and before God." See also Sternberg, *Poetics*, p. 288 ("the ten are thus branded as the would-be Hebrew rapists of Egypt," like Joseph the alleged violator of Potiphar's wife—but violators of *kin* is the narrower point).

The reader, Sternberg explains in *Poetics*, pp. 283–325, shares Joseph's curiosity over the relevance of the deep past, his doubt and suspense as to what alternatives the brothers will take in dealing with the demand for hostages, and his present surprise at Judah's sudden assumption of total responsibility. Sternberg observes that the reader knows that Reuben has tried and failed to take responsibility earlier, but that this fact is necessarily a surprise to Joseph. Judah, the youngest Leahite brother, ends up taking over for Reuben, the oldest one, in trying to protect a Rachelite brother—this time Benjamin: protect him from the unwanted and uncanny attention of the "knower" into whose hands they have so mysteriously fallen.

15. Others have also seen in the succession document the purpose of presenting the evidence for a revolution in political communications. See Sean E. McEvenue, "The Basis of Empire, A Study of the Succession Narrative," in *Ex Audite* 2, (1986):34–54, esp. 37–40.

Sternberg, *Poetics*, pp. 28–34, expounds the right presumed by the biblical author to know what God and the others have said or thought or known: to be "authoritative." Cf. Joseph Blenkinsopp, *Prophecy and Canon: A Contribution to the Study of Jewish Origins* (South Bend: University of Notre Dame Press, 1977), p. 147:"the canon is prophetic insofar as the claim to authority which underlies it in one way or another is the claim to a hearing actually staked by the prophets."

16. God remembers Abraham precisely when he remembers Abraham's relative Lot in Sodom (Gen. 19:29)—as He remembers Noah in the Flood (Gen. 8:1). For the Joseph-Judges analogy and the place of remembering-forgetting in the biblical narrative generally, see Nohrnberg, "Moses," in *Images*, ed. Long, pp. 47–50. For the "textual" theme, see the same author, "On Literature and the Bible," in *Centrum: Working Papers of the Minnesota Center for Advanced Studies in Language, Style, and Literary Theory* 2:2 (Fall 1974): 15:"Later generations apparently remembered what had been forgotten." For the specific case of Judges, cf. Gabriel Josipovici's chapter, "The Rhythm Falters," in *The Book of God: A Response to the Bible* (New Haven: Yale University Press, 1988), pp. 108–31. For Joseph see Gen. 40:23, "Yet did not the chief butler remember Joseph, but forgat him," with Gen. 41:9, "Then spake the chief butler unto Pharaoh, saying, I do remember my faults this day," Gen. 41:51, "And Joseph called the name of the firstborn Manasseh. For God, said he, hath made me forget all my toil, and all my father's house," and Gen. 42:9, "And Joseph remembered the dreams which he dreamed of them [his brothers]." See also Nohrnberg, "Moses," in *Images*, ed. Long, p. 40, on the symbolic conservation of the patriarchal inheritance and its conveyance, by means of Josephic *relictae*, to Mosaic Israel, and in general Gerhard von Rad, *Old Testament Theology*, vol. 1, *The Theology of Israel's Historical Traditions*, trans. D.M.G. Stalker (New York and Evanston: Harper &

Row, 1962), pp. 330–32, 347, and 69–84, chapter D, "Endeavours to Restore the Past."

17. For a comparable anticipation of the later history by the earlier one, cf. David Damrosch, "Leviticus," in *The Literary Guide to the Bible*, ed. Frank Kermode and Robert Alter (Cambridge: Harvard University Press, 1987), pp. 69–72, where the names of the two transgressing and stricken sons of the idolatrous Aaron, namely Nadab and Abihu (Lev. 10:1), are compared to the names of the sons of the idolatrous Jeroboam I: the idolatrous Nadab (1 Kings 14:20, 15:25) and the stricken Abijah (1 Kings 14:1ff). Nohrnberg, "On Literature and the Bible," in *Centrum*, pp. 9–12, 14–20, describes such "redundancies," "stretti," "metalepses," "typologies," and "compoundness," as principles of the Biblical text's mode, where there has been a loss "of the distinction between the inter-textual and the intra-textual" (p. 14).

18. See Gerhard von Rad, *Old Testament Theology*, pp. 154–60, "The Incursion and the Spread of Sin," and Nohrnberg, "On Literature and the Bible," in *Centrum* p. 12, for this analogy and some textual implications.

19. Sternberg, *Poetics*, pp. 394–400, esp. p. 397 on the doubled descriptive *beriot* (fat) in the narrative's first account of the dreams (that of the narrator), and p. 400 on the *rakot* (thin) cows and *rekot* (empty) ears in the narrative's third account (that of Joseph as interpreter).

20. The point is made by Joel Rosenberg, "1 and 2 Samuel," in *Guide*, ed. Alter and Kermode, p. 131.

21. For the "two fronts" in the narrative's linear temporality and its representation, I am indebted to a lecture by Meir Sternberg at the University of Virginia, "(Hi)story-telling as Fine Art: Chronology and Simultaneity in the Biblical Narrative"; a version of this lecture appears in *Book*, ed. Schwartz, pp. 81–145.

22. *The Tempest*, act 5, sc. 1, lines 27ff.

23. For Joseph: Gen. 42:24, 43:30, 45:2, 45:14–15, 50:1, 50:17; for David: 2 Sam. 1:24, 1:26 (Saul and Jonathan); 3:32 (Abner), 12:21–22 (Bathsheba's child), 13:36 (Amnon), 15:23, 15:30 (the people weeping over David's departure from Jerusalem, then David on Olivet weeping over Jerusalem), 18:33, 19:1 (Absalom). See now, for the case of David, the chapter of Josipovici, "David and Tears," in *Book of God*, pp. 191–209. As usual, Saul seems to anticipate the Davidic tears, with his son-in-law David in the cave at 1 Sam. 24:17; so also Jacob's twin Esau anticipates the Josephic tears, with his father Isaac at Gen. 27:38. For the parallel between the two scenes, see Alter, *Art*, pp. 36–37; for the ground of the parallel in biblical characterization, see Auerbach, *Mimesis*, p. 20, on the extremity of humiliation in the Bible (which is owed to the biblical God).

24. See, for the case of David, Joel Rosenberg, "1 and 2 Samuel," in *Guide*, ed. Alter and Kermode, pp. 128–32. Rosenberg's remarks have been quite influential here.

25. In other words, Eliab cut a kingly figure like that of Saul: cf. 1 Sam. 9:2, "a choice young man, and a goodly: and there was not among the sons of Israel a goodlier person than he." See Sternberg, *Poetics*, pp. 354–64, on stature and good looks in Saul, David, and Absalom, the first three aspirants to the kingship. The idea that David is legislating the correction of an injustice to camp-sitters, on the basis of his own experience, may be compared to the idea that Moses appoints the Levitical cities of refuge, from the standpoint of his status as a fugitive from the law, in the Midian. He is wanted for manslaughter in the jurisdiction of Egypt. For Midian is the domain of a priest, and Moses finds sanctuary there until the death of Pharaoh, as the manslayer enjoys the

Levitical city's protection for the life of its high priest (cf. also Nohrnberg, "Moses," in *Images*, ed. Long, pp. 56f). The narratives (about David's and Moses's early days) may well constitute inferences from the legislation's being "Davidic" or "Mosaic," which the stories' respective protagonists are thereupon called upon to pronounce. Good reasons for their having done so are planted in their early (hi)stories; these early anecdotes, in other words, have been conceived illustratively, though the causal connection is never made explicit by the narrative.

26. Rosenberg, "1 and 2 Samuel," in *Guide*, ed. Alter and Kermode, pp. 13lf.

27. Joseph recurs to his father explicitly or implicitly at Gen. 41:51, "God hath made me forget . . . all my father's house," and at Gen. 43:23, in speaking to his brothers. "Your God and the god of your father." But the indications of Joseph's specific inquiry after Jacob have been reserved for the report made in Judah's climactic speech to Joseph at Gen. 44:19:"My lord asked his servants, saying, Have ye a father, or a brother? And we said unto my lord, We have a father, an old man, and a child of his old age, a little one, and his brother is dead, and he alone is left of his mother, and his father loveth him." This expands greatly on the more elliptical profession originally made by the brothers: "And they said, Thy servants are twelve brethren, the sons of one man in the land of Canaan, and behold, the youngest is this day with our father, and one is not" (Gen. 42:13). It is after Judah's speech that Joseph reveals himself and thereupon asks (somewhat rhetorically, by this point), "doth my father yet live?" (Gen. 45:3).

28. For the equality of the plaintiff (the woman with the dead baby) and the defendant (the woman with the live baby), and the cognate observation that *we* never learn which—plaintiff or defendant—has perjured herself and which woman's maternal feeling wins custody of the child, see Sternberg's analysis, *Poetics*, pp. 166–69.

29. The parallel between these two narratives is the basis for the delicate balance between Sternberg's last two chapters; see *Poetics*, pp. 445–75 for the sons' rejection of Jacob in the matter of Dinah's rape, and pp. 482–515 for Samuel's rejection of Saul in the matter of the incomplete destruction of the enemy and his goods.

30. The scheme actually remembers four "Josephs," if we count "Josech" son of Joda and father of Semein, as analogous to Joseph father of Judas and grandfather of Symeon. The pattern of seventy-seven names, plus God, is constructed as eleven "genealogical weeks": the weeks of God, Enoch, Shelah, Abraham, Admin, David, a first Joseph, a first Jesus, Shealtiel, Mattathias, and a second Joseph, issuing in the final father-son pair Joseph-Jesus:

						Jesus
						Joseph
Joseph	Heli	*Matthat*	*Levi*	Melchi	Jannai	Mattathias
Mattathias	Amos	Nahum	Esli	Naggai	Maath	Shealtiel
Semein	Josech	Joda	Joanan	Rhesa	Zerubbabel	*Jesus*
Neri	Melchi	Addi	Cosam	Elmadam	Er	*Joseph*
Eliezar	Jorim	*Matthat*	*Levi*	Symeon	Judas	David
Jonam	Eliakim	Melea	Menna	Mattat	Nahum	Admin
Jesse	Obed	Boaz	Sala	Nahshon	Aminadab	Abraham
Arni	Hezron	Perez	Judah	Jacob	Isaac	Shelah
Terah	Nahor	Serug	Reu	Peleg	Eber	Enoch
Cainan	Arphaxad	Shem	Noah	Lamech	Methuselah	God
Jared	Mahaleel	Cainan	Enos	Seth	Adam	

For a scholar's comments, see I. Howard Marshall, *The Gospel of Luke: A Commentary on the Greek Text*, New International Greek Testament Commentary (Grand Rapids, Mich.: Wm. B. Eerdmans, 1978), pp. 159–61, and cf. 4 Ezra 14:11 for the idea of world-historical weeks. More of the numerology may be worked out as follows.

First, the names are variously interlocked. Both of the Josephs who are not Joseph the carpenter are seventh from a person named Jesus. The earlier Jesus is a genealogical "month" (the twenty-eighth generation) before the second Jesus (Jesus of Nazareth), and a genealogical month after Abraham (Jesus of Nazareth is thus two such months after Abraham). The first "Joseph" is the thirty-sixth generation before Jesus, as David is the thirty-sixth after God; and as the "week of David" issues in the first "week of Joseph" (Joseph, Judas, Symeon, Levi, Matthat, Jorim, and Eliezar), so the second such week of Joseph (Joseph, Jannai, Melchi, Levi, Matthat, Heli, and Joseph the carpenter) issues in Jesus of Nazareth. These we may call "priestly" weeks, given the preponderance of priestly names in them. David is a genealogical month after Enoch, and a genealogical month before Mattathias, whose name in its varieties is the most frequent in the list (at positions 3, 8, 13, 14, 31, and 40, where Joseph the carpenter is 1 and God is 77). The name Mattathias seems to recognize the period inaugurated by the sons of Mattathias, the Maccabees, as the name Shealtiel recognizes the period of the restoration of the Temple.

The scheme needs further explanation, but for the nonce we may note that the sequence Jonam-Joseph-Judas-Symeon-Levi-Matthat (the forty-second through the forty-seventh generations from God, or the thirty-first through thirty-sixth from Jesus) is subsequently duplicated in part by the sequence Joanan-Joda-Josech-Semein-Mattathias-Maath (the sixtieth through sixty-fifth from God, or the thirteenth through eighteenth from Jesus), and that these two sequences are separated by seventeen intervening names. The thirty-sixth from God would be David, who is the forty-second from Jesus: Jonam is thirty-sixth from Jesus and forty-second from God, and the "week of David" (David to Jonam) is thus the median week. In the middle of this week—thirty-nine names after God and thirty-nine names before Joseph the father of Jesus of Nazareth—is Menna. The Hebrew root *mnh* means "to number."

The two occurrences of the name Melchi are also separated by the mysterious seventeen-name interval, like the names Maath and Matthat, and the names Semein and Symeon, in the two sequences just given. So also the names Eliezar (father of the earlier Jesus) and Esli (the eleventh name from Jesus of Nazareth). The first Judahite, namely Perez (son of Jacob's son Judah), and Judas are also separated by seventeen names, and there are seventeen names between Judas the son of the first (earliest) Joseph and Josech the son of Joda, or between Joseph the father of this Judas and Joda the father of Josech. This is another way of saying that the pairs Judah-Perez, Joseph-Judas, and Joda-Josech, are placed at successive equal intervals (there are sixteen names between each pair): the pairs insist that the son of Joseph the carpenter will be "of Judah": for the seventeenth name from Joda father of Josech is Joseph father of Jesus of Nazareth. The first Levi, Matthat, and Joseph are each twenty-eight names before the second such names, establishing the two priestly weeks of Joseph (weeks seven and eleven); Symeon is a similar "genealogical month" before the second Melchi. And just as the first Melchi is ten names after Symeon, so the second Melchi is ten names after Semein (this recurrence helps show that Semein is a "second Symeon"). The later Melchi is the fifth generation before Jesus of Nazareth, the earlier one is the fifth generation after the earlier Jesus.

The significance of the number from "first" to "second" Melchi, Simeon, etc.—eighteen—would seem to be merely numerological: it is the sum of the overall factors of seven and eleven (or "days" and "weeks"). From the key priestly name Levi it is seventeen names to Mattathias, as it is one name to Matthat in the ultimate "week of Joseph." The pre-Davidic names in the "Levi" column are Sala (the father of Boaz), Judah (the Patriarch of the tribe of Judah), Reu, Noah (the just man in his generation), and Enos (the first generation to call on God). Thus a listing of the names by nines seems significant: almost all columns contain a "priestly" or tribal name twice:

Jesus	Joseph	*Heli*	Matthat	Levi	*Melchi*	Jannai	*Joseph*	Mattathias
Amos	Nahum	Esli	Naggai	*Maath*	Mattathias	Semein	*Josech*	*Joda*
Joanan	Rhesa	Zerubbabel	Shealtiel	Neri	*Melchi*	Addi	Cosam	Elmadam
Er	Jesus	*Eliezar*	Jorim	*Matthat*	Levi	*Symeon*	Judas	Joseph
Jonam	Eliakim	Melea	Menna	*Mattat*	Nahum	David	Jesse	Obed
Boaz	Sala	Nahshon	Aminadab	Admin	Arni	Hezron	Perez	*Judah*
Jacob	Isaac	Abraham	Terah	Nahor	Serug	Reu	Peleg	Eber
Shelah	*Cainan*	Arphaxad	Shem	Noah	Lamech	Methuselah	Enoch	Jared
Mahaleel	*Cainan*	Enos	Seth	Adam	God			

The doubled name Cainan reminds us that from Cain to Lamech I there were seven generations in the line of Cain, but from Adam to Lamech II, the parallel list, there were nine (through Seth).

Relisting the names by nines, we can show the effect of being ninth from God rather than from Jesus:

				Jesus	Joseph	*Heli*	Matthat	Levi
Melchi	Jannai	*Joseph*	Mattathias	Amos	Nahum	Esli	Naggai	*Maath*
Mattathias	*Semein*	*Josech*	*Joda*	*Joanan*	Rhesa	Zerubbabel	Shealtiel	Neri
Melchi	Addi	Cosam	Elmadam	Er	Jesus	*Eliezar*	Jorim	*Matthat*
Levi	*Symeon*	Judas	Joseph	*Jonam*	Eliakim	Melea	Menna	*Mattat*
Nahum	David	Jesse	Obed	Boaz	Sala	Nahshon	Aminadab	Admin
Arni	Hezron	Perez	*Judah*	Jacob	Isaac	Abraham	Terah	Nahor
Serug	Reu	Peleg	Eber	Shelah	*Cainan*	Arphaxad	Shem	Noah
Lamech	Methuselah	Enoch	Jared	Mahaleel	*Cainan*	Enos	Adam	God

Here the "enneads" are (reading right to left, and bottom to top): God-Lamech (Antediluvian), Noah-Serug (Postdiluvian), Nahor-Arni (Nahorite-Egyptian), Admin-Nathan (Numbers-Jerusalem), Mattat-Levi (Proto-Priestly I), Matthat-Melchi (Priestly I), Neri-Mattathias (Proto-Priestly II), Maath-Melchi (Priestly II), and Levi onward (Priestly III). In all of this it is necessary to remember, of course, that not only is Jesus the son of David (the name Nathan is chosen as the list's first "son of David" because the Nathan in question is listed in 2 Sam. 5:14 as the son of David born immediately before Solomon, after David had begun to reign over Israel in Jerusalem), but also that Jesus is a priest after the order of Melchi-zedeck (Luke's "Melchi," so to speak, is the first Melchior). Jesus is therefore in the line of the high priest Mattathias of 1 Maccabees 2:1:"Mattathias son of John, son of Simeon, a priest of the line of Joarib." We note, then, that not only is Semein the father of Mattathias, but also that the second Melchi is the father of the second Levi, and that the father of the first Levi was Symeon, the grandfather of the first Matthat. Being the son of a father bearing the Aaronic name Eliezer, the first Jesus bears a name anticipating that of the high priest Joshua or Jeshua in the days of Zerubbabel. The second half of the genealogy from which Luke's Jesus descends is indeed "a nation of priests and holy men."

Understanding the Bread

1. Albert Schweitzer, *The Quest of the Historical Jesus*, tr. W. Montgomery (London: A & C Black, 1911), p. 397.

2. John Drury, "Mark," in *The Literary Guide to the Bible*, ed. Robert Alter and Frank Kermode (Cambridge, Mass.: Harvard University Press, 1987), pp. 402–17.

3. Robert Lowth, *Lectures on the Sacred Poetry of the Hebrews* (1753), tr. Richard Gregory (1787), lecture 5, rpt. in *Critics of the Bible: 1724–1873*, ed. John Drury (Cambridge: Cambridge University Press, 1989), p. 77.

4. Edgar Wind, *Pagan Mysteries in the Renaissance* (New York: Norton, 1968), p. 15.

5. Anthony Collins, *Discourse of the Grounds and Reasons of the Christian Religion* (1724), rpt. in Drury, *Critics of the Bible*, p. 25.

6. Richard Ellmann, *James Joyce* (New York: Oxford University Press, 1959), p. 83.

Literary Exegesis of Biblical Narrative

1. Robert Alter, *The Art of Biblical Narrative* (New York: Basic Books, 1981), p. 120; J. P. Fokkelman, *Narrative Art and Poetry in the Books of Samuel*, vol. 2 (Assen: Van Gorcum, 1986), pp. 274–76; Peter D. Miscall, *The Workings of Old Testament Narrative* (Philadelphia: Fortress; Chico: Scholars, 1983), pp. 87–88.

2. Fokkelman also notes the "relevant" differences.

3. Even those not generally associated with literary exegesis have seen the value in this approach. For excellent examples, see Stanley D. Walters, "Hannah and Anna: The Greek and Hebrew Texts of 1 Samuel 1," *Journal of Biblical Literature* 107 (1988): 385–412; and Moshe Greenberg, "The Use of the Ancient Versions for Understanding the Hebrew Text: A Sampling from Ezek. II, 1–III,11," *Congress Volume, Gottingen 1977: Vetus Testamentum*, Suppl. 29 (1977):131–48.

4. Alter, *The Art of Biblical Narrative*, p. 120.

5. Miscall, *The Workings of Old Testament Narrative*, p. 87.

6. Fokkelman, *Narrative Art and Poetry in the Books of Samuel*, pp. 274–75.

7. Yair Zakovitch, "Mirror-Image Story—An Additional Criterion for the Evaluation of Characters in Biblical Narrative," *Tarbiz* 54/2 (1985): 165–76. Peretz Segal, in "The Inheritance of Eli," *Beth Mikra* 113/2 (1988): 179–83, has adopted Zakovitch's methodology in his analysis of the stories of Hannah and Rachel.

8. Moshe Garsiel, *The First Book of Samuel: A Literary Study of Comparative Structures, Analogies, and Parallels* (Ramat Gan, 1983), pp. 131–32; Miscall, *The Workings of Old Testament Narrative*, pp. 80, 87. See also James Nohrnberg's essay "Princely Characters" in this volume.

9. Joel Rosenberg, *King and Kin: Political Allegory in the Hebrew Bible* (Bloomington: Indiana University Press, 1986), pp. xii–xiii.

10. There is a hint of this in Fokkelman's wording: "invitation to the reader." Cf. also the remarks by Greenstein quoted below.

11. Alter, "Putting Together Biblical Narrative," Albert T. Bilgray Lecture, University of Arizona, 10 March 1988, pp. 17–18.

12. Actually, most source critics see in Genesis 37 more than a gloss; they see evidence of an independent source. A better explanation is provided by Israel Eph'al, *The Ancient Arabs* (Jerusalem, 1982), p. 236: "Since the Midianites and Amalekites were identified with the Ishmaelites, and the descriptions of the territories of the Ishmaelites and Amalekites correspond, it is probable that the Ishmaelites were at one time the leading confederation of nomads in southern Palestine, and that their name was occasionally attached to other groups."

13. David Damrosch, *The Narrative Covenant* (San Francisco: Harper & Row, 1987), pp. 200–201.

14. This is not the sadistic mutilation that one finds in, for example, the annals of Assurnasirpal: "I cut the limbs of the officers. . . . From some [living captives] I cut off their noses, their ears and their fingers." It is, rather, a folk-tale device, as when the queen instructs the hunter to take Snow White into the forest and kill her and bring back her heart (some versions have lungs and liver). In "The Origins of Infant Circumcision in Israel," *Hebrew Annual Review* 11 (1987): 355–70, William H. Propp notes that the Egyptians would sometimes take the genitalia of their uncircumcised foes as trophies (p. 361, n.22). Since Propp's discussion is about circumcision, he naturally cites both Genesis 34 and 1 Samuel 18. He says of the first that it is another example of the association of marriage and circumcision (p. 359); and of the second that "it is hard not to see here a burlesque allusion to an old-fashioned custom still remembered in the monarchic period" (p. 361). He is thus not far from the view of Damrosch, and I find him no more convincing.

15. Damrosch, *The Narrative Covenant*, p. 178.

16. He summarizes the views on the relationship between the Yahwist(s) and the Deuteronomist(s) on pages 144–81.

17. Damrosch, *The Narrative Covenant*, p. 303.

18. Damrosch, p. 180.

19. Damrosch, p. 205.

20. Edward Greenstein, "On the Genesis of Biblical Prose Narrative," *Prooftexts* 8 (1988): 351.

21. In addition to Damrosch's work, which has value despite the harsh criticism I have heaped upon it, see Marc Brettler, "The Book of Judges: Literature as Politics," *Journal of Biblical Literature*, forthcoming; Alexander Rofe, "The Vineyard of Naboth: The Origin and Message of the Story," *Vetus Testamentum* 38 (1988): 89–104; and the essays in *Empirical Models for Biblical Criticism*, ed. Jeffrey H. Tigay (Philadelphia: University of Pennsylvania Press, 1985).

22. Cf. my remarks in *Poetics and Interpretation of Biblical Narrative* (Sheffield: The Almond Press, 1983), pp. 15–21.

23. Similar thoughts were expressed by James Kugel in "On the Bible and Literary Criticism," *Prooftexts* 1 (1981): 217–36. Although I disagreed with some of his observations (cf. "On the Bible as Literature," *Prooftexts* 2 [1982]: 323–27), I did not disagree with his comments about the similarity between midrash and modern literary criticism of the Bible.

24. Compare Rosenberg's remarks on verbal correspondence, *King and Kin*, p. 203, and mine in *Hebrew Annual Review* 8 (1984): 8–10. Cf. also Michael Fishbane, *Biblical Interpretation in Ancient Israel* (Oxford: Clarendon, 1985), pp.

11–13, 287–91; and James Kugel, "The Bible's Earliest Interpreters," *Prooftexts* 7 (1987): 278–80. Seidel's "law" (in "Parallels between the Book of Isaiah and the Book of Psalms," *Sinai* 38 [1956]: 149–72, 229–40, 272–80, 333–54) that the reversal of terms indicates a quotation, actually shows only that word-pairs occur in reversed order. It is not a criterion for identifying quotations or allusions.

The Right Chorale

1. Bloomington: Indiana University Press, 1985; subsequent references will be provided in parentheses.

2. E. Auerbach, *Mimesis: The Representation of Reality in Western Literature* (Princeton: Princeton University Press, 1953), 3–23.

3. Such concern with theory is more likely to be present in commentaries attempting to make the results of scholarship available to a nonspecialist readership. For engaging examples: N. M. Sarna, *Understanding Genesis* (New York: Schocken, 1970); M. Greenberg, *Understanding Exodus* (New York: Behrman, 1969).

4. The dictum is Tannaitic. See its repeated exegetical application in *Mekhilta, Beshalaḥ* 7 (on Exod. 15:9) in the edition of H. Horowitz and I. Rabin, *Mekhilta d'Rabbi Ishmael* (Jerusalem: Bamberger and Wahrman, 1960), 139. See also *Siphre Num., Beha'aloteka*, 64 in the edition of H. S. Horowitz, *Siphre D'be Rab* (Jerusalem: Wahrmann, 1966), 61. In the Talmud, cf. *y. Šeqal.* 6.1; *y. Soṭa* 5.3; *b. Pesaḥ.* 6b.

5. R.H.M. Elwes, trans., *The Chief Works of Benedict de Spinoza*, 2 vols. (New York: Dover, 1951) 1.1–199. Subsequent references to Spinoza will be placed in parentheses in the text.

6. On Spinoza's contributions, see H. J. Kraus, *Geschichte der historisch-kritischen Erforschung des Alten Testaments* (2d ed.; Neukirchen-Vluyn: Neukirchener, 1969), 61–65. In immediate terms, the great advances in nineteenth century scholarship derive from the contributions of W.M.L. de Wette, who is the first "to use the critical method in order to present a view of the history of Israelite religion that is radically at variance with the view implied in the Old Testament itself." See J. Rogerson, *Old Testament Criticism in the Nineteenth Century: England and Germany* (London: SPCK, 1984), 29. At a more fundamental level, however, Spinoza's work is crucial for his rejection of the Mosaic authorship of the Pentateuch and his demonstration of textual corruptions and historical and conceptual inconsistencies within the Bible. As such Spinoza helps found and legitimate the historical and secular approach to Scripture; see L. Strauss, *Spinoza's Critique of Religion* (New York: Schocken, 1965), 35.

7. Most treatments of Spinoza reject his work as inimical to any notion of a biblically grounded hermeneutics; L. Strauss, *Spinoza's Critique of Religion* is the most obvious example. An independent approach to the whole of Spinoza's thought which I have found particularly instructive is provided by B. Polka: *The Dialectic of Biblical Critique* (New York: St. Martin's, 1986), 21–22, 25–27, 184–87; idem, "Spinoza and the Separation between Philosophy and Theology," *The Journal of Religious Studies* 16 (1990): 91–119; idem, "Ethics as Biblical Interpretation: Spinoza's Response to Descartes," vol. 2 of his "Dialectic and Interpretation" (5 vols.; Toronto: Department of History, York University; manuscript photocopy).

8. There is a critical translation error in the first sentence of the important chapter 15 (p. 190). That sentence should read, "Those who know not that philosophy and *theology* are distinct . . . ." not "philosophy and reason," as printed (B. Polka, personal communication).

9. Spinoza's double critique of Maimonides, pp. 114–18, in chap. 7, and of Alfakhar, pp. 191–92, in chap. 15, frames chaps. 7–15 as the unit concerned most specifically with biblical interpretation (7) and the relation between philosophy and theology (15).

10. E. Auerbach, *Mimesis*, 3–23 (see n.2 above); O. Barfield, *Saving the Appearances: A Study in Idolatry* (London: Faber and Faber, 1957) 107–15; K. Burke, "The First Three Chapters of Genesis," chap. 3 of his *Rhetoric of Religion* (Boston: Beacon, 1961) 172–272; E. Fromm, *You Shall Be As Gods* (New York: Holt, Rinehart and Winston, 1966); E. Voegelin, *Israel and Revelation*, vol. 1 of his *Order and History* (5 vols.; Baton Rouge: Louisiana State University Press, 1956–87); N. Frye, *Anatomy of Criticism: Four Essays* (New York: Atheneum, 1970), 141–46, 188–89, 315–26; idem, *The Great Code: The Bible and Literature* (New York: Harcourt Brace Jovanovich, 1982); H. N. Schneidau, *Sacred Discontent: The Bible and Western Tradition* (Berkeley: University of California Press, 1977); R. Alter, *The Art of Biblical Narrative* (New York: Basic Books, 1981).

11. Sternberg overlooks the nearly identical critique of medieval rabbinic exegesis provided earlier by M. Weiss in his *The Bible and Modern Literary Theory* (Jerusalem: Bialik Institute, 1967), 196 n.22 (Hebrew); English trans. *The Bible from Within* (Jerusalem: Magnes, 1984), 37 n.24. Weiss cites Ibn Ezra's body and soul simile for the relation of word to meaning and notes its origins in medieval Islamic literary theory. He also cites Kimḥi (Radak) on Gen. 24:39, rejecting the latter's restriction of repetition to lexical variation void of exegetical implications. The work of Weiss more broadly represents an important attempt to develop a literary approach to biblical poetic texts. He attempts to forge a system of "total interpretation," informed conjointly by European literary theory and the philological approach of biblical criticism. J. Unterman comments on Sternberg's not engaging the work of Weiss in "Sternberg's Ambiguity and the Bible's: With an Appendix on the Non-Ambiguity of the Killing of the Concubine (Judges 19:30)," *Hebrew Studies* 29 (1988): 194–205, especially 200–201.

12. There is a larger context that helps provide the rationale for Cassuto's "reducing" the significance of repetition. Cassuto maintained a constant polemic against the documentary hypothesis (source-criticism) for its reductive inattention to the coherence and final meaning of the text. His strategy was to argue from his extensive work on Ugaritic epic against conventional source-critical analysis: to argue that the very textual feature, repetition, basic to its separation of the sources is instead a *compositional* feature characteristic of ancient Near Eastern oral epic and the (biblical) literature he contends derives from it. See U. Cassuto, *The Documentary Hypothesis and the Composition of the Pentateuch* (Hebrew, 4th ed.; Jerusalem: Magnes, 1965), 60–70.

13. My Bible translations closely follow the highly literate *Tanakh: The Holy Scriptures* (Philadelphia: Jewish Publication Society, 1988) although I employ "Yahweh" for "LORD." In this instance two comments on the JPS rendering of this verse are necessary. First, the reference to "men" is not gender-specific in the Hebrew and means "humankind." Second, their translation of Gen. 6:7 reads "beasts" and obscures thereby the allusion to the identical Hebrew word in Gen. 1:24, which they render "cattle." In the narrative execution of Gen.

6:7 in 7:23, however, the same word is correctly translated as "cattle," which inconsistency in turn obscures the close link intended between the two verses.

14. The imagery inherent in the Hebrew verb is specifically that of erasure, in the first instance, textual (Num. 5:23; Exod. 32:32) but also more general wiping (2 Kings 21:13). For further discussion of the verb, see U. Cassuto, *A Commentary on the Book of Genesis* (2 vols.; Jerusalem: Magnes Press, 1961–64), 1.304–5. This motif of God's re-beginning from a *tabula rasa*, an enforced *ex nihilo* in response to human iniquity, is frequent in the Bible. It recurs in the debates between Moses and God following the episodes of the golden calf (Exod. 32:10) and the spies (Num. 14:11–12) and in the conception of the devastation of the autochthonous peoples of Canaan in order to create a new moral community bound by God's law (Lev. 18:24–30; 20:22–26). So characteristic is this motif of God's ominous duality as destroyer and creator that the early midrash retrojects it into the prehistory of Creation, positing a succession of other worlds as having been created and destroyed by God before he was, finally, content with this one: see *Genesis Rabbah* 3:7 in the edition of J. Theodor and Ch. Albeck, *Midrash Bereshit Rabba* (2d ed.; 3 vols.; Jerusalem: Wahrmann, 1965), 1.23.

15. The citation from Gen. 1:24 is, to be sure, not comprehensive but preserves in fixed order the only two substantives without the additional modifier, "of every kind."

16. Although the former does occur in Gen. 7:3. The Syriac Peshitta version is troubled by the inconsistent means of referring to the animals' gender and levels the lexical variation, thereby assimilating the lexicon of 7:1–5 to that of 6:17–22.

17. On the complexity of the chronology (which the Septuagint tries to minimize), see J. Skinner, *Genesis* (2d ed.; International Critical Commentary: Edinburgh: T. & T. Clark, 1930), 167–69; S. E. Loewenstamm, "The Flood," *Comparative Studies in Biblical and Ancient Oriental Literatures* (Alter Orient und Altes Testament 204; Neukirchen-Vluyn: Butzon & Bercker Kevelaer, 1980), 93–121, especially 110–14.

18. For a diagrammatic representation of the cosmology presupposed by Genesis 1, depicting the waters both supernal and subterrestrial, see N. M. Sarna, *Understanding Genesis*, 5.

19. On the Flood as a restoration of the pre-Creation watery chaos, or Gen. 7:11 as a reversal of Gen. 1:2, see: H. Gunkel, *Genesis* (Göttinger Handkommentar zum Alten Testament; 4th ed.; Göttingen: Vandenhoeck & Ruprecht, 1917), 77, 144; U. Cassuto, *A Commentary on the Book of Genesis*, 2.97; N. M. Sarna, *Understanding Genesis* (New York: Schocken, 1970), 55; M. Fishbane, *Text and Texture* (New York: Schocken, 1979), 33–34.

20. Sternberg briefly refers to the Flood story in several instances in the context of his analysis of the varieties and significance of repetition. He astutely points out the failure of Cassuto to resolve one of its repetitions (p. 376) and by way of contrast attempts to resolve other of its repetitions in terms of a deliberate narrative structure, the sequence of "forecast" and "enactment." He argues that the latter structure functions to elucidate the character of Noah: the narration of his obedient entry into the ark reveals what was implied in the proleptic description of Noah as "righteous" (p. 388; cf. 418, 439). In light of the analysis here, Sternberg's reference to a single sequence of forecast and enactment overlooks the pleonasm of double command and triple compliance.

21. The best classical literary-critical analysis on the Flood is H. Gunkel, *Genesis*, with exposition of the Yahwist's (J) version, pp. 59–77, the Priestly (P) version,

137–52, and the redactor's techniques for combining them, 139–40. The most thorough recent treatment is C. Westermann, *Genesis 1–11* (Minneapolis: Augsburg, 1984) 384–458. A valuable "primer" to source-criticism, with a discussion of Genesis 6–9, is N. C. Habel, *Literary Criticism of the Old Testament* (Philadelphia: Fortress, 1972), 29–42.

There has been a series of challenges to the source-critical analysis of Genesis 6–9: U. Cassuto, *A Commentary on the Book of Genesis*, 2.3–140; E. Nielsen, *Oral Tradition* (Studies in Biblical Theology 11; London: SCM, 1954), 95–103; G. J. Wenham, "The Coherence of the Flood Narrative," *Vetus Testamentum* 28 (1978): 336–48. An excellent critique of these and other attempts to disprove the documentary hypothesis is found in J. A. Emerton, "An Examination of Some Attempts to Defend the Unity of the Flood Narrative," *Vetus Testamentum* 37 (1987): 401–20 and 38 (1988): 1–21 (in two parts). Not included in Emerton's critique are two more recent works: I. M. Kikawada and A. Quinn, *Before Abraham Was: The Unity of Genesis 1–11* (Nashville: Abingdon, 1985), 83–106; G. A. Rendsburg, *The Redaction of Genesis* (Winona Lake, Ind.: Eisenbrauns, 1986), 9–13. For a refutation of the work of Kikawada and Quinn, see P. K. McCarter, "A New Challenge to the Documentary Hypothesis," *Bible Review* 4:2 (April 1988): 34–39. For an astute rebuttal of Rendsburg's methodology, see the review by M. Brettler, *The Jewish Quarterly Review* 78 (1987): 113–19.

An attempt to demonstrate difficulties in the source-critical approach while not altogether rejecting its validity is Loewenstamm, "The Flood," 93–121 (cf. n.17 above). That article is a translation of the Hebrew original published in 1960, unfortunately largely overlooked by scholarship.

22. The most comprehensive treatment of inner-biblical exegesis is M. Fishbane, *Biblical Interpretation in Ancient Israel* (Oxford: Clarendon, 1985), which provides a thorough bibliography. See also the ground-breaking study by N. M. Sarna, "Psalm 89: A Study in Inner-Biblical Exegesis," *Biblical and Other Studies*, ed. A. Altmann, (Brandeis Texts and Studies: Cambridge, Mass.: Harvard University Press, 1963), 29–46; G. Vermes, "Bible and Midrash: Early Old Testament Exegesis," *The Cambridge History of the Bible*, ed. P. R. Ackroyd and C. F. Evans (Cambridge: Cambridge University Press, 1970), 1.199–212; B. S. Childs, "Psalm Titles and Midrashic Exegesis," *Journal of Semitic Studies* 16 (1971): 137–50.

Converging with the above approach to inner-biblical exegesis are the important studies by Sanders and Childs of the ongoing reinterpretation and reapplication of the formative canon by Israelite authors. See J. A. Sanders, *Torah and Canon* (Philadelphia: Fortress, 1972) and, most recently, *From Sacred Story to Sacred Text: Canon as Paradigm* (Philadelphia: Fortress, 1987). See also B. S. Childs, *Introduction to the Old Testament as Scripture* (Philadelphia: Fortress, 1979), 69–83. For a critique of this approach: J. Barr, *Holy Scripture: Canon, Authority, Criticism* (Philadelphia: Westminster, 1983).

23. For the verse as redactional, see H. Gunkel, *Genesis*, 62–63; S. R. Driver, *The Book of Genesis* (12th ed.; London: Methuen, 1926), 90; this analysis is rejected by E. Nielsen, *Oral Tradition*, 98.

24. For interesting recent attempts to formulate the distinctiveness of ancient Israel in light of Jaspers's notion of "axial age breakthroughs," see the essays by S. Eisenstadt, B. Uffenheimer, M. Weinfeld, P. Machinist, and H. Tadmor, *The Origins and Diversity of Axial Age Civilizations*, ed. S. N. Eisenstadt (Albany: State University of New York Press, 1986), 127–224.

25. Sternberg does present his emphasis on the epistemological revolution

as something that has been overlooked, in contrast to more conventional formulations which stress "monotheism, the suppression of myth, the rise of ethics and personal responsibility" (46).

26. In the context of my use of Spinoza (pp. 133–35 above), I have to point out that Spinoza himself rejects the specific applicability of biblical "ceremonial law" to moderns in chapter 5 of the *Tractatus* (pp. 69–80). In doing so he distinguishes the binding intent of the law, morality, from its specific prescriptions.

27. Elsewhere (pp. 390–93, 431, 436) Sternberg notes the pattern of "repetition with variation" in Eve's reformulation (Gen. 3:2–3) of the original divine command (Gen. 2:16–17). A theological study whose subtle interpretations of this and other "retelling" within the story bear literary implications is D. Bonhoeffer, *Creation and Temptation* (London: SCM, 1966), 64–92.

28. Rashi, *Raschi: Der Kommentar des Saloma b. Isak über den Pentateuch*, ed. A. Berliner (Hebrew, 2d ed.; Frankfurt: J. Kaufmann, 1905), 1 [my translation]; cf. M. Rosenbaum and A. M. Silberman, trans., *Pentateuch with Targum Onkelos, Haphtaroth, and Rashi's Commentary* (5 vols.; London: Shapiro Valentine, 1929–34), 1.2.

Although the precise identity of the R. Isaac whom Rashi here cites is unclear, the problematic of the question is ancient and, at least in part, Tannaitic. The question concerning the justification for the Bible's beginning with cosmogony is found in *Genesis Rabbah* 1:2; see the edition of J. Theodor and Ch. Albeck, *Midrash Bereshit Rabba* (2d ed.; Jerusalem: Wahrmann, 1965), 4–5. For the comparative question about beginning with Creation rather than law, raised in the name of R. Isaac, Rashi's source in *Midrash Tanḥuma, Bereshit*, 11; see the edition of S. Buber, *Midrash Tanhuma* (Vilna: [n. p.], 1913), 7. The question is raised in nearly identical terms in the name of the third-century Amora, Yannai, in *Song of Songs Rabbah* 1:29; see the edition of S. Dunsky, *Midrash Rabba Shir ha-Shirim* (Tel Aviv: Dvir, 1980), 27. Also note *Midrash Leqaḥ Tov, Genesis*, on Gen. 1:1, ed. S. Buber (Vilna: Widow and Brothers Romm, 1884; reprinted, Jerusalem: [n.p.], 1959/60), 3 (reference courtesy of B. Walfish).

As for the identity of R. Isaac, there is some evidence that Rashi here honors his own father (cf. Rashi on Gen. 37:20). That the *Tanḥuma* also refers to R. Isaac, however, suggests a more ancient rabbi with the same name; so M. Kasher, *Torah Shelemah* (New York: American Biblical Encyclopaedia Society, 1949), 1.13, n.52. Resolution of this question awaits further progress on the manuscript history of the *Tanḥuma* family of midrashim.

29. "The Ox That Gored," *Transactions of the American Philosophical Society* 71:2 (1981): 13–14, 25–47. Finkelstein builds on the important article by M. Greenberg, "Some Postulates of Biblical Criminal Law," *Yehezkel Kaufmann Jubilee Volume*, ed. M. Haran (Jerusalem: Magnes, 1960), 5–28.

30. In references to biblical law that follow, my focus is on the civil and ethical laws of the Bible; the ritual laws have a somewhat different literary history.

31. G. R. Driver and J. C. Miles, *The Babylonian Laws* (2 vols.; Oxford: Clarendon, 1952), 1.53. The one citation of Hammurabi's Code found occurs in a political treaty nearly one thousand years after the Code's promulgation. Strikingly, the citation is not of the actual laws, but of the curses found in the poetic frame of the Code; see R. Borger, "Marduk-zākir-šumi I. und der Kodex Ḥammurapi," *Orientalia* n.s. 34 (1965): 168–69.

32. See S. E. Loewenstamm, "Law," *The World History of the Jewish People*, vol. 3, *Judges*, ed. B. Mazar (Rutgers: Rutgers University Press, 1971) 231–67. Loewenstamm's explanation, however, diverges from the one proposed here.

33. R. Westbrook, *Studies in Biblical and Cuneiform Law* (Cahiers de la Revue Biblique 26; Paris: J. Gabalda, 1988), 1–7.

34. For the general approach taken here, see Finkelstein, "The Ox That Gored" (cf. n.29 above). On the disjunction between the actual legal practice of Mesopotamia and the legal collections, see his article "Cuneiform Law," *Encyclopaedia Judaica* (2d printing; Jerusalem: Encyclopaedia Judaica, 1973), 16.1505f–1505k.

35. R. Polzin applies Vološinov's concept of "reported speech" to Deuteronomy's laws in *Moses and the Deuteronomist* (New York: Seabury, 1980), 47–69. Note Fishbane's productive use of voice in *Biblical Interpretation in Ancient Israel*, 260–61, 417–18, 530–31. With a different methodology, see the "total interpretation" of B. J. Schwartz, "A Literary Study of the Slave-Girl Pericope—Leviticus 19:20–22," in *Studies in Bible*, ed. S. Japhet (Scripta Hierosolymitana; Jerusalem: Magnes, 1986), 241–55. C. M. Carmichael has published a series of articles and books arguing for a literary approach to the laws of Deuteronomy; see most recently *Law and Narrative in the Bible* (Ithaca/London: Cornell University Press, 1985). Although he usefully emphasizes the theoretical component of Deuteronomy, there are methodological problems with his work. See my article, "Calum M. Carmichael's Approach to the Laws of Deuteronomy," *Harvard Theological Review* 83(1990): 227–57.

36. Among recent studies stressing the importance of literary theory and hermeneutics to the study of modern law is the collection of articles in "Symposium: Law and Literature," *Texas Law Review* 60 (1982): 373–586. Some of those articles are reprinted in the more comprehensive S. Levinson and Steven Mailloux, eds., *Interpreting Law and Literature* (Evanston: Northwestern University Press, 1988). Of extraordinary interest for its use of rabbinic texts to adduce hermeneutical principles which the author then applies to constitutional law is R. M. Cover, "The Supreme Court 1982 Term: Foreword: *Nomos* and Narrative," *Harvard Law Review* 97 (1983): 4–68.

37. P. J. Haas, "From Savigny to CLS: Legal Thought and the Biblical Text" (Nashville: Vanderbilt University, 1988; typescript photocopy), presented at the annual meeting of the Society of Biblical Literature, Chicago, 19–22 November, 1988.

38. This attribution is stressed in the important article by Greenberg, "Some Postulates of Biblical Criminal Law" (see n.29 above).

39. N. M. Sarna, "Bible: The Canon, Text, and Editions," *Encyclopaedia Judaica* (Jerusalem: Encyclopaedia Judaica, 1972), 4:817.

40. Textual stabilization begins approximately 2250–2225 B.C.E. in Mesopotamia; see A. L. Oppenheim, *Ancient Mesopotamia* (rev. ed.; Chicago and London: University of Chicago Press, 1977), 18. He discusses the contents and implications of the standardized written tradition on pp. 16–30.

41. M. Smith, "Pseudepigraphy in the Israelite Literary Tradition," *Pseudepigrapha T*, ed. K. von Fritz (Entretiens sur l'antiquité classique 18; Geneva: Vandoeuvres, 1971), 191–215 with ensuing discussion, 216–27, esp. 225–27; M. Fishbane, *Biblical Interpretation*, 260–72.

42. Cf. the formulation of the hermeneutical issue by Fishbane, *Biblical Interpretation*, 163.

43. See M. Haran, *Temples and Temple-Service in Ancient Israel* (Oxford: Clarendon, 1978), 322; H. L. Ginsberg, *The Israelian Heritage of Judaism* (New York:

Jewish Theological Seminary of America, 1982), 58; and Fishbane, *Biblical Interpretation*, 134–37, with greatest attention to the hermeneutical issues involved.

44. For the emphasis on the role of scribes, see M. Weinfeld, *Deuteronomy and the Deuteronomic School* (Oxford: Clarendon, 1972).

45. For detailed exegesis, see my *The Hermeneutics of Legal Innovation: The Impact of Centralization upon the Structure, Sequence and Reformulation of Legal Material in Deuteronomy* (Ann Arbor: University Microfilms International), 169–232.

46. G. Scholem, "Revelation and Tradition as Religious Categories in Judaism," *The Messianic Idea in Judaism* (New York: Schocken, 1971) 282–303. See the elaboration by G. H. Hartman, "On the Jewish Imagination," *Prooftexts* 5 (1985): 201–20, especially 210.

47. Although Scholem does not refer to it, the same issues arise with the sectarian Temple Scroll from Qumran which strikingly presents late sectarian innovations, interwoven with rearranged passages from the Pentateuch, as a divine pseudepigraph; as a result, Yahweh from Sinai proclaims the *halakha* of Qumran. See Y. Yadin, *The Temple Scroll* (3 vols.; Jerusalem: Israel Exploration Society, 1983), 1.71.

48. See the illuminating article of M. S. Jaffee, "The Pretext of Interpretation: Rabbinic Oral Torah and the Charisma of Revelation," *God in Language*, ed. R. P. Scharlemann and G. E. M. Ogutu (New York: Paragon House, 1987), 73–89.

49. On the issues involved in Scholem's pseudepigraphic dating of the *Zohar*, see D. Biale, *Gershom Scholem: Kabbalah and Counter-History* (Cambridge, Mass./London: Harvard University Press, 1979), 115–21.

50. See Fishbane, *Biblical Interpretation*, 257–66, 530–33, who builds on the article by Smith, "Pseudepigraphy," 191–215 (see n.41 above).

51. For an alternative, note Finkelstein's dialectical interpretation, *The Ox That Gored*, 7–8. In more explicitly philosophical terms, see B. Polka, "Interpretation and the Bible: The Dialectic of Concept and Content in Interpretative Practice," *The Journal of Speculative Philosophy* 4 (1990): 66–82.

52. See M. Foucault, "What Is an Author?" *Textual Strategies*, ed. J. V. Harari (Ithaca: Cornell University Press, 1979), 141–60.

53. H. Bloom, *The Anxiety of Influence: A Theory of Poetry* (New York: Oxford University Press, 1973). Deuteronomy's "misreading" of the Exodus lemma has further theoretical implications in light of Bloom's *A Map of Misreading* (New York: Oxford University Press, 1975).

54. I am grateful to a number of colleagues: D. Aaron (Wellesley College) and E. Wolfson (New York University) for consultation on rabbinic literature; M. Jaffee (University of Washington), G. Knoppers (Penn State) and J. Van Herik (Penn State) for comments on earlier drafts; and B. Polka (York University), B. Walfish (University of Toronto), and especially D. Charney (Penn State) for their detailed suggestions.

The Integrity of Biblical Pluralism

1. Review of R. Alter and F. Kermode, eds., *The Literary Guide to the Bible* (Cambridge, Mass.: Harvard University Press, 1987), in *The New Yorker*, 11 January 1988:94–98.

2. Hans Frei, *The Eclipse of Biblical Narrative* (New Haven: Yale University Press, 1974); David Kelsey, *The Uses of Scripture in Recent Theology* (Philadelphia: Fortress Press, 1975).

3. Childs, "Interpretation in Faith," *Interpretation* 18 (1964): 432–49; *Biblical Theology in Crisis* (Philadelphia: Westminster, 1970).

4. I have argued for a canonical-critical reading of the Bible (as both shape and function) in *Torah and Canon* (Philadelphia: Fortress, 1972) and numerous publications since (see below, notes 7, 8, and 12).

5. Sanders, *The Psalms Scroll of Qumran Cave 11:Discoveries in the Judaean Desert IV* (Oxford: Clarendon Press, 1965); and *The Dead Sea Psalms Scroll* (Ithaca: Cornell University Press, 1967). See also "Cave 11 Surprises and the Question of Canon," *McCormick Quarterly Review* 21 (1968): 284–98. Note that 4Q430 and 431 contain only non-Masoretic psalms: Eileen Schuller, *Non-Canonical Psalms from Qumran: A Pseudepigraphic Collection* (Atlanta: Scholars Press, 1986); cf. M. Baillet, *Qumran Grotte 4, III, DJD* 7 (Oxford: Clarendon, 1982).

6. See *Torah and Canon*, above, note 4.

7. More recently the thesis has been expanded to include the fact that the (hi)story that began in Genesis seems to end in the failure of those promises in 2 Kings 22 and 25, the demise of the northern and southern kingdoms. See Sanders, "Deuteronomy," in *The Books of the Bible*, ed. B. W. Anderson, vol. 1 (New York: Scribner's Sons, 1989), 89–102 as well as "Canon (OT)" in the forthcoming *Anchor Bible Dictionary*, ed. David Noel Freedman.

8. Sanders, "Adaptable for Life: The Nature and Function of Canon," *Magnalia Dei: The Mighty Acts of God: Essays on the Bible and Archaeology in Memory of G. E. Wright* (New York: Doubleday, 1976), 531–60.

9. Dominique Barthélemy, "Text, Hebrew, History of," *Interpreter's Dictionary of the Bible Supplement* (Nashville: Abingdon, 1976), 878–84; Sh. Talmon, "The OT Text," *The Cambridge History of the Bible*, vol. 1 (Cambridge: Cambridge University Press, 1970), 159–99.

10. *Critique textuelle de l'Ancien Testament*, Orbis biblicus et orientalis 50/1,2 (Fribourg: Editions universitaires, 1982, 1986).

11. See Sanders, "Hebrew Bible and Old Testament: Textual Criticism in Service of Biblical Studies," forthcoming in a compendium from the conference "Hebrew Bible or Old Testament" held at Notre Dame University, 9–11 April 1989.

12. "Text and Canon: Concepts and Method," *Journal of Biblical Literature* 98 (1979): 5–29, included in Sanders, *From Sacred Story to Sacred Text* (Philadelphia: Fortress, 1987), 125–51.

13. *Introduction to the Tiberian Masorah* (Atlanta: Scholars Press, 1980), 38.

14. Chadwyck-Healey Inc. has announced publication of *The Collective Catalogue of Hebrew Manuscripts* on microfiche covering 262,500 items in some 700 collections around the world; it purports to include catalogue data on the majority of Hebrew manuscripts (presumably other than the remaining unpublished Dead Sea Scrolls). Critical data of this sort is now more accessible than ever before.

15. A good recent example is Roger Beckwith, *The Old Testament Canon of the New Testament Church* (Grand Rapids: Eerdmans, 1985). Cf. Beckwith in ch. 2 of *Mikra*, ed. J. Mulder (Philadelphia: Fortress, 1988), 39–86; by contrast see J. Mulder in chap. 3 of the same volume, 87–135—a felicitous counterbalance to Beckwith.

16. L. Schiffman, *Sectarian Laws in the Dead Sea Scrolls: Courts, Testimony and*

the Penal Code (Atlanta: Scholars Press, 1983); B. Z. Wacholder, *Dawn of Qumran* (Cincinnati: Hebrew Union College Press, 1983); and the review by Sanders, *Journal of the American Oriental Society* 105 (1985): 146–48.

17. Kurt and Barbara Aland, *The Text of the New Testament* (Grand Rapids: Eerdmans, 1987), 78–79; Bruce Metzger, *The Canon of the New Testament: Its Origin, Development and Significance* (Oxford: Clarendon, 1987), 217.

18. The characteristics discerned in the canonical process have now been affirmed for the continuing canonical process in the early church by Cecil M. Robeck, Jr., "Canon, Regulae Fidei, and Continuing Revelation in the Early Church," in *Church, Word, and Spirit*, ed. J. Bradley and R. Muller (Grand Rapids: Eerdmans, 1987), 65–91, esp. 73, 80, 85–91.

19. Sanders, *Torah and Canon*, passim; "Adaptable for Life: The Nature and Function of Canon" (1976) and "The Hermeneutics of True and False Prophecy" (1977) in *From Sacred Story to Sacred Text*, 9–39 and 87–105.

20. P. Pokorny, "Das theologische Problem der neutestamentlichen Pseudepigraphie," *Evangelische Theologie* 44 (1984): 486–96.

21. Leland White, review of *From Sacred Story to Sacred Text* in *Biblical Theology Bulletin* 18 (1988): 37.

22. Sanders, "Canonical Hermeneutics," ch. 4 in *Canon and Community* (Philadelphia: Fortress, 1984), 46–60; *From Sacred Story to Sacred Text*, 61–73.

23. *Canon and Community*, 47ff.

24. J. C. Rylaarsdam, *Revelation in Jewish Wisdom Literature* (Chicago: Chicago University Press, 1946).

25. See Sanders, "The Strangeness of the Bible," *Union Seminary Quarterly Review* 42 (1988): 33–37.

26. See Richard Hays's brilliant study, *Echoes of Scripture in the Letters of Paul* (New Haven: Yale University Press, 1989), esp. 1–5.

27. 1 Kings 10 begins in majestic cadences. The alliterations in the Hebrew suggest a picture of the grand, royal caravan described in verse 2. But v. 1 ends with the statement, "but she came to test him with riddles," already anticipating the several human satans God will appoint to test Solomon beginning in chap. 11.

28. *Pace* B. Childs, *Introduction to the Old Testament as Scripture* (Philadelphia: Fortress, 1979), 46–106.

29. Morton Smith, *Palestinian Parties and Politics That Shaped the Old Testament* (New York: Columbia University Press, 1971).

30. It is something of a shock for a student of the Bible and other centuries-old religious canons to see the word "canon" used in fields other than religion, such as European and Western literature, as in vol. 10, no. 1 of *Critical Inquiry* (September 1983), the issue on "Canons," as well as articles in subsequent issues (December 1983, 301–47; March 1984, 462–542). As used by such scholars it apparently means lists of books which emerge as most often recommended as the "best" of Western letters; and such lists are apparently political in the sense that they represent the dominant and standard culture.

Genesis 22

1. This essay is an abridgment of a forthcoming study.

2. Bibliography on Genesis 22 is staggering. Claus Westermann lists numerous references from 1905 through 1978; see *Genesis 12–36, A Commentary* (Minneap-

olis: Augsburg Publishing House, 1985), pp. 351–54. James L. Crenshaw adds to this list, including his own essay, "A Monstrous Test: Genesis 22," *A Whirlpool of Torment* (Philadelphia: Fortress Press, 1984), pp. 9–29. Surveys of the history of interpretation appear in two articles: S. Kreuzer, "Das Opfer des Vaters— die Gefährdung des Sohnes: Genesis 22," pp. 62–70, and F. Neubacher, "Isaaks Opferung in der griechishen Alten Kirche," pp. 72–76, both published in *Schaut Abraham an, euren Vater! Festschrift für Professor Dr. Georg Sauer zum 60 Geburtstag, Amt und Gemeinde* 27:7/8 (1986). For a study of the Akedah in art, see Jo Milgrom, *The Binding of Isaac: The Akedah—A Primary Symbol in Jewish Thought and Art* (Berkeley: Bibal Press, 1988).

3. On rhetorical criticism, see the foundational document by James Muilenburg, "Form Criticism and Beyond," *JBL* 88 (1969): 1–18; for samplings of feminist hermeneutics, see *inter alia* Mary Ann Tolbert, ed., *The Bible and Feminist Hermeneutics*, Semeia 28 (Chico, Calif.: Scholars Press, 1983); Adela Yarbro Collins, ed., *Feminist Perspectives on Biblical Scholarship* (Chico, Calif.: Scholars Press, 1985); Letty M. Russell, ed., *Feminist Interpretation of the Bible* (Philadelphia: The Westminster Press, 1985).

4. For the classic literary analysis, see Erich Auerbach, "Odysseus' Scar," *Mimesis: The Representation of Reality in Western Literature* (Garden City, N.Y.: Doubleday, 1953). Most recently, cf. Francis Landy, "Narrative Techniques and Symbolic Transactions in the Akedah" and Jan. P. Fokkelman, "'On the Mount of the Lord There Is Vision,' A Response to Francis Landy Concerning the Akedah," *Signs and Wonders*, ed. J. Cheryl Exum (The Society of Biblical Literature Semeia Studies, 1989): 1–57.

5. All biblical citations refer to the book of Genesis, unless stated otherwise. Two translations of the Hebrew are used: mine and the Revised Standard Version. The former are left unmarked; the latter are designated RSV.

6. This literary reading follows the narrative in its final form rather than exploring the history of sources and traditions behind it. On that subject, see most recently Jean-L. Duhaime, "Le sacrifice d'Isaac (Gn 22, 1–19): l'heritage de Gunkel," *Science et Esprit* (1981): 139–56; Sean E. McEvenue, "The Elohist at Work," *Zeitschrift für die alttestamentliche Wissenschaft* 96 (1984): 315–32; Hans-Cristoph Schmitt, "Die Erzählung von de Versuch Abrahams Gen 22, 1–19* und das Problem einer Theologie der elohistichen Pentateuchtexts," *Biblische Notizen* 34 (1986): 82–109.

7. For the verb *nsh* with God as subject, cf. Exod. 15:25; 16:4; 20:20; Deut. 8:2,16; 13:3; 2 Chron. 32:31.

8. For an illuminating discussion of God as tester and provider (22:15), see Walter Brueggemann, *Genesis* (Atlanta: John Knox Press, 1982), pp. 188–94. Some commentators argue that the character of God (not just Abraham) is also tested here; see Kenneth R. R. Gros Louis, "Abraham: II," *Literary Interpretations of Biblical Narratives*, vol. 2, ed. Gros Louis with James S. Ackerman (Nashville: Abingdon, 1982), pp. 71–84 and Sidney Breitbart "The Akedah—A Test of God," *Dor le Dor* 15 (1986/87): 19–28. An altogether different reading of the verb *nissāh* as "uplifted" (from *nēs*) is proposed by Hirsch Patcas, "Akedah, The Binding of Isaac," *Dor le Dor* 14 (1985/86): 112–14.

9. E.g., King James Version. For a grammatical discussion of *hinnēh*, see Thomas O. Lambdin, *Introduction to Biblical Hebrew* (New York: Charles Scribner's Sons, 1971), pp. 170–71; for a literary analysis, with reference to its use by a narrator, see Shimon Bar-Efrat, *Narrative Art in the Bible* (Sheffield: The Almond Press, 1989), pp. 35–36.

10. Among others who have made this point, see Gerhard von Rad, *Genesis*

(Philadelphia: The Westminster Press, 1961), p. 239. For a discussion of links between Genesis 12 and 22, see Jonathan Magonet, "Abraham and God," *Judaism* 33 (1984): 160–70.

11. Such translations are designed to convey Hebrew vocabulary and syntax rather than felicitous English. Hyphens connecting words indicate a single word in Hebrew; they are used, however, only when deemed useful to the reader.

12. The phenomenon of repetition is important for understanding the structure, content, and meaning of Hebrew narratives. This phenomenon has numerous functions: to signal the boundaries and the connections of units, to aid memory, and to yield emphases. To indicate the presence of repetition in the relationships of words, phrases, clauses, and sentences, I employ a series of markers: e.g., <u>unbroken lines</u>, broken lines, and dots. These markers are arbitrarily chosen, but their use is purposeful and consistent.

13. Cf. von Rad, *Genesis*, p. 240.

14. Cf. the same reversal in 22:1.

15. The words, "took the knife," appear only twice in scripture, the other occurrence in Judges 19:29. On connections between these narratives, see Jeremiah Unterman, "The Literary Influence of 'The Binding of Isaac' (Genesis 22) on 'The Outrage at Gibeah' (Judges 19)," *Hebrew Annual Review* 4 (1980): 161–66.

16. The usual way of accounting for these two parts is to designate verses 15–19 a later addition. Westermann, e.g., writes that "one needs no deep insight to see the difference in style; vv. 15–18 are not narrative style" (*Genesis*, p. 363). True, but one does need deeper insight to discern the fit. The final form of the story may hold integrity. Cf. R.W.L. Moberly, "The Earliest Commentary on the Akedah," *Vetus Testamentum* 38 (1988): 302–23.

17. One usual way of explaining the unusual phrase "messenger of Yhwh" is to posit a redactor who altered the original text, "messenger of God." For an evaluation of this view, see Westermann, *Genesis*, p. 361. Rhetorically and theologically other interpretations prevail. Note the *inclusio* formed by the use of the Tetragrammaton at the beginning (22:11) and the end (22:14) of this unit. The inclusive emphasis underscores the character of the particular deity speaking to Abraham. Indeed, the switch from the generic Elohim (God), thus far used consistently in the story, to the divine name Yhwh highlights the self-revelation of the deity. If God is on trial also (cf. note 8), then Yhwh, the God of Abraham, discloses that this deity does not finally require child sacrifice.

18. On the deictic function of *kî*, see esp. James Muilenburg, "The Linguistic and Rhetorical Usages of the Particle *kî* in the Old Testament," *Hebrew Union College Annual* 32 (1961): 135–60; cf. Bar-Efrat, *Narrative Art in the Bible*, p. 30.

19. See Samuel Terrien, *The Elusive Presence* (San Francisco: Harper and Row, 1978), pp. 81–84.

20. This interpretation plays with three concepts: attachment, detachment, and nonattachment. The first two are interrelated, being positive and negative manifestations of an invalid mode-of-being in the world. This mode-of-being anchors existence in human relationships, rather than in God, with inevitable consequences of problems and sufferings. Nonattachment is a transcendent way of knowing and thinking. It moves human beings beyond interpersonal entrapments to a realization of the divine. Thus it offers a spiritual perspective that allows one to be in the world but not of it. In the language of Genesis 22, nonattachment is the fear of God. It frees human beings one from another so that they can be one with another. In addition to scriptural foundations, this interpretation builds on Zen Buddhism and Metapsychiatry. For further

clarification, see Venerable Gyomay M. Kubose, "Non-attachment," *Zen Koans* (Chicago: Henry Regnery Company, 1973), pp. 65–126 and Thomas Hora, *Beyond the Dream* (Orange, Calif.: PAGL Press, 1986), *passim*.

21. Cf. 22:3, 6, 9–10.

22. On sacrificial substitutions as a way to divert violence, see Rene Girard, *Violence and the Sacred* (Baltimore: Johns Hopkins University Press, 1977), pp. 4–6.

23. On Genesis 22 as the ratification of an eternal covenant between God and Abraham, with a particular focus on vv. 15–18, see T. Desmond Alexander, "Genesis 22 and the Covenant of Circumcision," *Journal for the Study of the Old Testament* 25 (1983): 17–22.

24. A full examination of this structure and content awaits the forthcoming longer study. It includes a comparison of the promise made here to Genesis 12 and 15.

25. On the particle *ya'an*, see D. E. Gowan, "The Use of *ya'an* in Biblical Hebrew," *Vetus Testamentum* 21 (1971): 168–85.

26. For a different treatment of the absence of Isaac, see James Crenshaw, "Journey into Oblivion: A Structural Analysis of Gen. 22:1–9," *Soundings* 58 (1975): 243–56.

27. Despite the salutary warning by Carol Meyers about problems inherent in the word *patriarchy*, the term appears likely to remain. As shorthand, it designates male-centered and male-dominated cultures and texts with an implied critique of them. It names a pervasive social system. Meyers rightly pleads for an understanding of historical specificities in descriptions and evaluations of patriarchy. See Carol Meyers, *Discovering Eve: Ancient Israelite Women in Context* (New York: Oxford University Press, 1988), pp. 24–46.

28. See, e.g., Louis Ginzberg, *Legends of the Bible* (Philadelphia: Jewish Publication Society of America, 1968), pp. 128–38; also Shalom Spiegel, *The Last Trial* (New York: Pantheon Books, 1967). Cf. Yaakov Elbaum, "From Sermon to Story: The Transformation of the Akedah," *Prooftexts* 6 (1986): 97–116. On ancient interpretations, Jewish and Christian, see, *inter alia*, P. R. Davies and B. D. Chilton, "The Aqedah: A Revised Tradition History," *Catholic Biblical Quarterly* 40 (1978): 514–46; Sebastian Brock, "Genesis 22: Where Was Sarah?" *Expository Times* 96 (1984): 14–17; C.T.R. Hayward, "The Sacrifice of Isaac and Jewish Polemic Against Christianity," *Catholic Biblical Quarterly* 52 (1990): 293–306.

29. Note that the verb laugh (*shq*) forecasts the name of the son, Isaac (*yshq*).

30. Note the parallel to Abraham's laugh in 17:17 and the corresponding play on the name Isaac. Note also other similarities and contrasts between Abraham and Sarah: "Abraham said in his heart" (17:17a); "Sarah laughed within herself" (18:12a). Two rhetorical questions by Abraham, asked inwardly (17:17), are matched in part by Sarah's one question, perhaps also asked inwardly (18:12b); cf. Bar-Efrat, *Narrative Art in the Bible*, pp. 63f.

31. For comments on these two stories, chapters 21 and 22, from the perspective of the abandonment of children, see John Boswell, *The Kindness of Strangers* (New York: Pantheon Books, 1988), *passim* but esp. pp. 141, 144–45, 155.

32. The thesis of this paragraph emerged in a discussion with Professor Tikva Frymer-Kensky of the Reconstructionist Rabbinical College, Wyncote, Pennsylvania.

33. Genesis 24:67 suggests that the problem of mother-son bonding continued even beyond Sarah's death.

34. For a womanist perspective on the Hagar and Sarah stories, see Renita

J. Weems, "A Mistress, a Maid, and No Mercy," *Just a Sister Away* (San Diego, Calif.: LuraMedia, 1988), pp. 1–19.

35. See Westermann, *Genesis 12–36*, pp. 366–67.

The Histories of David

1. Biblical scholarship, like any discipline, is not monolithic. In particular, recent interest in literary questions is beginning to make headway into the dominant methodology I characterize. See especially David Gunn, *The Story of King David* (Sheffield: JSOT, 1978), who argues that the so-called succession narrative is not best described as history writing; J. P. Fokkelman, *Narrative Art and Poetry in the Books of Samuel*, 2 vols. (Assen: Van Gorcum, 1981, 1986); Robert Polzin, *Samuel and the Deuteronomist* (New York: Harper and Row, 1989), who is explicitly bracketing the concerns that preoccupy traditional biblical scholars, see esp. pp. 1–17; Meir Sternberg, *The Poetics of Biblical Narrative* (Bloomington: Indiana University Press, 1985); and Peter Miscall, *1 Samuel: A Literary Reading* (Bloomington: Indiana University Press, 1986).

Furthermore, not all traditional biblical scholars who are interested in sources depict a developmental vision of history for the Samuel narratives. Among the notable exceptions is R. N. Whybray, *The Succession Narrative*, SBT 2nd Series 9 (London: SCM, 1968), who points out that there are too many personal scenes for this narrative to be characterized as history; instead, he regards it as political propaganda. But he detects in Samuel a far more coherent ideology than I do, one whose vision of consistency rivals developmental history's: "Every incident in the story without exception is a necessary link in a chain of narrative which shows how, by the steady elimination of the alternative possibilities, it came about that it was Solomon who succeeded his father on the throne of Israel" (pp. 20–21).

2. The two layers are the Dtr and non-Dtr. Dtr means the Deuteronomic and/or Deuteronomistic, the distinction being part of the dispute about the "nature and extent of the sources." The summary of positions is in Suzanne Boorer, "The Importance of a Diachronic Approach: The Case of Genesis-Kings," *Catholic Biblical Quarterly* 51 (1989): 195–208.

3. Robert Oden, Jr., *The Bible without Theology* (New York: Harper and Row, 1987), p. 6.

4. Georg Iggers, *The German Conception of History* (Middletown, Conn.: Wesleyan University Press, 1983), p. 9.

5. See Iggers's discussion of Droysen, p. 106.

6. Johann Gustav Droysen, *Outline of the Principles of History*, trans. and intro. E. Benjamin Andrews (Boston: Ginn and Co., 1897), pp. 15–16.

7. *Gesammelte Schriften* (Berlin, 1903–36), vol. 4, pp. 35–36.

8. Doris Summer writes of the concept of founding fictions in "Foundational Fictions: When History Was Romance in Latin America," *Salmagundi* 82–83 (1989): 111-41.

9. Julius Wellhausen, *Prolegomena to the History of Ancient Israel* (Cleveland: Meridian, 1957), p. 228.

10. Wellhausen, p. 231.

11. Quoted by Foucault, "Nietzsche, Genealogy, History" (1971), in *The Foucault Reader*, ed. Paul Rabinow (New York: Pantheon, 1984), pp. 86–87.

12. Martin Noth, *The Deuteronomistic History* (1967), trans. J. Doull et al. (Shef-

field: JSOT, 1981), pp. 80–81. Noth's thesis was considerably revised by Gerhard von Rad and Frank Cross who noted the positive elements in the Deuteronomistic history that conflicted with this sweeping principle. This critical history is summarized in P. Kyle McCarter, Jr., *2 Samuel, The Anchor Bible* (Garden City, N. Y.: Doubleday, 1984), pp. 4–8.

13. Foucault, "Nietzsche, Genealogy, History," p. 88.

14. Mieke Bal, *Death and Dissymetry: The Politics of Coherence in the Book of Judges* (Chicago: University of Chicago Press, 1988); see also her essay, "Dealing /with/Women," in *The Book and the Text: The Bible and Literary Theory*, ed. Regina Schwartz (Oxford: Basil Blackwell, 1990), pp. 16–39.

15. On King David, see Gunn, *The Story of King David* and Kenneth R. R. Gros Louis, "The Difficulty of Ruling Well: King David of Israel," *Semeia* 8 (1977): 15–33.

16. Claude Lévi-Strauss, *The Elementary Structures of Kinship* (1949; Boston: Beacon Press, 1969).

17. See Jon D. Levenson, "1 Samuel 25 as Literature and History," *Catholic Biblical Quarterly* 40 (1978): 11–28.

18. Lévi-Strauss, *The Elementary Structures of Kinship*, p. 68.

19. *Adultery in the Novel* (Baltimore: Johns Hopkins University Press, 1979), pp. 12, 13.

20. W.M.W. Roth, "NBL," *Vetus Testamentum* 10 (1960): 401.

21. Foucault, p. 89.

Esther Passes

1. Gerald Bruns, "Midrash and Allegory," *The Literary Guide to the Bible*, ed. Robert Alter and Frank Kermode (Cambridge, Mass.: Harvard University Press, 1987), 626, 633.

2. Joyce G. Baldwin, *Esther: An Introduction and Commentary* (Leicester: Inter-Varsity Press, 1984), 42.

3. Geoffrey Hartman, "Introduction," *Midrash and Literature*, ed. Hartman and Sanford Budick (New Haven: Yale University Press, 1986), xi; "Jeremiah 20:7–12: A Literary Response," *The Biblical Mosaic: Changing Perspectives*, ed. Robert Polzin and Eugene Rotham (Philadelphia: Fortress Press, 1982), 184.

4. While the *Interpreter's Bible* and RSV Esther retain the Hebrew name Ahasuerus, their first annotations state the equation: Ahasuerus is Xerxes.

5. *The Literary Guide to the Bible*, ed. Alter and Kermode, 668; Meir Sternberg, *The Poetics of Biblical Narrative: Ideological Literature and the Drama of Reading* (Bloomington: Indiana University Press, 1985), 470, 474, 498.

6. For philosophers and rhetoricians from Heraclitus to Hegel to Henri Morier, Gasché shows, in his "Reading Chiasms: An Introduction" to Andrzej Warminski's *Readings in Interpretation: Holderlin, Hegel, Heidegger* (Minneapolis: University of Minnesota Press, 1987), that chiasm expresses "harmony," "establishes the unity of opposites," i.e., "opposites are linked into pairs of parallel and inverted oppositions on the ground of an underlying unity, a *tauto*," and is therefore a figure of closure (xvi- xviii).

7. George A. Knight speaks of the "completeness," "integration," and "perfect harmony" of the book's chiasms, *Esther, Song of Songs, Lamentations: Introduction and Commentary* (London: SCM Press, 1955), 49; Michael Fox discovers "exact opposites" resulting in Esther's "symmetrical series," "The Structure of the Book

of Esther," *Festschrift to I. L. Seeligmann* (cited by Sandra Berg, *The Book of Esther: Motifs, Themes and Structure* [Missoula, Mont: Scholars Press, 1979], 106); Edward Greenstein writes of Esther as a "cartoon" with a "black and white portrayal of conflict," and "flat, cardboard caricatures," whose "uncomplicated plot" results in a "true reversal" that "will place the Jews precisely where their enemies wanted to be," "A Jewish Reading of Esther," *Judaic Perspectives on Ancient Israel*, ed. Jacob Neusner, Baruch A. Levine, and Ernest S. Frerichs (Philadelphia: Fortress Press, 1987), 231, 236; Jack Sasson finds "unambiguously drawn characters and fully resolved situations," "Esther," *Literary Guide*, 341; Werner Dommershausen pays attention to "symmetrie" and "parallelismus" alone, *Die Estherrolle: Stil und Ziel einer alttestamentlichen Schrift* (Stuttgart: Verlag Katholisches Bibelwerk, 1968), 149–50; Joyce Baldwin notes "symmetry" and "balance," *Esther*, 30, 31; and Gillis Gerleman sees only the book's "tautologischen Doppelausdrücke," *Studien zu Esther: Stoff-Structur-Stil-Sin," Biblische Studien 48* (1966), reprinted in Carey Moore's *Studies in the Book of Esther* (New York: Ktav Publishing House, 1982), 340–41. Yehuda Radday concedes "that the author of Esther did not follow" the rule of the "classical chiasm" which "would have demanded that . . . certain stylistic elements occur, for the sake of symmetry, twice only," but instead of the "expected 'dislegomena,'" we find a number of 'trislegomena,'" which nonetheless may be "disregarded," "Chiasm in Joshua, Judges and Others," *Linguistica Biblica 3* (1973): 9; and Sandra Berg admits that the "sequence of events does not present a precise chiasm," i.e., the positions aren't always strict, but they remain antithetical pairs. She speaks of "slight differences" which "contrast the pairs," and again observes "Esther is not a strict chiasm." However, she is more often concerned with the book's "inverse symmetry," "balance," and "uniform pattern of reversals," despite her report of a number of nagging, visible "seams" (162, n.99; 108; 95; 168; 186).

8. "Chiasm in Biblical Hebrew Poetry," *Chiasmus in Antiquity: Structures, Analyses, Exegesis*, ed. John W. Welch (Hildesheim: Gerstenberg, 1981), 52.

9. Namely Maurice Merleau-Ponty, Jacques Derrida, Paul de Man, Andrzej Warminski, and Rodolphe Gasché. Such an insistence on dissymmetry is "essential" in order to prevent "any neutralization of the . . . contradictions resulting from discursive inequalities and disparities," Rodolphe Gasché, *The Tain of the Mirror: Derrida and the Philosophy of Reflection* (Cambridge: Harvard University Press, 1986), 173. Regarding such neutralizing, Socrates explains that "When a person interchanges in his mind two things, both of which are, and asserts that one is the other," that person has judged "falsely," *Theaetetus*, trans. Francis Macdonald Cornford with an interpolation from the translation by B. Jowett, *The Collected Dialogues of Plato*, ed. Edith Hamilton and Huntington Cairns (Princeton: Princeton University Press, 1961), 189c. And Prov. 11:1 teaches: "A false balance is an abomination to the Lord, but a just weight is his delight."

10. Jacques Derrida, *Dissemination* (1972), trans. Barbara Johnson (Chicago: University of Chicago Press, 1981), 207, n.24.

11. *The Idea of Biblical Poetry: Parallelism and Its History* (New Haven: Yale University Press, 1981), 15, 31, 8. The "real nature" of biblical parallelism for Kugel, then, is what he terms the "differentiation" and "sharpness" of B's "emphatic seconding." He defines "sharpness" as "the delight in creating a B half which both connects with, and yet cleverly expands, the meaning of A"; it represents the "potential subtleties hidden inside juxtaposed clauses," it is "the highest advantage taken of parallelism, one might say the genius of the form" (12).

12. Kugel, 102, 109. Robert Alter follows Kugel, calling the predisposition

to symmetry "the greatest stumbling block in approaching biblical poetry," since "literary expression abhors complete parallelism, just as language resists true synonymity, usage always introducing small wedges of difference between closely akin terms," and that "poets understand more subtly than linguists that there are no true synonyms," "The Characteristics of Ancient Hebrew Poetry," *Guide*, 615; *The Art of Biblical Poetry* (New York: Basic Books, 1985), 10. J. P. Fokkelman is "challenged to look for differences" as a result of the chiasm ("Genesis," *Guide*, 46) and Luis Alonso Schökel admits chiasm's "calculated asymmetry" ("Isaiah," *Guide*, 169).

13. David J. A. Clines, *Ezra, Nehemiah, Esther* (Grand Rapids: Eerdmans, 1984), 316–17 (emphasis added).

14. *Dissemination*, 214, 221.

15. In his analysis of the "narratological chiasm" created by the baptisms of John and Jesus found in the prologue to the Gospel of St. Mark, John Drury identifies a similarly absent dividing element between the two: "So far [the river Jordan] has been the threshold of new beginnings, the thin line between contrasting states. But there is a thinner, the mathematical line, without thickness, where water touches land," "Mark," *Guide*, 408.

16. In his attempt to sell Xerxes on the pogrom, Haman claims: "We do not marry their daughters, and they do not marry ours," "The Second Targum (Targum Sheni) to Esther," translated from the Aramaic by P. S. Cassel and A. Bernstein, *The Targum to the Five Megilloth*, ed. B. Grossfeld, (New York: Hermon Press, 1973), 135. Racine's Assuérus is at first shocked at the revelation that Esther is "la fille d'un Juif!" that is to say, born of a "source impure," Jean Racine, *Esther*, ed. George Saintsbury (Oxford: Clarendon Press, 1886), lines 1036, 1039.

17. In his commentary, Charles John Ellicott writes: "Crucifixion was a common punishment among the Persians, especially on [*sic*] rebels (Herod. 3:120, 125, 159, etc.). The dead body of Leonidas was crucified by Xerxes's orders after the desperate stand at Thermopylae"; and "Doubtless the punishment intended for Mordecai was crucifixion, for hanging, in the common sense of the term, does not seem to have been in use among the Persians. The Greek word employed is the same used in the New Testament for our Saviour's cross (Acts. 5:30; 10:39; etc.)," *Ellicott's Bible Commentary* (Grand Rapids: Zondervan Publishing House, 1971), 368, 369. As I prefer the name "Xerxes" with the x's it bears, so this form of punishment, intended for Mordecai and visited upon Haman, fittingly reflects the book's chiastic overdetermination.

18. *Midrash Rabbah*, trans. and ed. H. Freedman and M. Simon (London: Soncino Press, 1939), 100, 115.

19. "The Second Targum (Targum Sheni) to Esther," 140.

20. *Die Estherrolle: Stil und Ziel einer alttestamentlichen Schrift* (Stuttgart: Verlag Katholisches Bibelwerk, 1968), 150.

21. *Studies in Biblical Law* (N.Y.: Ktav Publishing House, 1969), 104ff.

22. See Daube 116, 144; Maurice H. Farbridge, *Studies in Biblical and Semitic Symbolism* (N.Y.: Ktav Publishing House, 1970), 96; Erwin R. Goodenough, *Symbolism in the Dura Synagogue*, vol. 9 of *Jewish Symbols in the Greco-Roman Period* (Princeton: Princeton University Press, 1964), 185.

23. The law as codified in the Hebrew Bible actually acknowledges a dissymmetry, for example in the RSV Exod. 22:1: "If a man steals an ox or a sheep, and kills it or sells it, he shall pay five oxen for an ox, and four sheep for a sheep," which Daube understands as the law's provision for a "penal element,"

whereby a "multiple not simple restitution" is required ("Lex Talionis," 104, 134).

24. George A. Knight, *Esther, Song of Songs, Lamentations: Introduction and Commentary* (London: SCM Press, 1955), 43.

25. Marc Shell speaks of this "figurative basis of all commensuration" which "treats unreturnables as though returnable" as a "socially necessary fiction of identity," *The End of Kinship: "Measure for Measure," Incest, and the Ideal of Universal Siblinghood* (Palo Alto: Stanford University Press, 1988), 121, 123.

26. *Black's Law Dictionary* (St. Paul: West Publishing Company, 1959), 950.

27. Meir Sternberg calls the "drawn out" quality of the Book of Esther a "notorious exception" to the biblical narrator's typical adherence to "anti-suspense factors" which compel him to "foreclose the future," *Poetics*, 277.

28. In his discussion of Racine's *Esther*, Roland Barthes calls Xerxes's court a place "where glory always reveals some economic interest," *On Racine* [1960], trans. Richard Howard (New York: Performing Arts Journal Publications, 1983), 125.

29. Herodotus relates that "at posting stations every 14 miles or so waited messengers with fresh horses to speed the royal post on its way. A letter from Samaria or Damascus would reach the Persian king at whichever capital he was residing well within a week" (*Histories* 5.52), paraphrased by Clines (*Ezra*, 78). I am thinking here of Derrida's "teleguided speculation" on the always already "post," i.e., past, late, postal system and his specific reference to Esther and Cyrus in *The Post Card: From Socrates to Freud and Beyond* [1980], trans. Alan Bass (Chicago: University of Chicago Press, 1987), 60, 72, 75, 95, 123. Derrida calls Cyrus, Xerxes's grandfather, "the great 'conceptor' of the postal empire, the great master of order," *Post Card*, 114.

30. Deniability is of course the alibi former National Security Adviser Admiral Poindexter sought for President Reagan regarding knowledge of covert funds to the "contras." Poindexter obtained a subpoena for Reagan's White House diary—a book not unlike Xerxes's *Book of Memorable* (but secret) *Deeds*—"crucial to his strategy of showing that Mr. Reagan participated actively in the affair and approved of his [Poindexter's] activities"; Reagan's attorneys and the Justice Department refused to release the material, although Federal District Judge Harold H. Greene approved the order. In a report to Congress and attached letter to President Bush released on December 11, 1989, Iran-Contra Independent Counsel Lawrence E. Walsh requested that Bush intercede to prevent the existence of "an enclave of high public officers free from the rule of law." Bush and the Justice Department rejected Walsh's request. If pressed further to reveal his invisible diary, Reagan may have to claim executive privilege, that is to say, in this game of deniability, play his ace in the hole and silence his squealing Haman. (David Johnston, "Poindexter's Lawyers Assail Bush and Reagan over Trial," *New York Times*, 15 Dec. 1989: 15.) In his subsequent videotaped testimony, Reagan reportedly *denied* over one hundred times any knowledge of people and events connected with the affair.

31. Jacques Derrida, *Post Card*, 81.

32. Ps. 30:11. In a different context, Jean-François Lyotard writes of a similar transformation regarding the creation of Israel: "By forming the State of Israel, the survivors transformed the injustice [of the Nazis] into an injury and the *différend* into a litigation." "The *Différend*, the Referent, and the Proper Name," trans. Georges Van Den Abbeele, *Diacritics* (Fall 1984): 13. In Racine's drama, Zeresh, Haman's wife, reminds her husband:

Souvent avec prudence un outrage enduré
Aux honneurs les plus hauts a servi de degré.

(Often an outrage, with discretion borne,
Has served as a ladder to the loftiest palms.)
(842–43)

In a further attempt to placate her husband, Racine's Zeresh tells him: "De ce léger affront songez à profiter (Learn how to profit from this petty slight)," (886). Although hardly "léger," both Israel and Mordecai manage to do just that. *The Complete Plays of Jean Racine*, trans. and ed. Samuel Solomon, vol. 2 (New York: Random House, 1967).

33. Clines, 303.

34. Herodotus, *The Histories*, trans. Aubrey de Selincourt (Baltimore: Penguin, 1954), 8.85.

35. Berg, 73.

36. Another place where the book's artifice is revealed is its self-referentiality in 9:32: "And the decree of Esther confirmed these matters of Purim; and it was written in the book." Ellicott notes that the Vulgate calls this "book" the "Book of Esther itself, and so many scholars" *Commentary*, 371.

37. In the Targum Sheni, Xerxes "commanded that Queen Vashti should appear naked before him," and sent seven eunuchs with the following instructions: "Go and say to Queen Vashti: Arise from thy royal throne, strip thyself naked, put the crown upon thy head, take a golden cup in thy right hand and another in thy left, and thus appear before me and the hundred and twenty-seven crowned kings, that they may see that thou art the fairest of all women" (*Targum*; 92, 120). The Midrash Rabbah has Vashti disrobed (*Midrash*, 45, 54), and "I ordered Vashti to appear before me naked" (*Midrash*, 56). In a footnote, Josephus translator William Whitson paraphrases the "Chaldee paraphrast," asserting that Xerxes "intended to shew Vashti to his guests naked," "The Antiquities of the Jews," *Complete Works*, trans. William Whitson, foreword by William LaSor (Grand Rapids: Kregel Publications, 1960), book 9, chap. 6, 237.

38. *Histories*, book 1.

39. As Flavius Josephus attests in *The Antiquities of the Jews*, it is written in Lydian and Persian law that a wife's beauty should remain hidden from strangers: "But [Vashti], out of regard to the laws of the Persians, which forbid the wives to be seen by strangers, did not go to the king" (Josephus, 237).

40. Percy Neville Ure, *The Origin of Tyranny* (New York: Russell & Russell, 1962), 11–14.

41. Carey A. Moore, ed. and trans., *The Anchor Bible: Esther* (New York: Doubleday, 1971), xl. That the Book of Esther is dominated by kingly concerns is supported by Striedl's observation that the most repeated word in the book is *mlk*—meaning "to rule," "king": over two hundred fifty occurrences during the course of the one hundred sixty-seven verses (cited by Moore, *AB*, liv).

42. Seth Benardete, *Herodotean Inquiries* (The Hague: Martinus Nijhoff, 1969), 82.

43. D.J.A. Clines confirms: "The Persians prided themselves on their tolerance toward ethnic groups," *Ezra*, 296.

44. "Four Master Tropes," *A Grammar of Motives* (Berkeley: University of California Press, 1969), 508.

45. The Septuagint or B-Text and Megilla 13a both cast Esther and Mordecai as wed (*AB*, 21.)

46. *Encyclopedia Judaica*, vol. 6 (Jerusalem: Keter Publishing House, 1971), 907.

47. The king "ordered wine to be brought from a hundred and twenty-seven provinces for a hundred and twenty-seven kings who waited before him, in order that every one of them should drink the wine of his own country which would not injure him" (*Targum*, 92).

48. Carey A. Moore, *The Anchor Bible: Daniel, Esther and Jeremiah: The Additions* (New York: Doubleday, 1977), 173, 245.

49. The incuse coin has "on its reverse side the identical picture" of its obverse side, "but sunk in intaglio," Charles Seltman's *Book of Greek Coins* (1952), cited by Marc Shell in *The Economy of Literature* (Baltimore: Johns Hopkins University Press, 1978), 78. Shell observes that the chiastic "architecture of incuse coins unites or doubles obverse and reverse . . . incuse coins are associated with Pythagoras of Samos, the city where hollowcasting was invented" (*Economy*, 78–79). Shell cites George Thomson, who writes in *Studies in Ancient Greek Society* (1949–55): "the Pythagoreans believed that the upper and lower parts of the universe stood in the same relation to the centre, only reversed," symbolizing "the Pythagorean unity of opposites" (*Economy*, 78). I am attempting to argue against this unity in such chiastic exchanges. Erwin R. Goodenough, commenting on the four main Purim figures on the west wall of Dura, notes that "one of the earliest and most persistent parts of the Pythagorean tradition" was that the "number four was the symbol of justice," because, after Philo, the number four "is the first square," *Symbolism*, 185, n.53. The symmetry of this talionic "square deal" is misleading. Shell goes on to cite Oliver Codrington, who tells how, "in one early and very long Persian monetary poem, for example" (Shell), "one verse of the couplet is on the obverse and continues on the reverse of the coin: the poem begins at the top of the obverse and continues at the bottom of the reverse," *A Manual of Musalman Numismatics* (1904) in Shell, *Economy*, 79.

50. In her prayer to God, Racine's Esther claims: "Qu'à ces vains ornements je préfère la cendre (How ashes I prefer to such vain baubles)" (line 281).

51. Carey Moore tells us that the phrase—Esther had not revealed "her people and her descent" (2:10)—occurs "in reverse order in vs. 20, thus forming a chiasm, or crisscross pattern, which serves as an *inclusio* to bind together the subject matter of vss. 10–20. Another clear instance of chiastic structure serving as an *inclusio* is 'where I have found favor with the king and if it please the king' in v. 8 [,] rendered as 'if it please the king and if I have found favor before him' in viii 5. Here the chiasm frames the narrative of Esther's crisis," (*AB*, 22).

52. Clines, 288.

53. "*ḥwlk wgdwl*" (9:4, *AB*). As Sandra Berg notes by indicating the author's parallel use of the phrase "was growing and was great" here in 9:4 to describe Mordecai and in 1:4 to relate "the great wealth which accompanies" Xerxes's power, this is hardly a bland adjective; *Esther*, 71. Dommershausen calls our attention to its use to describe Moses in Exod. 11:3, *Estherrolle*, 113. In *Midrash Rabbah*, R. Hiyya also describes Mordecai's accrual of interest in Xerxes's court, saying that he "commences almost imperceptibly, but becomes continually more powerful" (*Midrash*, 123).

54. Carey Moore writes: "While Mordecai's rationale may reflect the personal

preference and religious scrupulousness of the author's Judaism, it does not reflect the actual practice in either the Persian or Hellenistic periods, inasmuch as Jews, like everyone else then, did obeisance," *Additions*, 204. *Midrash Rabbah* glosses Mordecai's refusal as owing to "the fact" that when the king "ordered that all should bow down to Haman, the latter fixed an idolatrous image on his breast for the purpose of making all bow down to an idol" (*Midrash*, 73).

55. Remarking on the sexual-political nature of this scene, Richard Howard in "Esther: Apart: Hearing Secret Harmonies" calls it a "condign phallic recognition," and asks: "Is this not an expression of a certain sexual understanding between suppliant and sovereign?" *Congregation: Contemporary Writers Read the Jewish Bible*, ed. David Rosenberg (San Diego: Harcourt Brace Jovanovich, 1987), 414. Jack Sasson says the scene "may well have erotic implications because of the submissive tone she adopts" ("Esther," *Guide*, 341). And see Robert Alter's discussion of Xerxes's "shaky scepter" in this volume.

56. Dommershausen has noted the book's marked hyperbole (*Estherrolle*, 35).

57. 35–36; 51, n.21.

58. Such exemplarity of restraint qualifies the Book of Esther as wisdom literature, improving upon the fate of Israel in 1 Samuel 15, who plundered Agag to Israel's subsequent detriment.

59. Moore, *Additions*, 157.

60. Racine's Esther remarks:

> Hélas! ignorez-vous quelles sévères lois
> Aux timides mortels cachent ici les rois?
> Au fond de leur palais leur majesté terrible
> Affecte à leurs sujets de se rendre invisible.

> (Alas! do you not know the rigorous laws
> That screen Kings here from all their timorous subjects?
> There awful majesty delights to be
> Invisible within their palace depths.)
> (lines 191–94, trans. Solomon)

See Marc Shell's discussion of "Invisibility and Tyranny" in "The Ring of Gyges" chapter of *The Economy of Literature*, 30f.

61. Herodotus reveals Xerxes's obsession for records written and at a safe distance: "Xerxes watched the course of the battle from the base of Mt. Aegaleos, across the strait from Salamis; whenever he saw one of his officers behaving with distinction, he would find out his name, and his secretaries wrote it down, together with his city and parentage" (*Histories*, 8.89).

62. Radday, "Chiasmus," 51.

63. Berg notes Michael Fox's curious choice for the book's turning point as 6:9 (*Esther*, 119, n.45).

64. His refusal owing, no doubt, to the still powerful enmity between the Kish and Agag factions each represents, and to Haman's idolatrous medallion (Targums 1 and 2 and Midrash Rabbah).

CONTRIBUTORS

Robert Alter is Class of 1937 Professor of Hebrew and Comparative Literature at the University of California at Berkeley. He is author of, among other works, *The Art of Biblical Narrative* and *The Art of Biblical Poetry*, and coeditor of *The Literary Guide to the Bible*.

Adele Berlin is Professor of Hebrew and Director of the Meyerhoff Center for Jewish Studies at the University of Maryland, College Park. Her publications include *Poetics and Interpretation of Biblical Narrative* and *The Dynamics of Biblical Parallelism*. She has just completed a book entitled *Biblical Poetry through Medieval Jewish Eyes*.

John Drury is Dean of King's College, Cambridge. A New Testament scholar, his publications include *Tradition and Design in Luke's Gospel, The Parables in the Gospels*, and contributions to the Alter/Kermode *Literary Guide to the Bible*.

Bernard M. Levinson is Assistant Professor in the Department of Near Eastern Languages and Cultures at Indiana University, Bloomington, where he specializes in cuneiform and Israelite religion and literature. He has recently published essays on hermeneutical issues in the legal corpus of Deuteronomy.

William T. McBride is Assistant Professor of English at Illinois State University, where he teaches the Bible, modern/postmodern drama, and critical theory. He has written on Augustine, Dracula, Bakhtin, and Beckett, and is working on a study of writing and violence entitled *The Terrible Alphabet*.

James C. Nohrnberg is Professor of English at the University of Virginia. He has taught the Bible at Harvard and Yale, and for the 1987 Princeton Gauss Seminars. The author of *The Analogy of the Faerie Queene*, he has published essays on Moses, the Old Testament, Homer, Dante, Spenser, Milton, Thomas Pynchon, and the Bible and literature.

261

Jason P. Rosenblatt is Professor of English at Georgetown University. He has published essays on Shakespeare, Milton, and Henry James, and is completing a book on law and gospel in *Paradise Lost*.

James A. Sanders is Professor of Intertestamental and Biblical Studies at the School of Theology at Claremont and at the Claremont Graduate School, and President of the Ancient Biblical Manuscript Center. He is the author of twelve books, including *Torah and Canon, Canon and Community*, and *From Sacred Story to Sacred Text*.

Regina M. Schwartz is Associate Professor of English at Duke University, where she teaches Renaissance literature, literary theory, and the Bible. She is the author of *Remembering and Repeating: Biblical Creation in "Paradise Lost,"* and the editor of *The Book and the Text: The Bible and Literary Theory*. She is currently writing a book on the Bible, *Can These Bones Live?*

Joseph C. Sitterson, Jr., is Associate Professor of English at Georgetown University. He has published essays on English Romantic poetry, biblical interpretation, and literary theory.

Meir Sternberg chairs the Department of Poetics and Comparative Literature at Tel-Aviv University. His publications include *Expositional Modes and Temporal Ordering in Fiction* and *The Poetics of Biblical Narrative*.

Phyllis Trible is Baldwin Professor of Sacred Literature at Union Theological Seminary, New York City. She is the author of *God and the Rhetoric of Sexuality* and *Texts of Terror*.